Anti-Semitism in American History

Anti-Semitism in American History

Edited by David A. Gerber

University of Illinois Press
Urbana and Chicago

Illini Books edition, 1987

© 1986 by the Board of Trustees of the University of Illinois
Manufactured in the United States of America
1 2 3 4 5 C P 5 4 3 2 1
This book is printed on acid-free paper.

Library of Congress Cataloging-in-Publication Data

Main entry under title:

Anti-Semitism in American history.

Bibliography: p.
Includes index.
1. Antisemitism—United States—History—Addresses,
essays, lectures.   2. United States—Ethnic relations—
Addresses, essays, lectures.   I. Gerber, David, A.,
1944–
DS146.U6A58   1986   305.8′00973   85-24488
ISBN 0-252-01214-3 (cloth)
ISBN 0-252-01477-4 (paper)

Contents

Introduction

David A. Gerber

Anti-Semitism and Jewish-Gentile Relations in American Historiography and the American Past

The Concept of Anti-Semitism

We may define anti-Semitism as:

1. the belief that Jews are different and alien, not simply in creed or faith, but in physiognomy and even more importantly in an inner nature or psychology;

2. the tendency to think of Jews in terms of negative imagery and beliefs which lead one to see them as power-hungry, materialistic, aggressive, dishonest, or clannish;

3. the fear and dislike of Jews based on their presumed alienness and on the understanding that these negative traits are not simply a response to past victimization or discrimination but rather a product of malevolence toward others, especially non-Jews;

4. the willingness to shun Jews, speak ill of them, subject them to social discrimination, or deny them social and legal rights afforded to society's non-Jews on the basis of a belief that Jews must be treated differently because they are different, alien, and malevolent.[1]

Many people whom we may call anti-Semitic accept at least part of this package. In particular, more people hold the views attached to the first three parts of the definition than practice

3

discrimination. Discrimination requires the cooperation of many others, and even of governments and social institutions, if it is to be effective, and it requires public behavior that may hold one up to censure. It is also possible for an individual to accept a part of the package, while refusing to accept or finding it inconvenient to accept the others. For example, someone may hold anti-Semitic opinions but find it expedient for professional reasons to belong to a business or civic club with Jewish members, or have no particular negative views of Jews but belong to a restrictive club because one's friends belong.[2] If such contradictory behavior were understood to be contradictory and regretted because one desired to be more consistently anti-Semitic, one may legitimately be considered an anti-Semite. Few people, however, fit all the parts of our definition, and even fewer people have wholly consistent or deeply rationalized views of Jews. Ambivalence—simultaneously rejecting and accepting, liking and disliking, fearing and not fearing—is today perhaps even more common than complete or near-complete compliance with the criteria of the definition.

When we think about anti-Semitism in the American past, and move the subject from individuals to past societies and cultures, we also find considerable evidence of ambivalence and complexity of motives toward Jews, as a number of the essays in this volume suggest. Indeed, the concept of anti-Semitism is too narrow to encompass all of the Jewish-Gentile interactions, even the negative and hostile ones, that the essays describe. This is not to say, however, that the concept of anti-Semitism is any less useful as a baseline from which to analyze Jewish-Gentile interactions which are conflictual and hostile. One example will suffice to suggest the problems with alternatives.

It has been contended that American hostility toward Jews in the past was a function of ethnocentrism or "nativism," the hostility of native-born white Americans toward all foreigners or representatives of foreign institutions.[3] On the face of it, the argument is attractive. During the colonial period, Jews suffered civil, political, and religious penalties as did such non-Jews as deists, atheists, and members of dissenting churches. During the era of mass immigration from the 1820s to the 1920s, Jews were certainly not the only immigrant people subjected to prejudice, hostility, and discrimination. Moreover, as American Jews have acculturated, becoming less visibly different in speech, dress, habits, and values, anti-Semitism has declined. Even so, this argument neglects an important reality of Jewish-Gentile relations in America: an ancient, aversive folklore—for example, the image of Shylock and the Christian belief concerning the guilt of the Jews as a people for the crucifixion—that had led to centuries of persecution in the Old World, followed them to the New. For this reason, and because of the unusually rapid socioeconomic mobility they experienced in America, Jews were unique among foreigners and became, as Oscar Handlin has said, "the most prominent and the most vulnerable of all [immigrant] minorities discriminated against."[4]

The limitations of the nativist conception of Jewish-Gentile hostilities are apparent when we consider the important practical matter of immigration restriction, which illustrates as well the difficulties we often have to face in sorting out various types of intergroup conflicts. After initially attempting without success to restrict Jewish immigration through manipulation of proposed literacy legislation in the 1890s, restrictionists did eventually adopt a broadly inclusive stance which sought to lessen dramatically the number of all "new immigrants," especially those from southern and eastern Europe. It must be noted that this shift seems more one of strategy than of heart, for many restrictionists continued to have deeply anti-Semitic responses to Jewish immigrants which, along with a less focused hostility toward southern Italians, proved most influential in providing the framework within which they conceived of the pressing need for restriction of many different peoples. Among restrictionists, too, even liberal assimilationists, who evinced an optimistic faith that Jews were ultimately assimilable, found traits they presumed to be Jewish not merely alien or different, but pernicious and disgusting, and they insisted that Jews must give these up before they could be recognized as Americans. Their response was not merely to Jews as foreigners, but to Jews as Jews.[5] As the historian Henry Feingold has said, "There is, after all, no way of being anti-Jewish other than to be anti-Semitic."[6]

But while anti-Semitism remains the most useful conceptual baseline from which to analyze the history of Gentile hostility toward Jews, it is necessary to be aware that there are types of Gentile behavior, which Jews have often perceived as hostile, that are not necessarily anti-Semitic. Two examples will suffice to demonstrate the limits of the concept in such instances. The first involves conversionism. Historians sometimes see Christian efforts to convert Jews as examples of anti-Semitism.[7] To be sure, conversionism has been based on the assumption that Judaism is obsolete and flawed because of its failure to accept Jesus as Messiah. Is this anti-Semitism? Aside from the fact that evangelical Christians have long debated among themselves whether such missionary activities were a Christian duty or an untoward and un-American interference, we must note that many missionaries have believed it would be anti-Semitic *not* to proselytize among Jews; it would imply that of all humanity, only the Jews were unable to become spiritual equals in Christ. Morever, missionaries commonly believed that the lowly, ostracized condition of the Jews was due to Christian error and hate, and that Christian guilt for this lamentable situation could only be alleviated by converting the Jews. Given this complex mixture of motives, it is no wonder that though Jews in the past were often offended by missionary efforts, some also showed understanding of the fact that missionaries were not as harmful to them as were anti-Semites, who approached them with the weapons of hate, not with the Christian Gospel.[8]

A second example of conflict which need not exist within the framework of anti-Semitism involves ethnocultural competition between religious and ethnic groups for bestowal of public legitimacy upon their doctrine or ritual. Throughout American history, pious Christians have sought legal guarantees for the sanctity of Sunday, the Christian Sabbath, or for hymn singing in the public schools at Christmastime. One may accuse them of forgetting about the doctrine of separation of church and state and of insensitivity to Jewish feelings, but one need not assume intentional hostility toward Jews in these actions, which have the potential to make use of heretofore latent anti-Semitism but are not necessarily motivated by it.[9] In fact, it is not difficult to believe that in an overwhelmingly Christian society, in which Jews have never been more than 3.7 percent (1937) of the population[10] and have been in the last century significantly concentrated in only a few areas and cities of the nation, many Christians seeking such public supports for Christianity have simply forgotten that Jews were in their midst. Jews in the past often understood the matter in this way. They reacted swiftly and with determination to assaults on their freedom of conscience and to attempts to gain public legitimacy for creedal impositions, and they reminded Christians that they, too, lived in America and that their feelings and rights had to be considered. But they have not necessarily assumed their adversaries were anti-Semites. They have been more correct than not. It is more profitable to see such episodes as an integral part of the continuing process of accommodation by which a pluralistic society develops and tests the rules that allow its various cultural communities to be true to themselves while simultaneously respecting their neighbors.[11]

It is necessary, therefore, to cast a critical eye at events, attitudes, beliefs, and motives in applying the concept of anti-Semitism. If based upon the recognition of the existence of ambivalence, of gray areas between anti-Semitism and philo-Semitism, and of the fact that all conflict and hostility are not necessarily bred of anti-Semitism, the concept provides a profitable way to approach the analysis of Jewish-Gentile relations in America. Without such cautions, the concept may obscure rather than clarify historical reality, a point to which we must soon return.

The Historiography of American Anti-Semitism

These assertions may well seem pedantic when addressed to a type of bigotry that has produced the greatest orgy of organized genocide probably ever committed by a government. Yet we are talking about the United States as well as about anti-Semitism; in this country, in contrast to Germany or Poland, anti-Semitism has been a distinctly minor feature of the nation's historical development. This fact is mirrored in the portrayal of anti-Semitism in general American historiography, or rather we should say the paucity of portrayal. As John Higham, one of the few generalists interested in the subject, has said, because "no decisive event, no deep crisis, no powerful social movement, no great individual is associated primarily with, or significant chiefly because of, anti-Semitism," historians of American social development have taken little interest in it. Indeed, such historians have considered the subject only as a by-product of other problems, deemed larger and more significant to explaining American development. Such was the case, as Higham has reminded us, in the scholarly discussions in the 1950s of anti-Semitism among the agrarian reformers of the 1890s; it was the place of the agrarian protest and of

Populist politics within the American liberal tradition, not the problem of anti-Semitism, that ultimately concerned the historians of the time.[12]

Historians of the American Jewish experience, themselves largely Jewish, have understandably been more concerned with anti-Semitism, but even for them it has been largely subordinate to other concerns: Jewish immigration; the evolution of Judaism, Jewish leadership, and Jewish institutions; the contributions of Jews to American life; and the settlement of Jews in the regions and localities of the nation.[13] Historians writing about these subjects have at times acknowledged anti-Semitism when they found it intruding on their primary concerns, but it was seldom the subject around which they organized their materials, even when it was present to a significant degree. When discovered, it was likely to be explained away as a transitory phenomenon, with a miniscule constituency of "crackpot" exponents and a minor impact on either American society or American Jews.

This situation placed the discipline of history in sharp contrast to those of social psychology and sociology in the period of World War II and after, when understanding the forces that created Nazism, a genocidal policy of extermination of European Jews, and western anti-Semitism more generally seemed imperative. Beginning in the late 1930s and continuing into the 1940s, the American Jewish Committee (AJC) and the Anti-Defamation League of B'nai B'rith (ADL), both Jewish defense organizations, subsidized research along two lines of inquiry: to explore the psychodynamics, particularly of mental disorder and neurosis, of those drawn to anti-Semitic mass movements and world views and to discover trends in popular attitudes toward Jews through public opinion sampling.[14] While questions have been raised about the methodologies and assumptions of the studies which resulted—the idea that anti-Semitism is evidence of personality pathology; the belief that people will tell the truth about their opinions when asked to reveal whether, in effect, they are bigots—from the perspective of historical analysis the studies were inadequate in a different way. While the attitude sampling and personality testing and evaluation offered pathbreaking insights into the social and psychological correlates of intolerant beliefs in the individual, they could not connect individual consciousness with daily social relations or with the movement of history. In short, they could not ask such questions about the development of anti-Semitism as "Why now and not then?"; "Why here and not there?"; and "Why the Jews and not another group?"[15] Yet American historians seemed no more ready to address these questions. They were preoccupied with other issues when examining the American-Jewish experience to the extent that over the course of thirty years of the postwar period, three historians—Bertram Wallace Korn (1951), Leonard Dinnerstein (1971), and Howard Rabinowitz (1980)—offered similar-sounding complaints about the lack of attention to anti-Semitism in American-Jewish historiography.[16]

In a recent analysis of the evolution of the subject of American anti-Semitism, Jonathan Sarna has offered a compelling explanation for this pattern of historiographical concerns. Sarna suggests that the root of the situation lies not in a lack of anti-Semitism in the American past, but in the concerns of historians. Prior to about 1945, he says, American-Jewish historians were concerned with demonstrating that Jews were "coworkers in the discovery, settlement, and development" of the United States and individual American communities. Such "fileopietistic" concerns, ultimately intended to stake Jewish claims to equality and civic participation, determined the particular way in which these historians approached anti-Semitism. They wanted not to reveal anti-Semitism in the past so much as to counter it in their own time "by showing that hatred of Jews was unpatriotic, a deviation from the country's noble past," which Jews, too, had played an integral role in shaping. Anti-Semitism was seen "as a bad habit, imported from Europe. If Americans would only return to the virtuous way of their forebears ... hatred would end."[17] After World War II, though the pattern of most monographic American-Jewish history remained the same, several important, broadly conceived efforts were made by scholars to rethink the historical study of American anti-Semitism, principally by Oscar Handlin, John Higham, and the liberal journalist Carey McWilliams. Each attempted to date the origins of anti-Semitism and locate it in particular social groups and individual regions and localities. All three agreed on the need to focus on the late nineteenth and early twentieth centuries when Jews were said to have emerged as scapegoats for the dislocations created by urbanization and industrialization and to have clashed with other groups in the intensified struggle for status and wealth which characterized the era. Although Higham's carefully crafted theoretical essays constituted a tremendous advance over previous explanations,[18] the works of these writers continued to reinforce a fundamental characteristic of older works: a liberal belief in American exceptionalism, which saw, said Sarna, "anti-Semitism as a late and alien phenomenon, largely attributable to outgroups, marginal groups, or groups whose status in society was declining, such as farmers, disaffected workers, and nativist patricians."[19] The emphasis was on the marginal place of anti-Semitism in American life, its lack of connection with the mainstream, whether social or ideological; and little attention was paid to its impact on American Jews. In this climate, the voice of Morris U. Schappes, arguing from a Marxist viewpoint that American-Jewish life had always been limited and distorted by capitalist social relations which spawned anti-Semitism, was a singular one, not only for its radicalism but for its insistence on the continuous, pervasive nature of anti-Semitism.[20]

Beginning in the 1970s, a sharp challenge was mounted against the liberal conceptual framework, causing a sudden explosion of writing in the field. Indeed, in 1980 when Rabinowitz was leveling his criticism of the paradigms of Jewish local histories, a wave of interest in American anti-Semitism was cresting. During the 1970s and early 1980s, several scholarly monographs and popular studies,[21] two popularly oriented surveys,[22] and even, for the first time in its long history, an entire special issue of the journal of the American Jewish Historical Society, *American Jewish History,* were devoted to the subject.[23]

Much of this new work was conceived in the 1960s and early 1970s when the notion of the benign exceptionalism of American society was being questioned by feminist, black, Chicano, anti-war, and New Left insurgencies. Amidst angry charges of sexism, racism, and class oppression and exploitation, American-Jewish history was now re-examined in a critical light. Moreover, a growing consciousness of the enormity of the Holocaust was taking shape at that time. In this climate, anti-Semitism was found to be older and more pervasive throughout the spheres of social life, and more widely distributed among many different social groups than had ever been previously imagined. Sarna has noted perceptively that the change in emphasis and understanding was evident when the last volume of Jacob Rader Marcus's important three-volume work on Jews in the American colonies was published in 1970. The first two volumes, which appeared in 1950 and 1953, recorded at length that civil, political, and sectarian disabilities existed against colonial Jews, but had rightly balanced off this acknowledgment by describing the extent to which these were shared with other groups of religious outsiders and the extent to which Jews were unconcerned with this discrimination. Marcus noted, too, the existence of a trend toward improvement in the Jews' position by the Revolution. He did not emphasize violence, harassment, or social prejudices and insults. The 1970 volume, while still even-handed in its judgments, now contained a chapter on "Rejection" which examined and developed these very themes.[24]

Works by Louis Harap and Michael N. Dobkowski found negative views and imagery about Jews, among respectable people as well as among outsiders and pathological anti-Semites, to be pervasive in the nineteenth and early twentieth centuries.[25] Saul S. Friedman even found evidence of the ancient blood libel (that Jews needed Christian blood for religious ceremonies) in a most unlikely place: Massena, New York, in 1928.[26] Other works, wholly or principally about Jews, re-examined the anti-Semitic propaganda campaign of Henry Ford,[27] discrimination in college and university admissions,[28] the influence of discrimination on Jewish socioeconomic mobility,[29] and American refugee policy before, during, and just after World War II.[30] Because this literature is deeply at odds with past emphases, it has caused bitter division among scholars in American-Jewish history and forced a productive questioning of past assumptions about the Jewish experience in a nation usually thought to be more hospitable than any other to diaspora Jews.

Stephen Whitfield, who is representative of those finding that the new scholarship wholly distorts the Jewish experience in America, seems to see this trend as an Americanized version of what Salo Baron called the "lachrymose conception" of the post-Biblical Jewish past: the view that the diaspora has been "a protracted nightmare . . . of trial and suffering."[31] Anti-Semitism, Whitfield says, has been so mild in America that Jewish leaders have been preoccupied with demanding that public officials protect Jews *abroad*. It is the "relative absence" of anti-Semitism, the fact that "it is the dog that did not bark," that must be noted. For Whitfield, it is not past anti-Semitism in this society but a deep vein of "historical pessimism" in Jewish culture which has made many American Jews unable to accept the "yes for an answer" that America has provided.[32]

Similarly, Sarna concentrates his attack on revisionist rhetoric and methods, which he claims work to vastly exaggerate the pervasiveness of anti-Semitism. He charges the revisionists with blowing up isolated incidents, such as the Massena episode, out of all proportion to their importance; failing to examine carefully Gentile motives, which are presumed a priori, as in the case of missionaries, to be anti-Semitic; creating false parallels between American and European events, which might succeed as dramatic devices but are analytically misleading; and emphasizing only negative views of Jews while neglecting to balance them off with equally pervasive positive ones, or to place negative views in a context which would lead us to appreciate the isolation of the speaker. Sarna urges careful conceptualization of anti-Semitism and more solidly empirically based generalizations.[33]

To these pointed criticisms, revisionists like Dobkowski and Friedman respond that the degree of Jewish acceptance in America has been exaggerated; that incidents and waves of anti-Semitism only seem innocuous in retrospect but were terrifying to those who lived in the midst of them; and that the negative regard in which Jews have been held throughout American history, even though not often actively expressed in dramatic form, has at least rendered society indifferent or hostile to Jewish interests—as, for example, when American political leadership and the public-at-large refused to change the nation's refugee policy during the immediate—World War II years to save European Jewry from the Nazis.[34]

Evaluating the claims of these parties is difficult precisely to the extent that monographic studies of anti-Semitism, especially at the level of the individual locality, are still lacking and that theoretical perspectives derived from this recent clash of opinions have not yet reached a very sophisticated plane. In such a context, especially given the weight of historiographical tradition and the hospitable climate in which American Jewry now lives, it is easy for historians to acknowledge anti-Semitism, indeed to list some of the problems it has caused Jews, but in the end to dismiss or minimize its *ultimate* importance. Thus, in a recent, pensive essay on anti-Semitism in American history, Henry Feingold states, "American anti-Semitism has most often been a painful personal experience," and that "at times, especially in the nineteenth century, it has had a collective effect on the Jewish sense of security." "But," says Feingold, "its impact on American-Jewish history has been minima[l] despite the fact that the Jewish community is very apprehensive about it." Later Feingold suggests that the proof of this contention is that Jewish survival in America has never been threatened by anti-Semitism. By this criterion certainly Feingold's assertion about the unimportance of anti-Semitism is proven. Yet even revisionists, who do indeed, as their frequent allusions to Europe suggest, seem haunted by the extermination of the majority of continental Jewry, would not claim threats to Jewish survival in America. More troublesome is the apparent failure in Feingold's formulation to confront the contradiction between implying, on the one hand, a culture formed amidst painful experiences of insult, hostility, rejection, insecurity, and apprehension, and, on the other, the minimal impact of anti-Semitism in American-Jewish history.[35]

While this volume cannot settle the debate, it responds to it in two ways. Most important, the essays themselves are often framed implicitly or explicitly against the background of disagreement with one or the other competing paradigms. Even so, the authors cannot easily be fitted into any one camp. A number of the essays find complexity in gentile motives toward and perceptions of Jews and Judaism, and they see crosscurrents of tolerance and even philo-Semitism intersecting with anti-Semitic hostility. Second, the balance of this introductory essay sketches briefly what we do know at this time about the forms and pervasiveness of anti-Semitism in the American past and relates the individual essays in this volume to disagreements, gaps, and working hypotheses that exist in the literature at the present time.

The Jews in American Society: Colonial and National History

The effort of historians in the past to see American anti-Semitism and other forms of hostility toward Jews as phenomena of the late nineteenth and early twentieth centuries clashes with the consensus of opinion among such historians of colonial Jewry as Jacob Rader Marcus, Richard B. Morris, and Abraham Vossen Goodman.[36] Nowhere in the British colonies did Jews receive equal status with professing Christians in law, and as Marcus has made clear, much informal prejudice and negative imagery surrounded colonial Jewry. Yet the pattern of Jewish-Gentile relations was undeniably complex, and it was informed by factors other than anti-Semitism. To a considerable extent, the position of Jews was connected to that of other minorities—atheists, deists, and dissenting Christians—with whom Jews frequently shared civil and political disabilities and the requirement of paying taxes for an established church, where one existed. Along with others who were not professing Christians, Jews experienced limitations upon their rights of settlement, naturalization, suffrage in colonial legislative elections (as opposed to town elections in which Jewish freeholders probably voted), officeholding, serving as witnesses or jurors, and practicing law. These disabilities were not present in all colonies, and few colonies practiced all of them at once. Furthermore, in South Carolina, Rhode Island, and New York, Jews and non-professing Christians at first had the right to vote but eventually lost it. It is not completely clear to what extent these laws were principally intended to strike out at Jews, nor is it clear whether Jews, who only numbered about 3,000 in 1790, outnumbered the population of those of Christian heritage so commited to atheism or deism that they went to the extraordinary lengths of refusing to declare themselves as Christians. Under any circumstance, along with other mechanisms of control fashioned in the Old World but unable to function in the New, these laws were quite often applied unevenly and without success. This was especially true of the laws regarding settlement. Jews were allowed, probably as a consequence of personal relations or the need for commercial services, to settle in locales where the residence of non-Christians was barred. Lack of economic opportunity, as a result of the stagnation of various colonial economies, rather than civil disabilities probably had more to do with establishing the pattern of where Jews did not settle. It must also be noted that nowhere in the British colonies were Jews forced into exile, or made to suffer the loss of economic freedom, or deprived of the freedom to practice their religion.[37]

With the American Revolution and the several decades of state and federal constitution-making which followed it, the pattern of Jewish life shifted rapidly from toleration to civil and political equality. Here, too, the fate of Jews was tied up with that of others, for they profited from, and reinforced, improvements in the status of other groups. After 1776, freedom came steadily, if unevenly, in state after state as new state constitutions removed test oaths and disestablished religion. Some states acted to accomplish these liberal reforms even before the final passage in 1791 of the Bill of Rights barred state support for religion and gave federal protection to freedom of conscience. Others later revised their constitutions so that they might conform to federal principles. Bitter controversy sometimes characterized the struggle for these new laws, particularly in Maryland, where the issue of Jewish civil and political emancipation was fought inconclusively between 1797 and 1826, when it was finally accomplished. Other states—Rhode Island (1842), North Carolina (1868), and New Hampshire (1877)—took even longer to grant Jews the rights to vote and hold office. In each of the four cases the issue was technically the status of non-Christians in general, but increasingly it was understood in the nineteenth century that the fate of the nation's small Jewish population was specifically at stake. Even so, while the advances in Jewish status were uneven, there may be no doubt that the Revolution and the liberal ideology sustaining it had set in motion powerful emancipatory forces where Jews were concerned.[38]

The creation of the new nation and the gathering of these forces provide an opportunity to step back from chronology and analyze those overlying factors in American historical development which so fundamentally separated the fates of American and much of European Jewry. Modern American-Jewish life has not evolved within a framework of oscillations between grudging toleration and violent, governmentally sanctioned, and broadly institutionalized anti-Semitism, as in eastern Europe. Jews here have not merely been tolerated but have been afforded full civil and political equality and substantial equality in the socioeconomic realm.[39] Nonetheless, a complex pattern of relations with gentiles and of acceptance and rejection outside the political-governmental realm has also been present.

Born in an age of religious laxity and skepticism and of republican distrust for clerical authority, the United States gave no legal sanction to religious bigotry from the dawn of its national existence. The Constitution and Bill of Rights created a political system institutionalizing creedal freedom. The resulting lack of legitimacy in the public sphere for anti-Semitism was a tremendous advantage for Jews. It created an egalitarian model for intergroup relations to which they could appeal against bigotry, and it guaranteed that prejudice and discrimination against Jews would remain random, informal, and unfixed in the private sphere and would be seen as an assault on the official values of the nation. Thus, while in Russia government created and implemented anti-Jewish quotas, here such quotas and less systematic forms of hostility would be imposed by private institutions, lacking government support for their practices and, it could then be argued, acting contrary to the liberal conscience at the foundation of the nation's political institutions. Furthermore, the emergence at the beginning of national history of a fully emancipated Jewry meant that, in contrast to blacks, for example, Jews never had a "place" to which, bigots might argue, they must be perpetually consigned. That Jews were emancipated, too, by general constitutional doctrine, applicable to all white residents, rather than by special legislation, as in western Europe, meant that no counterrevolutionary, anti-Semitic political movements aimed at revoking aspects of Jewish emancipation were able easily to take root here.[40]

The development of social processes and structures beneficial to Jews supplemented constitutional doctrine. Of utmost importance here is the pervasive ethnic and religious pluralism which has been a decisive force in the patterning of the American social system. The impact of pluralism upon Jewish status has been both ideological and social. Regarding ideology, even before the Revolution a cosmopolitan concept of white American identity was developing within the colonial melting pot, and it favored a broadly inclusive understanding of who and what was to be considered "American." Then, during the era of mass migrations from Europe, an ideology which placed high value on judging each person as an individual, but insisted at the same time on substantial communal cultural freedom for white ethnic and religious groups, gradually emerged. It was assumed that these groups would become more and more American, but at the same time, this ideology made the public expression of significant aspects of ethnic Jewishness or Irishness legitimate for groups and no necessary burden for the individual. To be sure, this was only one formulation, a culturally pluralistic one, of the meaning of "American." There were others, far less accommodating of diversity, but the more liberal, pluralistic view served as an important point of departure for the contention by Jews and their defenders that one could be, and should be allowed to be, both Jewish and American.[41]

Next, we have the implications of the actual sociological patterning of intergroup relations in the United States. A number of observers have noted the extent to which competition, rivalries, and asperities in the relations among a broad array of ethnic and religious groups have deflected hostility toward Jews. Throughout much of American history anti-Semitism has been less pervasive than hatreds and hostilities growing out of racial prejudice and domination, intersectarian divisions among Protestants, Protestant-Catholic animosity, and various ethnic tensions. In short, Jews have been one target, and most of the time a relatively minor one, among many. In addition, this pluralistic patterning of social hostilities has made it all the more difficult for the enemies of the Jews to unite in common cause.[42]

When pluralistic ideology and the pluralistic patterning of groups became institutionalized in politics, this, too, worked to the benefit of Jews. American political parties and electoral victories have often been fashioned out of broad coalitions of ethnic groups. This has been the case particularly in the major urban centers of immigrant settlement. During the era of mass migrations, the Democratic party emerged as the principal political protector of communal freedoms for recently arrived immigrant groups. It was able to attract the support of a number of such groups around generalized ethnocultural issues, such as opposition to the imposition upon society of American Protestant notions of Sabbath observation or of social control of liquor. At this level, the pluralistic patterning of politics functioned to increase awareness of groups that they had a stake in one another's protection. It also provided an important check against the use of the tactics of victimization of individual white ethnic and religious groups by politicians, whose welfare lay at least as much in attracting white groups as in scapegoating them.[43]

These social, constitutional, and political processes helped in combination to provide a basis for Jewish defense. While in Europe Jews were traditionally the least protected group in society, in the United States public officials have rarely sided with anti-Semites in active hostility against Jews. Not the least of the possibilities for protection came from the mechanisms America afforded Jews themselves for their own defense. Though they would disagree often on the tactics of self-defense, and though the difficulties of mobilizing waves of unacculturated, recently arrived immigrants were burdensome, Jews found that liberal ideology and civil and political freedoms provided ample opportunity to organize, seek legal redress, bring problems to the public's attention, lobby legislatures and public officials, and use the ballot against enemies. They have used such weapons of self-defense well throughout our national history from their memorials for repeal of test oaths and suffrage restrictions after the Revolution to the development in the twentieth century of the ADL, AJC, the American Jewish Congress, and local community relations bureaus—probably the most formidible array of professional white ethnic defense organizations ever existing in America.[44]

Finally, as Higham has reminded us, American Jews have benefited from a certain congruence between Jewish and mainstream American values. Jews quickly embraced American concepts of republican religious liberty because of their experiences with ecclesiastical oppression in Europe. Also, their historic pattern of decentralized congregational life meshed well with the pluralist and voluntarist pattern of much of American Protestant religious life. In this respect, Jews and Judaism were more acceptable than Roman Catholicism and Mormonism and their adherents, for the patterns of hierarchical organization and centralized, authoritarian leadership in both churches led them to be branded enemies of republican government. A similar congruence should be noted, too, regarding socioeconomic values. The emphasis on the bourgeois verities of "economic ambition, thrift, enterprise, and rational calculation" in secular Jewish culture was certainly compatible with American capitalism.[45]

Thus, much about American life placed anti-Semitism on the defensive and erected a formidable network of ideological, social, political, cultural, and constitutional impediments to persecution of American Jews. The problem remains to describe, according to our present knowledge, how, why, where, when, and by whom these impediments have been overcome.

Before doing so, we must note two issues in the interpretation of Jewish status in America, both of which function ultimately to qualify the general acceptance of Jews in America which has just been established. First, while one people among many, American Jews still have been highly visible because of their status as the most significant non-Christian religious minority. In an over-whelmingly Christian society, Jews are, to use Joel Carmichael's phrase, "indigestible,"[46] and this continuously evident reality provides an opportunity to view them not merely as different but as intruders and strangers, no matter how acculturated and otherwise assimilated they may become. As long as this perception of Jews as a people apart is accessible, the ancient myths attached to Jews can be, as Ben Halprin has said, continuously reinterpreted "to fit visible facts," whatever those facts may be: whether Jews are rich or poor, radical or conservative, powerful or impotent, religious or secular, successful or failures. Thus, depending on various social and historical circumstances, the Jewish capitalist may at times emerge in the public consciousness as Shylock, while the Gentile capitalist may be regarded as a cultural hero. To answer the question, "Why the Jews?" the possibility of anti-Semitism appears to be inherent in the very separateness of the Jews, particularly through Judaism but also through a historical peoplehood, which has been conditioned by secular culture and Gentile hostility as well as by religion. There may be grave or completely marginal anti-Semitism at various times in American history, but that there will ever be none, as long as there are people who call themselves Jews and live as Jews, is difficult to conceive.[47]

Second, for the very reason that American anti-Semitism has lacked governmental and constitutional sanction, it has been less consistent, comprehensive, and visible. Moreover, because it has lacked sanction in official ideology, its exponents to some extent have been inhibited from giving public expression to views lacking general respectability. Hence, American anti-Semitism has been somewhat insidious.[48] When and where it has existed, it has been more difficult to take seriously or even to detect than its European counterpart, because it has tended to lack a confident voice and has been most associated with demagogues and fringe elements willing to speak out publicly against the liberal consensus. Also, exceptions and inconsistencies in the presence of prejudice and discrimination, whether local, social, or chronological, lurk everywhere in the history of American anti-Semitism. In short, Jews here have received mixed and highly ambiguous signals. When added to the confusion over application of the concept of anti-Semitism, this particularly complex and subtle pattern has made the historical interpretation of American anti-Semitism that much more difficult. Combine these difficulties with a paucity of specialized works, whether monographic or theoretical, and one begins to understand the confusing claims made by both the recent revisionists and their critics. Left with rather little literature from which to deduce generalizations empirically, the contending parties have been forced to make general claims on the basis of *suspicions* about a singularly complex historical environment that is particularly resistant to being understood by inference and implication.

A Framework for the Study of American Anti-Semitism

Critical to understanding the scope, scale, and evolution of anti-Semitism in the American past is the differentiation between what we may call *ordinary* anti-Semitism, a common phenomenon of daily life, and the *extra-ordinary* anti-Semitism which has existed in periods of intense social crisis, strain, or change, whether for society in general or particular groups within it.[49] Both types have existed simultaneously at times and hence may be perceived as the same phenomenon. There are, however, essential differences between them. Ordinary anti-Semitism comprehends the usual daily experiences of prejudice, discrimination, and hostility Jews have continued, to one extent or another, to encounter since the founding of the Republic which accomplished their emancipation. Included here are

1. the appearance in literature, drama, art, and various facets of popular culture, such as cartoons, of negative imagery and stereotypes; or the informal verbalization of such negative views of Jews;
2. discrimination, most commonly in residence, employment, business, education, social clubs and other organizations that function to express and consolidate the social prestige of members, and quasi-public civic boards, such as boards of trade, museums, and symphony orchestras;
3. random harassment, whether verbal or physical.

Though practiced by a wide spectrum of social groups, ordinary anti-Semitism has existed without articulate public defense, let alone governmental sanction; even while practiced, it has probably been recognized to be inconsistent with official ideology. When and where it has existed, much of ordinary anti-Semitism has been so deeply institutionalized that it may be taken for granted by Jew and Gentile alike as part of the natural order of their relations with one another. Furthermore, given the inconsistencies, exceptions, and usual ideological illegitimacy of ordinary anti-Semitism, it has not been wholly unrealistic for individual Jews to seek strategies for circumventing it rather than confronting it, for substantial opportunities, in the form of other neighborhoods, or jobs, or businesses, to live free of social disabilities have existed. Their European experience amply prepared individual Jews for such strategies, and Jewish secular culture has been replete with folk wisdom on the subject. On the other hand, as we noted previously, organized and political, collective reponses to anti-Semitism have been present throughout the history of Jews in the United States.

What is extra-ordinary about the singular forms of anti-Semitism that have existed in times of social crisis, change, or strain, whether for society in general or particular groups, is not necessarily an increase in the scope and scale of ordinary anti-Semitism, which appears to have happened at some times but not at others. There is little evidence that the common types of prejudice, discrimination, and harassment increased significantly during the Civil War, when public officials, North and South, blamed Jews for problems encountered placing civilian economies on a wartime footing and publicly accused Jews of disloyalty. On the other hand, during the Great Depression and the international crises of the 1930s, harassment of Jews and verbalizations of prejudice appear to have increased substantially. Instead, what is extra-ordinary is that anti-Semitism becomes the core for the creation of ideologies that seek to blame Jews for the problems of society as well as for the establishment of movements that seek to enter the political mainstream. Accompanying these developments is an increase in the respectability of anti-Semitism within significant sectors of society. Influential figures in politics, the economy, the arts, or other endeavors are willing to articulate publicly prejudicial views and sanction discrimination against Jews on the basis of ideological conviction, or perhaps simply because it is now fashionable to do so. How generally the public conscience really shifts may not always be easily determined, but certainly Jews come to perceive a crisis in their relations with Gentiles. It is not surprising, then, that periods of extra-ordinary anti-Semitism have produced the most organized, sustained, and single-minded Jewish responses.

It was in such a period in the early twentieth century, which was compounded by increases in the scope and scale of common prejudice, discrimination, and harassment, that the two major Jewish defense organizations—the AJC (1906) and the ADL (1913)— were formed. During the 1930s, when movements with anti-Semitic ideologies seemed poised to enter the nation's politics, both Jewish national organizations and Jews in individual cities became engaged in organizing community relations bureaus and interfaith efforts to enlist Gentile organizations and neighbors against anti-Semitism.[50]

Ordinary Anti-Semitism: Prejudice, Discrimination, Harassment

We may conceive of ordinary anti-Semitism in the nineteenth century as a gradually broadening stream. During the first four decades of this century, however, that stream reached flood tide, only to contract into narrowing channels after 1950. In contrast with the view that ordinary anti-Semitism arises among society's elites and informally filters downward, or is intentionally imposed throughout the rest of the social system, the perspective here is that, as Higham has said, ordinary anti-Semitism exists simultaneously at various social levels, serving various functions for its varied constituencies.[51]

In the first three-quarters of the nineteenth century ordinary anti-Semitism existed within a context in which the Jewish population was small and grew only slowly. There were perhaps 3,000 Jews in 1790 and 230,000 in 1877, when Jews were scattered about the nation and were only about .5 percent of the American population. From the beginning the Jews generally avoided indigence, ultimately becoming firmly self-supporting and often quite prosperous. They were able to sustain communal institutions and charities. They soon adapted to American habits and customs. Such circumstances did not lend themselves to wholesale prejudice, discrimination, and harassment.[52] Nevertheless, the mostly German immigrant and minority, native-born Sephardic Jewish populations were subject to various types of daily anti-Semitic abuses. While positive comments about Jews as responsible, self-supporting citizens or as the progenitors of Christianity at times appeared in the press and elsewhere, from the first decades of the nineteenth century, negative religious and social stereotypes and images were quite common, whether on the symbolic-representational level in literature and on the stage or in daily social relations. Harap's study of the literary and dramatic exploitation of symbolic Jews, incarnations of greed, materialism, commercial double-dealing, and anti-Christian vengeance, illustrates how deeply European images were embedded in the American consciousness in the first half of the nineteenth century.[53] In an article reprinted in this volume, David Gerber demonstrates the way in which the durable Shylock image was reformulated at a critical juncture in American economic history to assist American commercial elites in dealing with newly emerging market conditions.[54] Sarna's biography of Mordecai Noah, a New York City literary figure and politician, reveals the use of these images and stereotypes in a concrete social situation. Noah's political opponents in the 1820s used anti-Semitic propaganda against him in political campaigns.[55] Discrimination and harassment of Jews in this period were rarely systematic and often involved the occasional intimidation of peddlers or harassment of immigrant Jews in urban neighborhoods.[56] The exceptions, however, presaged patterns that would evolve in more substantial form in the future. More systematic discrimination was found in realms of life—commercial relations between German-Jewish shopkeepers and merchants and American business elites controlling access to commercial credit; the long, troubled naval career of the Jewish officer Uriah Levy—in which Jews were seeking upward mobility and attempting to integrate themselves into major American institutions conferring social power and prestige.[57]

As both Higham and Handlin have noted, it was precisely this upward movement of Jews which produced the first sustained thrust toward broadening the stream of ordinary anti-Semitism in the last decades of the nineteenth century.[58] In the middle decades a few Jews had belonged to exclusive social clubs, civic boards, and business clubs; now, however, as many more of the German immigrants and their children grew affluent, they sought admission in ever-larger numbers to the social clubs, resorts, hotels, and college fraternities dominated by Gentiles. Gentiles rejected the notion of sharing with Jews the social prestige conferred by such places and organizations. The Jews were deemed socially unacceptable intruders who brought only money to the elevated circles to which they sought entrance. As Higham has said, social prestige was tenuous enough in mobile, fluid America, and socially elite Americans, as well as those who sought to emulate them, grew anxious at the thought of having to divide it with any foreigner with money enough to lay claim. A similar response led to the increased barring of Jews from boards governing museums, symphonies, and educational institutions. German Jews seeking to move to affluent neighborhoods found various formal and informal devices worked to bar their residence or restrict them to narrow enclaves. When wealthy Jewish capitalists moved to consolidate their financial power by seeking partnerships in American, mostly Yankee, banking houses, they were refused. In this context, it is not surprising that we find at this time the stereotype of the Jew as the graceless, pushy nouveau riche increasingly superimposed upon the older image of Shylock.[59]

Another, far more significant social process precipitating the increase of ordinary anti-Semitism was the mass immigration and resettlement of millions of eastern European Jews between the 1880s and 1914. By 1917, there were about 3.9 million Jews in the country, almost sixteen times the number only four decades before, and Jews were 3.3 percent of the population.[60] In contrast to the Germans who came before them, the eastern Europeans were poorer upon arrival; more prone to concentrate in the immigrant slums of the major northern cities; more troubled by such social problems as poverty, desertion, and unemployment; and more likely to be pre-modern in their habits and traditional in religious matters. Despite these problems, in the second generation especially they experienced startling socioeconomic mobility through strategies variously combining education, practice of the professions, ownership of small and medium-sized businesses, and movement to middle-class neighborhoods. The Gentile reaction to the aspirations and behavior of these immigrants and their children had a profound impact upon the scope and scale of ordinary anti-Semitism, which carried over well into the twentieth century, long after the close of mass immigration through the imposition of quotas in the 1920s.[61]

Two distinct patterns arose. First, there were the troubled intergroup relations arising out of daily political, economic, and spatial competition in the congested, immigrant working-class and lower-middle-class neighborhoods of the metropolis. In his detailed study of New York City in the 1930s, Ronald Bayor has analyzed the resulting conflicts, particularly between the Jews and the Irish, and the subsequent growth among the Irish, who came to America with traditional religious prejudices against Jews, of harassment and verbal abuse of the Jews around them as well as the development of anti-Semitic organizations. Bayor has illustrated how the desire to live among one's own people, on one's "turf," combined with a desire to leave decaying slums for better housing to produce conflict over residential space. He also notes how competition for influence over, or actual control of, political machines, political resources (such as patronage), and policies governing criteria for nonappointive public office further troubled Irish-Jewish relations.[62] That these relations had already been troubled for some time is evident, however, in the 1902 riots of Irish police and workers against Jews who marched in the funeral procession for Rabbi Jacob Joseph.[63] (See Leonard Dinnerstein's chapter in this volume.)

While working-class Jews did suffer job discrimination in competition with other immigrant groups, such blue-collar discrimination was not necessarily a consequence of anti-Semitism, though competition itself might have bred prejudice. Self-selection based on cultural values and European experience, not discrimination, appears to explain Jewish concentration in the needle trades and in middling, non-craft fields like the garment business and small shopkeeping. Jews were occasionally excluded from building trade unions, as in Cleveland and New York City, and hence from many jobs in new construction projects. That the impetus toward such exclusion was not anti-Semitism but a desire to control the job market is strongly suggested by the fact that, as their numbers increased to the point at which they could form rival independent unions, Jews were finally admitted to Gentile-dominated unions.[64]

A second pattern, which existed almost simultaneously, involved the response to the upward movement of the eastern European Jews and especially of their children. It paralleled the treatment received by the much more affluent German Jews but often took place at less elite levels of society and in newer sectors of the economy. The extraordinary movement of the immigrants' children into higher education, particularly in the Northeast where Jews were now greatly concentrated, led at first to discrimination on a wide scale in campus activities and organizations. Not too many years would pass before efforts, beginning with Columbia University during World War I but rapidly spreading outward to the Ivy League and eastern elite colleges in the 1920s, would be

..ade to curb Jewish enrollment through selective admissions procedures and quotas. As Marcia Synnott describes in her essay here, these mechanisms then spread, somewhat unevenly, to professional schools and, as eastern Jewish students attempting to circumvent restrictions at institutions in their own section sought admission, to non-northeastern colleges and universities. All these educational institutions feared that the rapid increase in Jewish enrollments, however hardworking and aspiring the Jewish students, would frighten away white Protestants, who were still conceived of as a natural constituency of higher education. Indeed it was the very ambitiousness and concern for achievement of the Jews which bothered many Gentile parents and educators, who continued to see higher education by nineteenth-century criteria, as a maker of men, rather than as a credentialing mechanism for careers and professions.[65] A pattern of discrimination in white-collar fields, from clerical through professional and corporate employment, followed aspiring young Jewish men and women into adulthood. Various analyses of employment agency listings and of want-ads between 1922 and 1926 have shown how frequently sales, bookkeeping, clerking, and secretarial positions were restricted.[66] Relative to their numbers among college graduates (8 percent) and national merit scholars (12–15 percent), by the 1950s Jews were vastly underrepresented in management in heavy industry, banking, transportation, insurance, and public utilities, and in newly emerging service industries such as advertising. In these areas, the very few Jews who obtained positions did so by masking their identities or by obtaining exclusively "Jewish jobs" in sales, data processing, and legal departments that were outside normal, management promotional tracks. Perhaps in direct proportion to this restriction, Jews became concentrated in law, medicine, garments, textiles, entertainment, publishing, and retailing, in all of which cultural predilection, European experience, and entrance in a field at a strategic, formative juncture in its history, or in a manner which protected them from discrimination, guaranteed them a foothold.[67] Notable, too, was a deepening and broadening of discrimination in middle-class urban neighborhoods and in suburbs as the second generation left the inner city and formed its own families.[68] A deepening of discrimination was also seen in social, professional, business, and service clubs. In 1950, for example, Jews were admitted to the Junior League in only 20 of 248 cities surveyed.[69] All of this Jewish upward movement and pressure for social integration obviously reinforced the popular perception of Jews as aggressive and intrusive nouveau riches.[70]

Were these patterns of prejudice, discrimination, and harassment spread evenly throughout the country in the late nineteenth and early twentieth centuries? Historians have speculated on the existence of regional and local variations, but because studies of local Jewish communities have not been greatly concerned with anti-Semitism, it is difficult to say. It has been contended that the South has displayed more ordinary anti-Semitism than other sections of the nation. After all, the Protestant South, it is said, has been characterized by great religious homogeneity and by considerably more xenophobia than other sections of the nation. The most violent incident of anti-Semitism in American history up to that time, the lynching of Leo Frank in 1913, took place in Georgia, and the agitation which accompanied the campaign against Frank helped to create the climate for the re-establishment of the Ku Klux Klan in 1915. It is well known, too, that in the mid-twentieth century, southern Jews, who were never able to embrace segregation with complete enthusiasm, were caught in the middle on the race question and angered their white Gentile neighbors to the extent that synagogue bombings took place in various cities. Despite these events, evidence for the existence of greater anti-Semitism in the South is ambiguous. Southern Jews may not have been among the South's most avid racists, but they were always included in the pre-1960s privileged caste of whites. Moreover, in an essentially underdeveloped economy, southern Jews were valued as merchants and petty tradesmen and were allowed to prosper in these roles. The few incidents of hostility to Jewish storekeepers by debt-ridden Mississippi and Louisiana farmers in the 1880s and 1890s seem uncommon when placed beside the record of acceptance in commerce in all types of southern communities. So well established were Jewish merchants that Klan efforts in the 1920s to boycott Jewish stores regularly failed. Jews were continually elected to office in the nineteenth and early twentieth centuries in the South. Finally, the patterns of exclusion from clubs, resorts, service organizations, and civic boards seemed no worse than elsewhere.[71]

Though in need of further refinement, an analysis which focuses not on sectional variations but on historical and social differences among localities is more promising. Gunther Plaut has suggested an approach to understanding local variations which is based on the comparison of Jewish experiences in St. Paul and Minneapolis, "twin cities" with widely different reputations for acceptance of Jews.[72] (John Higham has also worked, though in a less extended manner, on this comparison.)[73] Between approximately 1920 and 1945, Jews in Minneapolis, which Carey McWilliams in 1946 called "the capital of anti-Semitism in the United States,"[74] were excluded from all social organizations as well as from many fraternal and service clubs; they were never chosen for civic commissions, were never employed in public schools, major industries, or all but one of the hospitals, and were made to suffer unusually great residential discrimination. Such conditions were largely absent in neighboring St. Paul.[75] By way of explanation, Plaut has emphasized particularly the relatively late arrival of Minneapolis Jews and the less pluralistic ethnic and religious structure of that city. The first variable certainly seems to have applicability beyond this one case. Wherever Jewish settlement has been coterminous with the foundations of a settled community, as in the non-seaboard South and in the West, Jews have profited from early arrival. They have gained prestige by being considered local founders and pioneers, served on civic boards and occasionally belonged to largely Gentile social organizations, been elected to local office and to the state legislature, and have attained status and considerable wealth as proprietors of the first mercantile businesses.[76] As Moses Rischin has pointed out, between 1915 and 1931, Jews were elected governors in postfrontier Idaho, Utah, New Mexico, and Oregon, though only later in New York and Illinois, where there were many more of them.[77] Some studies, for example of Atlanta and Los Angeles, however, have shown a gradual deterioration of early, benign conditions after the decade 1890 to 1900 which they have attributed to the reaction to the arrival of the eastern European immigrants, so a "genetic" theory of local Jewish histories seems unable to account for the decisive impact of later developments.[78] In regard to the second variable, relatively less white ethnic and religious pluralism might make Jews more visible targets and their presence in a community that much more upsetting. In the South, however, this seems to have been compensated for by race, historically a far more significant source of social differentiation. Moreover, as Bayor has shown, the spectacular pluralism of New York City created conditions for interethnic hostilities, especially among working-class immigrants, that assumed anti-Semitic forms.[79] Since the studies of the Twin Cities have neglected consideration of such interethnic hostilities, it is impossible to evaluate the strength of this variable. Clearly, more local and comparative studies are needed to test these variables and discover new ones.

Extra-ordinary Anti-Semitism: Ideology, Conscience, and Politics

Because the brief Civil War experience of Jew-baiting by public officials[80] failed to survive the war, analysis of the development of ideological anti-Semitism and its political manifestations and of the breakdown of the usual moral, political, and cultural sanctions against the acceptance of anti-Semitic views among growing sectors of the population is best restricted to the period 1890 to 1950. During these years, several strands of ideological anti-Semitism took root at various times and gained legitimacy among various groups, for whom it served in varying degrees as the basis for a political orientation. Exact periodization is difficult because loose systems of ideals and subtle shifts of consciousness among vaguely defineable groups defy precise dating. The most relevant periods, peoples, movements, and ideologies appear to be (1) the early 1890s to 1914, during which in reaction to the various dislocations of modernization, patrician and "quasi-agrarian" anti-Semitic ideologies formed; (2) 1920 to 1927, the years of the ascendence of the revived Ku Klux Klan and of Henry Ford's anti-Semitic propaganda campaign against the so-called International Jew in the *Dearborn Independent,* which spawned other efforts with similar ideas and aims; and (3) the middle and late 1930s when quasi-fascist and anti-communist anti-Semitism which blamed Jews for the Great Depression and the international crises in Europe appeared and threatened for a time to become the basis of a mass political movement. The artificiality of these dates is suggested perhaps more than anything else by the fact that each of the latter two movements was built in part by ideas previously posited by the others. They were all, though to different degrees, also influenced by European anti-Semitic ideologies, which developed a strong presence during the same broad period of time but also failed to conform for the most part to any more particular periodization.

The extra-ordinary anti-Semitism of this period is the most developed area in the historical literature of American anti-Semitism, so it may be sketched briefly here. Higham has rightly used the term "pseudo-agrarian" to differentiate rural and small town anti-Semitic propagandists, most from the South, Midwest, and Great Plains, from agrarian political radicals of the 1890s such as the Populists, who were not particularly drawn to anti-Semitism.[81] Indeed, though a once-prominent Populist like Tom Watson in later years became an anti-Semitic publicist[82] and anti-Semitic demagogues like Theodore Bilbo could lay claim to Populist lineage,[83] quasi-agrarianism was a degeneration of Populist ideology of the type identified by C. Vann Woodward.[84] While Populists sought to understand the transformation of rural America and the decline of the family farm through analysis of modern capitalist market conditions and political forces, the pseudo-agrarian, xenophobic anti-Semites blamed vast conspiracies of monied, urban Jewish middlemen, bankers, and international finance capitalists, all nonproducers who lived off the toil of the American yeoman. They railed against the city, not only for its parasitism but for its cosmopolitanism, paganism, and modernity in manners and morals, and these traits, too, were attributed to Jewish influence, especially in the emerging mass communications industry.[85] Such ideas deeply influenced both the Ku Klux Klan, which periodically harassed Jews in the 1920s, and Henry Ford, whose ideology most historians see as an expanded, 1920s version of pseudo-agrarianism. Ford saw all of the dislocations of recent history—wars, revolutions, strikes, political corruption, and changes in morality—as the consequences of conspiracies of small cliques of rootless, or international, Jews, who at one and the same time were able to support plutocracy and bolshevism to further an insatiable appetite for power.[86]

Patrician anti-Semitism took root among northeastern Protestants of old, elite families and occasionally among those of lesser status who sought to emulate them. For patricians, somewhat paradoxically, Jews symbolized both the larger immigrant threat to American republican self-government and the threat, as Barbara Miller Solomon has said, of "a loss of fixed social distinctions"[87] in a fluid, modernizing society in which merit and money were replacing name and family background as standards for social status. Two variants of patrician anti-Semitism took shape. One, frequently associated with Henry Adams, found in the Jew as parvenu and ambitious striver a symbol of the materialistic forces which were reshaping the world in their own ugly and cynical image.[88] The other is associated with the Nordic and Anglo-Saxon ideologists—nativist publicists, racialist philosophers, and eugenicists—who increasingly saw immigrants, especially the presumably unassimilable Jews, threatening to outnumber the older northern European stock on which American political institutions were thought to depend for their proper functioning.[89] There was much overlap of both people and ideas between these two variants of patrician anti-Semitism. Representatives of both orientations came together in the Immigration Restriction League (1894), for which the menace of Jewish immigration loomed especially large. The league played an important role in changing consciousness on the wisdom of open immigration and, through the prominent support of Senator Henry Cabot Lodge, in drafting restriction legislation. Its efforts and those of its allies, such as organized labor which wished to limit the influx of low-wage labor, came to fruition in the 1920s with the imposition of quotas that discriminated against southern and eastern European migrants.[90] Patrician anti-Semitism declined with the gradual passing of the transitional generation which witnessed the reduction of its social authority. However, the influence of its ideas is thought to have lived on in the middle and upper reaches of the American State Department, where it affected in the 1930s and 1940s the making of American refugee policy which showed marked hostility toward assisting European Jews.[91]

The pseudo-agrarian tradition, however, blended ominously in the 1930s and 1940s with the ideologies of native right-wing movements which also took elements of their ideology from conservative Christian doctrine and from Nazism and Italian fascism. The 1930s were the high point of organized, ideological anti-Semitism in the nation's history. What such individuals and movements as George Sylvester Viereck, William Dudley Pelley and his Silver Shirts, Father Coughlin and the National Union for Social Justice, Fritz Kuhn and the German American Bund, the Christian Front, Gerald B. Winrod and the Defenders of the Christian Faith, and Reverend Gerald L. K. Smith had in common was an ideology linking Franklin Roosevelt, the New Deal, the Depression, and international crises and threats of war to international Jewish conspiracies, whether capitalist or communist or both. For a time in the mid-1930s, some of these movements threatened to coalesce into a mass political movement, but they proved too weak to survive an increasingly anti-Nazi shift of public opinion or, after the first Roosevelt term, to make significant inroads in the New Deal coalition which Roosevelt constructed.[92] The anti-Semitic constituencies of these groups are still somewhat obscure. Urban working-class ethnics, particularly Irish Catholics, were attracted to right-wing and quasi-populist movements like Social Justice and the violent Christian Front and Christian Mobilizers which combined hatred of Jews with defense of Catholicism.[93] The direct influence of Old World political movements is clear, too, in the case of Poles, Hungarians, and Germans, but the particular segments of these ethnic communities involved is known only among the Germans. Sandor Diamond has shown how the Bund was dominated by recent German immigrants of the 1920s, some of whom were veterans of postwar rightist militias and movements. Beyond these urban groups it is unclear what constituencies existed for ideological anti-Semitism at the time.[94]

Explanations for the relationship between groups espousing anti-Semitic ideology and the crises swirling around them have been based on two paradigms, one sociopsychological, the other social. The first focuses on the functions of anti-Semitism in alleviating frustration and deprivation in groups experiencing fundamental threats to normal expectations and security but unable to strike out at the source of their problems because it is obscure or beyond reach. A visible, vulnerable, and available substitute is sought as a scapegoat. Hence, Jews emerge through displacement and projective mechanisms of an endangered, collective psyche as the cause of all difficulties.[95] This paradigm may help us account for the activities of groups, but, in addition to the lack of historical grounding noted previously in regard to behaviorist paradigms of anti-Semitism, it is unable to explain the private behavior of individuals. It cannot demonstrate how such mechanisms of displacement and projection have been mediated through the individual consciousness in the past, nor explain the process by which individuals have attached themselves to anti-Semitic movements.[96]

As such, it remains a leap through a void, though a highly suggestive one which seems intuitively correct. Social explanations, such as those offered by Ronald Bayor, focus on extra-ordinary anti-Semitism as the by-product of objective problems in day-to-day intergroup relations, such as those that plagued Irish-Jewish relations in New York City in the 1930s.[97] Yet the jump from these objective differences to subjective fantasies of worldwide Jewish conspiracies seems too large; the latter is wholly out of proportion to the former. As Hannah Arendt rightly said, anti-Semitic projection is "an outrage to common sense."[98] Despite its difficulties, the sociopsychological paradigm, if not confused by an overly clinical perspective which sees anti-Semitism as necessarily a pathological condition in the individual personality, seems more explanatory, even for groups and individuals involved in daily competitive relations. In the case of both paradigms, too, it is necessary, as Jacob Katz has noted, to give more attention to another mechanism: the constant reinterpretation of historical images and stereotypes of Jews to fit evolving realities. Without such emphasis, Katz warns, the study of anti-Semitism becomes "de-Judaized," lost in the application of behaviorist hypotheses so generalized that the fact of Jewish victimization becomes "almost accidental."[99]

Post–World War II Trends

Since the late 1940s, there has been a significant decline in all forms of anti-Semitism. Discrimination has contracted to the point that private social clubs and quasi-social service organizations remain the only realms of life where there is any consistency of restrictive practices.[100] Public opinion polls have revealed a steady, if uneven from group-to-group and issue-to-issue, decline in anti-Semitic attitudes. The latest comprehensive study (1982) sampling attitudes shows that 45 percent of the population may be considered free of anti-Semitic views of any sort, while 23 percent, mostly older and less educated, hold on to the standard prejudices. Yet a much smaller percentage probably now sanction discrimination against Jews or would vote for an anti-Semitic candidate for office.[101] Ideological anti-Semitism and anti-Semitic mass politics have become marginal to the extent that no respectable public figure seems willing to use the old canards as a means of organizing people. The association of ideological anti-Semitism with violent and extremist groups like the Ku Klux Klan and the American Nazis has gone a long way toward destroying its respectability.[102] Indeed, right-wing anti-Semitism has lost its mass political power to the extent that since the 1960s Jews have been more apprehensive about the anti-Semitism of the Left, segments of which turned critical of Israel after 1967 and defended black radicals who denounced American Jews.[103] This decline in anti-Semitism has taken place in the midst of problems that, Jews feared, might rekindle hostility: McCarthyism, American commitment to Israel, desegregation, and the oil crisis.[104] Isolated, though recently increasing, incidents such as defacement of synagogues or cemetaries, which were common in the 1930s, now stand out for the infrequency with which they occur, and it remains unclear the extent to which they are a product of inchoate, anti-social vandalism rather than anti-Semitism.[105]

This turnabout may be attributed to both situational factors and underlying social and economic forces. In the immediate postwar period, in which all types of anti-Semitism remained strong, the gradually revealed horror of the Holocaust loomed large in the imagination of both Jews and Gentiles and provided a strong incentive for action. In spite of historical disagreements about strategy, the major Jewish defense organizations then expanded upon cooperation begun in the 1930s to push for an end to educational and employment discrimination, to sensitize public consciousness about stereotypes and negative images and to combat anti-Semitic political movements and demagoguery.[106] Jews profitted from the prevailing liberal consensus of the postwar years and from their role as particularly loyal partisans of the liberal wing of the Democratic party in gaining institutional, corporate, federal, and state action against discrimination.[107] The Holocaust, too, mobilized significant Jewish and Christian opinion leaders—journalists, novelists, ministers, and politicians—in the effort against anti-Semitism. The postwar years saw a number of films and books against anti-Semitism and many public efforts within Christian churches to reevaluate historical relations with Jews.[108]

Yet neither the Holocaust, nor for that matter sympathy for (or criticism of) embattled Israel, has had much long-term impact on the general public's recent attitudes and behavior toward Jews, as Charles Herbert Stember noted in 1966 after reviewing two decades of polls commissioned by the AJC.[109] For that reason, it

is necessary to focus on less-visible forces to explain the decline
of anti-Semitism. The rapid expansion of the postwar economy
played an important role in alleviating much, though not all,
corporate employment restrictions, because it created a shortage
of educated and skilled managers, technicians, and specialists of
many kinds, making skill and education necessary criteria in hiring.
However, Jews continue to be channeled into certain narrow
career tracks in some corporate fields.[110] Post-1945 prosperity
deeply affected the Gentile, white, urban working class, which
enjoyed new security and the benefits of consumerism and was
able to share in the American Dream in a substantial way for
the first time in its history. Its contacts with Jews were now less
competitive and conflictual. That this undercut the anti-Semitic
mass politics of the 1930s seems clear. It is attested to also by
the fact that blacks, who have in good and bad times alike continued
to lag behind in major indicators of well-being, are the only social
group in which anti-Semitism has increased since 1945. Seventy-
eight percent of blacks in a recent sample evidenced prejudiced
attitudes toward Jews. It is apparent that this phenomenon may
well be explained by lack of education and opportunity and by
unequal social and economic contacts with Jews. (Yet one must
also credit Jewish fears that a segment of black leadership, which
has a Third World orientation and is sympathetic to Palestinian
nationalism, has grown hostile to American Jews because of their
staunch support for Israel. Israel's ties with South Africa are
another irritant here. Moreover, the opposition of some Jewish
organizations to quotas in affirmative action programs has angered
many of these same blacks.)[111] The old ideological politics has
declined in other spheres, too. The eclipse of patrician anti-Semitism
has already been noted. While it has not disappeared from the
southern Bible Belt and Great Plains, the pseudo-agrarian tradition
has faded as the nationalization of marketing, media, and communications and the decentralization of industry have brought
rural and small-town America into the social mainstream.[112] Finally,
the end of Jewish mass immigration and the onward pace of
acculturation have made Jews considerably less visible and a much
less accessible target.[113]

So it is that while American Jews continue to be concerned
about anti-Semitism and to feel insecure, they have begun recently
to question whether intermarriage and a drifting away from Judaism

will pose greater difficulties than anti-Semitism for the future survival of American Jewry. Of course, as long as Jews remain at some level a distinctive people, anti-Semitism remains a social possibility, even in the benign environment of America. The decline of anti-Semitism, though, and the rise of these other concerns that are largely a consequence of the success of Jews in integrating into American society in the late twentieth century, surely open a new chapter in the long history of the diaspora.[114]

The Essays

The essays in this volume, all but one of them appearing in print for the first time, have been grouped according to categories derived from both traditional and new concerns in the historical literature on anti-Semitism and Jewish-Gentile relations. In the first section, "Mythologies, Images, and Stereotypes" are examined. Proceeding from an important insight of John Higham—that a significant difference has existed between the received or symbolic images of Jews (Sartre's "idea of the Jew")[115] and the perceived, daily, reality of flesh-and-blood Jews[116]—Jonathan Sarna investigates this tension among a number of groups and individuals in nineteenth-century America and analyzes the complex responses of Jews to Gentile ambivalence and hostility. Ellen Schiff considers the irony of Jewish support, at every level of theatrical endeavor, for the theater, even though it has been responsible for conveying a great deal of negative imagery about Jews, much of it created by Jewish playwrights themselves. Schiff develops the intriguing point that Jews have literally acted out, before Gentile audiences, their ambivalence about themselves; in the process they have exorcised not only their own demons, but those of Gentiles as well.

In section two, "Demogogues, Ideologues, Nativists, and Restrictionists," Robert Singerman questions Higham's contention that American anti-Semitic ideology has lacked a significant racial conception of Jews[117] and examines efforts made in America, generally within the patrician ideological framework, to fuse new theories of race with centuries-old anti-Semitic beliefs. Both Edward Shapiro and Glen Jeansonne take up case studies of the degeneration of agrarian radicalism by examining the anti-Semitic attitudes of Theodore Bilbo, John Rankin, and Gerald L. K. Smith, all of whom represent the immediate, post-war, pseudo-agrarian anti-

Semitism. Jeansonne develops his analysis in part within the context of a discussion of the perennial problem of Jewish defense and community organizations, which Bayor and others have noted, of the decision to ignore or confront (and then how to confront?) anti-Semitic demagogues and movements.[118] Shapiro notes no systematic racial basis in either Bilbo's or Rankin's anti-Semitism, for although both men blamed America's problems on Jews, they demonstrated the xenophobic rather than racist (in contrast to some patricians) basis of quasi-agrarianism by singling out for blame *northern* (especially New York City) Jews rather than their southern Jewish constituents. Alan Kraut and Richard Breitman challenge the view of a number of scholars that anti-Semitism among patrician and would-be patrician State Department officers played a significant role in forging the anti-refugee policy of the 1930s.[119] The authors find that although the important officials they examine generally disliked Jews, bureaucratic and political criteria were of greater importance than anti-Semitism in determining their approach to refugees.

In section three, "Social Discrimination," David Gerber calls attention to an aspect of discrimination—access to commercial credit—which was unexamined until just recently,[120] and in the process questions the established contention that antebellum Jewry was not hindered by important economic restrictions.[121] Sarna alerted us to the various processes by which the tension between the images of real and mythical Jews was addressed by gentiles in the nineteenth century; here, Gerber attempts to analyze one of them in the transformation of the ancient stereotype of Shylock to fit Jewish immigrant entrepreneurs of the antebellum period. Marcia Synnott's essay expands upon problems both she and Harold Wechsler addressed in excellent recently published works on the origins of quotas and selective admissions in higher education.[122] Using data never before brought together, Synnott examines the ways in which quotas spread from elite northeastern institutions outward to the rest of the nation, largely as a consequence of increased Jewish applications when paths were blocked in the East.

In section four, "Intergroup Relations in The City," Leonard Dinnerstein examines Irish-Jewish relations in turn-of-the-century New York City within the context of the riots accompanying the 1902 funeral of Rabbi Jacob Joseph. Like Kraut and Breitman,

Dinnerstein asks us to consider the extent to which institutional and professional values (in this case within the police) rather than anti-Semitism played a role in determining the course of intergroup hostility.

In section five, "Radicals and Reformers," Elinor Lerner and Arthur Liebman explore new ground largely opened to analysis as a consequence of the political movements and events of the 1960s and 1970s. The traditionally close relations between American Jews and reform and Left movements[123] have been marked, especially in the recent past, by inner tensions rooted ultimately in the problems that movements with universalistic ideologies and goals have experienced in accommodating particularistic ethnic needs. Lerner and Liebman do not share completely similar perspectives. Liebman is critical of the idea, which Lerner and a number of contemporary Jewish feminists share, that insensitivity to Jewish interests is a type of anti-Semitism. Lerner's essay is also controversial in its denial of the significance of the pluralist strain in American liberalism and, in particular, in liberal feminist thought.[124]

In section six, "Toward Christian Reevaluation and Interfaith Dialogue," David Singer and Egal Feldman provide sensitive examinations of the development of the twentieth-century American Christian conscience. Perhaps no institutions in Western society bear more fully the moral weight for anti-Semitism than the Christian churches, which, at best, have held deeply ambivalent views toward Jews throughout the history of Christianity. Nonetheless, in the years since the Holocaust painful yet unprecedented steps toward reformulation of attitudes and interfaith dialogue have been taken in the United States and elsewhere.[125] Both authors provide insight into the process of intellectual reconceptualization of these troubled historical relations from inside American Protestantism and Catholicism.

Notes

1. The definition is based on Melvin Tumin, *Anti-Semitism in America* (New York, 1966), excerpted in *Anti-Semitism in the United States,* ed. Leonard Dinnerstein, (New York, 1971), pp. 10–11; Harold E. Quiney and Charles Y. Glock, *Anti-Semitism in America* (New York, 1976), pp. 194–95; Carey McWilliams, *A Mask for Privilege: Anti-Semitism in America* (Boston, 1948), pp. 87–94; Hannah Arendt, *Antisemitism* (New York, 1951), pp. vii–xii.

In recent years the usage of the term "anti-Semitism" has perhaps been more controversial than the definition of the phenomenon. The technical flimsiness of the term for our purposes becomes immediately apparent to the extent that whether the word "Semite" is derived from biblical scholarship (the descendants of Shem) or linguistic studies (a subfamily of Afro-Asiatic languages), it refers to a number of peoples originating in southwestern Asia, including not only Jews but Arabs. In addition to its lack of precision, moreover, the term has an unsavory provenance. It was first developed by late nineteenth-century German ideologists of anti-Semitism who sought, in the face of criticism from liberals, to distinguish themselves from traditional religious bigots. They meant the term to carry racial connotations—to suggest, in other words, some racial essence or racial traits that were inherent in the group life and individual personalities of Jews. As such, of course, the term in itself carried some of the seeds of Nazi racial ideology.

The alternatives that have been suggested, however, either have failed to become established in conventional, American usage or do not really pose a meaningful or distinctive substitute. Thus, "anti-Jewish" and "Judeophobia" may appear more precise, particularly in fixing the target of abuse. The latter, however, carries rather more restrictive meanings, through the root "phobia," than does the customary usage. Under any circumstance, neither term has been able to establish itself in contemporary discourse. Perhaps the most widely employed substitute has been used by those who have sought to make the conventional term more precise by dropping the hyphen and the capital "S," thus producing "antisemitism." It is difficult to understand, however, how the new word that is said to develop out of this maneuver actually accomplishes its goal, since the source of the problem in the first place—"Semitism"—is left intact.

Because some scholars may have strong and well-considered objections to the customary usage, alternatives were discussed by the editor of the collection and editors from the University of Illinois Press. In addition, scholars in the field, but not involved in this collection, were consulted. Out of these discussions and consultations came the decision to opt for the convention, "anti-Semitism." In spite of its technical problems and the circumstances of its origins, "anti-Semitism" is still very widely employed in American literature and journalism, still sanctioned by American dictionaries, and still expected by American readers. (For more discussion of the rise of this debate over usage, see n. 67, p. 383 of Egal Feldman's essay in this volume.)

2. Tumin, *Anti-Semitism in America*, p. 11.

3. See the remarks in "Introduction," in *Anti-Semitism in the United States*, ed. Dinnerstein, pp. 2–3. This essay has been deeply influenced by all of the various works of John Higham cited and analyzed below, as will be obvious to the reader informed in American historiography. Higham is doubtless the leading theorist in the history of American anti-Semitism. The author's only significant disagreement with Higham is that, in general, Higham's works often seem to collapse anti-Semitism into a species of nativism; thus, it becomes not unlike other prejudices against American white ethnic groups. Anti-Semitism, however, seems to be better understood, in its content, history, and functions,

as a unique phenomenon even in the United States, where it has not been an important feature of the nation's historical development. What is particularly striking and unique about it is its durability and similarity of ideas across both the centuries and national boundaries.

4. Oscar Handlin, *Adventure in Freedom: 300 Years of Jewish Life in America* (New York, 1954), pp. 197–98.

5. Barbara Miller Solomon, *Ancestors and Immigrants: A Changing New England Tradition* (Cambridge, Mass., 1956), pp. 168–74, 201–7; Esther Panitz, "In Defense of the Jewish Immigrant," *American Jewish Historical Quarterly* (hereafter cited as *AJHQ*) 55 (Sept. 1965): 87–97; John Higham, "American Anti-Semitism, Historically Reconsidered," in *Jews in the Mind of America*, ed. Charles H. Stember et al., (New York, 1966), pp. 251–52; Moses Rischin, *The Promised City: New York City's Jews, 1870–1914* (Cambridge, Mass., 1962), p. 260.

6. Henry L. Feingold, "Anti-Semitism and the Anti-Semitic Imagination in America: A Case Study: the 1920s," in *A Midrash on American-Jewish History*, ed. Henry L. Feingold (Albany, N.Y., 1982), p. 178.

7. Thus, the September 1981 special issue of *American Jewish History* (hereafter cited as *AJH*), dedicated to anti-Semitism, contains two articles on missionaries: Jeffrey Gurock, "Jacob A. Riis: Christian Friend or Missionary Foe? Two Jewish Views," pp. 29–47; George L. Berlin, "Solomon Jackson's *The Jew:* An Early American Jewish Response to The Missionaries," pp. 10–28. Neither article is able to make the case that the missionaries were anti-Semitic; indeed only the latter comes close to suggesting the missionaries had any sort of explicitly negative view of Jews or Judaism, and this view can only dubiously be called anti-Semitic.

8. Jonathan Sarna, "America Is Different," *Midstream* 28 (Feb. 1982): 63, and "The American Jewish Response to Nineteenth Century Christian Missions," *Journal of American History* 68 (June 1981): 35–51; B. Zvi Sobel, "Jews and Christian Evangelization: The Anglo-American Approach," *AJHQ* 58 (Dec. 1968): 255–56; Gurock, "Jacob A. Riis: Christian Friend or Missionary Foe?" pp. 29–47; Berlin, "Solomon Jackson's *The Jew,*" pp. 10–28; Lloyd P. Gartner, *History of the Jews of Cleveland* (Cleveland, 1978), p. 177; David Max Eichhorn, *Evangelizing The American Jew* (New York, 1978).

9. Dennis Wrong, "The Rise and Decline of Anti-Semitism in America," in *The Ghetto and Beyond*, ed. Peter I. Rose (New York, 1969), p. 324; John Higham, "Another Look at Nativism," in his *Send These to Me* (New York, 1975), pp. 107–8; Anson Phelp Stokes, *Church and State in the United States*, 3 vols. (New York, 1950), 2:14–20, 3:153–76; Clifford S. Griffen, *Their Brother's Keeper* (New Brunswick, N.J., 1960).

10. Robert Gutman, "Demographic Trends and The Decline of Anti-Semitism," in *Jews in The Mind of America*, ed. Stember et al., p. 354.

11. Marshall Sklare et al., *Not Quite At Home: How an American Jewish Community Lives with Itself and Its Neighbors* (New York, 1969), p. 56; Joseph Brandes, *Immigrants to Freedom: Jewish Communities in Rural New Jersey since 1882* (Philadelphia, 1971), pp. 184–92; Peter R. Decker, *Fortunes and Failures: White Collar Mobility in Nineteenth Century San Francisco* (Cambridge,

Mass., 1976), p. 115; Isaac M. Fein, *The Making of an American Jewish Community: The History of Baltimore Jewry from 1773 to 1920* (Philadelphia, 1971), pp. 203–7; Steven Hertzberg, *Strangers within the Gate City: The Jews of Atlanta, 1845–1915* (Philadelphia, 1978), pp. 160–62; W. Gunther Plaut, *The Jews of Minnesota: The First Seventy-Five Years* (New York, 1959), pp. 263–64; Max Vorspan and Lloyd P. Gartner, *History of the Jews of Los Angeles* (San Marino, 1970), p. 15; Leonard Bloom, "A Successful Jewish Boycott of the New York City Schools—Christmas, 1906," *AJH* 70 (Dec. 1980): 180–88; Budd Westreich, *The Stow Affair: Anti-Semitism in the California Legislature* (Sacramento, 1981).

12. Higham, "American Anti-Semitism, Historically Reconsidered," p. 237. The controversy concerned Richard Hofstadter, *The Age of Reform* (New York, 1955), pp. 73–81. For a review of the relevant literature, see Walter T. K. Nugent, *The Tolerant Populists: Kansas Populism and Nativism* (Chicago, 1963), pp. 3–32.

13. See William Toll, "The 'New Social History' and Recent Jewish Historical Writing," *AJH* 69 (Mar. 1980): 325–27, 340–41, and Howard N. Rabinowitz, "Writing Jewish Community History," *AJH* 70 (Sept. 1980): 119–27, for analysis of the traditional concerns and their historiographical evolution with comments on the conceptualization of anti-Semitism.

14. Marshall Sklare and Theodore Solotaroff, "Introduction," in *Jews in The Mind of America*, ed. Stember et al., pp. 7, 11–12. Both organizations have sponsored research along each of these two lines. The printed works sponsored by the AJC have been Stember et al., *Jews in The Mind of America* and, in the "Studies in Prejudice," series, Theodore W. Adorno et al., *The Authoritarian Personality* (New York, 1950); Nathaniel Ackerman and Marie Jahoda, *Anti-Semitism and Emotional Disorder* (New York, 1950); Bruno Bettelheim and Morris Janowitz, *Dynamics of Prejudice* (New York, 1950); Leo Lowenthal and Nobert Grossman, *Prophets of Deceit: A Study of The American Agitator* (New York, 1949). Of the seven volumes in the ADL's "Patterns of American Prejudice Series," those most relevant to the study of anti-Semitism are Charles Y. Glock et al., *The Apathetic Majority: A Study Based on The Public Response to The Eichmann Trial* (New York, 1966); Charles Y. Glock et al., *Christian Beliefs and Anti-Semitism* (New York, 1966); Seymour Martin Lipset and Earl Raab, *The Politics of Unreason: Right Wing Extremism in America, 1790–1970* (New York, 1970); Gary T. Marx, *Protest and Prejudice: A Study of Belief in The Black Community* (New York, 1967); Gertrude J. Selznick and Stephen Steinberg, *The Tenacity of Prejudice: Anti-Semitism in Contemporary America* (New York, 1969); Rodney Stark et al., *Wayward Shepherds: Prejudice and the Protestant Clergy* (New York, 1971); Harold E. Quiney and Charles Y. Glock, *Anti-Semitism in America* (New York, 1979). That some of these works touch on other issues, too, is evident from a few of the titles, but less evident in other cases. Also, see Ernst Simmel, ed., *Anti-Semitism: A Social Disease* (New York, 1946).

15. Criticisms are found in Lucy Dawidowicz, "Can Anti-Semitism Be Measured?" *Commentary* 50 (July 1970): 36–43; Wrong, "The Rise and Decline of Anti-Semitism in America," pp. 314–19. Selznick and Steinberg, *The Tenacity*

of Prejudice, pp. xv, 189–90, provide a critique of the psychodynamic-psychopathology approach while defending attitude polling against its critics (pp. xvii–xxi).

16. Bertram Wallace Korn, *American Jewry and The Civil War* (Philadelphia, 1951), p. 156; Leonard Dinnerstein, ed., *Anti-Semitism in The United States,* p. 2; Rabinowitz, "Writing Jewish Community History," p. 127.

17. Jonathan Sarna, "Anti-Semitism and American History," *Commentary* 71 (Mar. 1981): 42. See also Leonard Dinnerstein, "The Historiography of American Anti-Semitism," *Immigration History Newsletter* 16 (Nov. 1984): 2–7.

18. Higham, "American Anti-Semitism, Historically Reconsidered," pp. 23–58, and "Anti-Semitism in The Gilded Age: A Reinterpretation," *Mississippi Valley Historical Review* 43 (Mar. 1957): 559–78. See also his "Ideological Anti-Semitism in The Gilded Age," pp. 116–37; "Social Discrimination against Jews, 1830–1930," pp. 138–73; "Anti-Semitism and American Culture," pp. 174–95, all in Higham, *Send These to Me.* These essays are revisions or reworkings of ideas found in earlier versions. "Social Discrimination . . ." is based on "Social Discrimination against Jews in America, 1830–1930," *Publications of The American Jewish Historical Society* (hereafter cited as *PAJHS*) (Sept. 1957): 1–33 but is so changed in its 1975 version that the latter alone will be cited. The other works are all so valuable in their own right that they will all be cited separately in their various versions.

19. Sarna, "Anti-Semitism and American History," p. 43.

20. Morris U. Schappes, *Documentary History of The Jews in America, 1654–1815* (New York, 1950), pp. xi–xiii, and "Anti-Semitism and Reaction, 1795–1800," *PAJHS* 38 (1948–49): 109–37.

21. See notes 25–29.

22. Nathan C. Belth, *A Promise to Keep* (New York, 1981); Ernest Volkman, *A Legacy of Hate: Anti-Semitism in America* (New York, 1982).

23. *AJH* 71 (Sept. 1981).

24. Sarna, "Anti-Semitism and American History," p. 43; Jacob Rader Marcus, *Early American Jewry,* vol. 1, *The Jews of New York, New England, and Canada* (Philadelphia, 1951); vol. 2, *The Jews of Pennsylvania and The South* (Philadelphia, 1953); vol. 3, *The Colonial American Jew, 1492–1776* (New York, 1970). It needs to be noted that the chapter following "Rejection" was entitled "Acceptance."

25. Louis Harap, *The Image of The Jew in American Literature from Early Republic to Mass Immigration* (Philadelphia, 1974); Michael N. Dobkowski, "American Anti-Semitism: A Reinterpretation," *American Quarterly* 29 (Summer 1977): 166–81, and *The Tarnished Dream: The Basis of American Anti-Semitism* (Westport, Conn., 1979).

26. Saul S. Friedman, *The Incident at Massena* (New York, 1978). The blood libel had existed within southern oral tradition, in ballad form, well into the twentieth century; Foster B. Gresham, " 'The Jew's Daughter': An Example of Ballad Variation," in *Jews in The South,* ed. Leonard Dinnerstein and Mary Dale Palsson (Baton Rouge, 1973), pp. 201–5.

27. Albert Lee, *Henry Ford and the Jews* (New York, 1980); Leo Ribuffo, "Henry Ford and *The International Jew, AJH* 69 (June 1980): 437–77; Robert Singerman, "The American Career of The *Protocols of the Elders of Zion,*" *AJH* 71 (Sept. 1981): 48–78.

28. Harold Wechsler, *The Qualified Student: A History of Selective College Admissions in America* (New York, 1977), esp., pp. 131–75; Marcia Graham Synnott, *The Half-Opened Door: Discrimination in Admissions at Harvard, Yale, and Princeton, 1900–1970* (Westport, Conn., 1979), pp. xvii–xx and passim.

29. David A. Gerber, "Cutting Out Shylock: Elite Anti-Semitism and The Quest for Moral Order in The Nineteenth Century American Market Place," *Journal of American History* 69 (Dec. 1982): 615–37; Stephen G. Mostov, "Dun and Bradstreet Reports as A Source of Jewish Economic History: Cincinnati, 1840–1875," *AJH* 72 (Mar. 1983): 333–53; Toll, "The 'New Social History' and Recent Jewish Historical Writing," pp. 340–41; Peter R. Decker, *Fortunes and Failures, White Collar Mobility in Nineteenth Century San Francisco* (Cambridge, Mass., 1976), pp. 18, 99–100. There are many quantitative studies of socioeconomic mobility that analyze Jewish mobility. I have included here only works which explicitly touch on questions of anti-Semitic discrimination.

30. Henry L. Feingold, *The Politics of Rescue: The Roosevelt Administration, 1938–1945* (New Brunswick, 1970); Saul S. Friedman, *No Haven for The Oppressed: U.S. Policy toward Jewish Refugees, 1938–1945* (Detroit, 1973); Arthur D. Morse, *While Six Million Died: A Chronicle of American Apathy* (New York, 1967); David Wyman, *Paper Walls: America and The Refugee Crisis, 1938–1941* (Amherst, Mass., 1968); Leonard Dinnerstein, *America and The Survivors of The Holocaust* (New York, 1982); David Wyman, *Abandonment of the Jews: America and the Holocaust, 1941–1945* (New York, 1984).

31. Salo W. Baron, *Social and Religious History of The Jews,* rev. ed. (New York, 1957), 6:232–34, and *Historians and Jewish History* (Philadelphia, 1964), pp. 88–89.

32. Stephen Whitfield, "The Presence of the Past: Recent Trends in American Jewish History," *AJH* 70 (Dec. 1980): 150–51.

33. Sarna, "Anti-Semitism and American History," pp. 43–47, and "America Is Different," pp. 63–64. Also see Sarna's exchanges with Michael N. Dobkowski, *Commentary* 81 (Nov. 1981): 12, and with Saul S. Friedman, *Midstream* 29 (Jan. 1983): 63–64. Also relevant here is Oscar Handlin, "A Twenty Year Retrospect of American Jewish Historiography," *AJHQ* 65 (June 1976): 307–8.

34. Michael N. Dobkowski, letter, *Commentary* 81 (Nov. 1981): 7–8; Saul S. Friedman, letter, *Midstream* 29 (Jan. 1983): 62–63.

35. Feingold, "Anti-Semitism and the Anti-Semitic Imagination in America: A Case Study: the 1920s," pp. 177, 187. Also see Lucy Dawidowicz, *On Equal Terms: Jews in America, 1881–1981,* (New York, 1982), p. 22, whose position resembles Feingold's but whose criteria for reaching her conclusions are somewhat better defined.

36. Marcus, *Early American Jewry,* vol. 1, *The Jews of New York, New England, and Canada,* vol. 2, *The Jews of Pennsylvania and the South,* and vol. 3, *The Colonial American Jew;* Abram Vossen Goodman, *American Overture:*

Jewish Rights in Colonial Times (Philadelphia, 1947); Richard B. Morris, "Civil Liberties and The Jewish Tradition in Early America," *PAJHS* 46 (Sept. 1956): 20–40.

37. Marcus, *Early American Jewry*, vol. 1, *The Jews of New York, New England and Canada*, esp. pp. 25–34, 54–63, 103–4, 128–29, 141–43, 156, 160–61; vol. 2, *The Jews of Pennsylvania and The South*, pp. 10, 12, 67–68, 125–28, 154–61, 166–69, 178–79, 182, 188, 217, 231–32, 246, 260, 270–72, 287, 293, 315, 318–19, 331–33, 337, 494–95, 514–29; vol. 3, *The Colonial American Jew*, pp. 1113–34, 1135–68; Morris, "Civil Liberties and The Jewish Tradition in Early America," pp. 20–40; Leon Hühner, "Jews in The Legal and Medical Professions in America prior to 1800," *PAJHS* 22 (1914): 149; Higham, "American Anti-Semitism, Historically Reconsidered," pp. 243–44.

38. Edward Eitches, "Maryland's 'Jew Bill'," *AJHQ* 60 (Mar. 1971): 258–78; Stanley F. Chyet, "The Political Rights of Jews in The United States, 1776–1840," *American Jewish Archives* 2 (Apr. 1958): 14–75; Fein, *The Making of An American Jewish Community: The History of Baltimore Jewry*, pp. 25–36; Marcus, *Early American Jewry*, vol. 1, *The Jews of New York, New England, and Canada*, pp. 156, 160–61; vol. 2, *The Jews of Pennsylvania and The South*, pp. 154–61, 217, 260, 271–72, 337, 529–37; Edwin Wolf and Maxwell Whiteman, *The History of The Jews of Philadelphia from Colonial Times to The Age of Jackson* (Philadelphia, 1956), pp. 146–64.

39. Ben Halprin, "Anti-Semitism in The Perspective of Jewish History," in *Jews in The Mind of America*, ed. Stember et al., p. 283.

40. Ibid., p. 282; Thomas F. O'Dea, "The Changing Image of The Jew and The Contemporary Religious Situation: An Exploration of Ambiguities," in *Jews in The Mind of America*, ed. Stember et al., pp. 305–6, 310; McWilliams, *A Mast for Privilege*, p. 48; Higham, "American Anti-Semitism, Historically Reconsidered," p. 253. Sarna, "Anti-Semitism and American History," pp. 46–47.

41. John Higham, "The Immigrant in American History," in his, *Send These to Me*, pp. 19–20; Handlin, *Adventure in Freedom*, pp. 73–74. See citations in n. 43 for related works on the organization of pluralism in American political attitudes in the nineteenth century.

42. Sarna, "Anti-Semitism and American History," p. 46; Higham, "Anti-Semitism and American Culture," pp. 178–79, and "Social Discrimination against Jews, 1830–1930," p. 164; Dinnerstein and Palsson, eds., *Jews in The South*, pp. 13–15; Harry Golden, *Our Southern Landsman* (New York, 1974), p. 101.

43. Michael F. Holt, *The Political Crisis of the 1850s* (New York, 1978), pp. 34, 155, 162; Ira Katznelson, *City Trenches: Urban Politics and The Patterning of Class in The United States* (New York, 1981), pp. 58, 65–67, 113–14, and *Black Men, White Cities: Race, Politics, and Migration in The U.S., 1900–1930* (New York, 1973), pp. 66, 86–104, 111–13; Edgar Litt, *Beyond Pluralism: Ethnic Politics in America* (Glenview, Ill., 1970), pp. 24–35; John Allswang, *Bosses, Machines, and Urban Voters: An American Symbiosis* (Pt. Washington, N.Y., 1977), pp. 36–42, 45–55; Paul Kleppner, *The Cross of Culture: A Social Analysis of Midwestern Politics, 1850–1900* (New York, 1970).

44. Sarna, "Anti-Semitism and American History," p. 43; Nathan Glazer,

"Jews," in *Ethnic Leadership in America,* ed. John Higham (Baltimore, 1978), pp. 30–31; Deborah Dash Moore, *B'nai Brith and The Challenge of Ethnic Leadership* (Albany, N.Y., 1981); Naomi Cohen, *Not Free to Desist: The American Jewish Committee, 1906–1966* (Philadelphia, 1972); Berlin, "Solomon Jackson's *The Jew,*" pp. 10–28; Sarna, "The American Jewish Response to Nineteenth Century Christian Missions," pp. 35–51.

45. Higham, "Anti-Semitism and American Culture," pp. 178–80. For interesting variations on this point, see Moses Klingsberg, "Jewish Immigrants in Business: A Sociological Study," *AJHQ* 56 (1966–67): 283–318, and Rudolph Glanz, "Jew and Yankee: A Historic Comparison," *Jewish Social Studies* 6 (1944): 3–30.

46. Joel Carmichael, "The Meaning of *Galut* in America Today," *Midstream* 7 (Mar. 1963): 11. Sartre makes the same point in *Anti-Semite and Jew,* trans. George S. Becker (New York, 1948), p. 83. ("Galut": Heb., "diaspora" or "exile".)

47. Halprin, "Anti-Semitism in The Perspective of Jewish History," p. 283. The example of post–World War II, and particularly recent eastern Europe, would seem to suggest that anti-Semitism may even be sustained when Jews are largely a distant memory of the national culture, and are resident only in very small numbers. See Paul Lendvai, *Anti-Semitism without Jews: Communist Eastern Europe* (Garden City, N.Y., 1971), and Lawrence Wechsler, *Poland in the Season of Its Passion* (New York, 1982), passim.

48. McWilliams, *A Mask for Privilege,* p. 48.

49. These categories resemble John Higham's distinction between "social anti-Semitism" ("a pattern of discrimination") and "political or ideological anti-Semitism" ("a power-hungry agitation addressed to the entire body politic, which blames the major ills of society on Jews") in "Ideological Anti-Semitism in The Gilded Age," p. 120, but there are substantive as well as semantic differences. The former will become clear in the next several pages. In general, I tried to create broader categories which were comprised of more, and related, phenomena. In regard to the latter, I find Higham's use of "social" too restrictive, apparently unable to include the "political or ideological."

50. Korn, *American Jewry and The Civil War,* pp. 122–55, 158–75, 175–88. On the background to the founding of both organizations see Cohen, *Not Free to Desist,* pp. 1–18, 37–53; Moore, *B'nai Brith,* pp. 102–8. As Moore states, while it was the 1913 lynching of Leo Frank that directly stimulated the creation of ADL, its B'nai Brith founders were particularly worried about ideological anti-Semitism and the ugly stereotypes which were connected with it. The AJC, on the other hand, was born of a concern for the deterioration of the condition of *Russian* Jews. Yet its first organized effort, as Cohen explains, was in fighting immigration restriction, an issue which always had an ideological edge to it. On interfaith efforts, see Haim Genezi, "American Interfaith Cooperation on Behalf of Refugees from Nazism," *AJH* 70 (Mar. 1981): 347–61; Louis J. Swichkow and Lloyd P. Gartner, *The History of The Jewish Milwaukee* (Philadelphia, 1963), pp. 304–5; Solomon Joshua Kohn, *The Jewish Community of Utica, New York, 1847–1948* (New York, 1959), p. 93.

51. Higham, "Social Discrimination against Jews, 1830–1930," p. 148;

McWilliams, *A Mask for Privilege,* pp. 17–21, 124–25; Oscar Handlin, "The Acquisition of Political and Social Rights by the Jews of The United States," *American Jewish Year Book* 55 (New York, 1955): 72, 74; Schappes, *Documentary History of The Jews,* p. xiii.

52. Stuart Rosenberg, *The Jewish Community of Rochester, 1843–1925* (New York, 1954), pp. 114–19; Vorspan and Gartner, *History of the Jews of Los Angeles,* pp. 14, 47–48; Robert Rockaway, "Anti-Semitism in An American City: Detroit, 1850–1914," *AJHQ* 64 (Sept. 1974): 42–47; Hertzberg, *Strangers in The Gate City,* p. 155; Louis J. Swichkow and Lloyd P. Gartner, *The History of The Jews of Milwaukee* (Philadelphia, 1963), pp. 19–20, 93–110, 157–66; Gutman, "Demographic Trends and The Decline of Anti-Semitism," p. 354; Handlin, *Adventure in Freedom,* pp. 54–57; Henry Feingold, *Zion in America: The Jewish Experience in America from Colonial Times to the Present* (New York, 1974), pp. 59, 63–64, 73–76; Marc Lee Raphael, "The Early Jews of Columbus, Ohio: A Study in Economic Mobility," in *A Bicentennial Festschrift for Jacob Rader Marcus,* ed. Bertram Korn (Waltham, Mass., 1976), pp. 435–51; Mitchell Gelfand, "Progress and Prosperity: Jewish Social Mobility in Los Angeles in The Booming '80's," *AJH* (June 1979): 408–33; Selig Adler and Thomas Connolly, *From Ararat to Suburbia: The History of The Jewish Community of Buffalo* (Philadelphia, 1960), pp. 105–59.

53. Harap, *The Image of The Jew in American Literature,* presents both positive and negative imagery about Jews. See also Oscar Handlin, "American Views of The Jew at The Opening of The Twentieth Century," *PAJHS* 40 (June 1951): 323, and *Adventure in Freedom,* p. 73; Gerber, "Cutting Out Shylock: Elite Anti-Semitism and The Quest for Moral Order in The Mid-Nineteenth Century Market Place," pp. 623–24, 629–33; Hertzberg, *Strangers in The Gate City,* pp. 176–7; Rosenberg, *The Jewish Community of Rochester,* pp. 114–19.

54. Gerber, "Cutting Out Shylock: Elite Anti-Semitism and The Quest for Moral Order in the Mid-Nineteenth Century American Market Place," pp. 615–37.

55. Jonathan Sarna, *Jacksonian Jew: The Two Worlds of Mordecai Noah* (New York, 1981), pp. 44–47, 54–55, 85–86, 119–25, 144. Philadelphia provides another example of anti-Semitism in early political campaigns; see Wolf and Whiteman, *The History of The Jews of Philadelphia,* p. 299. For Los Angeles, see Vorspan and Gartner, *History of the Jews of Los Angeles,* pp. 47–48; for Detroit, see Robert Rockaway, "Anti-Semitism in An American City: Detroit, 1850–1914," p. 45.

56. B. G. Rudolph, *From A Minyan to A Community: A History of The Jews of Syracuse* (Syracuse, 1970), pp. 48–49; Vorspan and Gartner, *History of The Jews of Los Angeles,* pp. 51–54; Fein, *The Making of An American Jewish Community: The History of Baltimore Jewry,* pp. 203–7.

57. Abram Karof, "Uriah Phillips Levy: The Story of A Pugnacious Commodore," *PAJHS* 39 (1949–1950): 8, 24–30, 51–52; Gerber, "Cutting Out Shylock: Elite Anti-Semitism and The Quest for Moral Order in The Mid-Nineteenth Century Market Place," pp. 625–34; Mostov, "Dun and Bradstreet Reports As A Source of Jewish Economic History," pp. 348–52; Higham, "Social Discrimination against Jews, 1830–1930," pp. 143–44.

58. Higham, "Social Discrimination against Jews, 1830–1930," pp. 148–151; Oscar and Mary Handlin, "Origins of Anti-Semitism in The United States," in *Race, Prejudice, and Discrimination,* ed. Arnold Rose (New York, 1951), pp. 26–30. For a contrasting view, emphasizing ideology and the cross-fertilization of ideas between America and Europe, see Naomi Cohen, "Anti-Semitism in the Gilded Age: The Jewish View," *Jewish Social Studies* 41 (1979): 190–98.

59. Feingold, *Zion in America,* p. 79; Jeffrey Gurock, *When Harlem Was Jewish* (New York, 1979), p. 14; Rischin, *The Promised City,* p. 261; Fein, *The Making of An American Jewish Community: The History of Baltimore Jewry,* pp. 203–7; Gartner, *History of The Jews of Cleveland,* pp. 83–84; John J. Appel, "Jews in American Caricature, 1820–1914," *AJH* 71 (Sept. 1981): 103–33, esp. 103–19. Appel largely holds that the cartoon images he analyzes aren't anti-Semitic, yet they certainly exploit traditional anti-Semitic metaphors. See also the slide series Appel and Selma Appel developed for the ADL, "The Distorted Image: Stereotype and Caricature in American Popular Graphics, 1850–1922" (New York, 1973). Dobkowski, *The Tarnished Dream,* pp. 78–112; Higham, "Social Discrimination against Jews, 1830–1930," pp. 146–47; Marshall Sklare and Joseph Greenbaum, *Jewish Identity on The Suburban Frontier: A Study of Group Survival in An Open Society* (New York, 1967), pp. 10–13; Vorspan and Gartner, *History of The Jews of Los Angeles,* pp. 81, 206.

60. Gutman, "Demographic Trends and The Decline of Anti-Semitism," p. 354.

61. Mark Zborowski and Elizabeth Herzog, *Life is With People* (New York, 1951); Rischin, *The Promised City,* pp. 19–47; Irving Howe, *The World of Our Fathers* (New York, 1976), pp. 67–118, 119–47, 148–68; Thomas Kessner, *The Golden Door: Italian and Jewish Immigrant Mobility in New York City, 1880–1915* (New York, 1977), pp. 59–65, 167–68, 173; Stephen Thernstrom, *The Other Bostonians: Poverty and Progress in An American Metropolis, 1830–1970* (Cambridge, Mass., 1973), pp. 145–73; Judith R. Kramer and Seymour Leventman, *Children of the Gilded Ghetto* (New Haven, Conn., 1961).

62. Ronald Bayor, *Neighbors in Conflict: The Irish, Germans, Jews, and Italians of New York City, 1929–1941* (Baltimore, 1979), p. 4, 25–29, 92–108, 113–21, 128–33, 135, 142, 145, 146, 150–63. See also Dennis Clark, "The Harp and The Mezuzah: Irish-Jewish Relations," in *Jewish Life in Philadelphia, 1830–1940,* ed. Murray Friedman (Philadelphia, 1983); Rudolf Glanz, *Jew and Irish: Historic Group Relations and Immigration* (New York, 1966). Rivka Lissak, "Myth and Reality: The Pattern of Relationship between the Hull House Circle and the 'New Immigrants' on Chicago's West Side, 1890–1919," *Journal of American Ethnic History* 2 (Spring 1983): 27–29.

63. Rischin, *The Promised City,* p. 91; Higham, "Ideological Anti-Semitism in The Gilded Age," pp. 135–36. The same tensions were indirectly mirrored in the 1908 controversy in New York City over the charge by the city's police commissioner that Jews were overrepresented in the crime statistics; see Arthur Goren, *New York Jews and The Quest for Community: The Kehillah Experiment, 1908–1922* (New York, 1970), pp. 24–30. Over three decades later, Jews were still complaining about the treatment they encountered at the hands of the Irish police; Bayor, *Neighbors in Conflict,* pp. 156–57.

64. Rischin, *The Promised City*, pp. 59–62, 188–89; Gurock, *When Harlem Was Jewish*, pp. 18–22, 66; Kessner, *The Golden Door*, pp. 59–65; S. Joseph Fauman, "Occupational Self-Selection among Detroit Jews," in *The Jews: Social Patterns of an American Group*, ed. Sklare (Glencoe, Ill., 1958), pp. 119–37; Joel Perlman, "Beyond New York: The Occupations of Russian Jewish Immigrants in Providence, Rhode Island, and in Other Small Jewish Communities, 1900–1915," *AJH* 72 (Mar. 1983): 384–94; Gartner, *History of The Jews of Cleveland*, pp. 134–35. For a contrasting position, pointing out the "rabid anti-Semitism" in factories and mines in the Pittsburgh area that limited Jewish employment options, see Ida Cohen Selavan, "Jewish Wage Earners in Pittsburgh, 1890–1930," *AJHQ* 65 (Mar. 1976): 272–73.

65. Synnott, *The Half-Opened Door*, pp. xvii–xx, and passim; Wechsler, *The Qualified Student*, pp. 131–75; Frederick Rudolph, *The American College and University*, (New York, 1962), p. 289; Moore, *B'nai Brith*, pp. 135–38. Harvey Strum, "Louis Marshall and Anti-Semitism at Syracuse University," *American Jewish Archives* 35 (Apr. 1983): 1–10. See also Oliver B. Pollock, "Antisemitism, The Harvard Plan, and the Roots of Reverse Discrimination," *Jewish Social Studies* 45 (Spring 1983): 113–22. For a different side of the same story, an institution which did not resist Jewish enrollment increases and became heavily identified with Jews, see Sherry Gorelick, *City College and The Jewish Poor, Education in New York, 1880–1924* (New Brunswick, N.J., 1981).

66. McWilliams, *A Mask for Privilege*, pp. 37, 158; Belth, *A Promise to Keep*, pp. 111–13. The standard work on the prevalence of, and devices used to achieve, discrimination in lower white-collar employment is Haywood Broun and George Britt, *Christians Only: A Study in Prejudice* (New York, 1931).

67. Cohen, *Not Free to Desist*, pp. 415–25; "Jews in America," *Fortune* 13 (Feb. 1936): 130, 133–316; Jerold S. Auerbach, *Unequal Justice* (New York, 1976), pp. 99–100, 122, 125–27, 209, 218; Daniel Pope and William Toll, "We Tried Harder: Jews in American Advertising," *AJH* 72 (Sept. 1982): 29, 31, 38. On "Jewish jobs," see Stephen L. Slavin and Mary A. Pradt, *The Einstein Syndrome: Corporate Anti-Semitism in America Today* (Washington, D.C., 1982), pp. 2, 8.

68. Vorspan and Gartner, *History of The Jews of Los Angeles*, p. 206; Gartner, *History of The Jews of Cleveland*, pp. 94–98; Swichkow and Gartner, *The History of The Jews of Milwaukee*, pp. 302–5; Albert I. Gordon, *Jews in Transition* (Minneapolis, 1949), pp. 43–68, and passim; Deborah Dash Moore, *At Home in America: Second Generation New York Jews* (New York, 1981), pp. 36, 38.

69. Vorspan and Gartner, *History of The Jews of Los Angeles*, pp. 245–47; Rudolf, *From a Minyan to a Community*, p. 245; John P. Dean, "Jewish Participation in the Life of Middle-Sized American Communities," in *The Jews: Social Patterns of an American Group*, ed. Sklare, pp. 304–20; Gartner, *History of The Jews of Cleveland*, pp. 299–303; Plaut, *The Jews of Minnesota*, pp. 273–75; Cohen, *Not Free to Desist*, pp. 426–28.

70. Appel, "Jews in American Caricature, 1820–1914," and "The Distorted Image"; Dobkowski, *The Tarnished Dream*, pp. 78–112.

71. Dinnerstein and Polsson, ed., *Jews in the South*, pp. 7–12, 13–15, neatly summarizes both sides of the question. See also Thomas D. Clark, "The Post–Civil War Economy in the South," *AJHQ* 55 (June 1966): 427–30; Leonard Dinnerstein, "A Neglected Aspect of Southern Jewish History," *AJHQ* 61 (Sept. 1971): 52–68, and "Southern Jewry and The Desegregation Crisis, 1954–1970," *AJHQ* 62 (Mar. 1973): 231–41; William Holmes, "Whitecapping: Anti-Semitism in the Populist Era," *AJHQ* 63 (Mar. 1974): 249; Melvin I. Urofsky, "Introduction," pp. xxii–xxiii, Raymond Arsenault, "Charles Jacobson of Arkansas," pp. 55–58; and Stephen Whitfield, "Jews and Other Southerners," pp. 82–86, all in *Turn to the South: Essays on Southern Jewry*, ed. Nathan M. Kaganoff and Melvin I. Urofsky (Charlottesville, Va., 1979); Leonard Dinnerstein, *The Leo Frank Case* (New York, 1968); Mark H. Elovitz, *A Century of Jewish Life in Dixie: The Birmingham Experience* (University, Ala., 1974), pp. 166, 169–70; Murray Friedman, "Virginia Jewry and The School Crisis: Anti-Semitism and Desegregation," in *Jews in The South*, ed. Dinnerstein and Polsson, pp. 341–50; Benjamin Kaplan, *The Eternal Stranger* (New Haven, Conn., 1957), pp. 84–85; Beverly S. Williams, "Anti-Semitism and Shreveport, Louisiana: The Situation in The 1920s," *Louisiana History* 21 (1980): 389–98.

72. Plaut, *The Jews of Minnesota*, pp. 273–79.

73. Higham, "Social Discrimination against Jews, 1830–1930," pp. 163, 165. See also Michael G. Rapp, "A Historical Overview of Anti-Semitism in Minnesota, 1920–1960" (unpublished Ph.D. diss., University of Minnesota, 1977).

74. Carey McWilliams, "Minneapolis: The Curious Twin," *Common Ground* 8 (Autumn 1945): 61–65.

75. Plaut, *The Jews of Minnesota*, pp. 273–79; Gordon, *Jews in Transition*, pp. 43–68.

76. William Toll, *The Making of An Ethnic Middle Class: Portland Jewry over Four Generations* (Albany, N.Y., 1982), pp. 8–11, 77–89, 134; Vorspan and Gartner, *History of The Jews of Los Angeles*, pp. 14, 47–48; Decker, *Fortunes and Failures*, pp. 114–18, 232, 238–39; Williams, "Anti-Semitism and Shreveport, Louisiana, The Situation in the 1920s," p. 389; Mark H. Elovitz, *A Century of Jewish Life in Dixie*, pp. 2–37; Charles Reznikoff and N. Z. Engelman, *The Jews of Charleston* (Philadelphia, 1950).

77. Moses Rischin, "Introduction" to the special issue on western Jewry, *AJH* 68 (June 1979): 394.

78. Hertzberg, *Strangers within The Gate City*, pp. 171, 175; Vorspan and Gartner, *History of The Jews of Los Angeles*, pp. 81–82, 103–4. Out of such patterns, Higham holds tentatively that there is "a direct correlation between discrimination and the degree to which the growth of the local Jewish community disturbed the existing social structure." He does recognize the difficulties with "so elastic" an explanation; see Higham, "Social Discrimination against Jews, 1830–1930," p. 165.

79. Bayor, *Neighbors in Conflict*, passim.

80. Korn, *American Jewry and The Civil War*, pp. 158–75, 175–88; Steven V. Ash, "Civil War Exodus: The Jews and Grant's General Orders, No. 11," *Historian* 44 (Aug. 1982): 505–23.

81. Frederick Cople Jaher, *Doubters and Dissenters: Cataclysmic Thought in America, 1885–1918* (New York, 1964), pp. 130–40; C. Vann Woodward, "The Populist Heritage and The Intellectual," *American Scholar* 59 (Winter 1959–60): 55–72; Norman Pollack, "The Myth of Populist Anti-Semitism," *American Historical Review* 68 (Oct. 1962): 76–80; Nugent, *The Tolerant Populists,* passim.; Higham, "Ideological Anti-Semitism in The Gilded Age," pp. 118, 123–24, and "American Anti-Semitism, Historically Reconsidered," p. 248. The principle text arguing the opposing point is Oscar Handlin, "American Views of The Jew at The Opening of The Twentieth Century," pp. 325, 328.

82. C. Vann Woodward, *Tom Watson: Agrarian Rebel* (New York, 1938), pp. 434, 438, 442–43, 445–46.

83. C. Vann Woodward, *The Origins of The New South, 1877–1913* (Baton Rouge, 1951), pp. 393–94.

84. Woodward, *The Origins of The New South,* pp. 392–94.

85. Higham, "American Anti-Semitism, Historically Reconsidered," pp. 247–48; "Ideological Anti-Semitism in The Gilded Age," pp. 123–24; "Anti-Semitism and American Culture," pp. 183, 187–88. Also see Arnold Rose, "Anti-Semitism's Root in City Hatred," *Commentary* 6 (Oct. 1948): 374–78.

86. Lee, *Henry Ford and The Jews,* pp. 6–7, 148–49: Singerman, "The American Career of *The Protocols of The Elders of Zion,*" pp. 48–78; Higham, "Ideological Anti-Semitism in The Gilded Age," p. 136, and "Anti-Semitism and American Culture," pp. 187–88; Seymour M. Lipset and Earl Raab, The *Politics of Unreason,* pp. 135–38; Allan Nevins and Frank E. Hill, *Ford: Expansion and Challenge, 1915–1933* (New York, 1957), p. 315; Feingold, "Anti-Semitism and the Anti-Semitic Imagination in America: A Case Study: the 1920s," p. 183. For a contrasting position—Ford as Progressive—see Ribuffo, "Henry Ford and *The International Jew,*" 471–77.

87. Solomon, *Ancestors and Immigrants,* p. 19. For observations on the relationship between the response to Jews and the conflict between merit and ascription that greatly shaped patrician resentments, see Stephen Steinberg, *The Ethnic Myth: Race, Class, and Ethnicity in America* (New York, 1981), pp. 230–46, who discounts ethnic factors but sees the Jews particularly as a potent symbol of the threat posed by new criteria of merit in modernizing society.

88. Dobkowski, *The Tarnished Dream,* pp. 113–38; Solomon, *Ancestors and Immigrants,* pp. 38–41. Kenton J. Clymer, "Anti-Semitism in The Late Nineteenth Century: The Case of John Hay," *AJHQ* 60 (June 1971): 344–54, provides an interesting exception-to-prove-the-rule: a wealthy, upwardly mobile, midwestern patrician and Henry Adam's best friend, who had nationalistic and nativistic views but was not an anti-Semite. It remained for Ezra Pound to combine both patrician and pseudo-agrarian perspectives. He blamed Jewish capitalists for warmongering *and* for the decline of aesthetic values; see Ben D. Kimpel and T. C. Duncan Eaves, "Ezra Pound's Anti-Semitism," *South Atlantic Quarterly* 81 (Winter 1982): 56–69.

89. Dobkowski, *The Tarnished Dream,* pp. 143–64; Solomon, *Ancestors and Immigrants,* pp. 171, 173–74, 201–2.

90. Solomon, *Ancestors and Immigrants,* pp. 82–151, 167–75, 195–207;

Panitz, "In Defense of The Jewish Immigrant," 87–89, 90–92. John Higham, in his classic work *Strangers in The Land: Patterns of American Nativism,* 2nd paperback ed. (New York, 1965), is not convinced of any particularly strong anti-Semitic *roots* of restrictionism but does present evidence of an increasingly anti-Semitic, as opposed to simply anti-foreign, component to restrictionist attitudes; see esp. pp. 102–3, 106, 112, 152, 162–63, 188, 204, 309–10, 313–14.

91. Solomon, *Ancestors and Immigrants,* pp. 205–9; Higham, "American Anti-Semitism, Historically Reconsidered," p. 252; Feingold, *The Politics of Rescue.* Perhaps one symptom of how well both the IRL's propaganda and popular anti-Semitism continued to exert influence on the question of restriction of Jews is found in Emory S. Bogardus, *Immigration and Race Attitudes* (Boston, 1928), pp. 24–25, a study of the acceptability of various peoples to native-born Americans of northern European origin. Jews ranked last of all white ethnic groups in seven different social contact situations in a survey of preferences taken among 1,725 such Americans.

92. Donald S. Strong, *Organized Anti-Semitism in America* (Washington, D.C., 1941); Leo Ribuffo, *The Old Christian Right: The Protestant Far Right from Depression to Cold War* (Philadelphia, 1983), pp. 52–63, 109–24, 146–57, 243–44, 256–57; Bayor, *Neighbors in Conflict,* pp. 57–86, 87–108, 109–25; Sander A. Diamond, *The Nazi Movement in The United States, 1929–1941* (Ithaca, N.Y., 1974). Mary C. Athans, "The Fahey-Coughlin Connection: Father Denis Fahey, C.S. Sp., Father Charles E. Coughlin, and Religious Anti-Semitism in the United States, 1938–1954," (unpublished Ph.D. dissertation, Graduate Theological Union, 1982); Myron I. Scholnick, "The New Deal and Anti-Semitism in America," (unpublished Ph.D. diss., University of Maryland, 1971). Several years later, the controversy over isolationism gave these groups a shortlived opportunity to reassert themselves; see Edward S. Shapiro, "Congressional Isolationism and Anti-Semitism, 1939–1941," *AJH* 74 (Sept. 1984): 45–65.

93. Bayor, *Neighbors in Conflict,* pp. 94–104, 112–14, 125.

94. Diamond, *The Nazi Movement in the United States, 1929–1941,* pp. 21–34, 55–84, 223–50; Swichkow and Gartner, *The History of the Jews of Milwaukee,* pp. 302–5. The difficulty with making generalizations about the attraction of right-wing anti-Semitism to eastern and central European ethnics is clear from the experience of Cleveland where Jews joined with Serbs and Czechs, who were usually not anti-Semitic, and Russians and Slovaks, who usually were, against local Nazis in the 1930s; Gartner, *History of the Jews of Cleveland,* p. 303.

95. Lewis Coser, *The Functions of Social Conflict* (New York, 1956), pp. 48–49, 105–8; Georg Simmel, *Conflict,* trans. Kurt H. Wolff, (Glencoe, Ill., 1955), pp. 27–28; Hubert Blalock, *Toward A Theory of Minority-Group Relations* (New York, 1967), pp. 43–44; Robin M. Williams, *The Reduction of Intergroup Tensions: A Survey of Research on Problems of Ethnic, Racial, and Religious Group Relations* (New York, 1947), pp. 40–41.

96. N. 15 contains the relevant citations to the critical literature.

97. Bayor, *Neighbors in Conflict,* pp. 166–67.

98. See Arendt, *Antisemitism,* pp. 3–10, for the chapter entitled, "Antisemitism

As An Outrage to Common Sense."

99. Jacob Katz, "Misreadings of Anti-Semitism," *Commentary* 76 (July 1983): 43–44.

100. Cohen, *Not Free to Desist*, pp. 426–428; Slavin and Pradt, *The Einstein Syndrome*, pp. 41–43; Dean, "Jewish Participation in the Life of Middle-Sized Communities," pp. 304–20.

101. The change in attitudes over time is traced in these works, listed chronologically: Charles Herbert Stember, "The Recent History of Public Attitudes [1938–1962]," in *Jews in The Mind of America*, ed. Stember et al., pp. 31–234, esp. pp. 208–18, 229 for summaries; Gertrude J. Selznick and Stephen Steinberg, *The Tenacity of Prejudice: Anti-Semitism in Contemporary America* (New York, 1969), esp. pp. 184–93; Harold E. Quiney and Charles Y. Glock, *Anti-Semitism in America* (New York, 1979), esp. pp. 185–90; Gregory Martire and Ruth Clark, *Anti-Semitism in The United States: A Study of Prejudice in The 1980s* (New York, 1982), esp. pp. 113–19.

102. Cohen, *Not Free to Desist*, pp. 374–82. Lacking a mass base, such organized anti-Semitism as exists has often adopted a new style. As Cohen makes clear, it now takes the form of quasi-respectable pressure groups and public education organizations and is less concerned with vast world conspiracies than current issues, among them Israel.

103. Volkman, *A Legacy of Hate*, pp. 225–33.

104. Feingold, "Anti-Semitism and the Anti-Semitic Imagination in America: A Case Study: The 1920s," p. 188, Moore, *B'nai Brith*, p. 103.

105. Murray Friedman, "Intergroup Relations," *American Jewish Year Book 1983*, 83 (New York, 1982): 67–68. The idea that such incidents as do take place constitute evidence of a high degree of latent, popular anti-Semitism in America, rather than inchoate vandalism, is explored in Oscar Cohen, *The Swastika 'Epidemic' and Anti-Semitism in America* (New York, 1960).

106. Leonard Dinnerstein, "Anti-Semitism Exposed and Attacked, 1945–1950," *AJH* 71 (Sept. 1981): 137–42; Moore, *B'nai Brith*, pp. 121–23; Cohen, *Not Free to Desist*, pp. 219–26.

107. Wechsler, *The Qualified Student*, pp. 194–204; Synnott, *The Half-Opened Door*, pp. 201, 221–22, 225; Gordon, *Jews in Transition*, pp. 55–66; Cohen, *Not Free to Desist*, pp. 415–25.

108. Dinnerstein, "Anti-Semitism Exposed and Attacked," pp. 142–48. Lester D. Friedman, *Hollywood's Image of the Jew* (New York, 1982), pp. 123–31.

109. Stember, "Recent History of Public Attitudes," pp. 171–95, 216.

110. Cohen, *Not Free to Desist*, pp. 415–25; Slavin and Pradt, *The Einstein Syndrome*, pp. 2, 4, 8, 25–40; Pope and Toll, "We Tried Harder: Jews in American Advertising," 42–43; R. L. Zweigenhaft and G. William Domhoff, *Jews in The Protestant Establishment* (New York, 1982). The persistence of corporate restriction and channeling is not necessarily a consequence of conscious anti-Semitism, but of patterns of recruitment within particular social networks; a belief that one's *clients* are prejudiced; a particular ideal-image of executives in the field in question, etc. See University of Michigan Institute for Social

Research, *Discrimination without Prejudice: A Study of Promotion Practices in Industry* (Ann Arbor, Mich., 1964).

111. Blue-collar attitudes have been more often measured than explained. What is clear is that blue-collar anti-Semitism has declined but more slowly than the anti-Semitism of upper income people, and that today's blue-collar anti-Semitism is less a function directly of income or occupation than of relatively low levels of education. See Selznick and Steinberg, *The Tenacity of Prejudice*, pp. 185–86; Stember, "Recent History of Public Attitudes," p. 227; Wrong, "The Rise and Decline of Anti-Semitism in the United States," pp. 328–29. On Afro-American attitudes and black-Jewish relations, the literature is now voluminous. See Ronald Tsukashima, "Chronological, Cognitive, and Political Effects in the Study of Interminority Group Prejudice," *Phylon* 44 (Sept. 1983): 217–31; Martire and Clark, *Anti-Semitism in the United States*, pp. 114–16; Robert G. Weisbord and Arthur Stein, *Bittersweet Encounter: The Afro-American and the Jew* (New York, 1970), pp. 19–35, 65–84, 85–110, 144–48; Albert Vorspan, "Blacks and Jews," in *Black Anti-Semitism and Jewish Racism*, ed. Nat Hertoff (New York, 1969), pp. 191–228; Nathan Glazer and Daniel P. Moynihan, *Beyond the Melting Pot* (Cambridge, Mass., 1963), pp. 71–77; Arnold Shankman, *Ambivalent Friends: Afro-Americans and the Immigrant* (Westport, Conn., 1982), pp. 111–37. The 1977 *University of California vs. Bakke* case has often been cited as a cause for tension because the AJC and ADL filed *amici curiae* briefs, along with other organizations, in Bakke's behalf. One should also note, however, the large number of Jewish attorneys and activists who, as individuals or in behalf of civil rights organizations, filed pro-quota briefs at the same time. See U.S. Commission on Civil Rights, *Toward An Understanding of "Bakke"* (Washington, D.C., 1979).

112. Feingold, "Anti-Semitism and The Anti-Semitic Imagination in America: A Case Study: The 1920s," pp. 188–89. As Lester D. Friedman suggests, small-town America has, in fact, taken Jews in recent films to its heart to the extent that Jewish ethnic types of the sort portrayed by Woody Allen are much loved in such places as Nebraska; Friedman, *Hollywood's Image of the Jew*, pp. 169–84. Ribuffo, *The Old Christian Right*, pp. 265–66, makes it clear that the nearest political phenomenon today to the Old Christian Right—the new Christian conservative movement, represented by the Moral Majority, for example—is philo-Semitic.

113. Feingold, *Zion in America*, pp. 302–4; Wrong, "The Rise and Decline of Anti-Semitism in America," pp. 325–27; Solotaroff and Sklare, "Introduction," *Jews in the Mind of America*, ed. Stember et al., pp. 17–18.

114. Morton Keller, "Jews and The Character of American Life Since 1930," in *Jews in The Mind of America*, ed. Stember et al., pp. 270–71; Feingold, "Anti-Semitism and The Anti-Semitic Imagination in America: A Case Study: The 1920s," p. 191. For an attempt to reformulate the definitions of "anti-Semitism" to accommodate a rapid decline in its historic bases, see Volkman, *A Legacy of Hate*, pp. 53–108, which unconvincingly develops the ideas of the anti-Semitism of insensitivity, and of indifference, to Jews.

115. Sartre, *Anti-Semite and Jew*, p. 16.

116. Higham, "Social Discrimination against Jews, 1830–1930," p. 139.

117. Ibid., pp. 170–71.

118. Bayor, *Neighbors in Conflict,* pp. 67–70, 104–7; Moore, *B'nai Brith,* pp. 115–18; Cohen, *Not Free to Desist,* pp. 129–34, 163–66.

119. Feingold, *The Politics of Rescue;* Wyman, *Paper Walls;* Morse, *While Six Million Died.*

120. Mostov, "Dun and Bradstreet Reports as A Source of Jewish Economic History," pp. 348–52; Decker, *Fortunes and Failures,* pp. 99–100.

121. Feingold, *Zion in America,* pp. 59, 79.

122. Synnott, *The Half-Opened Door;* Wechsler, *The Qualified Student.*

123. The definitive work is Liebman's *Jews and the Left* (New York, 1979), which, however, only briefly takes up the problem of anti-Semitism.

124. Among relevant contemporary Jewish feminist works are Letty Cottin Pogrebin, "Anti-Semitism in The Women's Movement," *MS* (June 1982), pp. 45–49, 62–72; the special issue of the Jewish feminist magazine, *Lilith* 7 (1980). Elinor Lerner's position on liberal assimilationists, however, bears a close resemblance to Sartre's striking characterization of the "French Democrat"; see Sartre, *Anti-Semite and Jew,* pp. 55–58.

125. Belth, *A Promise to Keep,* pp. 276–79; Cohen, *Not Free to Desist,* pp. 464–67; Hertzel Fishman, *American Protestantism and A Jewish State* (Detroit, 1973), pp. 53–63, 64–82, 140–50, 151–65, 178–83; Esther Yolles Feldblum, *The American Catholic Press and The Jewish State, 1917–1959* (New York, 1977), pp. 55–56, 91–106, 107–19. The latter two works have a considerably wider scope—and much greater interest in American attitudes and conditions—than the titles suggest.

Mythologies,
Images, and
Stereotypes

Jonathan D. Sarna

The "Mythical Jew" and the "Jew Next Door" in Nineteenth-Century America

"In the wilds of Tennessee, a mountaineer, who had just 'sperienced religion at a camp meeting, was coming down the road when he met a peddler. 'Say,' said the newly converted Tennessean, 'say, ain't you a Jew? I never seed a Jew but I calkalate you is one.'

"The peddler modestly answered the question affirmatively, ignorant of the results.

" 'Put your pack down,' said the Tennessean. 'Now I am going to knock hell out of yer,' and he proceeded to do as he had threatened.

" 'What you hit me for?' said the peddler.

" 'What fer?' said his assailant, 'what fer? Well that's a nice thing to ask a gentleman. You crucified our Lord, that's what you done.'

"Then the Jew explained that it had occurred nearly nineteen hundred years ago and that he had absolutely nothing to do with it.

" 'Scuse me,' said the mountaineer, 'I'm sorry I beat you. I was told up there at the camp meeting, that the Jews had crucified the Lord, and I calkalated you was one of the men that did it. I never heard of it before today.' "[1]

Such humor as can be found in this backwoods folktale comes from the absurdity of ignorant mountaineers confusing the Jew today with the Jew who lived back in the days of Jesus, and in blaming the former for misdeeds allegedly committed by the latter. Afro-American folklore contains a similar story but with roles reversed. The "good" Jew is the biblical one; the "bad" Jew a contemporary:

An old pious Negro mammy . . . expressed before her mistress the wish to see some of the Children of Israel, inasmuch as she could not visit the Land of Canaan. To humor her, the mistress, upon learning of the coming of a Jew peddler to the nearby village, told her servant that she might pay a visit there, and view the "Child of Abraham." The servant soon returned, and indignantly exclaimed: "Missus! dat's no Chillen o' Israel. Dat's de same ol' Jew peddler w'at sole me dem pisen, brass yearrings las' 'tracted meetin' time. Sich low down w'ite man as dat, he nevah b'long to no Lan' o' Cainyan."[2]

Both of these tales, at a deeper level, deal with a tension that affected far more than just the credulous and rural. Highly intelligent American Christians faced the same problem: how to reconcile the "mythical Jew," found in the Bible, recalled in church, and discussed in stereotypic fashion, with the "Jew next door" who seemed altogether different. Mythical Jews could, depending on the circumstances, personify either evil or virtue. Real Jews fell somewhere in between. Mythical Jews were uniformly alike. Real Jews displayed individuality, much as all people do. This tension between received wisdom and perceived wisdom, image and reality, posed little problem in colonial America; Jews were too few in number. But in the nineteenth century, America's Jewish population ballooned from 3,000 to almost 1 million and Jews spread throughout the country. As increasing numbers of Americans came in contact with Jews, reality began to impinge on previously unchallenged "truths." New questions emerged.

Americans coped with these new questions in various ways. While others have dealt with images of the Jew and the various, often contradictory myths—many dating back to antiquity—which shaped those images, here the focus more narrowly centers on the clash between myths and intruding realities. This clash assumed different forms at different times for different people, since both preconceptions and perceptions differed as circumstances did. Nevertheless, in structure if not in detail, the forms and responses were all variations on a common pattern.

The problem of the "mythical Jew" and the "Jew next door" was not confined to the nineteenth century, was not confined to America, and was not even unique to Jews; other stereotyped minority groups faced similar problems. If not unique, however, the problem in a nineteenth-century American Jewish context certainly displayed striking features, for it became intertwined with larger questions regarding the relationship of Jews past to Jews present. As such it not only affected the way Christians viewed Jews; ultimately, it also influenced the way Jews viewed themselves.

During the early days of the Republic, dissonance between the "mythical Jew" and the "Jew next door" frequently went unnoticed. Thomas Jefferson, for example, summarized his readings and reflections on the Jewish people as follows:

II. Jews. 1. Their system was Deism; that is, the belief in one only God. But their ideas of him and of his attributes were degrading and injurious. 2. Their Ethics were not only imperfect, but often irreconcilable with the sound dictates of reason and morality, as they respect intercourse with those around us; and repulsive and anti-social, as respecting other nations. They needed reformation, therefore, in an eminent degree.[3]

Elsewhere, Jefferson attacked Jewish theology "which supposes the God of infinite justice to punish the sins of the fathers upon their children, unto the third and fourth generation," and quoted approvingly to John Adams the conclusions of William Enfield in his epitome of Johann Jakob Brucker's *Historia critica philosophae:*

Ethics were so little studied among the Jews, that in their whole compilation called the Talmud, there is only one treatise on moral subjects. Their books of Morals chiefly consisted in a minute enumeration of duties. From the law of Moses were deduced 613 precepts, which were divided into two classes, affirmative and negative, 248 in the former, and 365 in the latter. It may serve to give the reader some idea of the low state of moral philosophy among the Jews in the Middle age, to add, that of the 248 affirmative precepts, only 3 were considered as obligatory upon women; and that in order to obtain salvation, it was judged sufficient to fulfill any one single law in the hour of death; the observance of the rest being deemed necessary, only to increase the felicity of the future life. What a wretched depravity of sentiment and manners must have prevailed before such corrupt maxims could have obtained credit! It is impossible to collect from these writings a consistent series of moral Doctrine.[4]

Yet, the same Jefferson saluted his friend Joseph Marx "with sentiments of perfect esteem and respect" and expressed to him what Marx termed "liberal and enlightened views" on Jewish affairs. He also declared himself "happy in the restoration of the Jews, particularly to their social rights" and lamented in a letter to Mordecai Noah that "public opinion erects itself into an Inquisition, and exercises its office with as much fanaticism as fans the flame of an *Auto-de-fe*." Jefferson championed the rights of Jews both in 1776, in a debate over naturalization in Virginia, and in 1785 when they gained protection under the Virginia Act for Religious Toleration. He consistently appointed Jews to public office. He took pride, as expressed in a letter to Isaac Harby, that his university "set the example of ceasing to violate the rights of conscience by any injunctions on the different sects respecting their religion."[5]

Jefferson thus displayed remarkable liberality when dealing both with Jews and with matters directly affecting their welfare. By contrast, his attitude toward what he believed Jews stood for— their theology, morality, and doctrine—was negative and scornful. These two simultaneous and contrasting approaches toward matters Jewish appear repeatedly among deists and freethinkers, and in most cases, Jefferson's among them, they seem to have stood virtually unreconciled.[6] Though Jefferson must have known that his Jewish correspondents and appointees differed from the Jews described in his readings, the fact gives no evidence of having troubled him.[7]

Abolitionist reformer Lydia Maria Child displayed even greater inconsistency in her attitudes toward Jews. In some of her letters, she invoked the typical stereotypes of her day, writing about "half-civilized Jews," and "a people so benighted and barbarous as the Israelites." Her description of the "Jewish Synagogue in Crosby street" (1841) was somewhat more sympathetic ("there is something deeply impressive in this remnant of a scattered people"), but still mentioned Jews' "blindness and waywardness" and found "spiritual correspondence" between old clothes dealers in New York and poor Jews in Judea. In her *Progress of Religious Ideas Through Successive Ages,* Child laid heavier stress on "the immense debt of gratitude" owed the Jews and spoke of their treatment as the "darkest blot" in the history of Christendom. Not long afterward, though, she described in a letter how Jews "have humbugged the world and dragged the wheels of progress." Child knew two myths about Jews: one positive, one negative. She invoked both, thereby unconsciously embodying the ambivalence of her age.[8]

In dealing with real Jews, however, Child ignored her preconceptions and treated them as objects of persecution, compared specifically in one case to "colored people." With obvious pride she related to Henry Ward Beecher's friend and associate, Theodore Tilton, how she stopped some boys who "were following a man with a long black beard, and calling after him 'I say, old Jew, got any ole clo's?'" Child reproved the boys, reminding them "that Moses and Solomon and St. Peter and St. Paul were Jews." On another occasion, she termed contemporary prejudice against the Jews "utterly absurd and wicked." However uncertain she was about the Jews in the past, she felt that the Jews around her deserved equal treatment.[9]

The case of James Russell Lowell offers a third and still more complex example of contradictory attitudes toward Jews. This youngest of the "Fireside poets" operated simultaneously with two versions of the "mythical Jew"—the noble ancient Hebrew and the medieval European scapegoat—and with two versions of the "Jew next door"—the talented, rich, and powerful Jew and the immigrant peddler. He eventually became obsessed with Jews and took delight "in the bizarre pastime of discovering that everyone of talent was in some way descended from Jewish ancestors. . . . He would play the game of 'detection' with a relish that approached monomania." Myth and reality blurred in Lowell's mind. Consequently, he both sought Jews out and avoided them, defended Jews and attacked them, admired Jews and feared them. His uncertainties about Jews paralleled his feelings about America in general and reflected, as Barbara Solomon has pointed out, larger social and intellectual concerns of his age—an age when perceived wisdom diverged from received wisdom on a whole range of issues, and when many old traditions broke down. If Lowell embodied the contradictions of his day, he neither recognized them nor solved them. Like Jefferson and Child, he held different views at different times about different Jews, and never reconciled them.[10]

Others in nineteenth-century America did recognize that their conceptions of the Jew differed from their perceptions. In 1816, for example, Philip Milledoler, later president of Rutgers, delivered a presidential address before the newly formed American Society for Evangelizing the Jews. He talked of Jews' "laxness of morals," claimed that "their religious exercises are scarcely conducted with the form, much less with the spirit, of devotion," lamented that "the female character among them holds a station far inferior to that which it was intended to occupy by the God of nature and of providence," and so on in a like vein. Then he suddenly put in a disclaimer: "In this description of the Jews it will be remembered that we are speaking in general terms. We do not by any means intend to say, that all which is here stated will apply to every individual and family among them: —we still hope better things of some of them, and especially of that part of the nation which is resident in this country."[11]

Milledoler was not alone in realizing that the Jews "in this country" did not quite comport with his analysis. During the 1819 debate over the Maryland Jew Bill ("to extend to the sect of people professing the Jewish religion, the same rights and privileges that are enjoyed by Christians"), Judge Henry M. Breckenridge recognized the same thing. He asked opposition speakers directly "whether the American Jew is distinguished by those characteristics" which they were ascribing to Jews generally. No answer is recorded.[12]

As the nineteenth century progressed, an increasing number of Americans made the vexing discovery that Jews formed too variegated a congregation to accord with any single stereotype. With the rise of Jewish immigration, it became clear not only that mythical Jews and real Jews diverged, but that in America not even all real Jews could be pigeonholed together. Writing in 1860, novelist Joseph Holt Ingraham still repeated the old refrain that "the Jew of Chatham Street, in this city, is, in every lineament, the Jew of Jerusalem today, and of the Jews of the days of Jesus." Even for him, however, that was only an article of faith. As a practical matter he had to concede that "in what this peculiarity consists, it is difficult to determine precisely. . . ."[13] If it was difficult to draw connections between the peddlers of Chatham Street and their ancient forebears, how much more so in the case of New York's wealthy Jews or the growing number of assimilated American Jews? The more Americans saw of Jews the less they understood them.

Tensions between the "mythical Jew" and the "Jew next door," or between received wisdom and perceived wisdom, resulted in what sociologists would later call cognitive dissonance, the realization that two items of knowledge do not fit together. "Dissonance produces discomfort," Leon Festinger wisely observed, "and correspondingly there will arise pressures to reduce or eliminate the dissonance."[14] In the case of Jews, dissonance was relieved in four ways: (1) suppression, (2) rationalization, (3) elimination, and (4) reconceptualization. Examples of all four may be found throughout the nineteenth century, seemingly from people in all walks of life. As might be expected, evidence suggests that most people sought easy ways to eliminate dissonance; *reconceptualization,* a difficult intellectual feat, took place infrequently. Still, by the end of the nineteenth century, the groundwork had been laid for the great intellectual revolution which raised Jews from a lowly religious status—allied in the popular mind wih infidels and deists—into a high one, membership in one of America's "three great faiths." General acceptance of the "Protestant-Catholic-Jew" model, of course, came only in the twentieth century.

Suppression meant ignoring feelings of dissonance and living with the resulting inconsistency.[15] As we have seen, Jefferson, Child, and Lowell did this; indeed, in their cases dissonance may never have reached consciousness. Philip Milledoler employed suppression explicitly. While ideally conscious and unconscious modes of suppression should be distinguished from one another, as a practical matter this is usually impossible. All that can be said with certainty is that throughout nineteenth-century America, much of the ambivalence found in perceptions of the Jew stemmed from one or another form of unresolved inconsistency. Positive and negative images stood side by side, each expressed on different occasions depending on the situation. The *New York Herald* could sometimes revile Jews as haters of Christianity, usurers, and second-hand clothes dealers who "deserve to be hung high as Haman for their charlatanism, pretension and folly," and yet on other occasions find them charitable and pious, "excellent men, excellent fathers, excellent husbands, excellent citizens."[16] The *Boston Sunday Gazette* summed up similar ambivalence in one succinct sentence: "It is strange that a nation that boasts so many good traits should be so obnoxious."[17]

Rationalization involved moving out beyond conscious or unconscious inattention to the anomaly of Jews who neither fit existing stereotypes nor resembled one another in order to search for solutions. The most obvious and popular of these simply dismissed the "non-conforming Jew" as "an exception to the rule." Thus William D. Howells wrote in his diary, "Dr. Kraus, Jew, but very nice."[18] Both Judge Henry Hilton and financier Austin Corbin admitted that there were "nice" and "well-behaved" people among the Jews, but since these were only exceptions, they did not allow them to affect their thinking. Hilton still excluded Jews as a class from the Grand Union Hotel and Corbin followed suit, refusing to admit them to his resort on Coney Island.[19] Even so grossly anti-Semitic a tract as *Tit for Tat* (1895), which claimed as fact that "the Jew is built expressly for that kind of cold-blooded heartless commerce in which sentiments take no part whatever" and then charged Jews with trying to "own the earth and reduce its occupants to starvation and beggary," still admitted that "there are honorable exceptions"—although they were allegedly few in number.[20] More commonly, as Nina Morais noted in 1881, the exceptional Jew found acceptance but did "not materially aid to negative [*sic*] the impression created by their less favored brethren." "You are a different kind of Jew," such a one was told, yet those who offered the praise continued to believe that to know one Jew was to know them all.[21]

Facts that do not comport with theoretical expectations do not by themselves overturn established paradigms. As Thomas Kuhn demonstrated in another connection, they may "be recognized as counterinstances and still be set aside for later work." We have seen that many nineteenth-century Americans handled seemingly anomalous Jews precisely this way. They noted their exceptional status, mentally filed it away, and yet kept established stereotypes intact. In other cases, "numerous articulations and *ad hoc* modifications" of stereotypes took place in order to rationalize apparent inconsistencies.[22] Some exceptional Jews, among them Mordecai Noah, Judah Touro, and later Simon Wolf, were termed "good Christians," the apparent implication being that they diverged from Jewish traits so much that they must not be completely Jewish. While the word "Christian" used in this fashion often meant no more than moral or ethical, as in the phrase "a Christian thing to do," literary evidence demonstrates that many genuinely viewed Jewish "good Christians" as Jews in name only, or "Christians in Jews' clothing." At least in novels, such characters frequently "saw the light" and converted.[23]

In "Judith Bensaddi, a Tale Founded in Fact," the young man, William Garame, describes Judith, the Jewish woman he loves, as "the most beautiful gem of humanity," a woman quite different from most members of the "accursed race": "In spirit and feeling she is a far better Christian than nine-tenths of those who make the loudest professions. She loves the rules and spirit of the Christian religion, and I have no doubt that she only needs to be placed in Christian society, and under Christian influence, to be soon persuaded to believe fully in Jesus of Nazareth." Although Garame is prevented from marrying her, Judith confirms his prediction less than a year later by converting.[24]

While benevolent Jewish males in American literature converted less often, possibly because nineteenth-century Americans classified religion as part of "women's sphere," "eminent men among the Israelites" regularly appear in anti-Semitic writings as Aryans or Christians in Jewish disguise, and hence no danger to prevailing stereotypes. Telemachus T. Timayenis's *The Original Mr. Jacobs,* a particularly notorious tract, sums up this standard apologia on page one of its opening chapter:

I admit that there have been eminent men among the Jews, as, for instance, their renowned lawgiver and leader in ancient times, Moses. But a careful examination of this anomaly (it is not an exception) will show that the great men among the Jews have drunk copious draughts of Aryan civilization, and have quickly either renounced Judaism or adopted a nominal, sometimes a real, Christianity. Thus their famous men—Heinrich Heine, Ludwig Borne, Edward Gans, Mose Mendelssohn, Disraeli, and Johann Neander—cannot be fairly called Jews; for either they became rank infidels, or they carefully tried to conceal their origin by a change of name, a practice followed to the present day.[25]

Interestingly, Timayenis also displays the obverse of this kind of rationalization, what might be termed "the Jew in Christian's clothing." He calls non-Jews who conform to his Jewish stereotype "Jews," evidence to the contrary notwithstanding: "Has ever a man of observation asked himself the question: 'Is there any Jewish blood in the veins of John D. Rockefeller?' We do not hestitate to affirm from an intimate knowledge of the man, that if Rockefeller is not actually a Jew, he has many Jewish traits.

. . . [T]he spirit of the Standard Oil Company is simply the spirit of the monopoly, of cruelty, of annihilation of all competitors, a spirit in fact such as manifests itself in the scandalous enterprises of the Jews."[26] Both the use of the name Shylock in connection with non-Jews, and the use of the word Jew in a non-Jewish context, meaning to bargain or cheat, imply the same sort of rationalization. Many apparently found it hard to admit that some non-Jews could exhibit supposedly "Jewish traits." Rather than divorcing behavioral traits from religious ones and abandoning stereotypes, they found it easier to adhere to existing stereotypes by making such "Jew-like" Christians into "Jews," just as they made "good Christian" Jews into "Christians."

While some Americans rationalized away dissonance by dismissing "uncharacteristic" Jews as "exceptions," and others did the same by ascribing to them "inner Christianity," still others sought to achieve harmony, consciously or unconsciously, by *elimination*. They sought to rid themselves of the problem by transforming reality to conform to expectations. Such attempts, similar to what scientists do when they destroy evidence that fails to fit in with their theories, led inevitably to what Jews saw as pernicious forms of anti-Semitism.

Three basic strategies for elimination emerged. The first involved doing in fact what others did in their literary imaginations: converting the Jew to Christianity. Conversionists did not restrict themselves to missionary work aimed at those whom they considered "uncharacteristic of the race," for they viewed any Jewish conversion to Christianity as a victory, a step toward solving the overall "Jewish problem." They need not even have been fully conscious of the degree to which they were reconciling what to them was the anomaly of the modern Jew. Some formal and many informal conversionist efforts did come to center on "exceptional Jews"; nevertheless, they were the most prized converts. Rabbi Bernhard Felsenthal, an opponent of all Christian missionary efforts, found this fact particularly disdainful:

You have every day occasion to meet members of the Jewish race. You know, perhaps, that there are Jews who enjoy excellent, sound positions, that some have become famous for their eminent learning, for their contribution to the treasures of science and art, for their literary attainments, for their acts of benevolence, for their deeds of grand philanthropy. Now approach such a Jew and say to him, "Oh, my poor friend, how I pity you! You are in such a forlorn condition. . . ." Speak in such a manner to your Jewish neighbor, and he will hardly understand you. He will sarcastically smile at you, thinking, perhaps, that there is a certain class of people who stick with wonderful tenacity to their notions, be they as unfounded as possible, and if he answers you he will say, "My friend, you are entirely mistaken."[27]

Jews insisted that they could be thoroughly modern and fully moral without converting, traditional Christian wisdom to the contrary notwithstanding. They urged Christians to change their stereotypes and leave the Jews alone.

The second strategy designed to harmonize received and perceived wisdom about Jews proceeded from an opposite tack: it sought to eliminate "uncharacteristic Jews" by treating them as inferior citizens and by degrading them until they eventually adhered to the expected stereotype simply because they had no other choice. This kind of self-fulfilling prophecy had commonly plagued Jews in the Middle Ages, where charters, for reasons as much social, political, and economic as religious, restricted Jews to precisely that accursed status supposedly foretold from on high. While nothing of similar magnitude occurred in America, moves in that direction, likewise undertaken for a variety of reasons— social, political, economic, and religious—were also not totally absent. Jews remained without full rights in New Hampshire until 1877, and throughout the nineteenth century they periodically had to battle against proposed Christian amendments to the Constitution aimed at rendering them second-class citizens. They also faced a host of discriminatory policies designed to restrict their educational and economic progress.[28]

The overall failure of all such efforts should not obscure their intended result: to put Jews in their place. Those who protested Jewish religious equality, ascribing to them a secondary status in Christian America, and those who thought as Austin Corbin did that Jews deserved "no place in first-class society" and should, therefore, be excluded, really were charging that Jews occupied a social position different from the one they supposedly "deserved." To resolve the contradiction, they sought to mold reality to fit their preconceived notions. They hoped that by treating Jews as second-class citizens, Jews would reassume their "rightful place," and so "proper" harmony, a harmony more closely comporting with their own social and economic expectations, would be restored. It wasn't.[29]

A final means of eliminating the problem posed by Jews was elimination of the Jews altogether; that way there would not be any "Jew next door," nor any dissonance either. Although such a suggestion received no serious consideration or support, in 1888 it did emerge in print:

"The Jew must go!" ... Let them go with all their ill-gotten gain, and let us forget that it was ill gotten—but let them go. ... We want no parasites among us; we will not have them; our social health demands that we purge ourselves of them. The Jew must go. Let the nation assert itself to this effect, not passionately, not bitterly, not vindictively; but from Maine to Louisiana, from New York to the Golden Horn, let the American people rise as one man, and assert in deep tones of calm, unwavering resolve, "We want no parasitic race among us: THE JEW MUST GO!"[30]

There remained another means of confronting the challenge that the "Jew next door" posed to nineteenth-century Americans and that was through *reconceptualization*. Where elimination involved forcing the "Jew next door" to conform to the "mythical Jew" or disappear, reconceptualization did the opposite. Old wisdom was pushed out; a new paradigm, one which took account of the realities of the day, replaced it. All evidence suggests that most people find it difficult to change long-standing cherished beliefs, regardless of the weight of the evidence. That Oliver Wendell Holmes and Mark Twain did so is, therefore, all the more remarkable.

Holmes admitted that he grew up with "the traditional idea" that Jews "were a race lying under a curse for their obstinacy in refusing the gospel." "The principal use of the Jews," he believed, "seemed to be to lend money, and to fulfill the predictions of the old prophets of their race." Later, as he came into contact with Jews, Holmes changed his mind. As he recounted in his poem, "At the Pantomime," he moved from "silent oaths" against "the race that slew its Lord" to a recognition that Christianity emerged from Judaism and that Jews remained an extraordinary people. More important, he adopted a pluralistic view of religion—one more commonly found in the twentieth century—urging Christians "to find a meaning in beliefs which are different from their own." Distancing himself from Christian triumphalism, he insisted that "in the midst of all triumphs of Christianity, it is well that the stately synagogue should lift its walls by the side of the aspiring cathedral, a perpetual reminder that there are many mansions in the Father's earthly house as well as in the heavenly one; that civilized humanity, longer in time and broader in space than any historical form of belief, is mightier than any one institution or organization it includes."[31]

Mark Twain (Samuel Clemens) underwent a similar transformation of views. In his autobiography he admitted that as a schoolboy he thought of Jews only in biblical terms: "They carried me back to Egypt, and in imagination I moved among the Pharaohs and all the shadowy celebrities of that remote age." His first Jewish schoolmates were persecuted by "the boys"—presumably including Sam Clemens himself—chased and stoned and taunted with cries of "Shall we crucify them?" It was only later, beginning in 1860, that his ideas began to change as he learned more about Jews and met a river pilot whose life had been saved by one. In subsequent years he came into contact with a great many other Jews, and in 1899, he published his famous essay entitled "Concerning the Jews." The essay, though overgeneralized and simplistic, nevertheless displayed what for its time was remarkable praise for Jewish characteristics and virtues while at the same time striving for balance. Some unfortunate stereotypes remained, most notably a comment on the Jew's alleged "unpatriotic disinclination to stand by the flag as a soldier," a charge corrected in a later postscript. What is really noteworthy about "Concerning the Jews," however, is its effort to make judgments based upon reliable facts rather than upon received myths. "Neither Jew nor Christian will approve of it," Clemens predicted when he wrote his essay, "but people who are neither Jews *nor* Christians will, for they are in a condition to know the truth when they see it." It is precisely this quest for verifiable truth that made the process of reconceptualization possible.[32]

By the end of the nineteenth century, the process of reconceptualization had also proceeded on other levels. Jews had won election to public office and held high appointive positions in government. The first pulpit exchanges between rabbis and ministers had taken place. Rabbis had delivered prayers before Congress and state legislatures. Liberal Jewish and Christian leaders had sat side by side at the meetings of the Free Religious Association. Jews had taken an active role in religious and women's activities connected with the 1893 World's Columbian Exposition.[33] Though isolated incidents, together these suggest that, however slowly, American Jews were winning acceptance on their own merit, myths notwithstanding. The process proceeded at a slow pace, cannot be said to have found widespread acceptance until after World War II,[34] and is not fully realized today. Nonetheless, pluralism—an attitude toward Jews quite different from that found earlier in the century—had at least begun to take hold, even as other means of confronting the "Jew next door" continued.

Although the problem of the "mythical Jew" and the "Jew next door" was seemingly a non-Jewish matter, involving Christian beliefs and perceptions, American Jews who interacted with their non-Jewish neighbors could hardly ignore it. After all, the problem concerned them; they *were* the Jews next door. They had to face embarrassing comments from neighbors who never had met Jews. They had to confront the challenge of wanting to become like everybody else while retaining Jewish identity intact. They had to grapple with rising social discrimination in many walks of life. By becoming involved in shaping their own image, American Jews sought to meet all of these challenges at once, demonstrating Judaism's complete compatibility with American life.

Not all Jews, of course, took part in this effort. Those who did, however, considered reconceptualization and elimination the best means of affecting negative Christian views. They presumably reasoned that if Christians would change their negative stereotypes at the same time as Jews showed how little they now resembled those stereotypes, then the so-called Jewish problem would be solved. For obvious reasons, Jews worried not at all about any positive preconceptions that Christians held regarding Jews; if anything, they sought to reinforce them.

A major thrust of the reconceptualization effort involved reinterpreting Jewish history so as to make the ancient Jew appear more respectable. This seemingly aimed both at easing the reconciliation of past Jews with present ones and at demonstrating that Christianity's mythical Jew lacked any historical basis whatsoever. In reinterpreting the biblical period, American Jews at first stressed Enlightenment concerns, endeavoring to prove that Judaism was far more reasonable and ethical than critics believed. Isaac Mayer Wise's *History of the Israelitish Nation,* for example, painted a Moses who might have been a *philosophe.* "Moses did not depart one step from the broad field of observation," Wise wrote. "He reasoned from facts; he started from observations on nature and history." "Moses gave a sanctity to virtue, to industry and labor, and awakened his people to the performance of human duties as men and citizens." While Moses did recommend "a careful study of the law . . . the study of the law is not the end and aim of it." Instead, "Divine service consists in obeying the laws, in doing what is good, noble and useful, and reforming the heart to desire the same; and shunning what is bad, ignoble or hurtful, and educating the heart to despise the mean, the bad, and ignoble desire." In case anyone missed the modern parallel, Wise made it explicit: "Liberty, justice and fraternity were his watch words, now the nations re-echo them; mental, moral and physical strength constitute the proper man, to which superstition, immorality, opulence and luxury are the greatest enemies. . . . This is the doctrine of Moses, which the world now begins to understand."[35]

Later in the nineteenth century, American Jews, basing themselves on ideas worked out in Germany, shifted the tone of their revisionism to confront charges leveled by higher biblical criticism. Striving to negate the stereotyped picture of an ancient Jew, steeped in legalism if not paganism and offering sacrifices to an angry Lord, they stressed Prophetic Judaism which, by no coincidence, displayed lofty universalistic values thoroughly consonant with contemporary Social Gospel ideals. "Not the law . . . but the prophetic principles constitute the essence of Judaism," Rabbi Emil G. Hirsch declared, "for the Law operates largely, especially in its priestly conceits, with institutions based upon ante-Jewish and often anti-Jewish conceits, while the Prophetic vision and ardor is instinct with a new view and outlook, interpreted as a proclamation of those hopes and assurances, of those maxims and principles upon which the fate of humanity, as humanity, depends."[36] Prophetic Judaism thus permitted reconciliation between Israel past and Israel present. It offered all-embracing universalism in place of tribalism. It gave Jews a biblical heritage which they could affirm with pride, even when attacked.

A similar effort underlay revisionist accounts of Christianity's birth. The mythical Jew, described in countless Christian works, belonged to a degenerate race, unremittingly orthodox in its devotion to legal minutiae, that rejected and persecuted the savior of mankind, and then finally crucified him screaming "his blood be upon us and upon our children." Jews, particularly in the late nineteenth century, sought to effect a change in this myth. They apparently hoped that a reconceptualization of their part in Christianity's past would create a more favorable climate for harmonious Jewish-Christian relations in the present.

The revisionist view that Jews put forward, largely based on Jewish and Christian scholarship in Germany, stressed that Jesus was born a Jew and remained one throughout his life. He was, Isaac Mayer Wise insisted in 1888, "an enthusiastic and thoroughly Jewish patriot, who fully understood the questions of his age and the problems of his people, and felt the invincible desire to solve them." Wise had by then discarded his earlier doubts as to whether Jesus existed and had determined that Christianity's founder was actually a "Pharisean doctor of the Hillel School."[37] Moritz Loth, Wise's disciple and the first president of the Union of American Hebrew Congregations, went further, calling Jesus "the greatest king that emanated from the loins of Jacob."[38]

Having reclaimed Jesus, Jewish revisionists proceeded to explain away the crucifixion, usually blaming it on the Romans, and to insist that Christianity, far from being a sharp break from Judaism, was merely what Mordecai Noah had earlier called "our laws, our principles, our doctrines . . . beneficially spread throughout the world under another name." The relationship of Judaism to Christianity was, to Rabbi Solomon Schindler, the relationship of a mother to her daughter: "The daughter soon severed all connections with her mother. She went her own way; for she had a mission of her own to fulfil; a mission which neither Judaism nor Hellenism could have fulfilled with success: she had to civilize a world of barbarians."[39] It followed from the writings of Schindler and others that Jews and Christians had once been united and could be reunited; that Christian beliefs about first-century Judaism were wrong, as witnessed by the fact that Jesus was a Jew; and that the "Jew next door" was the heir of those who provided the spiritual foundation upon which Christianity was built. As with Prophetic Judaism, so too with first-century Judaism, revisionism had refashioned the past to meet what it saw as contemporary needs.

While revisionism stressed the continuity of Jewish history, and sought to improve the image of Jews in earlier centuries in order to help Jews in the nineteenth century, elimination did the opposite. It stressed the discontinuity of Jewish history and sought to distinguish modern Jews from their predecessors by casting off "excrescences." Reform Jewish leaders made their break with the past explicit. The Pittsburgh Platform of 1885, which Isaac Mayer Wise properly termed a "Declaration of Independence," rejected "all such as are not adapted to the views and habits of modern civilization" and eliminated many traditional laws and ceremonies as "altogether foreign to our present mental and spiritual state." Ten years later, the Central Conference of American Rabbis officially declared "that our relations in all religious matters are in no way authoritatively and finally determined by any portion of our Post-Biblical and Patristic literature."[40]

Most other efforts to transform American Jews, including Reform Jewish ones, more prudently sought legitimation in history. Their supporters, therefore, claimed either to be revitalizing forgotten relics of bygone days or to be conforming to natural historical processes. In deeds, if not in words, they too sought to effect changes that would render the modern Jew quite distinct from his pre-modern stereotypical counterpart. Some worked to direct Jews into "productive" professions, particularly agriculture, in order to counteract the image of the Jews as merchants and middlemen. Others, especially late in the century, took up Zionism, a different attempt to change the Jewish image and transform Jewish life.[41] Still others, perhaps those with more modest ambitions, thought it sufficient to change the Jewish name. They hoped that modern "Yahvists," "Hebrews," or "Israelites" could be distinguished from pre-modern "Jews," and that stereotypes connected with the latter would not be applied to the former.[42] The means differed, but the desired end remained the same: the modern Jew sought to make himself as different from the mythical one as possible.

In counteracting Christian myths, reconceptualization and elimination thus manifestly worked at cross purposes: the one aimed at maintaining ties to the past while the other sought to sever them. At the same time, the two strategies also worked nicely in tandem. Reconceptualization aimed at improving the Christian's image of the historical Jew, while elimination aimed at improving that of the contemporary one. The latter consistency needs no explanation. Jews sought the best possible image of themselves, past and present, much as any minority group does. The inconsistency, however, is much more revealing. Jews' simultaneous desires to both identify and break with their past express a basic tension in American Jewish life: the tension between tradition and change. Ambivalence about the past reflects ambivalence about the past's religious legacy, ambivalence about the Old World heritage, and ambivalence about assimilation. Many nineteenth-century American Jews displayed conflicting attitudes in all three cases.[43]

And so a final paradox: without realizing it, Christians and Jews in nineteenth-century America faced a common problem. Both had trouble reconciling traditions received from the past with the changed Jewish situation that they perceived in the present. The nature of the received myth differed in the two cases as did the means used to overcome dissonance, but the problem itself— the relationship of the Jewish past to the Jewish present—was never truly resolved, not in the nineteenth century and not today.

Notes

I am grateful to the American Council of Learned Societies for its support of my research, and to Professors Benny Kraut, Jacob R. Marcus, Michael A. Meyer, and Henry Shapiro, and Rabbi Lance Sussman, as well as to the editor, for comments on an earlier draft of this work.

1. Rudolf Glanz, *The Jew in the Old American Folklore* (New York, 1961), pp. 134–35.

2. Ibid., p. 130.

3. Jefferson to Benjamin Rush (Apr. 21, 1803) in *The Writings of Thomas Jefferson,* ed. Andrew A. Lipscomb (Washington, D.C., 1904), 10: 382. Robert M. Healey's "Jefferson, Judaism, and the Jews: Divided We Stand, United We Fall!" *American Jewish History* 73 (June 1984): 359–74 appeared after this essay was in proofs.

4. Jefferson to Ezra Stiles (June 25, 1819) in *The Writings of Thomas Jefferson,* ed. Albert Ellery Gergh (Washington, D.C., 1904), 15: 203; Jefferson to John Adams (Oct. 12, 1813) in *The Adams-Jefferson Letters,* ed. Lester J. Capon (Chapel Hill, N.C., 1959), 2: 383.

5. Joseph L. Blau and Salo W. Baron, *The Jews of the United States, 1790– 1840: A Documentary History* (New York, 1963), pp. 12, 13, 605, and passim;

Max J. Kohler, "Unpublished Correspondence Between Thomas Jefferson and Some American Jews," *Publications of the American Jewish Historical Society* (hereafter cited as *(PAJHS)* 20 (1911): 11–30; Lee M. Friedman, *Jewish Pioneers and Patriots* (Philadelphia, 1942), pp. 31–42, 377–79; Morris U. Schappes, *A Documentary History of the Jews in the United States 1654–1875* (New York, 1971), pp. 157, 605, and passim.

6. Jonathan D. Sarna, "The Freethinker, The Jews, and The Missionaries: George Houston and the Mystery of *Israel Vindicated*," *AJS Review* 5 (1980): 101–14, esp. n. 33.

7. In contrast with Jefferson's attitudes toward blacks, see David Brion Davis, *The Problem of Slavery in the Age of Revolution 1770–1823* (Ithaca, N.Y., 1975), pp. 166–84; John C. Miller, *The Wolf by the Ears: Thomas Jefferson and Slavery* (New York, 1977). A rigorous comparative study of attitudes toward Jews and blacks in America would be valuable.

8. Patricia G. Holland and Milton Meltzer, eds., *Guide to the Collected Correspondence of Lydia Maria Child, 1817–1880* (New York, 1980), s.v. "Jews," esp. letters to Louisa Gilman Loring (Sept. 4, 1846) and Ellis Gray Loring (Mar. 5, 1854); Lydia Maria Child, *Letters From New York* (New York, 1846), pp. 37–47, and *The Progress of Religious Ideas Through Successive Ages* (New York, 1855); Louise Abbie Mayo, "The Ambivalent Image: The Perception of the Jew in Nineteenth Century America" (unpublished Ph.D. diss., City University of New York, 1977), p. 54.

9. Child to Mrs. S. B. Shaw (1859), *Letters of Lydia Maria Child* (Boston, 1882), p. 141; Child to Theodore Tilton (Apr. 10, 1862); Child to Robert Purvis (Aug. 14, 1868) in *Collected Correspondence*, ed. Holland and Meltzer (microfiche).

10. Martin Duberman, *James Russell Lowell* (Boston, 1966), pp. 307–10; Barbara M. Solomon, *Ancestors and Immigrants: A Changing New England Tradition* (Cambridge, Mass., 1956), pp. 17–20; Louis Harap, *The Image of the Jew in American Literature from Early Republic to Mass Immigration* (Philadelphia, 1974), pp. 96–99; Edmund Wilson, *A Piece of My Mind: Reflections at Sixty* (New York, 1958), pp. 85–107.

11. *Religious Intelligencer* 1 (1816): 535–37.

12. E. Milton Altfeld, *The Jews Struggle for Religious and Civil Liberty in Maryland* (Baltimore, 1924), pp. 77, 119; Edward Eitches, "Maryland's Jew Bill," *American Jewish Historical Quarterly* 60 (Mar. 1971): 258–79.

13. Joseph Holt Ingraham, *The Sunny South* (Philadelphia, 1860) as quoted in Harap, *Image of the Jew*, p. 58. For somewhat different perspectives on the Jewish image, see Harold Fisch, *The Dual Image* (New York, 1971) and Michael D. Dobkowski, *The Tarnished Dream: The Basis of an American Anti-Semitism* (Westport, Conn., 1979); the latter cites earlier literature on the subject.

14. Leon Festinger, *When Prophecy Fails* (New York, 1956), p. 26, and *A Theory of Cognitive Dissonance* (Stanford, Calif., 1965); for the use of this theory in another historical context, see Henry Shapiro, *Appalachia on Our Mind* (Chapel Hill, N.C., 1978), esp. pp. xvi, xvii.

15. "Social scientists tend to underestimate the ease with which people can live with cognitive dissonance. . . . People professionally concerned with ideas and with the logic of social relationships may elevate the general significance

of logic and consistency in human affairs." Neil J. Smelser, *Sociology: An Introduction* (New York, 1973), p. 524.

16. *New York Herald* (Nov. 2, 13, 1837); Jonathan D. Sarna, *Jacksonian Jew: The Two Worlds of Mordecai Noah* (New York, 1981), pp. 119–20.

17. Quoted in John Higham, *Send These to Me: Jews and Other Immigrants in Urban America* (New York, 1975), p. 124.

18. William D. Howells, *Selected Letters,* ed. Thomas Wortham (Boston, 1981), 4: 151.

19. *Coney Island and the Jews* (New York, 1879), pp. 17, 28.

20. "Prof. Pal. Sylvanus," *Tit for Tat: Satirical Universal History* (Chicago, 1895), pp. 30, 57, 18.

21. Nina Morais, "Jewish Ostracism in America," *North American Review* 133 (1881): 273. For a parallel case, see Gary B. Mills, "Miscegenation and the Free Negro in Antebellum 'Anglo' Alabama: A Re-examination of Southern Race Relations," *Journal of American History* 68 (June 1981): 32. See also Maxwell Geismar, ed., *Unfinished Business: James N. Rosenberg Papers* (New York, 1967), pp. 267–68.

22. Thomas S. Kuhn, *The Structure of Scientific Revolutions,* 2nd ed. (Chicago, 1970), pp. 82, 78. See also David A. Hollinger, "T. S. Kuhn's Theory of Science and Its Implications for History," *American Historical Review* 78 (1973): 370–93.

23. Sarna, *Jacksonian Jew,* p. 133; Leon Huhner, *The Life of Judah Touro* (Philadelphia, 1946), p. 109; *Selected Addresses and Papers of Simon Wolf* (Cincinnati, 1926), p. 24; David A. Brener, "Lancaster's First Jewish Community, 1715–1804, The Era of Joseph Simon," *Journal of the Lancaster County Historical Society* 80 (1976): 276; Sarna, "The Freethinker, the Jews and the Missionaries," 107.

24. Harap, *Image of the Jew in American Literature,* pp. 72–76; Curtis Carroll Davis, "*Judith Bensaddi* and the Reverend Doctor Henry Ruffner," *PAJHS* 39 (1949): 115–42. Henry Ruffner, *Judith Bensaddi: A Tale* has recently been reprinted with an introduction by J. Michael Pemberton as part of the Library of Southern Civilization (Baton Rouge, La., 1984). For other examples, see Mayo, "The Ambivalent Image," pp. 93–104.

25. [Telemachus T. Timayenis], *The Original Mr. Jacobs* (New York, 1888), p. 1; Leonard A. Greenberg and Harold J. Jonas, "An American Anti-Semite in the Nineteenth Century," in *Essays on Jewish Life and Thought Presented in Honor of Salo W. Baron,* ed. J. L. Blau (New York, 1959), pp. 265–83. For a later and more extreme form of this type of rationalization, see William H. Montgomery, *Jesus Was Not A Jew* (New York, 1935), and Jacob E. Conner, *Christ Was Not A Jew* (n.p., 1936).

26. [Timayenis], *The Original Mr. Jacobs,* pp. 283–85; for an earlier example, see Eitches, "Maryland's Jew Bill," p. 275.

27. Bernhard Felsenthal, *The Wandering Jew* (Chicago, 1872), p. 4; see other literature cited in Jonathan D. Sarna, "The American Jewish Response to Nineteenth Century Christian Missions," *Journal of American History* 68 (June 1981): 35–51.

28. Naomi W. Cohen, "Pioneers of American Jewish Defense," *American Jewish Archives* 29 (Nov. 1977): 116–50; Cohen, "Antisemitism in the Gilded

Age: The Jewish View," *Jewish Social Studies* 41 (1979): 187–210; Allan Tarshish, "Jew and Christian in a New Society: Some Aspects of Jewish-Christian Relationships in the United States, 1848–1881," in *A Bicentennial Festschrift for Jacob Rader Marcus*, ed. Bertram W. Korn (Waltham, Mass., 1976), pp. 565–83; all survey anti-Semitism during this period citing earlier sources.

29. *Coney Island and the Jews*, pp. 21–22; see [Telemachus T. Timayenis], *The American Jew: An Exposé of his Career* (New York, 1888), esp. pp. 21, 218–19; Robert T. Handy, *A Christian America* (New York, 1971); F. M. Szasz, "Protestantism and the Search for Stability: Liberal and Conservative Quests for a Christian America, 1875–1925," in *Building the Organizational Society*, ed. Jerry Israel (New York, 1972), pp. 88–102.

30. [Timayenis], *The American Jew: An Exposé of his Career*, pp. 218–19.

31. Philip Cowen, *Prejudice Against the Jew* (New York, 1928), pp. 15–23; Harap, *The Image of the Jew in American Literature*, pp. 87–90.

32. Samuel Clemens, "Concerning the Jews," in *The Complete Essays of Mark Twain*, ed. Charles Neider (Garden City, N.Y., 1963), pp. xxii, 235–50; Harap, *The Image of the Jew in American Literature*, pp. 349–57. For another example of reconceptualization, see Paul Engle, "Those Damn Jews," *American Heritage* 30 (1978): 72–79.

33. Allan Tarshish, "Jew and Christian in a New Society: Some Aspects of Jewish-Christian Relationships in the United States, 1848–1881," pp. 565–87; Bertram W. Korn, "The First Jewish Prayer in Congress," in *Eventful Years and Experiences* (Cincinnati, 1954), pp. 98–124; Benny Kraut, "Francis E. Abbot: Perceptions of a Nineteenth Century Religious Radical on Jews and Judaism," in *Studies in the American Jewish Experience*, ed. Jacob R. Marcus and Abraham J. Peck (Cincinnati, 1981), 1:90–113; Rebecca T. Alpert, "Jewish Participation at the World Parliament of Religions, 1893," in *Jewish Civilization*, ed. Ronald A. Brauner (Philadelphia, 1979), pp. 111–21; Ellen Sue Levi Elwell, "The Founding and Early Programs of the National Council of Jewish Women: Study and Practice as Jewish Women's Religious Expression," (unpublished Ph.D. diss., Indiana University, 1982), pp. 49–82.

34. *American Jewish Year Book* 42 (1941): 296; Koppel Pinson, "Antisemitism in the Post War World," in *Essays on Antisemitism*, ed. Koppel Pinson (New York, 1946), pp. 3–16; Will Herberg, *Protestant-Catholic-Jew* (Garden City, N.Y., 1960).

35. Isaac M. Wise, *History of the Israelitish Nation* (Albany, N.Y., 1854), pp. 161–68, 189–90; for other examples see Sarna, "American Jewish Response to Christian Missions," p. 40.

36. Quoted in W. Gunther Plaut, *The Growth of Reform Judaism* (New York, 1965), p. 228; see also D. R. Schwartz, "History and Historiography: 'A Kingdom of Priests' As a Pharisaic Slogan," *Zion* 45 (1980): 96–117 with the subsequent exchange with Michael Meyer in *Zion* 46 (1981): 57–60; Jacob B. Agus, *Jewish Identity in an Age of Ideologies* (New York, 1978), pp. 282–333; Yosef Hayim Yerushalmi, *Zakhor: Jewish History and Jewish Memory* (Seattle, Wash., 1982), p. 86.

37. Quoted in James G. Heller, *Isaac M. Wise: His Life, Work and Thought* (New York, 1965), p. 645; see Samuel Sandmel, "Isaac Mayer Wise's 'Jesus Himself,'" in *Essays in American Jewish History* (Cincinnati, 1958), pp. 325–

58; Walter Jacob, *Christianity Through Jewish Eyes* (Cincinnati, 1974), pp. 67–82; Benny Kraut, "Judaism Triumphant: Isaac Mayer Wise on Unitarianism and Liberal Christianity," *AJS Review* 7–8 (1982–83): 179–230.

38. Moritz Loth, *Pearls From the Bible* (Cincinnati, 1891), p. 17.

39. Mordecai M. Noah, *Address Delivered at the Hebrew Synagogue in Crosby-Street, New York, on Thanksgiving Day to Aid in the Erection of the Temple at Jerusalem* (Jamaica, N.Y., 1849), p. 11; Solomon Schindler, *Messianic Expectations and Modern Judaism* (Boston, 1886), p. 56; for other examples see Plaut, *Growth of Reform Judaism,* pp. 178–90 and sources cited in n. 37.

40. Plaut, *Growth of Reform Judaism,* p. 34; see also Sefton D. Temkin, *The New World of Reform* (Bridgeport, Conn., 1974); *CCAR Yearbook* 5 (1895), p. 63; Marc Lee Raphael, "Rabbi Jacob Voorsanger of San Francisco on Jews and Judaism: The Implications of the Pittsburgh Platform," *American Jewish Historical Quarterly* 63 (Dec. 1973): 185–203.

41. See Uri D. Herscher, *Jewish Agricultural Utopias in America, 1880–1910* (Detroit, 1981), and Melvin I. Urofsky, *American Zionism from Herzl to the Holocaust* (Garden City, N.Y., 1976) which cite earlier literature.

42. This subject merits a study of its own. See, meanwhile, Adolph Moses, *Yahvism and Other Discourses* (Louisville, Ky., 1903), pp. 1–10; Heller, *Isaac M. Wise,* pp. 519–21; Harap, *Image of the Jew in American Literature,* pp. 58, 345; Abraham S. Schomer, *The Primary Cause of Antisemitism* (New York, 1909), esp. pp. 76–77; and H. L. Mencken, *The American Language* (New York, 1937), pp. 297–300; Harold R. Isaacs, *Idols of the Tribe* (New York, 1975), pp. 71–92.

43. Fisch, *The Dual Image,* pp. 77–79.

Ellen Schiff

Shylock's *Mishpocheh**:
Anti-Semitism on
the American Stage

A few years ago, Tyrone Guthrie speculated that were Jews to withdraw from the American theater, the institution would "collapse about next Thursday." Guthrie was no doubt assessing Jewish contributions at every level of show business from artists, to administrators, to "angels." He must have been thinking, too, of audiences, for enthusiastic Jewish patronage extends from Broadway to the most remote regional and summer playhouses. In view of the degree of Jewish involvement with the theater, how ironic it is that the American stage nourishes to this day a centuries-old tradition of anti-Semitism.

There is a nice bit of theatrical foreshadowing in the fact that the very first play with a Jewish character to appear in America was *The Merchant of Venice*. Shylock, the archetype of the stock Jew, made his colonial debut in Williamsburg, Virginia, the quintessentially American community. That premiere in 1752 ushered in the remarkably successful career of stereotyped Jews on the American stage.

As befits the prototypical Jew, Shylock flourished in the New World. His descendants in American drama became purveyors not only of every kind of desirable merchandise, but also of prestigious services like heroic surgery, impeccable justice, and

---

* Hebrew and Yiddish: family; familiarly: clan, lineage

careers in the movies. His voluptuous, saucy granddaughters parlayed their charms to princessdom. Perhaps it was the family's successes on the American stage that eventually enticed their Yiddish-speaking co-religionists, the *schlemiel** and the *schnorrer**, to join them. And from the rib (or the funny bone) of Shylock's progeny, the American theater fashioned several new stock types, including the libidinous hustler, the full-time neurotic, and, most formidably, the Jewish mother.

Curiously, during precisely the same decades that Shylock's *mishpocheh* have been fruitful and multiplying in the United States, that country has become the home of the largest and most secure Jewish population in history. So apparently contradictory a situation invites comment. To begin, a qualification: stereotypes compose only a segment of the throng of Jewish personae who have filled the theaters of this country, particularly since World War II.[1] It is the stereotypes and the negative attitudes they nurture, however, that command center stage in this discussion because its focus is anti-Semitism, a phenomenon which rests upon the dissemination of simplistic, distorted, and emotionally freighted depictions of the Jew. How to account for the ostensible paradox that formulaic Jews persist and proliferate in the conspicuously Jewish theater of a society in which the spectrum of life models is ubiquitous? Several conjectures suggest themselves: first, that the portrayal of the Jew in the popular arts often has very little to do with the actuality of the Jew in society; second, that Jews may not only be powerless to banish disagreeable theatrical images, they may indeed even contribute to them; and third, that the Jew frequently serves a unique function in drama which is historically and irrevocably rooted in rejection. An examination of the fortunes of Jewish roles and images on the American stage supports all three assertions.

The 1752 production of *The Merchant of Venice* transported significant cultural baggage to the American stage. Some 150 years earlier, the genius of Shakespeare had created masterful personae out of myths about the Jews already ingrained in European dramatic tradition. Shylock bears the complement of conventional Jewish attributes. He embodies the image of the Jew as murderer and mutilator, as worshipper of Mammon, and as haughty challenger

---

* *schlemiel*: simpleton, a born loser, misfit
 schnorrer: moocher, chiseler

of Truth. At his side there is Jessica, another icon, and a complex one. The comely and intriguing Jewess incorporates at the same time the ultimate promise of Judaism, a Savior, with the stigma of membership in a deicidal race. Blinded by the wrongheaded vision of her people, she requires only a Christian lover to open her eyes. Together, Shylock and Jessica flesh out the classic conception of the Jew as a creature apart, at once repulsive and magnetic, frightful and comic. That Shakespeare was able to endow them with such authoritative dimensions in the England from which Jews had been banished for some three hundred years vividly demonstrates that the presentation of the Jew on stage is a matter unrelated to his real presence in society.

The same phenomenon is evident in the early American theater where the Jew is represented as he appeared in the mind rather than as he existed in the midst of his countrymen (not that Jews were conspicuous; there were not more than three thousand in this country at the time of the Revolution[2]). Hence, one is not surprised to find in Massachusetts Tory Jonathan Sewell's *A Cure for Spleen* (1775) a reference to "the Jews, a head-strong, moody, murm'ring race. . . ."[3] The first native American play to contain Jewish characters, Susanna Haswell Rowson's *Slaves in Algiers* (1714), has its Jewish villain describe himself as "a forger and crook . . . [who] cheated the Gentiles, as Moses commanded."[4] Predictably, the blackguard has a wondrously beautiful daughter who manifests the desire, if not the courage, for apostasy.

These early examples multiplied with discouraging regularity as accounts of plays presented in Albany, Annapolis, Baltimore, Boston, Charleston, Hartford, New York, Philadelphia, and Providence indicate.[5] The American stage in the first hundred years of national life faithfully aped the European tradition from which it had sprung. However, this was hardly a golden age for the theater in general. Indeed, there is poetic justice in the fact that the plays which were so outrageously pirated in this era before copy- and stagerights were almost uniformly melodramatic mediocrities. Nonetheless, the mindless confections, both imported and domestic, swarmed with the habitual anti-Semitic slurs, clichés, and caricatures. With the embarrassing exception of Richard Cumberland's Sheva (in the enormously popular *The Jew,* 1794), whose radical virtue renders him lifeless, Jews are the customary bad lot. They never lose sight of their money, a monomania which makes them treacherous or funny or both. Rapacity and insidiousness are often communicated by non-Jews in Jewish disguises, a not terribly original subterfuge freely adopted by would-be scoundrels. Plays shown on the early American stage make use of a device effective since its introduction in medieval Church drama: they exploit the comic of forcing the Jew to do good for the very people he had intended to harm. The Jew is regularly made ludicrous by his funny accent, if not altogether corrupt dialect, a contrivance which clearly marks him as alien, for a person who cannot speak like others appears incapable of thinking like them. Although the very notion of the Jew as foreign, a thoroughly conventional attitude, responds particularly well to the distinctly American need to have fun at the expense of the newest arrivals, it is astonishing to learn that an *American* Jew is not depicted in drama until the mid-nineteenth century.[6]

The degree to which formulaic references were respected may be gauged by the fact that they went unchallenged by the first American Jewish playwrights, Mordecai Manuel Noah, Samuel B. H. Judah, Jonas B. Phillips, and Isaac Harby. These authors, whose melodramas enjoyed popular success during the first half of the nineteenth century, met prevailing expectations in the most circumspect way: they eschewed Jewish characters and subjects altogether.[7]

Disparaging references, stereotypical personae, and caricatured behavior mark the first century of theater in America as routinely anti-Semitic. One hastens to add that the acceptance and continuation of established prejudices appear to be a product of cultural habit and insensitivity rather than of deliberate ill will toward Jews. Coleman writes about the Jews he observed on the American stage between 1752 and 1821 that "none of these characters bears any relation, political, social or cultural, to the condition of Jews in America." Then he adds insightfully, "Nevertheless, we record them here because in them the American audiences for the first time saw what they believed to be real Jewish characters."[8] The real offense lies in the American theater's persistence in ignoring the increasingly visible human nature it might have mirrored—on the eve of the Civil War there were 150,000 Jews in the United States, some 22,000 below the Mason-Dixon line and 40,000 in New York alone—sticking instead to prefabricated images, with all the bias and bigotry they embody.

The end of the nineteenth century and the first decades of the twentieth brought events crucial to the depiction of the Jew in the arts. The first was the unprecedented era of expansion. Waves of immigrants more than tripled the population of the United States between 1870 and 1930. Of particular importance to the present consideration was the heightened conspicuousness of two kinds of Jews: the earlier German émigrés, who by the end of the last century bid fair to become business and social competitors in the mainstream of American life, and the 2 million Russian and East European Jews who arrived between 1880 and 1920, establishing in New York a vibrant center of Jewish life in which the stage played a vital role.

Other major influences on the popular representation of the Jew came from within the theater itself in the form of two roughly contemporaneous though radically dissimilar developments. One was the world revolution in dramaturgy; the other, the advent of vaudeville. In the wake of the great iconoclasts—Ibsen, Strindberg, Chekhov, and Shaw—dramatists increasingly turned for their subjects to social issues and to what were intended as everyday stories about everyday people. Meanwhile, the establishment of the first American vaudeville house in 1883 and the rise of pre-dominantly Jewish impresarios and syndicates opened wide the stage door to Jewish personae.

That all these factors combined to transform the representation of the Jew on the popular stage is indisputable, but trying to explain *how* they did so makes one appreciate actress Fannie Kemble's remark that unlike music, painting, sculpture, and architecture, the art of the theater "has no basis in positive science." Indeed, in the convoluted manner in which the stage comes to express its social roots, it frequently appears the life is imitating art instead of the other way around.

Take for example the case of the stereotypical outsider. For centuries, the foreignness of the stage Jew reflected not the banishments and wandering of his people, but their peculiar exclusivity and incompatible beliefs. The influx of immigrants to the United States made the Jew as foreigner a literal reality. On stage, the persona of the immigrant Jew simply absorbed the older image of the alien whose standard attributes—the tortured English, the maladroitness, the oily opportunism, and the heavy clothing which appeared to conceal heaven only knew what goods or tricks—

fitted him to a "T." Similarly, generations of petty Shylocks and Barabases gave way to old-clothes men, fences, loan sharks, and devious merchants whose tag line was "pizness is pizness." How can we not see in these Joseph Pennell-Jacob Riis-style personae theater's ready-made reference, however exaggerated, to the countless enterprising immigrants who became peddlers, merchandising whatever they could lay their hands on?

The Jew was not, of course, the only newcomer to these shores. Moreover, the popular comedies and vaudeville acts of the late nineteenth and early twentieth centuries were almost exclusively populated by stock types. The era's dramatis personae included a whole variety of ethnic caricatures which exploited the traits familiarly associated with the Irish, Germans, French, Swedes, and that irresponsible burlesque concoction, the stage Negro. The Jew figured as an ethnic among ethnics in entertainment which appealed to more settled Americans' need to laugh at the stumbling of greenhorns as well as to the newcomers' need to be recognized, no matter how mockingly. Irving Howe calls the popular arts of a century ago "a sort of abrasive welcoming committee" which built on "the tradition of American demotic contempt for refinement."[9]

The immigrant Jew made his way into this motley scene trailing behind him many of the typical maligning characteristics. He was grotesque and vulgar, he was always selling something shady, but most of all, he was ludicrous. Therein lay a significant departure: unlike the stereotyped Jew who served as the hapless butt of universal derision, the immigrant Jew made audiences laugh by laughing at himself, a notable innovation.[10] The caricatured comic Jew who pokes fun at himself (and everything else) as one ethnic among others is essentially an American Jewish creation. Responding both to opportunity (theaters by the turn of the present century were largely controlled by Jews) and to cultural conditioning (sarcastic humor and wry self-deprecation have historically served among the few Jewish defenses against hideous fortune), Jewish performers scored conspicuous success in vaudeville and burlesque as well as in drama. The team of Bert and Leon in the late 1870s is credited with initiating the Hebrew comic,[11] an institution which, in the hands of such as David Warfield (Wohlfelt), Smith and Dale (Sulzer and Marks), and Montague Glass's characters Abe Potash and Mawruss Perlmutter, grew to impressive proportions and quality. It is noteworthy that so many of the entertainers whose names come immediately to mind as the early great Jewish comedians and comediennes—Tucker, Brice, Cantor, Jessel, Burns—launched their careers with a bag of borrowed tricks that bespoke their awareness of themselves and their audiences as ethnics. With other diversions, they offered " 'Dutch' (German) dialect routines, Irish imitations, Yiddish parodies"[12] and, with remarkable regularity, blackface.

Early in the century, the Jew who entertained in blackface may have been thinking only of giving the public what it liked. Eight decades later, the image of the Jew playing at being a stage black seems prophetic and so merits a brief digression. There is more than a little irony in one historically despised and maltreated minority adopting the identity of another, even when the disguise has no relevance outside the theater. Irving Howe is surely correct in suspecting that more than the desire to please crowds motivated so many Jews to put on black face, and in supposing that "some deeper affinity was also at work."[13] As one studies the increasingly sophisticated plays by blacks and Jews which have enriched the American repertory in the twentieth century, one is struck not just by how often each group writes about the other, but also by how strenuously stereotyping is avoided. In the face of other evidence of black anti-Semitism (e.g., Candice van Ellison's oft-cited statement that blacks belonged to the mainstream by virtue of their "sharing a national prejudice"; Amiri Baraka protesting his tolerance of Jews even as he quotes his own vilifying poetry), the theater adopts quite a different stance. On the stage, blacks and Jews demonstrate a decided preference for treating one another if not always with approbation, at least as individuals rather than as types.[14] The prevalence of this practice explains the omission of the work of black dramatists from this discussion of anti-Semitism. There is good reason to believe that, as Howe posits, when the early Jewish entertainers put on blackface, "black became a mask for Jewish expressiveness, with one woe speaking through the voice of another."[15] Furthermore, subsequent theater history shows that such transference worked reciprocally as black playwrights began to vent their own concerns through Jewish personae and situations.

Nowhere did the woes and concerns of Jews in America receive more concentrated treatment than in the Yiddish theater whose spectacular career on New York's Lower East Side was launched in the last decade of the nineteenth century. An eclectic institution, it offered plays from the European repertory, along with a good deal of *shund* (cheap drama designed for mass appeal), domestic drama, and *tsaytbilder* ("loosely documentary, highly sensationalized portrayals of current events"[16]). Some playwrights, like Jacob Gordin and Leon Kobrin, were influenced by the realistic masters of modern drama who wrote of the commonplace and the mean; few ignored ticket-buyers' delight in seeing their own lives reflected on the stage. If the Yiddish theater did not regularly present Jews with any remarkable psychological depth, it at least showed a whole array of Jews, and in this it took a giant stride toward verisimilitude. Beneath even its most extreme sentimentalizing or brutalizing, the Yiddish theater drew on genuine Jewish experiences.

For the first time, Jews had ample opportunity to depict themselves on stage. Significantly, the self-portraits designed for this esoteric theater were far from uniformly flattering. The Yiddish stage demonstrated in every conceivable way that, as a Sholom Aleichem title states, it is *Hard To Be a Jew*. Life's exigencies or adversities could make a mother abandon her child (Lateiner's *The Jewish Heart*) or dominate her offspring (Gordin's *Mirele Efros*); an innocent girl could unwittingly be lured into degradation by her own father (Asch's *God of Vengeance*); a parent could force his daughter to marry a man she does not love (Anski's *The Dybbuk*); encouraged by such a victory, a husband could then make his wife terrified enough to kill him (Gordin's *The Slaughter*). With its wide variety of dramatis personae, the Yiddish stage undermined the domination of the monomaniacal merchant and his daughter, the tainted oriental beauty. It showed that Jews were real people, which meant they could be good and noble, yes, but they could also be bounders, scoundrels, whores, debauchees, sybarites, fake rabbis, bums, infighters, and, in doubtless the most drastic departure from stage tradition, poor. Unpleasantness never daunted the Yiddish theater. In 1927, well into the decline of the institution, a Yiddish play remorselessly mirrored the world beyond it, "the old generation helplessly regarding the new—the new generation impatiently watching the old."[17]

The diverse personae on the Yiddish stage were surely as authentic as any Jews ever to appear in the American theater.

They were drawn from Jewish life rather than from the legends and myths of the Christian world. They were created by playwrights free to give rein to Jewish imaginations, writing for playgoers who, as audiences go, have to be considered a homogeneous group. The prominence of unpleasant, even grim portraiture is not surprising. In a theater which reflects the lives of a people who have experienced everything that can possibly happen to human beings, one would scarcely expect a preoccupation with gaffes and peccadilloes. However moderate the influence of the Yiddish stage on the American theater, it is essential to note that with it, Jews themselves inaugurated another tradition of unflattering Jewish images.

The stages from which Jews representing themselves held far more sway were those in vaudeville, the borscht belt, and the burlesque circuit. Here the entertainer's stock in trade included making all of Jewish life the subject of parody. Nothing was sacred, not teachers, not rabbis, and certainly not parents. Al Jolson and Eddie Cantor mimicked their cantor fathers. In George Jessel's sketch "Mama in the Box," his *Yiddishe momma*'s stubborn boorishness disrupts a performance at the Comédie Française.[18] Buddy Hackett reported his consternation when, the first time he ate a meal away from his mother's table, he didn't get heartburn and feared that he was going to die because his fire had gone out. Whatever else these depictions of Jews were, they were obviously not intended as anti-Semitic. The Jewish entertainers, Irving Howe writes, "wanted to amuse, not attack, to please, not preach."[19]

How they have been perceived is something else again. Once the Jewish-originated negative images of Jews entered into the public domain, they were subject to imitation by anyone and, therefore, to censure by those who feared that Jews were blithely arming their enemies. A furious James Fuchs stormed in 1927 that the only "legitimate function" allowed Jews in America "is to afford entertainment of the farcical kind to the mentally disinherited majority of their fellow-citizens."[20] Obviously sobered by hindsight, Irving Berlin wrote to Groucho Marx in the 1950s cautioning that some of his songs ought not to be done anymore since they would no longer be understood as they were intended to be.[21] It is patently impossible to determine how much harm Jews may have done themselves by exercising their wit and their freedom of expression. What seems easier to establish is the probability that had Jews taken great care to project only benign images of themselves, their popular depictions would have been just as derisive, but distinctly less versatile. In any event, the first criterion in responsible aesthetic criticism cannot be, Is it good for the Jews? In assessing the portrayal of distasteful Jews in American theater, we need to distinguish carefully between those delineations intended to mock, degrade, or malign an entire people and those where the creative imagination feeds on what it sees as true, however spontaneous and indiscreet the results.

The point can be made by contrasting one of the few blatantly anti-Semitic works in the American repertory with a play about an unscrupulous Jewish protagonist which was nonetheless produced by the markedly Jewish Group Theater. The first is Theodore Dreiser's Zolaesque *The Hand of the Potter* (1918). It unfolds the story of Isadore Berchansky, mentally disturbed as a result of inferior genes and his slum environment, who molests little girls and ultimately kills one. At first there seems no special reason why Berchansky should be Jewish, nor, for that matter, why he should not be. Dreiser's ethnic designation appears less circumstantial after Berchansky commits suicide in a boarding house run by one Samuel Elkas, a contemporary Shylock complete with winsome daughter. This niggardly landlord protests vigorously when he is refused the reward posted for Berchansky, begrudges the very gas his tenant had used to do himself in, and demands that the bereaved, indigent father settle his son's unpaid rent on the spot. By incorporating the stalest of stereotypes into his cast of naturalistic Jewish wrecks and cripples, Dreiser suggests that Jews cannot escape the forces which have traditionally impoverished them spiritually, physically, and psychologically, and disqualified them as positive characters in literature. Or as the play's Irish newspaperman puts it, "If ye're made up right, ye work right; if ye're naht, ye don't an' that's aal there is to it."[22]

John Howard Lawson's *Success Story* (1932) is hardly more savory. The plot centers on the fanatic careerism of Sol Ginsberg who, finding Marxism too slow a route, lacking the nerve to become a gunman like his brother, and having no time for ethics, forges his way to money and power by superhuman effort, steely will, and blackmail. Lawson's play uses Jews quite differently from Dreiser's. To begin, there is a sound reason for the protagonist of *Success Story* to be Jewish. The subtext is rooted in the havoc wrought by the Depression even in the lives of those with pedigrees or established seats in the inner circle. What more apt a David to pit his ingenuous determination against this Goliath than a punk of a Jew rebelling against his place in life, resolved that "I'm going someplace; anyone stands in my way I'll smash 'em"?[23] Moreover, the figure of the driven opportunist in *Success Story* is thrown into relief by two other Jewish characters. One is Sonnenberg, an impressively cultured and highly respected Wall Street banker who vainly tries to teach Ginsberg something about moderation; the other is the beautiful Sarah whose love for Sol miraculously survives his betrayal of her and of the values they once shared. Ironically, Sarah accidentally shoots and kills Ginsberg just at the moment when he seems to be on the verge of repentent self-awareness. Among other things, Lawson's play acknowledges that good and evil are not the exclusive province of Gentile or Jew.

Success Story, as it opened the 1932 season of the Group Theater and starred three major Jewish actors (Luther Adler as Sol Ginsberg, Stella Adler as Sarah, and Morris Carnovsky as Sonnenberg), exemplifies plays which appeared on the American stage between the world wars. Many of the works were efforts of producing units like the Group Theatre, the Provincetown Players, and the Theatre Guild which naturalized the new realism energizing world drama. Jews were abundantly involved in every aspect of these productions, many of which explored the social, economic, and political concerns of their era. Notable examples include the Provincetown Players' 1920 production of Michael Gold's *Money,* in which obsession with the title commodity very nearly proves the undoing of five immigrant Jews, and the Group Theatre's 1935 premiere of Clifford Odets's *Awake and Sing!* a landmark work by virtue of its authentic portrayal of three generations of a Jewish family, all of them restless and discontent.

The contemporary preoccupations these plays dramatized represented a distinct rupture in American theater tradition, a transformation widely attributed to Jewish influence. Critic John Corbin discusses the point in a piece entitled "Drama and the Jew," published in *Scribner's* in 1933. Tartly acknowledging the talent and energy responsible for the preeminence of Jews in the commercial and artistic spheres of the institution, Corbin laments what he perceives as the consequent uprooting of American theater from its Anglo-Saxon heritage. Although Corbin praises through clenched teeth Jacob Adler's Yiddishization of Shakespeare and the plays "these Yids wrote . . . first-hand out of their daily experience and thought,"[24] he rejects the triumph on the commercial stage of what he sees as a Jewish-inspired naturalism, the acid intelligence and eroticism of which were polluting the mainstream of this country's theatrical tradition. He rails at Elmer Rice's *Counsellor-at-Law* (1931), whose Jewish eponym's generosity of spirit and integrity do not shield him from manipulation by his upperclass Gentile wife and his patrician rival. He censures the satiric treatment, however richly deserved, of what he calls Anglo-Saxondom in the plays of George S. Kaufman. Corbin saw only the indictment of "the elder stock" in *Counsellor-at-Law* and of American presidential elections in *Of Thee I Sing.* He missed entirely Rice's delineation of his protagonist's struggle to reconcile the Jewish values he cherishes with opportunities to advance in legal circles. Similarly, the critic avid for proof that Jews were using the theater to avenge themselves on those who had ridiculed them for centuries overlooked the manifest instances of the sarcastic Kaufman's characteristically Jewish self-criticism, like the arrogant composer in *On Your Toes,* or the extravagant, thoroughly ridiculous movie moguls in *Once in a Lifetime.*

The watchdogs of tradition were, of course, not the only ones keeping an eye on Jews, both onstage and off, as the greatest cataclysm in Jewish history was building. In Los Angeles in 1935, pro-Nazi hoodlums attacked the director of *Till the Day I Die,* a work by Jewish author Clifford Odets, whose communist hero is methodically destroyed by Nazis.[25] Harold Clurman, a director and later chronicler of the Group Theatre, records how the sense of Lawson's *Success Story* was distorted by the rise of Hitler. People felt it inopportune to put on stage "a demoniacally ambitious Jewish boy."[26]

In 1933 Richard Maibaum wrote the first American play about Nazism. Entitled *Birthright,* it was based on a story the playwright had heard from a German refugee about National Socialism's anti-Jewish measures.[27] *Birthright* signaled a flood of plays about Germany and Hitlerism, virtually all of which accepted sub-textually as a given Nazi persecution of Jews and "chromosome hunting" without developing the theme through affected Jewish characters. American drama of the late 1930s and early 1940s skirted Nazi anti-Semitism. At least until the German-Soviet non-aggression treaty (1939), it was the fate of communists, not Jews, at the hands of Nazi excesses that inspired plays.[28] Two German works had limited success here. Friedrich Wolf's *Professor Mamlock,* which delineates the cruelties endured by a surgeon at the hands of the Nazis, was produced by one of the units of the Federal Theater Project but became more widely known in a subsequent film version. The 1934 Theatre Guild production of Ferdinand Bruckner's *Races,* which depicted the divisive effect on youth of the Nazi party's rise to power, closed after its out-of-town tryout.[29]

What did get to the New York stage were such plays as S. N. Behrman's *Rain from Heaven* (1934), which pits spunky artistic mentality against totalitarianism. Then there was Elmer Rice's *American Landscape* (1938), where a Bund group is blocked from buying land for a training camp in Connecticut, and Clare Booth's *Margin for Error* (1940), in which no less than three characters have solid motivation for the murder of a Bund chief who is shot, poisoned, and stabbed. Lillian Hellman warned of the dangers involved in outwitting fascists (*Watch on the Rhine,* 1941) and in trying to appease them (*The Searching Wind,* 1944). Doubtless there are a number of reasons that explain the American stage's disinclination to confront directly the worsening menace to European Jews, among them isolationism, apathy, ignorance, fear of fanning anti-Jewish sentiment, and concern for the box office. Yet another factor was a hard-to-despise innocence, of which an early example informs the review Burns Mantle, drama critic for the *New York Daily News,* wrote of Elmer Rice's *Judgment Day* (1934), a melodrama (Rice's term) based on the Reichstag Fire trials: "Even the frankest propaganda play must be believable to its audience. It matters very little that Mr. Rice can bring into court evidence to prove that he has not, either from bias or author's enthusiasm, overstated the case of Hitler, who is obviously the target of his wrath. The audience does not believe it humanly possible for so vicious and brazen a travesty of justice to have taken place in any civilized state, whatever its revolutionary adventures.[30]

Only after the United States had entered the war, when naiveté about the fate of European Jewry was no longer possible, anti-Semitism gradually began to be considered thoughtfully on stage. Arthur Laurents's *Home of the Brave* (1945) treats a Jewish soldier's paralyzing guilt over his relief at the battleground death of a gentile friend whom he suspected of secretly harboring prejudicial feelings. A related theme, a Jew witnessing a Gentile become the sacrificial other, is worked through by Arthur Miller in *Incident at Vichy* (1964).

There are few American authors who, like Arthur Miller, have accepted the challenge of writing drama about the Holocaust. While the impact of the Nazi genocide on Jewish identity shapes the behavior of the lawyer in Herman Wouk's *The Caine Mutiny Court-Martial* (1954), as well as that of the survivor of persecution in Lanford Wilson's *Talley's Folly* (1979), it is clear that staging any part of the event itself—still so incomprehensible to the civilized mind in general, the more so to sheltered Americans—constitutes an awesome feat. Probably the earliest in the small body of American works dealing forthrightly with Holocaust episodes became the subject of a prolonged, ugly battle. At its center was Anne Frank's *Diary of a Young Girl,* discovered in its French translation and adapted for the stage by Meyer Levin in the early 1950s. Shortly after, Frances Goodrich and Albert Hackett wrote another dramatization of the diary. These authors, apparently in league with Lillian Hellman and Kermit Bloomgarden, among others, were instrumental in having the first version legally suppressed. According to Levin in his book *The Obsession,* his rivals' objections stemmed from their left-wing political ideology, inimical to his pro-Zionist, "too Jewish" stance. Levin's script *is* richer in Jewish content than Goodrich and Hackett's which aims for universal relevance by downplaying ethnic specificity. The lamentable Jewish infighting over a precious Jewish text cannot be undone, but Levin's work should be allowed to speak for itself. Anne Frank has entered the consciousness of civilization. Like Cleopatra and Joan of Arc, she must be expected to inspire more than one theater artist.

While no other American work about Nazi anti-Semitism has achieved the international renown of the Goodrich and Hackett *Diary of Anne Frank,* other stageworthy plays on the subject have appeared. Some outstanding examples are Harold and Edith Lieberman's *Throne of Straw* (1975), the story of the Lodz ghetto and the monomaniacal Chief Elder of its Jewish Council; Arthur Miller's adaptation of *Playing for Time* (1980), Fania Fénelon's memoir of her membership in the inmates' orchestra at Auschwitz;

and Martin Sherman's *Bent* (1978), which argues that homosexuals were treated even more inhumanely than Jews by the Nazis. Moreover, in the last several years, the American stage, like the television and movie industries, has demonstrated a markedly increased, indeed sometimes too eager, interest in dramatizing the Hitler era.

However skillfully the horrors are dramatized, the public's interest in plays about the Holocaust is more quickly satisfied than its appetite for more palatable subjects and less gruesome Jewish characters. There is still much sobering truth in James Fuchs's 1927 charge that "the nation does not want to be informed about . . . Jews—it wants to be entertained by them, and it wants, for the sake of authenticity, Jewish writers to furnish the entertainment."[31] In the pursuit of that goal, Jews have not lost the promising start they had made by the turn of the century. But what fantasies they have fabricated, perhaps in spite of themselves and often quite irrespective of the degree to which they knowledgeably or accurately reflected Jewish psyche and experience.[32] One wonders, for example, how any of the famous "Jewish gangsters"—Paul Muni, Edward G. Robinson, John Garfield—would feel to hear activist Amiri Baraka recall, "So heavy was the Garfield mystique of . . . [the] early 40s tough guys he had portrayed that I knew he could kick any nut's ass *and I would help him.*"[33]

It is a startling fact of American stage (and film) history that Jews have had a hand in creating virtually all the prevailing contemporary Jewish stereotypes. Nowhere is this better illustrated than in the images of the two women who dominate the idea of the Jewess in popular culture. The first is the Jewish mother, sentimental, pushy, tireless, and infinitely resourceful in coping with the misfortunes which afflict her life with predictable regularity. The other is the equally spirited, eternally restless, libidinous, and reliably gorgeous young woman whom it is convenient to call the *belle Juive.* The former is a modern, primarily indigenous phenomenon; the latter, the American stage's variation of a European myth embodying the nexus of Christian attitudes toward Judaism.

If Shylock paved the way for generations of moneymen, Jessica announced a long line of sensuous Jewesses eager to abandon both father and the morality of the fathers for upward mobility in one Belmont or another. As an aggressive voluptuary, usually endowed with special wisdom, the *belle Juive* is a well-established figure in European drama and no doubt made her way to the New World in imported plays. In the 1930s she turns up in the works of Odets, the Spewacks, Lawson, and Whedon and Kaplan as an opportunistic, sexually active conniver. These fictionalized Jewesses, reinforced by the stage personae of Fannie Brice and Sophie Tucker—brash and brassy—evolve into the contemporary image of the Jewess as a synonym for carnality, an image so widely understood that nothing beyond a Jewish name is needed to account for the behavior of Woody Allen's Doris Klein (*God*), David Mamet's Deborah Soloman (*Sexual Perversity in Chicago*), and Albert Innaurato's .Bunny Weinberger (*Gemini*).

By contrast with the legendary *belle Juive*, the *Yiddishe momma* is a twentieth-century caricature. Here, too, it is essential to recognize and acknowledge the Jewish origins of a popular stereotype. Elsewhere I have noted that the Jewish mother was fashioned "from the fabric of immigrant life, her image shaped (or stretched) by the emotionalism of the Yiddish theater, the humor of borscht belt comedians, and the prejudices of American-Jewish authors."[34] On the English-speaking stage, we find her, strangely enough, in some of the same plays that launched in American drama her putative daughter, the *belle Juive:* Odets's *Awake and Sing!, Paradise Lost,* and *The Flowering Peach*, Sam and Bella Spewack's *Spring Song*. Here, too, the literary image was reinforced by the stage personae of actual Jewish women. If Stella Adler balked at playing the mother in *Paradise Lost* because she wanted to avoid identification with the part she had done so succesfully in *Awake and Sing!* other actresses cultivated just such typecasting. Far and away the outstanding example was Gertrude Berg whose best-know *momma* was Molly Goldberg, a persona Berg created and brought to life on radio, stage, and television and one who represents the quintessence of Jewish motherhood in the popular mind.[35] Like any good stereotype, the *Yiddishe momma* travels indefatigably, undergoing appropriate modifications through the years. During the 1982 New York season, for example, she appeared in WASPish façade to shore up her faltering son, the writer (Jules Feiffer's *Grown Ups*), and, in one of her most challenging roles to date, attempted rapprochement with her son, the gay, a professional transvestite (Harvey Fierstein's *Torch Song Trilogy*).

Like these Jewish women, many Jewish men on today's stage

bear traces of their origins in Jewish-formed molds. We have only to look at Odets's *Awake and Sing!* whose entire cast of characters has, amazingly, shaped the subsequent stage images of Jews. The males include Myron Berger and Sam Feinschreiber, the sympathetic bunglers; Ralph, the whining idealist; Jacob, the impotent revolutionary; Uncle Morty, the hedonist; and Moe Axelrod, the sharp, big-talking, physical and emotional cripple. These men have exercised a different sort of influence than the females in their play. Where the American theater has adopted the entire characterization of the *Yiddishe momma* and the *belle Juive* from plays like *Awake and Sing!*, it has instead borrowed various traits from the men and standardized them as Jewish traits. These it has combined with the attributes of the *schnorrer* and the *schlemiel* on the one hand, and the distinctive features of the stand-up comedian on the other. What results are the male protagonists of plays by Neil Simon, Jules Feiffer, Murray Schisgal, and Herb Gardner, among others, Jews easy to recognize but harder to classify than the female types. Woody Allen provides excellent examples with his personae, chief among whom is the persona Allen himself projects. These are Jews with individualized human dimensions who also bear formulaic characteristics (e.g., they are oversensitive, overambitious, and oversexed), wisecracking self-deprecators afflicted with the syndrome Saul Bellow calls "Pagliacci gangrene."

Although the Jewish male on the contemporary stage does not always lend himself to ready categorization as a type, he nonetheless often continues a tradition that is fundamentally anti-Semitic. His faults—like those of the most monstrous stage Jews throughout history—are emphatically human faults. Following the example of the "Hebrew" comedian, he palliates his failings, at the same time ingratiating himself with other people, by being wildly and wittily articulate about them. The impact of Jewish humor and the Jewish comic type in Protestant America has been splendidly documented,[36] and we need only probe the reasons for their amazing success to understand why essentially ridiculous (and reproachable) stage Jews endure.

From the first, Jewish comedians and comediennes have provoked laughter by breaking the rules. They are loud and vulgar; they shamelessly call attention to their physicality. These entertainers join their audiences in laughter at their own expense. They ridicule themselves, their families, the environment that made them what they are, and the world with which they cannot seem to sustain contact. Of course their mordant humor is double-edged: more often than not they make fun of their audiences. How many variations have there been on the sneering, "You think *I'm* crazy? Who paid to get in here?" The comic Jews are, in short, all the things it's not nice to be, and what is more, they are these things in public. What excites laughter—and it is frequently shocked, embarrassed laughter—is spectators confronting the open affirmation of the inadequate, uncouth, ignoble traits they know they too possess.

The Jew in the limelight surrounded by those who, applauding from the shelter of a darkened auditorium, recognize in him all the nasty secrets they know to be true of themselves occupies a position everyone simultaneously craves and fears. We all yearn to be the center of attention, true; at the same time, we shrink from the possibility of being exposed and ridiculed as the weak, inept sinners that we are. So we let the Jew in the limelight do it for us, joining him in mocking what we reject about ourselves.[37] Such transference—or exorcism—of various elements of human nature is, of course, basic to the relationship between actors and audiences. However, by putting on a Jewish mask, the actor enhances his role as a target onto which the spectator can project guilt, shame, and alienation because, as Jonas Barish points out, Jews and actors alike have traditionally been regarded as pariahs whose presence good society regulates or excludes.[38]

Despite the fact that the theater in our day has grown infinitely more hospitable to humanized images of Jews, showing them to be representative of mankind in many acceptable and admirable ways, it has, by its very nature and purview—as an institution that entertains while demonstrating something about how people behave—at the same time perpetuated its distinct brand of anti-Semitism. The Jew type on stage in the last half of the twentieth century serves much the same function he did in Church drama of the thirteenth: he is a negative reference point, an objectification of that part of himself man needs to control by laughter, derision, or worse. No milieu lends itself more naturally than the theater to the illusion that he can do so.

Notes

1. For a demonstration of the range of humanized Jews in dramatic literature since 1945, see my *From Stereotype to Metaphor: The Jew in Contemporary Drama* (Albany, N.Y., 1982).

2. One estimate puts 400 Jews in New York City and 300 in Philadelphia on the eve of the Revolution. "Life in Early America: The Jews in the Colonies," *Early American Life* (Feb. 1978), pp. 24, 25.

3. Edward D. Coleman, "Plays of Jewish Interest on the American Stage, 1752–1821," *Publications of the American Jewish Historical Society* 33 (1934): 172.

4. Ibid., p. 181.

5. See Coleman, "Plays," and Louis Harap, "The Drama," in *The Image of the Jew in American Literature from Early Republic to Mass Imigration,* 2nd ed., ed. Louis Harap (Philadelphia, 1978), pp. 200–238.

6. Harap, "The Drama," p. 202.

7. The omission of Jews from the work of Harby and Noah is especially telling since Harby was a leader of Reform Judaism in his native Charleston and Noah was an active Jew and an early Zionist. See Sol Liptzin, *The Jew in American Literature* (New York, 1966), pp. 22–28, and Harap, "The Drama," p. 264–69.

8. Coleman, "Plays," p. 198.

9. Irving Howe, *World of Our Fathers* (New York, 1976), p. 402.

10. It was an achievement that did not travel easily. M. J. Landa, that admirable first-hand commentator on the Jew in the British theater, recounts the story of the fate in London of *Sam'l of Posen,* whose eponym is an early example of a loyal, honest, and funny immigrant Jew. The play, written by George H. Jessop in 1881, enjoyed great success across America and catapulted its star, M. B. Curtis, to fame. In London, by contrast, *Sam'l of Posen* open and closed on—ironically—July 4, 1895. Landa observes that *Sam'l* was "beyond the grasp of London's playgoing *cognoscenti* and *intelligentsia* because they had not yet gone through a course of 'Hebrew' comedians in the music-halls. . . . Not that Sam'l was absolutely novel. But it was still the law in the theatre that the people were to laugh *at* the Jew beyond the footlights, not *with* him." The anecdote also illustrates the contribution of vaudeville to the evolution of audience expectations of the stage Jew. See M. J. Landa, *The Jew in Drama* (1926; rpt. New York, 1969), p. 201.

11. Harap, "The Drama," p. 220.

12. Howe, *World of Our Fathers,* p. 561.

13. Ibid., p. 563.

14. For a discussion of this phenomenon, see my "The Inside of the Outsider: Blacks and Jews in Contemporary Drama," *Massachusetts Review* 21 (1980): 801–12.

15. Howe, *World of Our Fathers,* p. 563.

16. Nahma Sandrow, *Vagabond Stars: A World History of Yiddish Theatre* (New York, 1977), p. 114.

17. Lillian Krieger, review of M. Adelschlager's *Greenberg's Daughter,* a melodrama about the return of the prodigal daughter presented by Maurice Schwartz's Yiddish Art Theatre, *Reflex* 1 (Oct. 1927): 127.

18. Irving Howe includes a version of "Mama in the Box" in *World of Our Fathers,* p. 564.

19. Ibid., p. 565.

20. James Fuchs, "Facts and Fictions," *Reflex* 1 (Sept. 1927): 14.

21. Howe, *World of Our Fathers,* p. 562.

22. Theodore Dreiser, *The Hand of the Potter* (New York, 1918), p. 199.

23. John Howard Lawson, *Success Story* (New York, 1932), p. 147.

24. John Corbin, "Drama and the Jew," *Scribners' Magazine* 93 (1933): 295.

25. Malcolm Goldstein, *The Political Stage: American Drama and Theatre of the Great Depression* (New York, 1974), p. 98.

26. Harold Clurman, *The Fervent Years* (New York, 1957), p. 132.

27. Joseph Mersand, *Traditions in American Literature: A Study of Jewish Characters and Authors* (New York, 1939), p. 193.

28. See Goldstein, *The Political Stage,* pp. 209–12.

29. Ibid., p. 106. The late actor Fitzroy Davis, whose memory of this era was uncanny, wrote me of having seen one of the few New York showings of *Races* with Virginia Stevens in the spring of 1935.

30. Quoted by Mersand, *Traditions in American Literature,* p. 195.

31. Fuchs, "Facts and Fictions," p. 14.

32. Sometimes American-Jewish authors' voices lack authenticity. Robert Alter makes the point that they have inadvertently continued the tradition of ignorant observers writing about Jews: "Ironically, what most American-Jewish writers are outsiders to is that very body of Jewish experience with which other Americans expect them to be completely at home. . . . The American writer of Jewish descent finds himself utilizing Jewish experience of which he is largely ignorant and so the Jewish skeletons of his characters are fleshed with American fantasies about Jews. The result is a kind of double sentimental myth: the Jew emerges from fiction as an imaginary creature embodying both what Americans would like to think about Jews and what Jews would like to think about themselves." See Alter, "Sentimentalizing the Jews," in his *After the Tradition: Essays on Modern Jewish Writing* (New York, 1969), p. 39.

33. Amiri Baraka, "Confessions of a Former Anti-Semite," *Village Voice* (Dec. 17–23, 1980).

34. "What Kind of Way Is That for Nice Jewish Girls to Act? Images of Jewish Women in Modern American Drama," *American Jewish History* 52 (Sept. 1980): 106.

35. For example, consider this description of her in the musical comedy *Molly:* "The lovable Molly Goldberg . . . guides her children Samuel and Rosalie through adolescence, her husband Jake through unemployment and her entire Bronx neighborhood through the Depression and its attendant but—for Molly— always solvable problems." See Otis L. Guernsey, Jr., ed., *The Best Plays of 1973–74* (New York, 1974), p. 348.

36. See, for example, Robert Alter, "Jewish Humor and the Domestication

of Myth," in *Veins of Humor,* ed. Harry Levin (Cambridge, Mass., 1972); Sarah Blacher Cohen, ed., *Comic Relief* (Urbana, Ill.,1978); Albert Goldman, *Freakshow* (New York, 1971); Howe, *World of Our Fathers,* esp. Chap. 17; Anthony Lewis, "The Jew in Stand-up Comedy," in *From Hester Street to Hollywood,* ed. Sarah Blacher Cohen (Bloomington, Ind., 1983); Earl Rovit, "Jewish Humor and American Life," *American Scholar* 36 (Spring 1967): 237–45.

37. On the transposition of the watcher and the watched, see Jonas Barish, *The Anti-Theatrical Prejudice* (Berkeley, Calif., 1981), p. 476.

38. Ibid., pp. 464–65.

Demagogues,
Ideologues,
Nativists, and
Restrictionists

Robert Singerman

The Jew as Racial Alien: The Genetic Component of American Anti-Semitism

"In the final analysis," Adolf Hitler once declared, "the Jew is actually an Asiatic, not a European."[1] A similar ideology can be traced in the writings of immigration restrictionists and eugenicists who joined forces in the first three decades of the twentieth century to maintain the United States as an Anglo-Saxon preserve. They opposed Jewish immigration from eastern Europe on racial grounds; specifically, they contended that the Jews were racially Asiatics, wholly incapable of successful assimilation because of their alleged Mongol-Khazar blood. Although racial opposition to the Jews faded as the eugenics movement declined, American anti-Semitism had a clearly identifiable genetic component inextricably linked with the restriction of the "new" immigration of white ethnics from southern and eastern Europe prior to 1924.

In his highly illuminating essay "Social Discrimination Against Jews, 1830–1930," John Higham has isolated the primary difference between racism in America and Europe. Whereas in Europe racists typically distinguished between Aryans and Jews, "American racists differentiated principally between Anglo-Saxons or Nordics and every other variety of human being, Jews along with the rest." The view expressed here unreservedly confirms this assessment, but nonetheless takes exception to Higham's premise that while ideological anti-Semitism in the United States may be explained partly on racial grounds, Jews were traditionally identified only as Caucasians.[2]

At this juncture, it is essential to point out that in earlier decades the term "race" was used loosely to designate virtually any physical, linguistic, or ethnic group, while modern usage limits its primary meaning to a "local geographic or global human population distinguished as a more or less distinct group by genetically transmitted physical characteristics."[3]

Five influential Europeans who during the last half of the nineteenth century speculated on the Jews' racial distinctiveness warrant a brief review because of their influence on the evolution of American racist ideology.[4] To Count Joseph Arthur de Gobineau (1816–82), the reputed father of racist ideology, "the Semites were a white hybrid race bastardized by a mixture with blacks."[5] Of prime importance is his conceptualization of racial mongrelization as the cause of a superior nation's degeneracy and ultimate downfall as seen in ancient Greece and Rome. Another Frenchman, Ernest Renan (1823–92) helped to popularize the erroneous notion that the Aryans and Semites form distinct, antithetical races, and seems to have been the first person to question the ethnic purity of the Jews in eastern Europe because of their alleged Khazar antecedants.[6] Referring to the Jews of southern Russia and the Danubian lands, Renan's essay *Le judaisme comme race et comme religion* (1883) startled the world with the declaration: "These regions contain Jewish masses which, in all probability, have nothing or next to nothing Jewish in the ethnic sense of the expression." To Renan, these Jews appeared to have so much foreign blood that from the biological point of view, the very meaning of the word "Jewish" was now in dispute.[7]

Using the cephalic index as a measure of racial superiority, Georges Vacher de Lapouges (1854–1936) elevated the Aryans into *Homo Europeus,* a master race whose biological superiority was under attack by racially inferior peoples such as Asiatics and Jews. Vacher de Lapouges stressed the peril of racial degeneration confronting longheaded (dolichocephalic) Aryan civilization through mixture with roundheaded (brachycephalic) non-Aryans, thereby shrouding his racism in a cloak of pseudo-scientific "anthroposociology." His studies were introduced to American readers in the late 1890s, and the French anthropologist found an eager interpreter in the person of one Carlos C. Closson.[8]

Another writer was Houston Stewart Chamberlain (1855–1927), a naturalized German born in England, whose *Foundations of the Nineteenth Century* (originally written in German in 1899) depicted the satanic Jews as a bastardized race engaged in mortal combat with Germanic Aryandom.[9] A second German worthy of consideration here was Werner Sombart (1863–1941), an economic historian best known for his *Die Juden und das Wirtschaftsleben* (1911). To Sombart, the Jews were an oriental race of wandering nomads transplanted into northern Europe where, bound by Talmudic Judaism and an avaricious love of money, they fostered the rise of capitalism.[10] Sombart devotes an entire chapter to "The Race Problem" in his widely discussed classic, permeated with images of Jewish rootlessness and financial acumen. It is highly significant that a new English edition of Gobineau's *The Inequality of Human Races* appeared in 1915, preceded by English translations of Chamberlain's *Foundations* (1910) and Sombart's *The Jews and Modern Capitalism* (1913), all within a relatively short period and coinciding with the rise of racial anti-Semitism in the United States.

One of the earliest Americans to reflect on the racial origin of the Jews was Josiah Clark Nott, a surgeon practicing in Mobile, Alabama. In his review-essay "Physical History of the Jewish Race" (1850), Nott cast the Jews as an immutable race which for four thousand years had kept its blood so pure from foreign mixture that the modern Jew has "the same features which the Almighty stamped on the first pairs which he created."[11] Drawing on the notion that the Jews are an unadulterated stock that preserved its "original type" against all adversity and in all climates, subsequent writers concluded that the Jews were unassimilable, in large part because of their rabbinic strictures against intermarriage. James K. Hosmer, an American chronicler of the Jews, echoed this belief in his characterization of them as a "Semitic flotsam and jetsam thrown upon the Aryan current." Hosmer found support from Rabbi Felix Adler who explained the Jews' oriental "peculiarities of disposition" as owing to the "Asiatic blood in their veins." Just as oil and water can never mix, Hosmer looked upon the Jews as "soluble by no saturation, not to be pulverized or ground away by the heaviest smitings, unabsorbed, unoverwhelmed, though the current has been rolling for so many ages ever westward, until at length the West is becoming East"; and he asked, are they "to subsist forever apart, or will [they] some time melt into the stream that bears [them]?"[12]

Throughout the last quarter of the nineteenth century, more and more investigators speculated on the racial history of the Jewish people. In England, the Jewish folklorist Joseph Jacobs argued for the existence of a definable Jewish race, and he validated the widely accepted notion of a "superior prepotency of the Jewish blood." Through their racial endogamy, Jacobs argued, the indelible Jewish racial type was transmitted over the generations and emerged dominant even in spite of marriages with non-Jews and in defiance of marginal racial admixture.[13]

In America, the definitive work on race at the century's end was William Z. Ripley's *The Races of Europe*.[14] Based in large part on the latest ethnographic investigations appearing in the anthropological journals of Europe, Ripley correctly dispelled any scientific foundation for the existence of an Aryan race. He did, however, divide the Europeans into three distinct races: a northern race of blond Teutonic longheads; an Alpine race of Celto-Slavic roundheads; and a longheaded Mediterranean race.[15] Although he did not attach any hierarchic value to these "racial" groups, nativists used Ripley's research to denigrate the Slavs and Latins as biologically inferior to the Nordics or Teutons of Scandinavia, Germany, and the British Isles. As for the Jews, Ripley properly arrived at the conclusion that they are not biologically a distinct race, a progressive view at that time and contrary to Joseph Jacobs's arguments for a Jewish racial homogeneity.[16] Nevertheless, in an otherwise enlightened treatment of the subject, Ripley could not resist interjecting statements on the Jews' "physical degeneracy" as measured by their short stature and deficient lung capacity. He could point to Poland as a great "misery spot" where he attributed the stunted height of the Poles as being "largely due to the presence of the vast horde of Jews, whose physical peculiarity drags down the average for the entire population."[17] Referring to the Jews, Ripley feared that this "great Polish swamp of miserable human beings . . . threatens to drain itself off into our country as well, unless we restrict its ingress."[18]

In his subsequent writings, Ripley's bias appeared on more than one occasion in the fear that with unrestricted immigration from eastern Europe, the superior Anglo-Saxon in America might disappear along with the buffalo and the vanquished American

Indian. Indeed, successful American biological amalgamation with lower European stocks was by no means assured as Ripley raised the possibility that the superior American people might revert to a more primitive physical type through intermarriage with the new immigrants.[19]

Throughout his chapter on "The Jews and Semites" in *The Races of Europe,* Ripley generously cited Anatole Leroy-Beaulieu's *Les Juifs et l'antisemitisme* (Paris, 1893), translated two years later into English as *Israel Among the Nations.* Perhaps borrowing from his countryman Ernest Renan, Leroy-Beaulieu raised the question of the Khazars and how perhaps thousands of Russian and Polish Jews could trace their lineage to "the old nomads of the steppes."[20] Repeating a theme that continued unchanged in the writings of American nativists and eugenicists, Leroy-Beaulieu was horrified by the "apparent degeneration of the race" as he wrote of the east European Jews. He lamented:

Their physical strength, their muscular power, has diminished in each generation; their blood has become poorer, their stature smaller, their shoulders and chests narrower. Many Jews of the large Jewries have an emaciated, pallid look. Many of them show signs of racial decline and degeneracy. . . . The Jew is, moreover, often misshapen; few races have so many men who are deformed, disabled, or hunch-backed, so many who are blind, deaf mutes, or congenital idiots. The reason for this lies not only in their early marriages and their marriages between near relations, but also, and above all, in their age-long confinement, their lack of exercise, of pure air and wholesome nourishment.[21]

Taken as a whole, the text just presented is also indicative of a broader ideological current alluded to earlier. To counter a perceived state of racial degeneration and to improve the biological fitness of the human species, eugenicists, beginning with the movement's founder, Sir Francis Galton (1822–1911), advocated a rational program of mate selection and breeding so as to perpetuate the very best hereditary qualities while reducing, as through involuntary sterilization, reproduction among criminals and society's mental and physical defectives. Charles Darwin (1809–82), of course, popularized the concept of natural selection but this was applied by him only to the animal kingdom; it remained for Herbert Spencer (1820–1903) to extend Darwinism to the societal realm with a philosophy soon to be popularized as an anti-egalitarian "Social Darwinism" based on the "survival of the fittest." The eugenics movement, spurred by the rediscovery of Mendelian genetics and its application to agriculture and animal breeding, flourished in the United States in the first three decades of the twentieth century, a period also coinciding with the peak in east European immigration to America.[22]

Beginning in the early 1900s, the extremist writings of some eugenicists and white supremacists became increasingly shrill about the superiority of Anglo-Saxons and the peril of mongrelization confronting the American people through amalgamation with inferior stocks, the Jews being counted among the undesirable classes of aliens whose Asiatic blood, some claimed, could never be genetically absorbed. The relationship between a nation's supposed purity of blood and racism is well known. In America, laws against interracial miscegenation were justified as necessary for the maintenance of social harmony, while Hitler's Germany and inquisitorial Spain sustained broad-based crusades against the Jews in the name of preserving national blood purity.[23] To David Starr Jordan, a proponent of eugenics and biologist turned president of Stanford University, the nation's very vitality was linked to the survival of the fittest in the struggle for existence. As he put it, "The blood of a nation determines its history" and, conversely, "the history of a nation determines its blood."[24] As the annual immigration from Europe approached and exceeded the one million mark in 1905, more and more "old stock" Americans recoiled with horror as they contemplated the newcomer's "bad blood" entering the American gene pool. Hybrids were often pointed to as inferior to either parent, and it was commonly pointed out that racial mixture, while raising the lower race, invariably pulls the higher one down.[25] Americans were frequently warned of the biological consequences of unrestricted immigration, with analogies readily drawn from the animal kingdom, as in the following passage:

The foal of a Percheron dam by a Percheron sire is, of course, a Percheron. The children of negroes are negroes, with the negro's black skin, thick lips, prognathous jaw and kinky hair. The children of Jews have their parent's prominent nose and other physical attributes. Like breeds like, and when the unlike mate together the progeny have some of the characteristics of both parents. It is beyond question that the vast infusion of southern European blood which is each year passing into American veins is certain to work marked changes in the physical appearance of

Americans. It is reasonable to conclude that the future American will be shorter in stature, swarthier of skin, that his skull will be shorter and broader, that probably his nose will be more prominent than is the case to-day.[26]

In the last three decades of the nineteenth century, the Slavs, Latins, and Jews were also singled out as particularly undesirable and wholly unassimilable to American ways.[27] Jews were typically believed to be exceedingly resistant to Americanization because of their pronounced racial solidarity. To most writers, the immigrant's race consciousness was a trait carried in the blood, and "no injection of Americanism will be able to get it out of the system." Similarly, racial solidarity was thought to be "strongest in people who have no country which they can call their own," as demonstrated by the Jews and the Poles.[28] Prejudice could be condoned by placing the blame on the Jew for his natural isolation, usually by pointing to him as "largely a race apart, an alien in our midst." Whether one called it race consciousness or racial isolation, it was highly resistant to amelioration. Increasing the number of Jews in the United States would only aggravate an existing problem "for racial prejudice increases with numbers by a sort of geometrical proportion."[29]

Racial explanations for Jewish distinctiveness were abundant, often couched in descriptions of the Jews as a non-Caucasian, oriental people, inherently incapable of absorbing Anglo-Saxon ideals. In twentieth-century America, this imagery can be traced to an article written in 1903 by one Roger Mitchell, who combined orientalism with images of the physical deterioration so often associated with the immigrant Jew. Mitchell's description of New York's Jewish ghetto was highlighted by the Jews' vulnerability to chronic disease and physical breakdown. According to Mitchell, "Jewish immigrants of a military age who could pass our army requirements for recruits are comparatively rare. . . . Among the Jews also, senile decay is pronounced at an age when the German, Englishman or Scandinavian is still in his physical and mental prime. . . . The mental standard of the Jewish immigration fails to offset its physical inferiority. . . ."[30] He alerted his readers to the "moral degradation" associated with the wave of Jewish immigration and addressing himself to the Hebrew mentality in general, offered the following observation: "They have a nervous make-up that is not easily susceptible to the formation of habits of body or thought, and it would often appear that their mental processes were not of the western order, but, after all, the Hebrew is only a more or less modified Oriental still."[31]

Not a few doctors singled out the Jews on medical grounds, with some pointing to their "racial incest" as the cause of "a racial tendency toward, or characteristics of, mental instability and predisposition to a neurotic and psychopathic constitution."[32] Others warned of "hidden sexual complexes among Hebrews."[33] Also the scourge of tuberculosis was indelibly associated with the immigrant Jewish community in New York City.[34] To Alfred C. Reed, an assistant surgeon affiliated with the United States Public Health and Marine Hospital Service in New York City, the

... Jews of different nationalities differ considerably in their physical status and aptitude for American institutions, and for amalgamation with our body politic. No race is desirable which does not tend to lose its distinctive traits in the process of blending with our own social body. It would seem from history that the Jew only blends inadvertently and against his conscious endeavor and desire. Hence the process of true assimilation must be very backward. Moreover, in origin, racial traits, instincts and point of view, the Hebrew race is essentially oriental, and altogether there is at least ground for objection to unrestricted Jewish immigration.[35]

In a book issued under the auspices of the Council of Women for Home Missions, Mary and Lemuel Barnes had no doubts about the Jews ("thoroughbred Asiatics") who are "avowedly not Christians." The Jews were seen as a dominant factor in American business and trade, while their assimilation was by no means assured owing to their not-so-remote Asiatic origin. As the Barneses viewed the Jewish problem, the Jews "have persistently kept themselves a distinct and distinguished Asiatic race in spite of the massive and cruel forces which would have submerged or at least merged any occidental breed of humanity."[36] Others praised the Jews for their so-called abhorrence of promiscuous racial mongrelization and attributed this apparent fact as the source of their commercial success.[37] A contrary position was advanced by J. G. Wilson in his article "The Crossing of the Races," a discussion of racial amalgamation and the question of unlimited immigration.[38]

In time, Wilson argued, the Poles, Slavs, Hungarians, and Italians would be absorbed, but history has shown that the Jew has been "a source of worry and discomfort to every nation in which he has ever settled in *any numbers.* . . ."[39] The crux of the problem was racial identity and tribal clannishness which precluded Jewish-Gentile intermarriage, Wilson's prime requisite for successful amalgamation. He praised the Reform Jews in America for marrying out of their race, yet this process was too slow because the "old superstitions" were buttressed by the ever-increasing number of Orthodox Jewish arrivals from the European ghettos. In the end, all peoples could be amalgamated as long as they didn't arrive in an overwhelming tide, but a "complete racial substitution" and the loss of "our inherited Anglo-Saxon ideals" were to be feared if the mass immigration continued unabated.[40]

Another restrictionist, Edward A. Steiner, argued for the cessation of all Jewish emigration from eastern Europe to the United States, though he did concede that the Jewish physical "type," although disagreeable when very pronounced, was capable of successful genetic assimilation. Steiner reassured Americans that the "issues of intermarriage are exceptionally good and the resultant types normal."[41] On the issue of intermarriage, Maurice Fishberg, a physical anthropologist and a Jew, informed a conference of eugenicists and all "those interested in improving the human breed" that "the flow of Jewish blood into the veins of the European and American peoples does not infuse any new racial elements. . . ."[42] His assurances would hardly be required today, but given the racial character of everything ethnic in the America of his day, they are indicative of articulated perceptions of Jewish blood as unwholesome, foreign, and racially debilitating. Consider, for instance, that Charles Benedict Davenport, the founder of the eugenics movement in America, viewed the offspring of Jewish and non-Jewish couples as "halfbreeds"![43]

In the early years of the twentieth century, it seemed that race explained everything, and superior nations rose and fell on the strength of their racial purity. Americans were warned that the ancient civilizations of Egypt, Greece, and Rome all had decayed from within because of the infusion of degenerate blood.[44] Mongrelization was the ultimate eugenic horror, with the analogy of the village dog pound close at hand:

If we must have a symbol for race mixture, much more accurate than the figure of the melting pot is the figure of the village pound. If one can imagine a pound from which no dog was ever rescued, and in which all the denizens were free to interbreed at will, and into which dogs of every variety were introduced continuously for many dog generations, he will have an excellent representation of the racial situation of a country which receives all races of immigrants indiscriminately. The population of the pound, after a few generations, would be composed, aside from the newcomers, exclusively of mongrels.[45]

Additionally, Prescott F. Hall, a prominent foe of unrestricted immigration, wrote in 1908 that the "physical degeneration of the Jew in New York and Philadelphia has been accompanied to some extent by a moral and political degeneration." Assimilation of the Jews into American society was "often a mingling rather than a fusion" because of the Jew's desire for "race and religious purity" which prevented his intermarriage with other races.[46] Hall was later converted to eugenics and his world view became increasingly one of the higher races competing for survival with the lower races whom he compared to bacteria.[47] An American army medical officer, Charles Edward Woodruff, similarly stated the racial problem in biological terms. Persecution of the Jews in Europe was merely a "process of disinfection." Woodruff's powerful imagery presented the Jews as bacilli "which may be beneficial if few and in place, but deadly if numerous and out of place." Persecution was defended as "an extermination of an invading disease" whenever the Jews in Europe became unproductive economic parasites. New York City was becoming infested with Jews and if their number were not controlled, America would suffer the fate of Poland, a nation that perished from "this ethnic infectious disease."[48]

What should be done, however, with the Jews already in America? This question was tackled by "Junius Aryan" who divided all of mankind into four races, the Aryan, Semitic, Mongolian, and Negro, with the latter three seen as posing an imminent peril to the biological purity of the United States through miscegenation. In what must be one of America's more bizarre specimens of racist literature, "Junius Aryan" cited the animal breeding arguments advanced by the eugenicists in his call for the segregation of the non-Aryan races within the United States, with the eventual removal of each group to its respective country of origin to follow in due course. A national miscegenation law was proposed to help improve and increase the pure-blooded Aryan race, only the members of which should be permitted to speak a language with Aryan roots or to bear Aryan names.[49]

Proponents of eugenics frequently contributed to the public's jaundiced image of the Jews. This was certainly the case with Charles B. Davenport, America's best known eugenicist, who summarily dismissed the latest Jewish arrivals: "There is no question that, taken as a whole, the hordes of Jews that are now coming to us from Russia and the extreme southeast of Europe, with their intense individualism and ideals of gain at the cost of any interest, represent the opposite extreme from the early English and the more recent Scandinavian immigration with their ideals of community life in the open country, advancement by the sweat of the brow, and the uprearing of families in the fear of God and the love of country." In an exceedingly candid letter to Madison Grant written in 1925, Davenport contemplated the desirability of a genocidal solution to America's Jewish problem: "Our ancestors drove Baptists from Massachusetts Bay in to Rhode Island but we have no place to drive the Jews to. Also they burned the witches but it seems to be against the mores to burn any considerable part of our population."[50]

Another eugenicist, Paul Popenoe, the editor of the American Genetic Association's *Journal of Heredity,* uncharitably regarded the Jewish race as an example of urban selection in the survival of the fittest: "In a community of rascals, the greatest rascal might be the fittest to survive. In the slums of a modern city the Jewish type, stringently selected through centuries of ghetto life, is particularly fit to survive, although it may not be the physical ideal of an anthropologist."[51]

A similar argument, also emphasizing the tenacious ability of the Jews to survive in a competitive urban environment, was fused with a portrait of conquest through immigration. Albert E. Wiggam, a popularizer of eugenics and Nordic supremacy (*The Fruit of the Family Tree*), speculated that "other races will be out-bred and supplanted by the Jew, or by some other race even better adapted to city life. . . .[52] Another unflattering portrait, aptly entitled "The Conquest of America," presented an America being conquered by the alien Jew. Comparing nations to organisms, Herman Scheffauer admonished: "In a cosmic sense and to the eye of historical time nations are but vast and loosely constructed organisms subject to all natural laws of growth and decay, and to many ills and disasters, and for each in turn the great clock of eternity must strike twelve. This is true even of the once-dominant race within a nation. When it is no longer strong or worthy to rule, then conquest comes, though it may not come as of old, by fire and sword, but by a gradual permeation of vigorous alien people."[53]

Opposition to the new immigration from southern and eastern Europe, as we have seen, was frequently articulated on biological and racial grounds. At the forefront of this powerful movement was the Immigration Restriction League, founded in 1894 in Boston and dominated from its inception by Prescott F. Hall, a lawyer, and Robert De Courcy Ward, a professor of climatology at Harvard.[54] Both became staunch advocates of a national eugenics policy through their domination of the Committee on Eugenics of the American Breeders' Association; they even considered changing the name of their Immigration Restriction League to the Eugenic Immigration League.[55] To Ward, a national eugenics policy required "the prevention of the breeding of the unfit native, as well as the prevention of the immigration and of the breeding after admission of the unfit alien."[56] In terminology strongly reminiscent of Houston Stewart Chamberlain, the immigration problem was seen as a racial problem; the depth of this sentiment was conveyed with scientific authority in the eugenicist literature of the day:

We are allowing race mixing to proceed on a large scale without definitively knowing, for instance, which characteristics of the white, the yellow, and the black breeds are dominant; without having a knowledge of whether certain undesirable physical and psychic characters of other races are not so strongly dominant as to breed out some of the most desirable and distinctive characteristics of the aryo-germanic race, which took possession of this continent, assumed domination over it and planted in it its civilization, institutions and ideals, [and yet] is ... in danger of being mixed with the blood of other races to the degree of obliteration if the present influx of immigration from the far east, from southern and southeastern Europe and from Asia Minor is allowed to go unchecked. ... *The final test, which is inevitably approaching, will not consist in assimilating this or that other race but in dominating the complicated network of heredity in what threatens to become a blood-chaos* [italics added].[57]

The immigrant Jews, as we have seen, were not infrequently the object of castigation as undesirable aliens on genetic grounds. In the mind of Madison Grant ("The high Priest of racialism in America"[58]), mongrelization between any superior and inferior race resulted in reversion to the "more ancient, generalized and lower type," as exemplified in the following instances: "The cross between a white man and an Indian is an Indian; the cross between a white man and a negro is a negro; the cross between a white man and a Hindu is a Hindu; and the cross between any of the three European races and a Jew is a Jew."[59] Similarly, Grant deplored "the Jew, whose dwarf stature, peculiar mentality, and ruthless concentration on self-interest are being engrafted upon the stock of the nation."[60] Another perspective was advanced by Seth K. Humphrey in an attack on "depreciated mixtures of peoples" of slight hereditary value. Yes, an exceptional person may emerge from immigrant stocks, as in the case of the poet Mary Antin, but one instance "does not compensate for the tens of thousands of Russian Jews who never get beyond a driving acuteness in small trade, and range down from that to gunmen for wages and incendiaries for insurance."[61]

A novel variation of the Jew-as-Asiatic theme was promoted by anti-communists who parlayed the bugaboo of Asiatic communism with Asiatic Semitism. The Immigration Restriction League's Prescott F. Hall saw bolshevism as a "movement of oriental Tartar tribes led by Asiatic Semites against Nordic *bourgeoisie*."[62] One of the most vivid expressions of this theme was tendered by Robert Tuttle Morris, a nationally known surgeon and son of a former governor of Connecticut, as he described a meeting addressed by Emma Goldman:

Many of the Jews present possessed hair and eyes of colour suggesting that the men and women were not purely Semitic. Immediately there came the thought that these anarchists and ultra Socialists were largely Eurasians, representing hybrids of the sort which the naturalist already knew to represent an unstable element in all governments. If this view proves to be correct on further examination of the subject it will allow us to make rational classification of Jews who do not add to that great credit which we freely give to the best and purest Semitic element. Because Trotsky and so many of his Bolshevik colleagues are Jews the question of their being Eurasian hybrids becomes important in a special way in relation to Russia.[63]

With the passage of time, however, racialists must have perceived that their threadbare conceptualization of the Jews as racially
inferior Asiatics was losing whatever potency it had as a stereotyped
epithet. The popular imagination overwhelmingly conceived of
the Jews as Europeans, not as Asiatics or Bedouin-like nomadic
Semites.[64] New ground was broken in 1911 with the appearance
of Maurice Fishberg's *The Jews: A Study of Race and Environment*
which demonstrated that the Jews are genetically a heterogenous
people akin to the varied physical types among whom they have
lived throughout the Jewish diaspora and are neither a pure-
blooded race nor a distinct sub-race.[65]

In the early 1920s, the restrictionists, in league with the eugenicists and all other upholders of Anglo-Saxon purity, mounted
their final assault to close the immigration door to all so-called
inferior racial types. (The Chinese and Japanese were effectively
barred through earlier exclusionary acts and so-called gentlemen's
agreements.) A victory was won in 1921 with a provisional law,
later renewed and extended to 1924, limiting immigration to 2
percent of each nationality in the United States according to the
1910 census.[66]

Beginning in 1922, racialists discarded their generalized descriptions of the Jews as "Asiatic elements," a phrase used in
1921 by Lothrop Stoddard,[67] and replaced it with the more specific
term, Mongoloid Khazars. In his 1899 review of Ripley's *The
Races of Europe,* Joseph Jacobs had already noted that those
"who contest the purity of the Jewish race lay great stress upon
the Chozars as forming the nucleus of the Russian Polish Jews.
. . ."[68] John R. Commons, by no means sympathetic to the Jews
in his *Races and Immigrants in America* (1920), followed Ripley
in denying the Jews any status as a race of pure descent owing,
in part, to the native tribes in early Russia who converted to
Judaism.[69] The Khazars were again identified by name in 1922 in
two restrictionist texts. In one, Kenneth L. Roberts seized upon
the *Jewish Encyclopaedia*'s article on the "Chazars" as he concocted
a new imagery blending the "Yellow Peril," the "Jewish Peril,"
and the Mongol horde: "It must not be forgotten, moreover, that
the Jews from Russia, Poland and nearly all of Southeastern Europe
are not Europeans: they are Asiatics and in part, at least, Mongoloids. California long ago realized the importance of barring

Mongoloids from white territory; but while they are barred in the West, they pour in by millions in the East."[70]

The second book was Clinton Stoddard Burr's *America's Race Heritage,* containing favorable words about the aristocratic German Jews and the Sephardim who formed the "old" Jewish immigration but sheer contempt for the eastern European Jews whom he regarded as the Ashkenazim. Why were Burr's "Ashkenazim" so loathsome? It was their mongrel blood, their "mixed racial type" traced by Burr to the Khazars of Mongolian origin which distinguished them from the admirable and purer type of genteel western European Jew.[71]

The myth of the invading Mongol-Khazar horde was once more broadcast, this time by Burton J. Hendrick in 1923. The "Eastern Jews," he wrote, "have never been Europeanized," so as candidates for American assimilation, these Jews, "as they land at Ellis Island, are about as promising as a similarly inflowing stream of Hindus or Syrian Druses."[72] Painting the immigrant Jew as permanent racial aliens ("always and necessarily aliens"[73]), he elaborated: "Thus the blood of this Turkish or Mongol people flows extensively in the veins of the Eastern Jew of today. A further large Slavic mixture makes the Eastern Jew racially alien to Jews from other parts of Europe. Thus the masses that comprise one fourth the present population of New York City trace their beginnings, in considerable degree, to certain tribes that roamed the steppes of Russia in the Middle Ages and happened to accept the religion of Judah as their own."[74] As for their level of social, economic, and political advancement, the situation was equally dismal: it was nothing short of "primitive, tribal, Oriental."[75]

T. Lothrop Stoddard, a lawyer with a doctorate from Harvard, also helped to implant the durable Khazar myth in the body of American racist thought. Whereas in 1921 he had portrayed the Jews as "Asiatic elements," Stoddard's *Racial Realities in Europe* (1924) benefited mightily from the investigations of others whose grim conclusions he shared. Absorbing the pseudo-anthropological prattle of Madison Grant and the gloomy portrait of worthless biracial hybrids painted by the eugenicists, Stoddard singled out the "disharmonic combinations" so commonly observed in the eastern European Jews with their "dwarfish stature, flat faces, high cheekbones, and other Mongoloid traits" traceable to the

Mongolian Khazars.[76] He repeated this theme in "The Pedigree of Judah," an article published in *The Forum* and read by countless thousands who might otherwise never be exposed to such blatant racial nonsense, including Stoddard's observation about the "Negroid strain . . . in Jewry; to it the frizzy or woolly hair, thick lips, and prognathous jaws appearing in many Jewish individuals are probably due."[77] From Stoddard's article came a curious British variation upon the Khazar myth wherein it was asserted that imbecile mongolism (Down's Syndrome) in Jews is associated only with Jews of Khazar Mongoloid ancestry through one or both parents.[78]

In 1926, the Ku Klux Klan's imperial wizard, Hiram W. Evans, exploited the Khazars to illustrate his premise of the unassimilable American Jews who are not true Jews.[79] The non-Semitic Khazar Jews who falsely claim the title Jew also figure prominently in a tract by an advocate of Anglo-Israelism, the true author of which may be none other than William Cameron, the compiler of the infamous *International Jew* series in Henry Ford's *Dearborn Independent*.[80] By 1933, long after the mass immigration from Europe had ceased, Madison Grant summarized his movement's obsession with the Jews as one of the lesser breeds threatening the racial unity of a Nordic America. Under the heading "The Alien Invasion," Grant's *The Conquest of a Continent* boldly summarized the Khazar origin of the Ashkenazim and declared: "It is doubtful whether there is a single drop of the old Palestinian, Semitic-speaking Hebrew blood among these East European Jews. They are essentially a non-European people."[81] As currently embellished, the Khazar theory is widely promoted by anti-Zionists who contend that Palestine can never be a Jewish homeland because the Khazars didn't originate in Palestine and therefore have no legitimate claim to it.[82]

It would appear that all the individuals whose writings have been examined were old-stock Americans invariably of northern European ancestry, university-trained professionals, and financially secure. In maintaining that "race" was synonymous with "nation," these Anglo-Saxon standard-bearers were all to varying degrees white supremacists and xenophobes, with eugenics providing an appealing rationale for barring all non-whites as well as eastern and southern Europeans from America.[83] The Jewish "problem," it may be noted, was a minor preoccupation even among such widely-published authors as Madison Grant or T. Lothrop Stoddard, and none of the individuals examined here could be regarded as professional Jew-baiters or full-time propagandists against the Jews, domestic or foreign. To the extent that the restrictionists specifically attacked the Jews, they all agreed that the immigrant Jews were entirely unassimilable with explanations for this perception to be sought in the emerging pseudo-science of racial biology. Racial anti-Semitism was by no means a widely disseminated ideology when viewed in the context of the more widely known conspiratorial International Jew—"half banker and half Bolshevik"—theme that dominated the literature of American anti-Semitism following World War I.[84] The conceptualization of the Jew as an Asiatic Khazar never took hold in the popular imagination nor was it reinforced in cartoons or caricatures. Nonetheless, in the long-fought campaign for the passage of the Immigration Restriction Act of 1924, the major victory of the eugenics movement in America, arguments stressing the racial inferiority of immigrants from eastern or southern Europe were commonly accepted as valid.[85]

It may be noted that while racialists singled out the Jews as unassimilable aliens on racial grounds, a few distinguished between the Americanized, economically productive German and Sephardic Jews who generally had been in America for many decades and the impoverished Orthodox arrivals from the tribal ghettos of eastern Europe. This is most clearly observed in Burton J. Hendrick's *The Jews of America* (1923), a text fully exploiting the Khazars and the menace of the Polish Jews but otherwise full of praise for the western Jews who "represent a vastly higher stage of achievement in business, in politics, in literature, and the arts. . . ."[86] This selectivity may further help to clarify the relationship between the immigration restriction movement and racial anti-Semitism in the years preceding 1924. While the restrictionist movement cannot be studied without reference to the eugenics movement that helped to fuel it, racial anti-Semitism was a simply contrived propaganda ploy wielded by a handful of writers in the overall campaign to bar all cultural aliens, not just Jews, from America's shores. The primary issue, we are led to conclude, was not a presumed racial peril but cultural homogeneity. As elaborated by John Higham, "At the deepest level, what impelled the restriction movement in the early decades of the twentieth century was the discovery that immigration was undermining the unity of American culture and threatening the accustomed dominance of a white Protestant people of northern European descent. The science of the day, together with America's traditional susceptibility to race feelings, made the language of race an impelling vehicle for thinking and talking about culture."[87]

Not surprisingly, the Jews, Slavs, and Mediterranean peoples that were once perceived as a degenerate breeding stock have since been culturally Americanized and physically absorbed into the American gene pool through intermarriage. Racial anti-Semitism in America, predicated on an alleged Jewish biological inferiority, was a manifestation of the closely allied eugenics and immigration restriction movements. The triumph of racial nationalism in the passage of the Immigration Restriction Act of 1924 was preceded by a propaganda campaign capitalizing on biological arguments to demolish the myth of the "Melting Pot."[88] Anti-Semitism was an integral part of the overall effort to exclude most aliens from eastern and southern Europe. Following 1924, these biological arguments virtually disappeared from the American scene.

Notes

1. Quoted in Horst Von Maltitz, *The Evolution of Hitler's Germany; The Ideology, the Personality, the Moment* (New York, 1973), p. 110.

2. John Higham, "Social Discrimination Against Jews, 1830–1930," in his *Send These to Me: Jews and Other Immigrants in Urban America* (New York, 1975), pp. 170–71. A similar position is taken by Isacque Graeber, "An Examination of Theories of Race Prejudice," *Social Issues* 20 (1953): 268–69, who contends that since the Jews are not a biological race, "anti-Semitism is not really a phenomenon of racial hostility." It is important to recall Eric Voegelin, "The Growth of the Race Idea," *Review of Politics* 2 (1940): 283–84, who distinguishes between the "race concept" as used in the natural sciences and the "race idea" of the racialists, typified by the Nazis. According to Voegelin, "The race idea with its implications is not a body of knowledge organized in systematic form, but a political idea in the technical sense of the word. A political idea does not attempt to describe social reality as it is, but it sets up symbols, be they single language units or more elaborate dogmas, which have the function of creating the image of a group as a unit." Conclusive research on the subject demonstrates that the Jews do not form a distinct racial or genetic group. See Raphael Patai and Jennifer Patai Wing, *The Myth of the Jewish Race* (New York, 1975).

3. *American Heritage Dictionary of the English Language*, s.v. "Race." For an understanding of "racism," I have been guided by Van den Berghe who defines it as "any set of beliefs that organic, genetically transmitted differences

(whether real or imagined) between human groups are intrinsically associated with the presence or the absence of certain socially relevant abilities or characteristics, hence that such differences are a legitimate basis of invidious distinctions between groups socially defined as races." See Pierre L. Van den Berghe, *Race and Racism: A Comparative Perspective,* 2nd ed. (New York, 1978), p. 11.

4. Referring to the racial doctrines of Gobineau, Renan, Vacher de Lapouges, and Chamberlain, Oscar Handlin had observed that their impact, though indirect, was of considerable magnitude: "These ideas were by no means fully absorbed or consciously accepted, but they left definable traces in the minds of thousands of Americans. Meshing with consciousness of color and consciousness of nationality, they helped to produce an American racial ideology." See Oscar Handlin, *Adventure in Freedom: Three Hundred Years of Jewish Life in America* (New York, 1954), p. 194.

5. Hannah Arendt, *The Origins of Totalitarianism* (New York, 1951), p. 174. The standard work in English on Gobineau is by Michael D. Biddiss, *Father of Racist Ideology: The Social and Political Thought of Count Gobineau* (New York, 1970).

6. Leon Poliakov, *The Aryan Myth: A History of Racist and Nationalist Ideas in Europe* (New York, 1978), pp. 132–50; S. Almog, "The Racial Motif in Renan's Attitudes Towards Judaism and Jews," *Zion* 32 (1967): 175–200 (in Hebrew); Edward W. Said, *Orientalism* (New York, 1978), pp. 132–50.

7. Ernest Renan, "Judaism: Race or Religion?" *Contemporary Jewish Record* 6 (1943): 445–46. The Khazars, a seminomadic tribe inhabiting the Volga basin north of the Caspian and Black Seas, converted en masse to Judaism in the early eighth century. Upon the collapse of the Khazar empire in 965, the Jewish Khazars, it has been speculated, drifted westward into Hungary and Poland where they formed the nucleus of Askhenazic East European Jewry. A controversial book supporting this theory is by Arthur Koestler, *The Thirteenth Tribe: The Khazar Empire and its Heritage* (New York, 1976). The Khazar origin of Ashkenazic Jewry is challenged by Bernard Dov Weinryb, "The Beginnings of the East-European Jewry in Legend and Historiography, *Studies and Essays in Honor of Abraham A. Newman* , , , (Leiden, 1962), pp. 445–502, and by Bernard Rosensweig, "The Thirteenth Tribe, the Khazars and the Origins of East European Jewry," *Tradition* (Fall 1977), pp. 139–62.

8. The cephalic index (head breadth divided by head length times 100) is the most commonly used index of the human body in racial studies; the lower the index, the longer the head. On the "anthropo-sociology" of Vacher de Lapouges, see Frank H. Hankins, *The Racial Basis of Civilization: A Critique of the Nordic Doctrine* (New York, 1926), pp. 101–40. According to George L. Mosse, *Toward the Final Solution: A History of European Racism* (New York, 1978), p. 62, "De Lapouge's influence in France far exceeded Gobineau's because he succeeded in integrating Darwinism and racism." Two of Vacher de Lapouge's early appearances in American journals are his "The Fundamental Laws of Anthropo-Sociology," *Journal of Political Economy* 6 (1897): 54–92, and "Old and New Aspects of the Aryan Question," *American Journal of Sociology* 5 (1899): 329–46, supplemented by Carlos C. Closson, "The Hierarchy of European Races," *American Journal of Sociology* 3 (1897): 314–27.

9. Chamberlain is now the subject of an important work by Geoffrey G. Field, *Evangelist of Race: The Germanic Vision of Houston Stewart Chamberlain* (New York, 1981).

10. Werner Sombart, *The Jews and Modern Capitalism* (London, 1913).

11. Josiah Clark Nott, "Physical History of the Jewish Race," *The Southern Quarterly* 1 (1850): 436. Nott, it may be noted, elsewhere asserted that "no Negro or Indian or other nonwhite man could show evidence of high intelligence unless he had at least one white ancestor." See Thomas F. Gossett, *Race, The History of an Idea in America* (Dallas, 1963), p. 65. Nott's role in the early development of American racism is discussed by Reginald Horsman, *Race and Manifest Destiny: The Origins of American Racial Anglo-Saxonism* (Cambridge, Mass., 1981), pp. 129–37 passim.

12. James K. Hosmer, *The Story of the Jews* (New York, 1886), pp. 367–68.

13. Joseph Jacobs, "On the Racial Characteristics of Modern Jews," *Journal of the Anthropological Institute of Great Britain and Ireland* 15 (1886): 23–56; Jacobs, "Are Jews Jews?," *Popular Science Monthly* (Aug. 1899), pp. 502–11. The major nineteenth-century conclusions on the Jewish "race" are summarized by Patai and Wing, *Myth of the Jewish Race*, pp. 21–39. Our knowledge of how the American scientific community dealt with the "Who are the Jews?" question is greatly enhanced by George W. Stocking, "American Social Scientists and Race Theory, 1890–1915" (unpublished Ph.D. diss., University of Pennsylvania, 1960), pp. 135–55.

14. William Z. Ripley, *The Races of Europe: A Sociological Study* (New York, 1899).

15. Ibid., pp. 103–30.

16. Ibid., p. 400; on Jacobs, see n. 13.

17. Ibid., p. 379.

18. Ibid., pp. 372–73.

19. William Z. Ripley, "Races in the United States," *Atlantic Monthly* (Dec. 1908), pp. 754–58; Ripley, "Race Progress and Immigration," *The Annals, American Academy of Political and Social Science* 24 (1909): 130–38; Ripley, "The European Population of the United States," *Journal of the Royal Anthropological Institute of Great Britain and Ireland* 38 (1908): 221–40.

20. Anatole Leroy-Beaulieu, *Israel Among the Nations: A Study of the Jews and Antisemitism* (New York, 1904), p. 118.

21. Ibid., pp. 163–64. For a comparable American description of Jewish immigrants and their perceived physical inferiority, see Edward Alsworth Ross, *The Old World in the New: The Significance of Past and Present Immigration to the American People* (New York, 1914), pp. 285–89. The Jewish community, it may be noted, perceived Ross, a noted sociologist at the University of Wisconsin, as anti-Semitic. See "Prof. Edward A. Ross's Persistent Anti-Semitism," *Jewish Advocate* (Boston), (Sept. 4, 1914), p. 2.

22. Four major studies of the eugenics movement in America are available: Kenneth M. Ludmerer, *Genetics and American Society: A Historical Appraisal* (Baltimore, 1972); Mark H. Haller, *Eugenics; Hereditarian Attitudes in American Thought* (New Brunswick, N.J., 1963), particularly chapter 10, "Eugenics and

Race"; Donald K. Pickens, *Eugenics and the Progressives* (Nashville, 1968); and Daniel J. Kevles, *In the Name of Eugenics: Genetics and the Uses of Human Heredity* (New York, 1985), especially valuable for an up-to-date appraisal of Charles Davenport and his prejudices. One can gauge the extent of the eugenicist's preoccupation with "race suicide" and whether or not the human race is degenerating by consulting Samuel J. Holmes, *A Bibliography of Eugenics* (Berkeley, 1924). The racist overtones of Social Darwinism are explored by Robert C. Bannister, *Social Darwinism: Science and Myth in Angle-American Social Thought* (Philadelphia, 1979), pp. 180–200; Richard Hofstadter, *Social Darwinism in American Thought*, rev. ed. (New York, 1959); and Gossett, *Race*, pp. 144–75. Jewish interest in and support for eugenics may be gauged by the following: W. M. Feldman, *The Jewish Child: Its History, Folk-lore, Biology and Sociology* (London, 1917), pp. 20–45; Maurice Fishberg, "Eugenics in Jewish Life," *Journal of Heredity* 8 (1917): 543–49; Max Reichler, *Jewish Eugenics, and Other Essays* (New York, 1916); Arthur Ruppin, *The Jews in the Modern World* (London, 1934), pp. 261–64; R. H. Salaman, "Heredity and the Jew," *Journal of Genetics* 1 (1910): 273–92; J. Snowman, "Jewish Eugenics," *Jewish Review* (London) 4 (1913): 159–75.

23. The American tradition of blood purity is examined by John G. Mencke, *Mulattoes and Race: American Attitudes and Images, 1865–1918* (Ann Arbor, Mich., 1979).

24. David Starr Jordan, "The Blood of the Nation; A Study of the Decay of Races Through the Survival of the Unfit," *Popular Science Monthly* (May 1901), p. 90. Of related interest is Jordan's "Biological Effects of Race Movements," ibid., (Sept. 1915), pp. 267–70.

25. Edwin Grant Conklin, "Some Biological Aspects of Immigration," *Scribner's Magazine* (Mar. 1921), p. 353. An erudite study of racial hybrid degeneracy in nineteenth-century scientific thought is by Nancy Stephan, "Biological Degeneration: Races and Proper Places," in J. Edward Chamberlin and Sander L. Gilman, *Degeneration: The Dark Side of Progress* (New York, 1985), pp. 97–120.

26. Paul Leland Haworth, *America in Ferment* (Indianapolis, 1915), pp. 98–100. Not all observers, however, viewed the "new" immigration as an unmitigated polluting flood. Comparing successful assimilation to blood circulation, one writer saw immigration as a source of invigoration if and only if immigrants received a thorough medical screening and were then dispersed so as to prevent the formation of clot-like "foreign colonies." See "Keeping the New Blood Pure," *Outlook* (New York), (Jan. 28, 1905), pp. 219–21.

27. There is no comprehensive history of Jewish immigration to the United States in all of its phases, but an excellent overview of the mass-immigration period is provided by Esther Panitz, "In Defense of the Jewish Immigrant (1891–1924)," *American Jewish Historical Quarterly* 55 (1965–66): 57–97. On American images of the unassimilable Jew, see Michael N. Dobkowski, *The Tarnished Dream: The Basis of an American Anti-Semitism* (Westport, Conn., 1979), pp. 143–69. American perceptions of the Slavs were just as unfavorable when compared to the negative imagery associated with the Polish-Russian Jews. See Joseph S. Roucek, "The Image of the Slav in U.S. History and in Immigration Policy," *American Journal of Economics and Sociology*, 28 (1969): 29–48. For immigration

restriction as an expression of American nativism, the standard work remains John Higham, *Strangers in the Land: Patterns of American Nativism, 1860–1925* (New Brunswick, N.J., 1955), now supplemented by Thomas J. Curran, *Xenophobia and Immigration, 1820–1930* (Boston, 1975). For an understanding of how selected Caucasian immigrant groups came to be regarded as *racially* inferior, consult Ronald M. Pavalko, "Racism and the New Immigration: A Reinterpretation of the Assimilation of White Ethnics in American Society," *Sociology and Social Research* 65 (1980–81): 56–77.

28. Peter Roberts, *The Problem of Americanization* (New York, 1920), p. 30.

29. Edward R. Lewis, *America, Nation of Confusion: A Study of Our Immigration Problems* (New York, 1928), pp. 369–70.

30. Roger Mitchell, "Recent Jewish Immigration to the United States," *Popular Science Monthly* (Feb. 1903), p. 342.

31. Ibid., p. 340.

32. Alfred C. Reed, "Immigration and the Public Health," *Popular Science Monthly* (Oct. 1913), p. 325. A recent study demonstrates that the immigrant Jew in the period from 1880 to 1914 was in fact much healthier than commonly assumed. See Jacob Jay Lindenthal, "*Abi Gezunt:* Health and the Eastern European Jewish Immigrant," *American Jewish History* 70 (1980–81): 420–41.

33. Thomas W. Salmon, "Immigration and the Mixture of Races in Relation to the Mental Health of the Nation," in *The Modern Treatment of Nervous and Mental Diseases by American and British Authors,* ed. William A. White and Smith Ely Jelliffe, 2 vols. (Philadelphia, 1913), 1:258.

34. Henry L. Shively, "Immigration, a Factor in the Spread of Tuberculosis in New York City," *New York Medical Journal and Philadelphia Medical Journal* 77 (1903): 222–26; Albert Allemann, "Immigration and the Future American Race," *Popular Science Monthly* (Dec. 1909), p. 594. The linking of contagious disease to the influx of allegedly unwholesome foreigners is a persistent theme in attacks on unrestricted immigration.

35. Alfred C. Reed, "The Medical Side of Immigration," *Popular Science Monthly* (Apr. 1912), pp. 390–91.

36. Mary Clark Barnes and Lemuel Call Barnes, *The New America: A Study in Immigration* (New York, 1913), pp. 106–7.

37. Alfred P. Schultz, *Race or Mongrel: A Brief History of the Rise and Fall of the Ancient Races of Earth; A Theory that the Fall of Nations is Due to Intermarriage with Alien Stocks; A Demonstration that a Nation's Strength is Due to Racial Purity; A Prophecy that America Will Sink to Early Decay Unless Immigration is Rigorously Restricted* (Boston, 1908), pp. 34–44.

38. J. G. Wilson, "The Crossing of the Races," *Popular Science Monthly* (Nov. 1911), pp. 486–95.

39. Ibid., p. 493.

40. Ibid., pp. 494–95. The Orthodox Jew from eastern Europe came to New York "five hundred years from the middle ages," bringing "his tribal instincts and his tribal conception of God with him, and the first thing he does is to attempt to set up and continue his tribal institutions." So declared Ray

Stannard Baker, "The Disintegration of the Jews," *The American Magazine* (Oct. 1909), p. 592.

41. Edward A. Steiner, *The Immigrant Tide, Its Ebb and Flow* (New York, 1909), p. 285.

42. Maurice Fishberg, "Intermarriage Between Jews and Christians," in *Eugenics in Race and State,* vol. 2, *Scientific Papers of the Second International Congress of Eugenics held at the American Museum of Natural History* . . . (Baltimore, 1923), pp. 132–33.

43. Ibid., p. 457 ("Discussion"). Davenport repeatedly deplored miscegenation and the physical, mental, and temperamental "disharmony" that he believed ensued. He tersely summarized the consequences: "A hybridized people are a badly put together people and a dissatisfied, restless, ineffective people." See his "The Effects of Race Intermingling," *Proceedings of the American Philosophical Society* 56 (1917): 367.

44. Charles W. Gould, *America, A Family Matter* (New York, 1922).

45. Henry Pratt Fairchild, *The Melting-Pot Mistake* (Boston, 1926), p. 125. Fairchild also shared the widely held conviction of his day that "the qualities of race are carried in the germ plasm," thus negating any remediation through Americanization programs (p. 113).

46. Prescott F. Hall, *Immigration and Its Effects Upon the United States,* 2d ed., rev. (New York, 1908), pp. 51–52.

47. Prescott F. Hall, "Immigration Restriction and World Eugenics," *The Journal of Heredity* 10 (1919): 126.

48. Charles Edward Woodruff, *Expansion of Races* (London & New York, 1909), pp. 382–85. Woodruff's *Expansion of Races,* it may be noted, was regarded by one admirer as "one of the most important books brought out since Darwin's *Origin of Species.*" See Woodruff's obituary, *American Medicine* 21 (1915): 336. Drawing on his study *The Effects of Tropical Light on White Men* (New York, 1905), Woodruff asserts in "The Complexion of the Jews," *American Journal of Insanity* 62 (1905–6): 327–33, that the Jews, for the most part brunettes, possess a pigmentation favoring their survival in the sunny, treeless American cities. In time, these Jewish city dwellers will supplant the extinction-bound Aryans whose blond complexion leaves them "progressively feebler in every generation of city life." An in-depth study of Woodruff's influence on American racial thought and the extent of his alliances in anthropological and army medical circles appears to be justified.

49. "Junius Aryan," *The Aryans and Mongrelized America: The Remedy* (Philadelphia, 1912), pp. 50–63 passim.

50. Charles Benedict Davenport, *Heredity in Relation to Eugenics* (New York, 1911), p. 216 text from Davenport to Grant letter quoted in Charles E. Rosenberg, *No Other Gods: On Science and American Social Thought* (Baltimore, 1976), pp. 95–96. On another occasion, Davenport wrote of the "Jewish segregate" in America to characterize "an alien people in the country where they have dwelt and reproduced so unrestrictedly." See Davenport's "Hereditary Influence of the Immigrant," *Journal of the National Institute of Social Sciences* 8 (1923): 64. Davenport's support for the exclusion of inferior human breeding stock bore

fruit in the Immigration Restriction Act of 1924. See Carroll Ann Smith, "Anglo-Saxon Science: The Scientific Rationale for Immigration Restriction" (unpublished Master's thesis, Columbia University, 1958), pp. 15–34. The considerable political influence of eugenicists, led by Davenport and others of a racist or anti-Semitic persuasion, is analyzed by Kenneth M. Ludmerer, "Genetics, Eugenics, and the Immigration Restriction Act of 1924," *Bulletin of the History of Medicine* 46 (1972): 59–81; Richard Rene Rivers, "American Biological Opposition to Southeastern European Immigration 1900–1924: Ideas, Policies and Implications for Teaching" (unpublished Ph.D. diss., Illinois State University, 1978); Joseph H. Taylor, "The Restriction of European Immigration and the Concept of Race," *South Atlantic Quarterly* 50 (1951): 25–37.

51. Paul Popenoe and Roswell Hill Johnson, *Applied Eugenics* (New York, 1918), p. 133.

52. Albert Edward Wiggam, *The Next Age of Man* (Indianapolis, 1927), p. 386.

53. Herman Scheffauer, "The Conquest of America," *Contemporary Review* (Feb. 1914), p. 252.

54. The history of the Immigration Restriction League is told by Barbara Solomon, *Ancestors and Immigrants: A Changing New England Tradition* (Cambridge, Mass., 1956).

55. Higham, *Strangers in the Land*, p. 152.

56. Robert De C. Ward, "Our Immigration Laws from the Viewpoint of National Eugenics," *National Geographic Magazine* (Jan. 1912), p. 39.

57. "Race Genetics Problems," *American Breeders' Magazine* 2 (1911): 232.

58. Gunnar Myrdal, *American Dilemma: The Negro Problem and Modern Democracy* (New York, 1944), p. 114. Grant's indebtedness to Gobineau and Chamberlain is traced by Charles C. Alexander, "Prophet of American Racism: Madison Grant and the Nordic Myth," *Phylon* 23 (1962): 73–90.

59. Madison Grant, *The Passing of the Great Race; or, The Racial Basis of European History* (New York, 1916), pp. 15–16.

60. Ibid., p. 14.

61. Seth K. Humphrey, *Mankind: Racial Values and the Racial Prospect* (New York, 1917), pp. 176–77.

62. Prescott F. Hall, "Immigration and the World War," *Annals, American Academy of Political and Social Science* 93 (1921): 193.

63. Robert T. Morris, *The Way Out of War: Notes on the Biology of the Subject* (Garden City, N.Y., 1918), pp. 157–58. From 1898 to 1917, Morris was a professor of surgery at the New York Post-Graduate Medical School and Hospital. See *The National Cyclopaedia of American Biography* 39 (New York, 1954): 467–68.

64. "Yet, taking all factors into account, and especially their type of civilization, the Jews of to-day are more truly European than Asiatic or Semitic," confirmed the United States Immigration Commission, *Reports of the Immigration Commission,* 41 vols. (Washington, D.C., 1911), 1:246.

65. Fishberg's conclusion that the Jews are not a race was challenged by Abram Lipsky, "Are the Jews a 'Pure Race'?" *Popular Science Monthly* (July 1912), pp. 70–77. See also the more balanced review, "Will the Jews Ever Lose

Their Racial Identity?" *Current Opinion* (Mar. 1911), pp. 292–94. The pervasiveness of racial anti-Semitism was noted at the time by Nahum Wolf, "Are the Jews an Inferior Race?" *North American Review* (Apr. 1912), pp. 492–95.

66. John Higham, "The Politics of Immigration Restriction," in his *Send These to Me,* p. 54. Upholders of Anglo-Saxon racial integrity hailed their temporary victory in 1921, while continuing to press for permanent legislation, as typified by Henry Pratt Fairchild, "The End of Race Migrations," *Yale Review* n.s., 11 (1922): 827–33, and Edward A. Ross, "The Menace of Migrating Peoples," *The Century* (May 1921), pp. 131–35.

67. Lothrop Stoddard, *The Rising Tide of Color against White World Supremacy* (New York, 1921), p. 165.

68. Compare Ripley, *The Races of Europe,* p. 377, with Jacobs, "Are Jews Jews?" p. 505. Ripley (ibid., p. 390), in turn, acknowledged Ernest Renan (see n. 6) as his source for the Khazar origin of the putative Jews of Russia and the Danubian lands.

69. John R. Commons, *Race and Immigrants in America,* new ed. (New York: Macmillan, 1920), p. 93.

70. Kenneth L. Roberts, *Why Europe Leaves Home* (Indianapolis: Bobbs-Merrill, 1922), pp. 117–18. For an analysis of Roberts's widely read series on immigration in the *Saturday Evening Post,* later reprinted in book form as *Why Europe Leaves Home,* see Gary Frank Hoffman, "Ethnic Prejudice and Racial Ideology in the Immigration Articles of Kenneth L. Roberts" (unpublished Master's thesis, Michigan State University, 1979).

71. Clinton Stoddard Burr, *America's Race Heritage* (New York, 1922), pp. 121, 171, 212, 291, 293, 310. In his *Mankind at the Crossroads* (New York, 1923), p. 310, Edward M. East likewise praised the innate superior hereditary stock of the English and German Jews "who furnished a high percentage of greatness to our country," in marked contrast to the poor grade stock represented by the recent Jewish arrivals from eastern Europe.

72. Burton J. Hendrick, *The Jews in America* (Garden City, N.Y., 1923), p. 96. The evolution of Hendrick's attitudes toward the Jews can be traced in his articles "The Great Jewish Invasion," *McClure's Magazine* (Jan. 1907), pp. 307–21, "The Skulls of Our Immigrants," ibid. (May 1910), pp. 36–50, and "The Jewish Invasion of America," ibid. (Mar. 1913), pp. 125–65.

73. Hendrick, *Jews in America,* p. 138.

74. Ibid., p. 96.

75. Ibid., p. 99.

76. Lothrop Stoddard, *Racial Realities in Europe* (New York, 1924), pp. 171–72.

77. Lothrop Stoddard, "The Pedigree of Judah," *Forum* (Mar. 1926), p. 326. The only other anti-Semitic work suggesting a Negro ancestry of the modern Jews with which I am familiar is Arthur T. Abernethy, *The Jew a Negro, Being a Study of the Jewish Ancestry from an Impartial Standpoint* (Moravian Falls, N.C., 1910). After tracing the physical intermingling of the Jews with the Hamitic Egyptians and Ethiopians in ancient times, Abernethy concludes that "the Jew of to-day is essentially Negro in habits, physical peculiarities and tendencies" (p. 105). Only America's preoccupation with the "Negro question," he writes,

has delayed urgent federal legislative action to check the "alien Hebrew whose fomentings have given internal disruption to the ancient empires of the world, and who, producing nothing, has lived always the parasitical existence" (p. 107).

78. F. G. Crookshank, *The Mongol in Our Midst: A Study of Man and His Three Faces,* 3rd ed. (London, 1931), pp. 75–80, 100–103.

79. Hiram Wesley Evans, "The Klan's Fight for Americanism," *North American Review* (Mar./May 1926), p. 60.

80. Reuben Herbert Sawyer, *The Jewish Question* (Mere, Wilts., n.d.), pp. 5–6. The identification of Sawyer as William Cameron is made by Albert Lee, *Henry Ford and the Jews* (New York, 1980), p. 89.

81. Madison Grant, *The Conquest of a Continent; or, The Expansion of Races in America* (New York, 1933), p. 225.

82. For an extended review of anti-Zionism as it relates to the Khazar canard, see Morris Kominsky, *The Hoaxers: Plain Liars, Fancy Liars, and Damned Liars* (Boston, 1970), pp. 143–61.

83. The clearest and most concise identification of "race" with "nation" was made by Madison Grant who wrote, "Our institutions are Anglo-Saxon and can only be maintained by Anglo-Saxons and by other Nordic peoples in sympathy with our culture." See Madison Grant, "America for the Americans," *Forum* (Sept. 1925), p. 351.

84. Higham, "Social Discrimination Against Jews," p. 171.

85. I do not wish to leave the impression that eugenics is intrinsically a racist movement or that all geneticists identified themselves with the racist views of some of their outspoken colleagues. Along these lines, see Ludmerer, *Genetics and American Society,* pp. 121–34, where he discusses the repudiation of eugenics. Ludmerer's "American Geneticists and the Eugenics Movement," *Journal of the History of Biology* 2 (1969): 337–62, may also be profitably consulted.

86. Hendrick, *Jews in America,* p. 139. Burr, *America's Race Heritage,* p. 310, contrasts the German element ("the true Jews who have earned an enviable record in the United States") with the Eastern ghetto Jews who besmirch "the good name of the Chosen People." Although Burr exploited the Mongol-Khazars and the mixed racial type represented by their descendants (p. 121), one cannot escape the conclusion that his anti-Semitism and that of like-minded restrictionists was predicated on the failure of the ill-mannered Polish and Russian Jews to adopt American manners. Burr was particularly troubled by "their uncleanly habits, their custom of living in congested communities, their litigious spirit, and their insolence upon being endowed with freedom and prosperity" (p. 310).

87. Higham, "Politics of Immigration Restriction," p. 47.

88. This is amply documented by Ludmerer's "Genetics, Eugenics, and the Immigration Restriction Act of 1924."

Edward S. Shapiro

Anti-Semitism
Mississippi Style

Students of the South have differed regarding the importance of anti-Semitism in Dixie. The journalist Harry Golden, for example, wrote of the philo-Semitism of southerners, and the prominent social psychologist Thomas F. Pettigrew has argued that the South has been one of the least anti-Semitic regions of the country. W. J. Cash's classic *The Mind of the South,* in contrast, contended that Judeophobia was central to the southern experience, resulting from the hold which the "savage ideal," "the patriotic will to hold rigidly to the ancient pattern, to repudiate innovation and novelty in thought and behavior, whatever came from outside and was felt as belonging to Yankeedom or alien parts," had over the southern mind. For Americans, the Jew was the alien "and in the South, where any difference had always stood out with great vividness, he was especially so. Hence it was perfectly natural that, in the general withdrawal upon the old heritage, the rising insistence on conformity to it, he should come in for renewed denunciations; should, as he passed in the street, stand in the eyes of the people as a sort of evil harbinger and incarnation of all the menaces they feared and hated—external and internal, real and imaginary."[1]

Leonard Dinnerstein, a leading authority on southern anti-Semitism, agreed with Cash. Dinnerstein attributed the famous Leo Frank case of 1913–14 to the insecurity and anxiety of southerners experiencing the social instability resulting from rapid industrialization, urbanization, and the decline of agriculture and rural life. The Jew symbolized the external forces transforming the cherished South, while anti-Semitism provided southerners with both an outlet for relieving their frustrations and an explanation for their social and economic afflictions.[2]

One clue to the relative importance and nature of anti-Semitism in the South is the careers of the two most vitriolic anti-Semitic national politicians in recent American history: Senator Theodore G. Bilbo and Congressman John E. Rankin. Residents of Mississippi, they gained notoriety as anti-Semites during and immediately after World War II. Bilbo and Rankin had first won national attention as political insurgents representing what passed for left-of-center politics in Mississippi. This involved appeals to extreme racism and demands for public electric power, control of corporations, close supervision of Wall Street, and economic leveling. Rankin and Bilbo capitalized on the same popular frustrations responsible for the emergence of Huey Long, Father Charles Coughlin, Gerald L. K. Smith, and the other messiahs of the 1930s. Unlike these demagogues, however, Rankin and Bilbo never had any grandiose national ambitions nor, as good Democrats, did they contemplate establishing competing political parties or movements. Their racism limited their influence, and even in the South they were viewed as bizarre. Despite the fears of their northern protagonists, neither Rankin nor Bilbo was able to attract a national following. They remained provincial politicians concerned with their own political survival and the interests of those constituents with white skins.

Bilbo had begun his political career as a staunch follower of James K. Vardaman, the leader of Mississippi Populism at the turn of the century. During the 1940s Bilbo was known chiefly for his ferocious racism, sexual peccadilloes, membership in the Ku Klux Klan, and attraction to the fast buck. Yet while governor of Mississippi for eight years, the "Bilbonic Plague" had recognized, as his biographer noted, that "state government must accept its social responsibility; indeed, his impulses in this regard were much in advance of his time." Bilbo was not a mossback during the 1930s. "Folks are restless," he declared at the depths of the Depression. "Communism is gaining a foothold. . . . In fact, I'm getting a little pink myself."[3] As a senator from 1935 until his death in 1947, Bilbo was a loyal New Dealer, supporting the Democratic national agenda except where race relations were involved.[4] Many observers considered Bilbo to be the Senate's worst member, with Senator Robert A. Taft describing him as a disgrace to the upper house. Non-Mississippians, particularly northerners, characterized him as a foul-mouthed, lecherous demagogue embodying the most retrograde aspects of southern politics. In contrast, Reinhard H. Luthin's study of twentieth-century American political demagoguery claimed that had it not been for Bilbo's racism, northern liberals "would have hailed him as a great humanitarian" in the mold of Claude Pepper, Hugo Black, and Lister Hill.[5]

John E. Rankin had first been elected to Congress in 1920 from the area encompassing Tupelo in the northeast corner of Mississippi. He continued to be reelected until 1952 when reapportionment forced him to run against a younger and more popular incumbent. Rankin's thirty-two-year Congressional career can be conveniently divided into two parts. During the 1920s and 1930s he was one of Congress's more prominent Progressives. During the 1940s and early 1950s he was Congress's foremost racist and anti-Semite.[6]

Influenced while young by the Populist movement, Rankin went to Washington as an opponent of big business and as a spokesman for agrarian interests. His major claim to legislative fame was sponsoring, along with Senator George Norris of Nebraska, the law establishing the Tennessee Valley Authority. "Cheap Juice John," as Rankin came to be known, was a New Dealer during the 1930s, and the journalist Stanley High bracketed him with the likes of Maury Maverick, Jerry Voorhis, Tom Amlie, Vito Marcantonio, and Herman Kopplemann.[7] In 1933 Rankin unsuccessfully sought election as Speaker of the House. Running as "a progressive Democrat," he attacked "the forces of reaction" and "the old reactionary crowd" controlling Congress. Three years later he was a candidate for floor leader of the House Democrats. When he withdrew from this race, he announced he would throw his support to "some other liberal" candidate.[8]

By the 1940s both Rankin and Bilbo saw themselves, and were seen by others, as "conservatives." Opposing the labor union movement, an intrusive federal bureaucracy, and internal subversion, Rankin and Bilbo's metamorphosis was characteristic of that of many southerners who had originally welcomed the New Deal as a means to alleviate some of the South's economic problems and to rectify the economic imbalance between the South and the North. The belief that the South was at the mercy of external forces remained in the 1940s, but the large northern corporation was no longer the favorite whipping boy. Because of the growing assertiveness of southern blacks, southerners now focused their ire on northern philanthropists, labor unions, and civil rights organizations for undermining southern social patterns. Southerners also attacked the labor union movement and wage-and-hours legislation for weakening the incentives for industry to relocate to the South. Southern public opinion was accustomed to thinking it was being exploited by foreign banks, insurance companies, railroads, and Wall Street. For Bilbo and Rankin the external enemy took on another form: the New York Jew.[9]

Rankin's anti-Semitism also had a more personal source. All his political ambitions of the 1930s had been unsuccessful. In addition to his campaigns for Speaker of the House and House Democratic floor leader, he had tried and failed to interest Democratic leaders in his availability for the vice-presidential nomination in 1936 and 1940. By the 1940s Rankin was frustrated and embittered. The New York Jew symbolized for him those social and economic forces responsible for the defeat of his political goals and for the weakening of racial segregation.[10]

The public first became aware of this new emphasis in Rankin's thinking in the late 1930s and early 1940s. He, along with other prominent politicians who had been influenced by southern and midwestern Populism, was an isolationist. Some, including Senator Burton K. Wheeler of Montana and Rankin, were unable to resist the temptation to blame American Jews for the growing national opposition to the Axis powers. In 1939, two months after the outbreak of World War II, Rankin claimed that "99 percent of the Christian people of America" wanted to stay out of the European conflict. He pleaded for retention of the arms embargo and warned his House colleagues that "a certain international element that has no sympathy for Christianity was spending money by the barrel" in order to get America committed to the aid of England."[11]

Rankin's attacks on International Jews escalated in April 1941. At that time he singled out Walter Lippmann as a prototype of the International Jew who was more concerned with international Jewry than with American welfare. Rankin differentiated between Lippmann and his ilk and the majority of American Jews who were patriotic "and who must now suffer for the misconduct of these international Jews who are always stirring up trouble for them. In my opinion they are making the greatest blunder since the Crucifixion." According to the Mississippian, Lippman spoke for a clique of international Jewish financiers "who own or control the gold supply of the world" and, under the leadership of the Rothschilds, "are now crucifying civilization on a cross of gold." They had "crucified the German Republic" prior to the emergence of Hitler and had now turned their hired pens on Franklin Roosevelt because he refused to declare war on Germany.[12]

Two months later Rankin's accusations regarding international Jewry had tragic consequences. On June 4 he gave a one-minute speech in the House in which he charged "Wall Street and a little group of our international Jewish brethren" with harassing Roosevelt and Congress into declaring war on Germany. M. Michael Edelstein, who represented New York City's Lower East Side, immediately challenged Rankin. He compared Rankin's rhetoric with Hitler's, noted that very few American bankers were Jewish, and charged Rankin was using Jews as scapegoats. "I say it is unfair and I say it is un-American. . . . All men are created equal, regardless of race, creed, or color; and whether a man be Jew or Gentile he may think what he deems fit." Deeply agitated, Edelstein promptly left the House chamber, suffered a massive heart attack in the Capitol lobby, and died almost instantaneously.[13]

Edelstein's death shocked most House members, and for once Rankin, whose verbosity in the House had earned him the sobriquet "the great American earache," was nonplussed. It wasn't until nearly two years later that he discussed Edelstein's death. This occurred during an anti-Semitic tirade occasioned by his defense of the murder of two Polish Jewish socialists by the Soviet Union. "Let me say this here and now," he ranted, "I have never at any time attacked an American Jew. I have known them all my life. The old line American Jews are just as patriotic as you or I. Many of them are worried to death about this communistic group in this country and all over the world that is stirring up this trouble for them." "I have refrained from mentioning the question here on the floor," Rankin concluded, "even in the face of the slime that was smeared throughout the country two years ago. . . . These Communists are what I am complaining of and not the patriotic Americans."[14]

Rankin, Bilbo, and other anti-Semites of the period were convinced that Jews exercised an inordinate influence within the Roosevelt administration. Jews, Bilbo claimed, had received "more consideration" under the New Deal than any other nationality. For Rankin, Felix Frankfurter was the prime example of the insidious and excessive influence of Jewry in Washington. Frankfurter was a perfect foil for Rankin. He was foreign-born, a former resident of New York, a professor at the Harvard Law School, and a defender of Sacco and Vanzetti, everything which the self-professed spokesman for "the white Anglo-Saxons of the South" detested. When Rankin wished to attack the "communist crackpots" who had infiltrated the Roosevelt administration, he focused attention on what he termed "this Frankfurter bureaucracy."[15]

By World War II Rankin was equating communists with Jews. The support of American Jews for the civil rights movement, which Rankin believed to be a communist plot, strengthened this equation. The basis of atheistic Jewish communism, according to the Rankin gospel, was hatred of Christianity. This required him to sharply differentiate Jews from Christians and to deemphasize the Jewish roots of Christianity. Rankin traced modern Jewry partially back to the Khazars, a central Asian tribe that had adopted Judaism in the seventh century. "Atheistic communism," Rankin told the House of Representatives, "is largely composed of a racial minority that has swarmed into Europe through the Urals in the last 100 or 300 years. . . . They seem to be more akin to Pharoah than they are to Moses."[16]

Strangely enough, Rankin's surrealistic interpretation of Jewish history led him to defend Stalin during the early 1940s. According to the Mississippian, the Russian revolution had been conceived and carried out by Jews, while Stalin was leading a counterrevolution against the Jewish disciples of Leon Trotsky. The Russian dictator's wartime repudiation of the Soviet Union's antireligious campaign revealed the antirevolutionary intentions of the former Russian Orthodox seminary student. "The Bible," Rankin claimed, "says teach a child the way he should go and when he is old he will not depart therefrom. It was but natural therefore that when Stalin got into power he should open the churches." After the war's end there will be "a real democracy in Russia, in which these White Russians and Ukrainians will dominate, and . . . they will see to it that the Russian people will never again be subjected to such persecution as they have endured in the past."[17]

During the postwar years Rankin dropped his admiration for Stalin, but he still continued to claim that communism was an instrument of world Jewry to extirpate Christianity. In his most vicious calumny, he informed doubting congressmen that the murder of 30 million European Christians had been carried out by "the same gang that composed the fifth column of the crucifixion. They hounded the Saviour during the days of His ministry; persecuted Him to his ignominious death; derided him during the moments of his dying agony; and then gambled for His garments at the foot of the cross." For nearly two millenia Jews have attempted "to destroy Christianity and everything that is based on Christian principles. They have overrun and virtually destroyed Europe. They are now trying to undermine and destroy America. God save our country from such a fate."[18]

The issue, simply put, was "Yiddish Communism versus Christian civilization." "Remember," he told his colleagues in 1950, "communism is Yiddish. I understand that every member of the Politburo around Stalin is either Yiddish or married to one, and that includes Stalin himself." Congressman Jacob Javits answered Rankin's canard. He noted that only one of the twelve members of the Soviet Politburo was Jewish, and that it was virtually impossible to secure information about the ethnic and religious background of the wives of Politburo members or their influence on their husbands. Rankin's speech, Javits stated, resembled "the dangerous propaganda technique, popularized by Hitler, Goebbels, and Stalin, of the sweeping lie constantly reiterated." Rankin's sentiments threatened "our essential freedom and domestic peace." Congressman Clifford Case of New Jersey seconded Javits's views. "I think it terribly important that the country as a whole and the world should know that in this sad and sordid departure the gentleman from Mississippi stands alone."[19]

Rankin returned to the fray two years later when he accused "a little gang of yids" of dominating the communist governments of the Soviet Union, Poland, Czechoslovakia, and other Iron Curtain nations. Jews, he contended, had not only been responsible for the starvation of millions of Ukrainian peasants during the 1930s and the murder of Polish Christians during the Katyn massacre, but they had also been behind the infamous Nuremberg trials. Rankin described the court which tried the Nazi war criminals as having "perpetrated more outrages than any other organization of its kind that ever sat." It was horrible that Soviet communist Jews, who had been responsible for the killing of tens of millions of Christians, should sit in judgment of "German soldiers, civilians and doctors, 5 or 6 years after the war closed."[20]

The founding of the state of Israel provided Rankin with another opportunity for equating communists with Jews. His opposition to Zionism had been longstanding. During the war he argued that a strong British empire was vital if the "Anglo-Saxon peoples" were to retain their political and economic dominance and check the nationalistic and racial aspirations of the colored peoples. He berated Wendell Willkie, Drew Pearson, and other critics of British imperialism, but most of his venom was reserved for Zionism which, he contended, was a racial movement opposed to the interests of Anglo-Saxons. In 1944, for example, Rankin warned that American support for a Jewish homeland would disrupt relations with 400 million Moslem and Christian Arabs, would weaken England's control over India, would undermine the British military effort, and would strengthen communism in Palestine. Aid to Zionism resembled "waving a red flag in the face of the British Empire." Instead of going to Palestine, Jews should instead take up Stalin's offer and move to the Soviet Union, "possibly east of the Urals." Such an arrangement for the Zionists could be "easily worked out, and since practically every Communist among them came from Russia, I am sure they would not protest— especially after they got over there."[21]

Rankin's knowledge of Zionism was minimal. He claimed that the Irgun, a nationalistic Jewish underground organization in Palestine, was pro-communist, that the only Americans who sympathized with Zionism were radical Jews who did not represent "the better element of American Jews," and that American politicians supported Zionism only because they were seeking Jewish votes in the 1948 election. On one occasion he contended that the United Nations had supported the partition of Palestine solely because Jews had bribed some of the ambassadors, while other ambassadors had been warned that a negative vote would result in the cutting off of Marshall Plan aid to their nations. (Rankin referred to the Marshall Plan as the "Baruch-Marshall" plan, implying that it was of Jewish origin.) Rankin predicted the ejection of England from Palestine would result in "the collapse not only of Britain but probably of all western Europe; then communism, the greatest menace civilization has ever known, would overrun the whole European continent." The decision of "this international Sanhedrin up here in New York" to divide Palestine, he warned, would touch off "a race war in Palestine" in which anywhere from one million to five million American soldiers would be sacrificed defending the Zionist state, "a branch of the Communist movement." Rankin furthermore claimed that European Jews had no right to settle in Palestine since they were descended from the Khazars and not from the Jews of the Bible. Rankin's source for this was Benjamin H. Freedman, whom Rankin termed "a great American Jew." In truth, Freedman was a wealthy renegade Jew who on one occasion had praised Adolf Hitler. Two weeks after the birth of Israel in May 1948, Rankin claimed that "Russian Communists" were pouring into the new state in order to establish "a Russian bridgehead" in the Middle East. He proposed that the United States provide Great Britain with atomic bombs in order to stop the spread of communism in the Middle East and other areas vital to the British Empire.[22]

International factors were not, however, the basis for the anti-Semitism of Rankin or Bilbo. Bilbo, in fact, admired Zionism, and proposed it as a model to American blacks whom he was eager to see migrate to Africa. All of Bilbo's anti-Semitism and most of Rankin's could be traced to their image of the northern, and particularly the New York Jew, as the ally of the American Negro. Mississippi politics during the era of Rankin and Bilbo largely concerned the social and economic place of the Negro, and no Mississippi politicians were more extreme on the race issue than they. Bilbo, for example, predicted the passage of an anti-lynching bill by Congress in 1938 would "open the flood-gates of hell in the South. Raping, mobbing, lynching, race-riots, and crime will be increased a thousand fold; and upon your garments . . . will be the blood of the raped and outraged daughters of Dixie, as well as the blood of the perpetrators of these crimes that the red-blooded Anglo-Saxon white southern men will not tolerate." In 1947 Bilbo published *Take Your Choice: Separation or Mongrelization,* a lengthy exposition of his racial views. He modestly claimed the book was the result of having studied "practically all the records and everything written throughout the entire world on the subject of race relations, covering a period of close on to thirty thousand years." Here he defended his 1939 proposal to provide a homeland in Liberia for American blacks willing to leave the United States, examined the threat to America from white amalgamation with a race several thousand years behind in physical, mental, and cultural development, surveyed the racial theories of Madison Grant, Arthur de Gobineau, Lothrop Stoddard, and Robert B. Bean, and warned against the "mongrel poison" being spread by communists and communist sympathizers. The United States, he concluded, "is now standing at the crossroad, and we must choose between a white or mongrel America of the future." On other occasions Bilbo was more graphic in analyzing the race question. The "nigger is only 150 years from the jungles of Africa" where he ate "some fried nigger steak for breakfast." The undermining of white supremacy would transform the United States into a replica of South America inhabited by "mestizos, mulattoes, zambos, terceroones, quadroons, cholos, musties, fusties, and dusties."[23]

Rankin, if anything, was more extreme in his racial attitudes. While Bilbo was a politician working the redneck precincts, Rankin was a true believer. He predicted that Congressman Herman Kopplemann's bill to eliminate segregation in the District of Columbia would encourage "the brutal Negroes to assault white women in every section of the city," force whites to move into the suburbs, and terrify law-abiding blacks. Kopplemann's proposal was part of the Jewish communist plan to "force Negro equality or mongrelization upon the white people of the South" and to destroy American civilization. "Every time that someone high up socially or politically comes out and advocates social equality or racial amalgamation," Rankin cried out, "some innocent white girl in Washington pays with her life, or suffers humiliation that is worse than death."[24]

Rankin's racism extended to Orientals. He interpreted the war with Japan as a racial and religious struggle in which "Christianity has come in conflict with Shintoism, atheism, and infidelity." The United States was defending Caucasian civilization against "those yellow reprobates" and the "yellow peril." In order to guarantee the security of Hawaii and California and ensure racial purity, Rankin favored the internment of all Japanese-Americans and their deportation to Japan after the conclusion of the fighting, even if they were fourth-generation citizens. "Once a Jap always a Jap," is how the Mississippian described it. "You cannot change him. You cannot make a silk purse out of a sow's ear." You could no more change a Japanese into a white man than you could "reverse the laws of nature." Rankin was so incensed by the Japanese that he introduced a congressional resolution in April 1943 to change the name of the cherry trees located around the District of Columbia's Tidal Basin to "Korean cherry trees."[25]

At times Rankin's racism was bizarre. In 1942, for example, he attributed unrest among American blacks to "Japanese fifth columnists." He accused "the crackpots, the communists, and parlor pinks" of seeking to "mongrelize" the American blood stream by removing racial labels from Red Cross blood plasma. Behind this scheme were "alien doctors" and "a radical communistic element" which had flooded into America from eastern Europe. Mongrelization would destroy America because, as Rankin told the House of Representatives, "mongrels, as a rule, do not propagate."[26]

Rankin, Bilbo, and many other southerners of the 1940s believed that racial discontent among blacks was caused by outsiders. Southerners claimed that they understood blacks, that they had always provided for their basic needs, and that blacks were essentially content in the South. Rankin, for instance, proclaimed himself to be "one of the best friends the Negro ever had." Furthermore, Negroes supposedly lacked the political skills, education, and intelligence to mount an effective campaign in their own behalf. Thus white southerners looked elsewhere for the sources of racial unrest. At various times they blamed misguided northerners, crackpot reformers and philanthropists, labor union agitators, demagogic northern politicians, communists, and, in the case of Rankin and Bilbo, Jews for disrupting harmonious southern race relations.[27]

Of all the various guises which the Jews assumed in the minds of Rankin and Bilbo, none was more prominent or more nefarious than the ally of the Negro. Both men were careful to distinguish between the "good" Jews, many of whom lived in the South and backed white supremacy, and New York Jews who supported the National Association for the Advancement of Colored People.

Bilbo's reply to a Jew critical of his opposition to a fair employment practices commission was typical. Most American Jews were "fine American citizens," the Mississippi senator declared, but there were "a few of you New York Jew 'Kikes' that are fraternizing and socializing with Negroes for selfish and political reasons." He warned American Jews that their continuing involvement in the civil rights movement would result in their removal from America to Palestine where they could agitate all they wanted.[28]

Bilbo's differentiation between "good" Jews and "Kikes" was based on his belief that the Jewish people were part of the white race. His anti-Semitism never extended as far as Rankin's, and it lacked Rankin's evangelical fervor and ideological underpinnings. Anti-Semitism for Bilbo was merely a by-product of his racism and was mainly a political ploy. On other occasions he attacked Catholic priests, Polish-Americans, and Italian-Americans for harboring doubts about white supremacy.[29]

Bilbo uttered his most famous racist statement in July 1945. It was directed at Josephine Piccolo of Brooklyn who had written him to protest his opposition to equal employment opportunities for blacks. She stated that she was neither a Jew nor a Negro, "but that does not make you less my enemy." "I find it hard to believe," she declared, "that you are an American citizen, and much, much harder to believe that you are allowed to enter the doors of the United States Senate. Every man and woman who cast a vote for you should hang his head in shame." Bilbo's response to Miss Piccolo began with "Dear Dago." Italian-Americans were infuriated by Bilbo's slur, and Congressman Vito Marcantonio of New York demanded an immediate apology to Miss Piccolo. Bilbo then took out after Marcantonio. "When and by whom were you appointed as the judge and arbiter ... of any letter that I might write ... to a nasty, insulting letter?" Bilbo avowed that he would be the last person to question the loyalty and patriotism of the "splendid citizens of Italian descent of this republic, but of course there are some exceptions." Bilbo concluded by claiming that "Dago" was a longstanding and nondisparaging southern term used to describe swarthy southern Europeans.[30]

For Bilbo it was no coincidence that Miss Piccolo was from New York City. New York harbored all that was evil in American life. It was the center of American liberalism and Harlem, as well as the home of large numbers of supposedly unassimilated immigrants, of the offices of the major civil rights organizations, and of the major opponents of politics Mississippi-style. Bilbo described New York's population as "a mongrel, motley bunch of Negroes and aliens" who think "they are sitting on top of the world." In responding to a Jewish soldier who wrote Bilbo to criticize his "Dear Dago" letter, Bilbo characterized him as "a 'Bowery inmate' from the slum sections of New York City and . . . a very common 'kike.' " Actually his correspondent was from Toledo, Ohio, but Bilbo assumed any Jewish critic had to be from the deracinated, unassimilated, polyglot population of New York. "To a citizen like myself, who has been born and reared in a State where there are more genuine white Caucasians than possibly in any State in the Union," Bilbo wrote, "I am sure I would feel very much at a loss" in New York. He portrayed Congressman Marcantonio as a "political mongrel" representing a "sin-soaked communistic" area. By focusing their animus on New York City, Bilbo and Rankin continued a long history of New York-baiting. Southern and western agrarian spokesmen had for decades described cities in general, and New York in particular, as unnatural, parasitical, materialistic, pagan, alien, and corrupt. In 1896 William Jennings Bryan had accused the American metropolis of exploiting the farmer. In the 1940s Rankin and Bilbo accused New Yorkers, particularly radical Jews, of seeking to mongrelize the South.[31]

There was no doubt in Rankin's mind that communist "long-nosed reprobates" were behind the civil rights movement. At times Rankin admitted there were many anti-communist Jews in the South and elsewhere, loyal members of the white race, who opposed the schemes of their New York co-religionists. "The better element of the Jews, and especially the old line American Jews throughout the South and West," he said in 1943, "are not only ashamed of, but they are alarmed at the activities" of Jewish communists responsible for the rapes and murders of white girls by "vicious Negroes." On other occasions Rankin implied that "Jew" and "communist" were virtually synonymous. Thus he described the Fair Employment Practices Committee as "the most dangerous and brazen attempt to fasten upon the white people of America the worst system of control by alien or minority racial groups that has been known since the Crucifixion." The FEPC was a product of "alien influences directed by a foreign comintern . . . that is based upon hatred for Christianity."[32]

In 1950, Rankin read off a list of communist sympathizers which included the Rosenbergs, David Greenglass, and Lee Pressman. "Not a single one," he told his startled congressional colleagues, "has ever been a member of a Christian church. There is not a white gentile in the entire group, and the same may be said of at least seventy-five percent of the Communists in this country." These persons "have been stealing our atomic secrets . . . and plotting the overthrow of this government and the destruction of our Christian civilization." On one occasion Rankin even included Klaus Fuchs among the Jewish atomic traitors even though Fuchs had been raised as a Lutheran.[33]

Rankin's anti-Jewish diatribes continued virtually until his last days in Congress. In 1952 he recommended that every American should read the anti-Semitic tract *Iron Curtain over America* by John Beaty of Southern Methodist University. As a parting shot, Rankin warned America about "those insidious alien enemies who are now plotting the overthrow of the American way of life, and the wiping of Christianity from the face of the earth." Rankin was equally as spiteful toward Jewish congressmen who answered these calumnies. He accused Abraham Multer of representing "more Jewish Communists than any other man in Congress" and attacked Arthur G. Klein for abusing both the British Empire and America's whites by supporting Zionism and the elimination of school segregation in the District of Columbia. In describing Samuel Dickstein, he declared, "I do not want any such man to . . . pretend to speak for me or for those old-line Americans that I have the honor to represent."[34]

Rankin had a celebrated confrontation with Emanuel Celler of Brooklyn. In April 1943, Rankin referred on the floor of the House of Representatives to Celler as "the Jewish gentleman." Celler immediately accused the Mississippian of intolerance, malice, and cruelty, and of deliberately seeking to promote religious divisiveness. "He glories in such strife. It tickles his vanity to create racial animosities." Rankin responded that Celler had been "doing the Jews of this country immeasurable harm" by "attacking the white people of the South ever since he has been in Congress." Rankin then warned Celler that he would "probably be expelled" if he continued making such attacks on members of Congress. At this point the Speaker of the House warned the southern congressman to be more careful or he would be disciplined.[35]

Two years later the two congressmen had another encounter. This was occasioned by Celler's protest against a purported recommendation by the American Dental Association to limit the admission of Jews to dental schools. "I am getting tired of the gentleman from New York raising the Jewish question in the House," Rankin harangued while shaking a fist at Celler. "Remember that the white gentiles of this country have some rights." A few months later Rankin again referred to Celler as the "Jewish gentleman" and, when Celler protested, he asked whether Celler objected to being called "Jewish" or "gentleman."[36]

These attacks on Celler were mild compared to what Rankin said about other Jews critical of his racial and diplomatic stances, particularly the radio and newspaper columnist Walter Winchell. Rankin claimed Winchell's real name was "Lipshitz" (this was incorrect), that he was a "loathsome" Jew, and that he was part of the clique persecuting America's white Christians. This "little communistic 'kike' " resembled a "ghoul at night, that invades the sacred precinct of the tomb, goes down into the grave of a buried child, and with his reeking fingers strips from its lifeless form the jewels and mementoes placed there by the trembling hands of a weeping mother." How much longer, Rankin cried out, "will the decent, patriotic Jews of America have to endure the punishment he is to bring upon them? How much longer will patriotic gentiles have to endure his infamous persecutions?"[37]

In order to prevent further "persecution," Rankin introduced legislation in 1949 amending the Communications Act of 1934 to make it easier for private individuals to sue the radio and television networks for defamation. As might be expected, Bilbo shared Rankin's animus towards Winchell. After Winchell discussed the "Dear Dago" letter on his radio show, Bilbo wroted him a nasty letter describing him as a "limicolous liar and notorious scandalizing kike," a "rabble-rousing, strife-breeding Communist" who spews "venom and hate and if anybody calls your hand you immediately try to hide behind your race and yell 'persecution.' "[38]

Rankin charged Winchell with working closely with the Anti-Defamation League of B'nai B'rith to defame America's white Gentiles. The ADL, he claimed, was a "subversive organization" responsible for leaking information to Winchell about George Patton's slapping of hospitalized soldiers in Sicily during World War II. This was supposedly done to discredit the anti-communist general. In order to protect the nation from this "Yiddish Ku Klux Klan" and "Communist-front organization," Rankin introduced legislation in 1949 to outlaw the ADL. Anyone belonging to the ADL or participating in its activities could be imprisoned for up to one year and fined a maximum of $10,000. Rankin believed "an organization of white Gentile Americans" was needed to combat this alien "gestapo of an organization." He proposed such an organization to the anti-Semitic, retired general George Van Horn Mosely, requesting assistance in fighting "those insidious, treacherous influences that are trying to undermine and destroy our country as well as our Christian civilization."[39]

Rankin's hatred for Winchell was exceeded only by his enmity toward Sidney Hillman, the foreign-born head of the CIO's Political Action Committee. For Rankin, Hillman represented those alien social and political influences infecting the South with wage-and-hours laws, equal pay for Negroes, militant labor unions, and anti-poll tax agitation. Hillman's "oriental mug" reflected his un-American makeup. He was a "communist agitator" and a labor "racketeer." Rankin had never been sympathetic toward the labor movement, believing it threatened southern industry, small business, and white supremacy. The prominence of Hillman the Jew within the CIO merely strengthened Rankin's aversion to labor unions.[40]

By the mid-1940s Rankin had discovered a concerted Jewish conspiracy to dominate and pervert American culture through control of the mass media. He was a member of the House Committee on Un-American Activities and, more than any other person, was responsible for the investigation of communist influences in Hollywood during 1945 and 1946. He described the motion picture industry as the scene of "one of the most dangerous plots ever instigated for the overthrow of the government" and "the greatest hotbed of subversive activities in the United States." Jews had "virtually driven Christian American actors and actresses from the moving-picture field." Hollywood, for Rankin and his ilk, was a center of debauchery, social and racial experimentation, and advanced ideas, the very antithesis of, say, Tupelo, Mississippi. From Hollywood there emanated the poison undermining morality, Christianity, and white supremacy. The purveyors of such filth were Trotskyites who spoke in "broken English." He singled out such subversive figures as David Daniel Kamisky (Danny Kaye), Edward Iskowitz (Eddie Cantor), Emanuel Goldenberg (Edward

G. Robinson), and Melvyn Hesselberg (Melvyn Douglas). These, and others like them, sought "to bring to the Christian people of America the murder and plunder that has taken place in the Communist-dominated countries of Europe." While eager to investigate Hollywood, Rankin refused to allow HUAC to examine the Ku Klux Klan. "After all," he noted, "the Klan is an American institution, its members are Americans. Our job is to investigate foreign issues and alien organizations."[41]

Convinced that American communists were mostly Jews and other aliens, Rankin zealously opposed any modification of the nation's immigration laws to accommodate the post–World War II refugees. In fact, he wished to put an end to what he termed the "immigration racket" so that "riffraff" and the "long-nosed" do not flood the nation, bringing with them "atheism, anarchy, infidelity, and hatred of our form of government." During the war he proposed cutting off all immigration, and in 1945 he introduced a bill forbidding immigration until the number of unemployed Americans was less than 100,000.[42]

Rankin consistently opposed anything which reeked of foreign influences. He portrayed foreign aid as benefiting "long-nosed grafters" and warned against surrendering American sovereignty to the United Nations, "an international Sanhedrin" controlled by "a gang of long-nosed internationalists." The pacifist and internationalist Albert Einstein also infuriated the Mississippian. Einstein, Rankin declared, was "one of the greatest fakers" in history and should be deported immediately. In addition to equating Jews with communism and internationalism, Rankin also characterized them as international bankers. The distrust of metropolitan bankers, especially those of New York, had long been a staple of midwestern and southern demonology. Rankin's complaint regarding the "shylocks" exploiting farmers and small businessmen thus was not original, but it was explosive when uttered within the context of the intense anti-Semitism of the 1930s and 1940s.[43]

At one time or another Bilbo and Rankin expressed most of the anti-Semitic stereotypes popular in twentieth-century America. Jews were international bankers, communists, urban slum dwellers, polluters of American culture, and enemies of Christianity. In turn, contemporary Jewish spokesmen described the two Mississippi politicians as the most degenerate politicians in Washington. Rabbi Stephen S. Wise, president of the American Jewish Congress, called Rankin "the most treasonable enemy of American democracy." The Jewish War Veterans of the United States termed Rankin and Bilbo "un-Americans" and called for their removal from Congress. Not surprisingly, Rankin and Bilbo were viewed as American versions of Hitler.[44]

There were, however, crucial differences between Rankin and Bilbo and the Nazis, stemming from the critical fact of Mississippi politics: the division between whites and Negroes. Jews had white skins and hence were part of a racial aristocracy. These two Mississippi anti-Semites never argued that Jews were undesirable because of ineradicable biological characteristics; rather, Jews were resented because of their supposed cultural and political traits. Rankin and Bilbo never disowned all Jews, and they always held out to Jews the possibility of acceptance if only they would change their nefarious agitation on racial issues. "God knows I got nothing against the Jewish people," Bilbo said. "The Jews we got in Mississippi are fine people. They are some of the finest people we got. They're natives. They fought on our side in the Civil War." Bilbo always claimed that the "high-class Jews" of Mississippi voted for him, while Rankin alleged that "the better element of the Jews" was ashamed of, and alarmed by, the activities of Jewish radicals. Their enemies were, of course, the Hillmans, Cellers, Kopplemanns, and Winchells. They were also aware of other types of Jews such as the man who worked in Bilbo's 1946 reelection campaign, or Judah Benjamin, the Confederate secretary of state, or David Cohn, the southern writer. The anti-Semitism of Bilbo and Rankin was also held in check by the war with Germany. Unwilling to be identified with the nation's mortal enemy, or with a Nazi ideology so alien to America, Bilbo and Rankin continued to espouse a racism that remained traditional to the South: the racism of white supremacy.[45]

It is not surprising that anti-Semitism in the South has diminished over the past several decades. No longer is the Jew the alien, the radical, the fomenter of racial discord. The outward transformation of southern racial attitudes and practices has blunted whatever overt anti-Semitism might have existed because of the close identification of Jews with the 1960s civil rights movement. Furthermore, the state of Israel had diminished the identification between Jews and radicalism. Perhaps in no part of the country is there as much admiration for the martial virtues and opposition to communism than in what the historian John Hope Franklin had called "the militant South." There the Israeli may be seen not as the insidious subversive of Rankin's imagination, but rather the gallant warrior holding back the tide of communism and Arab radicalism. Support for Israel also rests upon the reservoir of southern religious fundamentalism which, as Harry Golden liked to remind us, contains a deep strain of philo-Semitism. The nationalization of American culture resulting from the impact of the mass media and demographic mobility has diminished the southern sense of regional distinctivenes as well as the South's perception of being persecuted by the Yankees. If anything, it is the North which feels oppressed by the economic and political challenge of the sun belt. The anti-Semitism of a Rankin and a Bilbo, which fed on the identification of the Jew and the city, is difficult to sustain when the fastest growing metropolis in the nation during the last several years has been Houston and when San Antonio is now larger than Pittsburgh, Boston, or Cleveland. The Populist rhetoric and radicalism which lay at the heart of Bilbo and Rankin's Judeophobia is a thing of the past. One would be foolhardy to predict the complete demise of southern anti-Semitism, but one can safely surmise that, if and when anti-Semitism again rears its ugly head in southern politics, it will not resemble that of Bilbo and Rankin.

Notes

Research for this essay was made possible by grants from the Seton Hall University Faculty Research Council and the Lucius Littauer Foundation.

1. Thomas F. Pettigrew, "Parallel and Distinctive Changes in Anti-Semitic and Anti-Negro Attitudes," in *Jews in the Mind of America,* ed. Charles H. Stember (New York, 1966), pp. 390–91; W. J. Cash, *The Mind of the South* (New York, 1941), pp. 327, 342.

2. Leonard Dinnerstein, *The Leo Frank Case* (New York, 1968), p. 70; Dinnerstein, "A Note on Southern Attitudes Toward Jews," *Jewish Social Studies* 32 (Jan. 1970): 43–49; Dinnerstein, "A Neglected Aspect of Southern Jewish History," *American Jewish Historical Quarterly* 61 (Sept. 1971): 52–68; Allan Peskin, "The Origins of Southern Anti-Semitism," *Chicago Jewish Forum* 14 (Winter 1955–56): 83–88; Stanley Meisler, "The Southern Segregationist and His Anti-Semitism," ibid., 16 (Spring 1958): 171–73.

3. A. Wigfall Green, *The Man Bilbo* (Baton Rouge, La., 1963), pp. 123–25.

4. Arthur M. Schlesinger, Jr., *The Crisis of the Old Order* (Boston, 1956), pp. 204–5; Reinhard H. Luthin, *American Demagogues: Twentieth Century* (Gloucester, Mass., 1954, 1959), pp. 63–65; *New York Times*, Feb. 10, 1937, p. 15; ibid., July 9, 1939, p. 6; Raymond G. Swing, *Forerunners of American Fascism* (New York, 1935), Chapter 4.

5. Luthin, *American Demagogues,* p. 75; Raymond J. Zorn, "Theodore G. Bilbo," in *Public Men In and Out of Office,* ed. J. T. Salter (Chapel Hill, N.C., 1946), pp. 293–96; Allan A. Michie and Frank Ryhlick, *Dixie Demagogues* (New York, 1939), esp. Chapter 5. Jews found it highly ironic that Bilbo, in the last year of his life, went to the Touro Infirmary in New Orleans for treatment for cancer of the jaw. The hospital had been named for Judah Touro, a nineteenth-century Jew from New Orleans.

6. Rankin's district was extremely poor. Only 1 percent of his constituents had attended college, less than one-third had completed high school, and less than two-thirds had finished grammar school. The district had few Catholics, immigrants, or Jews. Approximately 15 percent of its population was black. Rankin was not popular statewide. He finished last among the five Democrats running to fill Bilbo's seat in 1947 and even failed to carry his own district. Easton King, "Why Rankin Got Licked," *ADL Bulletin* (Sept. 1952), pp. 3–4, 8; *New York World-Telegram,* Nov. 5, 1947; Russell Whelan, "Rankin of Mississippi," *American Mercury* 59 (July 1944): 31–37.

7. Stanley High, "The Neo-New Dealers," *Saturday Evening Post* (May 22, 1937), p. 105; Walter Davenport, "Big Wind From the South," *Collier's* (Dec. 1, 1945), pp. 81–83; *New York Times,* Apr. 23, 1933, p. 25, July 11, 1935, p. 4, Sept. 1, 1935, p. 3, Jan. 16, 1938, p. 2, June 6, 1938, p. 2. The relationship between Populism and anti-Semitism has been debated by historians since the publication of Oscar Handlin's "American Views of the Jew at the Opening of the Twentieth Century," *Publications of the American Jewish Historical Society* 40 (June 1951): 323–44, and Richard Hofstadter's *The Age of Reform: From Bryan to F.D.R.* (New York, 1955). Handlin and Hofstadter argued that the Populists attributed the source of many of rural America's ills to an internal Jewish financial conspiracy. Irwin Unger's *The Greenback Era: A Social and Political History of American Finance, 1865–1879* (Princeton, N.J., 1964) supported this line of thought, while strong dissents were voiced by C. Vann Woodward, "The Populist Heritage and the Intellectual," *American Scholar* 29 (Winter 1959–1960): 55–72; Walter T. K. Nugent, *The Tolerant Populists: Kansas Populism and Nativism* (Chicago, 1963); Norman Pollack, *The Populist Response to Industrial America: Midwestern Populist Thought* (Cambridge, Mass., 1962); Pollack, "Handlin on Anti-Semitism: A Critique of 'American Views of the Jew,' " *Journal of American History* 51 (Dec. 1964): 391–403; Pollack, "Hofstadter on Populism: A Critique of 'The Age of Reform,' " *Journal of Southern History* 26 (Nov. 1960): 478–500; and Pollack, "The Myth of Populist Anti-Semitism," *American Historical Review* 68 (Oct. 1962): 76–80. As of November 1982, Rankin's papers were still closed and Bilbo's papers had not yet been catalogued. The precise influence which the populist mentality might have had on shaping the nature and intensity of their anti-Semitism is thus rendered more difficult, if not impossible, to determine.

8. Arthur M. Schlesinger, Jr., *The Coming of the New Deal* (Boston, 1958), p. 11, and *Crisis of the Old Order*, p. 299; *New York Times*, Jan. 1, 1933, p. 8, Nov. 13, 1934, p. 20, Nov. 13, 1936, p. 4, Nov. 20, 1936, p. 22, Jan. 3, 1938, p. 38.

9. Walter Goodman's description of Martin Dies fits Rankin as well. Dies, Goodman wrote, "stood for the small town populated by a few hundred neighborly descendants of early settlers and against the big cities with their polyglot masses. He stood for a style of life that was being shaken by industrial unions, by the Negro awakening, by revolutionary currents of every sort. He stood for fundamentalist enthusiasm against the radical enlightenment. He stood for Western insularity and against Eastern cosmopolitanism, for a strong legislature and against a strong executive, for the old verities and old slogans and against the new slogans and new demands. He stood, practically alone, he rapidly persuaded himself, for capitalism and the Constitution and God, and these were under attack from Pennsylvania Avenue and from New York City as much as from Moscow." Walter Goodman, *The Committee: The Extraordinary Career of the House Committee on Un-American Activities* (Baltimore, 1969), p. 163.

10. Rankin's racism eclipsed his earlier image as a liberal and advocate of public power. Harold Ickes noted that Rankin had undermined the cause of public power in Congress because other congressmen didn't want to be associated with him. "Rankin has almost gone crazy in his hatred of Jews and Negroes," the secretary of the interior commented. Ickes Diary (July 4, 1943), pp. 7947, 9756; Ickes Papers, Reel 6, Library of Congress, Washington, D. C.

11. U.S. *Congressional Record* (hereafter cited as CR), 76th Cong., 2nd Sess., Nov. 1, pp. 1939-940.

12. CR, 77th Cong., 1st Sess., Apr. 24, 1941, pp. 3280-81.

13. CR, 77th Cong., 1st Sess., June 4, 1941, pp. 4726-27.

14. CR, 77th Cong., 1st Sess., June 4, 1941, pp. 2727-28, June 5, 1941, p. 4761, June 11, 1941, p. A2789, June 18, 1941, pp. A2910-11, A2913, A2915, A2927, A3056; 78th Cong., 1st Sess., April 7, 1943, p. 3064.

15. CR, 78th Cong., 2nd Sess., June 20, 1944, p. 6253; 77th Cong., 2nd Sess., Nov. 5, 1942, pp. 8717-18; 79th Cong., 1st Sess., Feb. 19, 1945, pp. A693-94.

16. CR, 81st Cong., 1st Sess., Feb. 9, 1949, p. 1044.

17. CR, 77th Cong., 1st Sess., June 8, 1942, p. A2337; Irving Howe and Lewis Coser, *The American Communist Party: A Critical History (1919-1957)* (Boston, 1957), p. 433.

18. CR, 81st Cong., 1st Sess., Feb. 9, 1949, p. 1044.

19. CR, 81st Cong., 2nd Sess., Feb. 13, 1950, p. A1010, Mar. 1, 1950, p. 2594.

20. CR, 82nd Cong., 2nd Sess., Mar. 11, 1952, pp. 2106, 2110.

21. *New York Times*, Oct. 8, 1942, p. 3; CR, 78th Cong., 2nd Sess., Mar. 8, 1944, p. 2374; 79th Cong., 1st Sess., Oct. 16, 1945, p. 9675.

22. CR, 80th Cong., 1st Sess., Mar. 3, 1947, pp. 1622, 1631; 80th Cong., 2nd Sess., Jan. 15, 1948, pp. 204-5, May 24, 1948, p. 6350; U.S. Congress, House, Subcommittee on Legislation of the Committee on Un-American Activities, *Hearings on Proposed Legislation to Curb or Control the Communist Party of*

the United States, February 5, 6, 9, 10, 11, 19 and 20, 1948, 80th Cong., 2nd Session, 1948, pp. 154, 206.

23. Zorn, "Bilbo," p. 289; Theodore G. Bilbo, *Take Your Choice: Separation or Mongrelization* (Poplarville, Miss., 1947), pp. v, 283; Greene, *Bilbo,* pp. 103–5.

24. *CR,* 77th Cong., 2nd Sess., May 28, 1942, p. A1985; 77th Cong., 1st Sess., Aug. 15, 1941, pp. 7184–85.

25. *CR,* 77th Cong., 2nd Sess., Feb. 18, 1942, pp. 1419–20, Jan. 23, 1942, p. 605, Feb. 23, 1942, pp. A768–69, May 5, 1942, pp. A1868–69; 78th Cong., 1st Sess., Apr. 17, 1943, p. 3536.

26. *CR,* 77th Cong., 2nd Sess., Feb. 23, 1942, pp. A768–69, May 23, 1942, p. A2985, June 5, 1942, p. A2146, Oct. 14, 1942, p. 8192.

27. *CR,* 78th Cong., 1st Sess., Dec. 15, 1943, p. 10732.

28. *New York Post,* July 26, 1945.

29. *New York Post,* July 27, 1945.

30. Green, *Bilbo,* pp. 102–3; *New York World Telegram,* July 21, 1945.

31. *New York Times,* July 25, 1945, p. 23; *New York Post,* July 27, 1945: *PM,* Aug. 15, 1945; Arnold M. Rose, "Anti-Semitism's Root in City Hatred," *Commentary* 6 (Oct. 1948): 374–78.

32. *CR,* 78th Cong., 1st Sess., July 1, 1943, p. A3371; 79th Cong., 1st Sess., Nov. 21, 1945, p. 10886; 80th Congress, 1st Sess., Feb. 13, 1947, p. 1014.

33. *CR,* 81st Cong., 2nd Sess., Aug. 29, 1950, pp. 13725–27.

34. *CR,* 82nd Cong., 2nd Sess., June 30, 1952, p. 8633; 80th Cong., 2nd Sess., May 19, 1948, p. 6109; Goodman, *The Committee,* p. 117.

35. *CR,* 78th Cong., 1st Sess., Apr. 2, 1943, pp. 2880, 2885, 3062–66.

36. *CR,* 79th Cong., 1st Sess., Feb. 7, 1945, p. 872; *New York Times,* Feb. 8, 1945, p. 17. See also *CR,* 79th Cong., 1st Sess., Oct. 24, 1945, p. 10032.

37. *PM,* Jan. 27, 1944; *CR,* 78th Cong., 2nd Sess., Feb. 21, 1944, pp. 1925–26; 79th Cong., 2nd Sess., Feb. 11, 1946, p. 1225.

38. *CR,* 81st Cong., 1st Sess., May 9, 1949, p. A2763; Green, *Bilbo,* p. 102; *CR,* 79th Cong., 1st Sess., Aug. 1, 1945, pp. A3702–703.

39. *CR,* 81st Cong., 2nd Sess., Jan. 4, 1950, p. A28; 79th Cong., 1st Sess., Feb. 2, 1945, p. 758; 81st Cong., 1st Sess., June 13, 1949, p. A3647, Oct. 19, 1949, p. 15103; John E. Rankin to George Van Horn Mosely, Nov. 18, 1947, Moseley Scrapbook, Mosely Papers, Library of Congress, Washington, D.C.

40. *New York Times,* July 27, 1937, pp. 1, 11; *CR,* 78th Cong., 2nd Sess., May 18, 1944, pp. 4640; June 23, 1944, p. A3389.

41. *CR,* 81st Cong., 1st Sess., Oct. 19, 1949, p. A6677; 79th Cong., 1st Sess., July 9, 1945, pp. 7371–72, July 18, 1945, p. 7737; 80th Cong., 1st Sess., Nov. 24, 1947, p. 10792; Ellen H. Posner, "Anti-Jewish Agitation," *The American Jewish Year Book 5707,* ed. Harry Schneiderman and Julius Maller (Philadelphia, 1946), p. 183.

42. *CR,* 79th Cong., 2nd Sess., Mar. 20, 1946, p. A1527; 80th Cong., 1st Sess., Mar. 17, 1947, p. 2142; 82nd Cong., 1st Sess., Oct. 2, 1951, p. 12494; 78th Cong., 1st Sess., Oct. 29, 1943, p. 8880; 79th Cong., 1st Sess., May 22, 1945, p. 4913.

43. *CR,* 80th Cong., 1st Sess., June 6, 1947, p. 7747; 82nd Cong., 1st Sess., May 7, 1951, p. 4987; 77th Cong., 1st Sess., Apr. 25, 1941, pp. 3328–29; 81st Cong., 2nd Sess., Feb. 13, 1950, p. A1022.

44. *New York Times,* Apr. 26, 1946, p. 15; Nov. 26, 1946, p. 23.

45. Harry Henderson and Sam Shaw, "Bilbo," *Collier's* (July 6, 1947), p. 20; "Senator Bilbo Meets the Press," *American Mercury* 63 (Nov. 1946): 534.

Glen Jeansonne

Combating Anti-Semitism:
The Case of Gerald L. K. Smith

Much has been written about anti-Semitism in its various manifestations. In almost every study, however, Jews are depicted as
victims while little has been written about the organized Jewish
response: strategies, disagreements within the Jewish community,
and the ultimate effectiveness of such strategies when emanating
from a united front. This is important because only when the
Jewish response is considered can the phenomenon of anti-Semitism
be viewed analytically. Indeed, the decline of anti-Semitism from
virulence in the 1930s to less threatening manifestations in the
late 1940s can be attributed largely to the effectiveness of the
Jewish community in combating anti-Semitism. This demonstrates
that Jews have not been helpless when confronted with an onslaught
of anti-Semitic activity, but rather that they have been more successful in counteracting bigotry than is generally believed. The
underestimation of organized Jewish effectiveness has resulted
partly from a paucity of sources available to historians.

Of great significance is the public and covert effort of the
Jewish organizations, especially the American Jewish Committee
and the Anti-Defamation League of B'nai B'rith to blunt the
impact of the most notorious anti-Semite of the 1930s and 1940s,
Gerald L. K. Smith. This period marked a decline in anti-Semitism
paralleling the decline of the rabble-rousing career of Smith. In
the 1930s he was a highly publicized confederate of Huey P. Long,
Father Charles E. Coughlin, William Lemke, and Dr. Francis E.
Townsend, but by the end of the decade of the 1940s Smith's

following had dwindled from a mass movement to a sidelight limited to the lunatic fringe.

There are several reasons for the simultaneous decline of Smith's influence and of anti-Semitism in general. The most important factor was World War II. It may have been respectable to oppose the foreign policies of the Roosevelt administration from an isolationist viewpoint prior to the war, but continued isolationist hysteria, frequently mixed with anti-Semitism, was considered unpatriotic if not actually treasonous in wartime.

From an individual perspective, Smith's decline followed his unsuccessful race for the United States Senate in Michigan in 1942. Repudiated by the electorate, Smith became discouraged about his own political prospects and disillusioned about operating through the established political process. After his defeat he realized that he had no reasonable opportunity to win political office by appealing to a right-of-center constituency in the mainstream. Thereafter, he directed his appeals to the fringes. With each increasingly shrill attack on Jews, he found himself condemned by moderates. Such criticism provoked him to further attack those who had denounced him. This vicious cycle shaped Smith's career, and he became a particularly vicious anti-Semite in the postwar era. Witnessing his prospects decline, he angrily concluded that there must be a Jewish plot to repress him.[1]

Indeed there was a Jewish *plan* ("plot" is too strong a word), and it was more effective than many of Smith's opponents anticipated. The strategy devised was to deny Smith any publicity. This plan evolved after several years of spirited debate within the Jewish community; it required a herculean effort to convince and coordinate the press as well as fellow Jews. Although never completely effective, the strategy reduced Smith from a highly publicized public figure in the 1930s to a pariah in the postwar period. More important is the question of whether such tactics can be successful against all bigots. Clearly, tactics must be tailored to circumstances. A combination of the "silent treatment" and restraint in the use of militant tactics such as picketing, heckling, invading meetings, holding counter-rallies, and issuing defensive propaganda holds positive potential for the general effort to combat anti-Semitism. The most persuasive argument for these tactics is that they succeeded with Smith.

After a career as a successful Disciples of Christ minister,

Smith had soared to fame between 1933 and 1935 as a Share-Our-Wealth organizer for Louisiana's United States Senator Huey P. Long. So skilled an organizer and so brilliant an orator was he that H. L. Mencken considered Smith a more charismatic speaker than the Louisiana Kingfish himself.[2] Smith roamed the hill and bayou country of Louisiana as Long's disciple before expanding his efforts into other southern states. At the time of Long's assassination in 1935, Smith was preparing to manage a presidential campaign for the Louisianian in 1936.[3] Unfortunately for his plans, Smith's charisma had provoked envy and suspicion among Long's remaining henchmen. Collectively, they prevented him from becoming Long's successor and banished him from Louisiana.[4]

Prior to this, Smith's efforts had been oriented chiefly toward furthering the Kingfish's panacea for the Great Depression, the Share-Our-Wealth Society. His ego inflated by this taste of political power, Smith did not return to the ministry after 1935 but rather sought to apply his oratorical talents to other political movements. He gravitated first to Dr. Francis E. Townsend and his crusade to provide generous pensions to the elderly, who in turn would prime the depressed economy by spending. Smith had been told that the elderly physician had obtained Long's mailing list; by the time he learned otherwise, he had opportunistically joined Townsend's staff. Townsend's collaboration with Father Charles E. Coughlin in 1936 behind Union party presidential candidate William Lemke brought Smith to the pinnacle of his career. At successive conventions staged by Townsend and Coughlin, he eclipsed them and unleashed his persuasive oratory upon a national audience. Lemke's candidacy flopped, but it made Smith a national figure.[5]

Smith exploited his fame by organizing a "Committee of One Million" to fight Jews, communists, and labor unions. Headquartered in Detroit, partially subsidized by Henry Ford, Smith toured the Midwest and addressed large audiences in an effort to undermine labor unions. At first most of his tirades were directed at communists and labor leaders and were only secondarily anti-Semitic. Smith's conversion from populist economic exponent to outright anti-Semite has never been fully explained. Some historians assumed that Smith had always been an anti-Semite, or that his anti-Semitism was contrived, but this was not the case. His evolution into an anti-Semite began during his childhood.[6]

Smith grew up in rural Wisconsin, the second child and only son of devout parents. His education was limited to the rudiments of math, science, English, and history. He read little but biblical literature.[7]

There were few Jews in rural Wisconsin. Both his parents, however, condemned Jews abstractly on religious grounds. Jews had refused to worship Christ, and then had crucified Him; they could never be forgiven. Later, as an adult in Louisiana, Smith acquired more tangible hatred. Smith believed that Carl Austin Weiss, the physician who assassinated Huey Long, was Jewish, although Weiss was in fact Gentile. The man responsible for expelling Smith after Long's death was a Jew, Seymour Weiss. Smith's subsequent association with Father Coughlin accentuated his developing anti-Semitism. Smith was further influenced by Henry Ford, for he idolized the anti-Semitic flivver king. He read Ford's paper, the *Dearborn Independent,* and his book, *The International Jew.* Ford introduced Smith to *The Protocols of the Learned Elders of Zion,* a notorious forgery describing a Jewish plot for world conquest.[8]

During Smith's transition from anti-communism and labor-baiting to obsessive anti-Semitism, he experienced two "visions" which revealed to him the "iniquity" of the organized Jew. He dreamt that he had been selected by God to reveal a Jewish plot against Christianity. In an "Open Letter" to his mother, published in his monthly, *The Cross and the Flag,* Smith discussed his "call" to become an anti-Jewish crusader. "One day I experienced a call. It was more definite, it was more real, it was more vivid than any spiritual experience that I had ever had. . . . And what was it? It was to save my Christian America from the invasion of the enemies of Christ."[9]

After Smith's "conversion," anti-Semitism became the ruling passion of his life. Once converted, Smith never wavered. The fact that there was no real evidence of a Jewish plot he also attributed to the diabolical cunning of the Jews. Smith committed his reputation and livelihood to his bigotry; he would never yield a single point or concede that he might be wrong. His dogmatism intensified his bitterness as irrationality pyramided and fed hatred.

The catharsis Smith experienced was only temporary; like an addict returning to a narcotic, he repeatedly turned to hatred. He wanted to be strong, but he felt weak and vulnerable, the victim of plots by sinister conspirators he could not control.[10]

It was not until after his defeat in a race for the United States Senate in Michigan in 1942 that Smith became completely consumed by anti-Semitism. Stung by his expulsion from Louisiana, smarting from his subsequent repudiation by the electorate of Michigan, he was ripe for a conspiracy theory. He did not become, as some interpreters have claimed, simply an opportunist operating a lucrative racket; rather, he came to genuinely hate Jews. In the midst of a calm interview with this writer, he became agitated when he mentioned Jews and then launched into a half-hour tirade. This bigotry was compulsive and uninhibited, not contrived or calculated. He lived for his anti-Semitic work and plowed back into his movement most of his income. He labored until he collapsed from exhaustion. Some days he did nothing but work and sleep. This was not the pace of a hedonistic opportunist, but that of a driven man.[11]

In the early stages of Smith's career, he had been a demagogic but relatively ordinary political figure, a gadfly to more prominent leaders but not an independent power. In the late 1930s and early 1940s, however, he began staging rabidly racist meetings and publishing diatribes against Jews. The Jewish community understandably considered him a threat. They were, however, divided over how to respond. Some favored confrontations in each city where Smith spoke and advocated picketing his meetings, denying him meeting halls, and heckling. They wanted to turn the harsh glare of publicity on Smith's bigotry, for they argued that he could not survive scrutiny. When his bigotry was unmasked, his movement would wither. Jews, blacks, and unionized laborers would hold mammoth anti-Smith meetings attracting larger crowds than he did. Such principled militancy would anger Smith, undermine the morale of his followers, and galvanize opposition. Publicity would destory Smith.[12]

Jewish groups, World War II veterans, labor unions, liberal churches, socialists, and communists combined to stage large protests in many cities. Smith's organizing efforts in California particularly provoked huge, hostile demonstrations. Anti-Smith actors and actresses attracted 14,000 supporters to a rally while Smith himself spoke to a much smaller audience. The liberals hoped, by such tactics, to discourage Smith from opening his headquarters in Los Angeles.[13]

At one anti-Smith demonstration in Los Angeles, 200 police officers were required to restore order. Several hundred pickets were arrested, and dozens of injured were hospitalized. Equally militant if smaller groups of pickets confronted Smith in other cities. In St. Louis, war veterans seized the municipal auditorium in a futile effort to prevent Smith from speaking.[14] A major riot erupted during a Smith meeting in Chicago which featured Father Arthur V. Terminiello, a suspended Birmingham, Alabama, priest whom Smith promoted as "the Father Coughlin of the South."[15]

These demonstrations reaped enormous publicity. Smith attempted to turn the opposition to his own advantage by posing as a martyr. He himself might suffer prison or assassination but would never cease his crusades. He claimed that Jewish, black, and communist thugs had tried to imprison him, shoot him, and poison him, since he constituted the last redoubt of Christian civilization. The charges were ludicrous, but his persuasive talent was so great that he often convinced the credulous.[16]

Counter-demonstrations did not cause attendance at Smith's meetings to diminish or the ardor of his followers to cool; in fact, they generated sympathy for Smith among civil libertarians who argued that Smith had a right to speak regardless of his views.[17] His audiences grew, and he collected thousands of dollars which he used for travel, advertising, and printing.[18]

At the same time, there was another faction among Smith's opponents, one that believed militant tactics were counterproductive. They argued that a more effective tactic would be to limit news about his activities, thus denying him the opportunity to display his showmanship.[19] In a radio address in 1946, Los Angeles Mayor Fletcher Bowron commented:

Those left-wing groups that shout so much about civil liberties attempted then through demonstrations, picket lines, insults and actual violence to prevent free speech. They got just what they wanted—publicity, notoriety and the apparent satisfaction they get out of demonstrations such as they indulge in. Had it not been for that, Gerald L. K. Smith would have come to Los Angeles, talked to a few of his kind, received little notice, and left without even causing a ripple of interest or excitement.[20]

Bowron's strategy was advocated by other groups opposing Smith. A peace group calling itself "The Society of World Equiteers, Inc.," argued that it would be wrong to fight Smith by emulating his methods:

There is neither wisdom nor practicality, nor justice, nor equity in the behavior of those who hatefully oppose and seek to obstruct the public meetings of that hate monger. That method is unwise, because it covers the hate monger with the glory of martyrdom, which is welcomed and coveted by Smith and his emulating followers. It is impractical, because instead of stopping those meetings, it increases them in size and intensifies them in spirit. It is unjust, because it is without due process of law.[21]

These leaders reasoned that Smith thrived on publicity, and so by physically opposing him they created a martyr. They believed that Smith secretly reveled in their opposition, and this in fact was true. In 1947 Smith wrote to Mrs. Catherine Brown, leader of an isolationist group, the Blue Star Mothers: "I think it would be a good idea to stir the elements in Philadelphia and here is how it can be done: Rent a very respectable hall like the Town Hall or some public place—one that you know will be cancelled. Rent it for an anti-Communist rally under the auspices of some well named committee. Then after you have rented it announce it to the press and watch the thing go off."[22] He instructed Mrs. Brown to reserve an alternate site she knew they could use: "It will give you a lot of publicity and make everybody realize that the pot is boiling and the fat is in the fire and that we are all working together fighting atheistic Communism."[23]

Prior to an address in Buffalo, Smith confided to the president of the local sponsoring group that any kind of publicity would increase his attendance. He wrote: "As far as newspaper publicity is concerned, you can make sure that we will get some, even though it will be unfavorable. Whatever it is, it will aid attendance."[24]

To combat Smith, Rabbi S. A. Fineberg of the American Jewish Committee advocated a strategy he called "dynamic silence" or the "silent treatment." Fineberg believed that if nothing at all were written about Smith, his following would dwindle. He realized that convincing opponents of Smith to ignore him would require patience, restraint, and more discipline than would "exposing" him. It would necessitate nationwide work to persuade journalists to deny Smith publicity and let him wilt in obscurity.[25] Fineberg wrote: "A rabble-rouser can no more be blown out of his racket with blasts against him than an electric light can be blown out by one's breath. The one thing rabble-rousers cannot overcome is that which would close any show on Broadway—a lack of publicity in the general press."[26]

Fineberg advanced his position against considerable opposition. He patiently corresponded with hundreds of journalists and published a book entitled *Overcoming Anti-Semitism.*[27] In 1946 Jewish leaders debated in *Commentary* the most effective means of dealing with Smith. In September Rabbi Fineberg argued against mass demonstrations.[28] The November issue carried opposing viewpoints written by Irwin Lee Glaustein, director of the Hillel Foundation and an associate professor of religion at the University of Oklahoma, and Irving Howe, the socialist writer and editor.[29]

Glaustein stated that it would be impossible to silence the press completely because right-wing papers such as the Hearst, McCormick, and Gannett chains would provide Smith coverage whether he were picketed or not. Moreover, by demonstrating, Smith's opponents publicized their own cause. A policy of silence would be demoralizing to them if they must passively watch him spread hatred. The success of militant behavior should not be judged solely in terms of increasing or diminishing Smith's audiences, but also on the effect it had in unifying the anti-Smith coalition.[30]

In his rebuttal Fineberg pointed out that the ultimate aims of the militants were vague. What did they hope would be the result of their demonstrations? They probably would not stop Smith from talking. By violent confrontation they would not change the minds of any Americans who were not already convinced that Smith was a menace.[31]

Fineberg wrote that Smith's attendance and monetary contributions were smallest in cities where he attracted the least opposition. For example, Smith had received no publicity in Pittsburgh on three visits there and had not returned. On the other hand, in Oakland, California, where he had drawn only forty persons the first time he spoke, he addressed an audience of over a thousand when he returned following a public effort to deny him a high school auditorium.[32]

Fineberg persuaded his own organization, the American Jewish Committee, and then convinced the American Jewish Congress and the Anti-Defamation League of B'nai B'rith to try the silent treatment. The results were dramatic. In 1945 Smith had attracted thousands of pickets and thousands of listeners; his listeners in 1947 numbered only in the hundreds. Few young people attended, and there was a marked decline in enthusiasm. Part of Smith's attraction had been the excitement of his perfervid oratory and the hostile response he evoked by pitting the "patriotism" of his followers against "un-American" opposition. Lacking a villain seeking to suppress Smith, his audiences were not moved to rise up in indignation. His monetary collections dwindled. Without the glamour of martyrdom, he was an irrelevant bore.[33] Without scapegoats to be used to titillate his audiences, he was merely a minor curiosity. He complained bitterly about being ignored.[34]

In the early 1940s Smith had made news practically every day, but the silent treatment ended that. He no longer rated front-page publicity. Examination of the morgues of a half-dozen major dailies reveals a marked contrast: the later stories are fewer, shorter, and less dramatic. Even in cities where papers were not officially cooperating with Fineberg, Smith's coverage diminished. If unpublicized in one city, he became a less important subject in the next city he visited. Journalists began to consider him a "has-been."[35]

The application of the silent treatment produced a watershed in Smith's career: it marked the beginning of a permanent decline in his mass rallies. He no longer toured the country attracting huge audiences with his forensic brilliance. For nearly two decades Smith had earned his living by pandering to prejudice. His lies had been so transparent that it seemed surprising that anyone took him seriously, yet thousands had, not only the middle-aged matrons who usually cheered him, but local officials and citizens who sought to ostracize him and prevent him from speaking.

Was there ever a chance that Smith would achieve political power? There were some who thought so, and they directed their energies against Smith. In the immediate aftermath of World War II, in a time of racial tension, paranoia about communism, suspicion of internationalism, labor unrest, and economic dislocation, Smith may have been a minor threat. Americans are not immune to irrational appeals, but in this case patience and common sense eventually prevailed.

The growing effectiveness of the silent treatment in the 1950s does not explain entirely Smith's decline, which was partly the result of the endless repetition of his rhetoric. His exaggerated, bellicose, Bible-thumping oratory became dated. The kinds of speeches that thrilled audiences during the Depression seemed antiquated. Without President Roosevelt to scapegoat, Smith lost some of his appeal. His charges that the conservative Eisenhower represented a leftist threat were hardly credible. Moreover, Smith was aging. Although by no means frail, he was no longer the robust orator of the 1930s who could deliver a three-hour declamation, change his sweat-soaked suit, and deliver a similar tirade a few hours later in another city.

People might go once to hear Smith out of curiosity, but he could not compete with television to lure people from their homes on a regular basis. Political oratory in general was waning because of competition from television, and Smith never learned to exploit the medium. His rambling speeches were too long and disorganized for an effective televised presentation. At his best among screaming zealots, he was out of his element before more sophisticated audiences. The more he raved, the more ridiculous he appeared; even his homilies seemed corny.[36]

Smith's influence never entirely faded, however. He continued to write, and he developed a direct-mail, fund-raising operation which foreshadowed political action committees. Smith's tracts sold well on the extreme Right. His monthly, *The Cross and the Flag,* which carried no advertising and was not sold on newsstands, had a circulation of about 25,000 in the 1960s and 1970s. The inside front page of each issue was devoted to a religious essay written by Smith. The remainder of the hate-sheet consisted of commentary on the national news in the form of one-paragraph messages, reprinted speeches by public figures Smith admired, and occasionally longer articles on current events.[37]

Smith also wrote hundreds of pamphlets even more sensational than *The Cross and the Flag.* Titles such as "Ike Eisenhower (Swedish Jew)," "Benjamin Franklin and the Jews," "The Bible of the Antichrist," "Jews Strive for World Control," "Jesus vs. the Jews," "The Jew Created Communism," and "Zionism: The Hidden Tyranny" lured credulous readers. Smith lived comfortably until his death in 1976 on contributions he received from his readers, but the excitement of his halcyon days never returned.

Smith's diminished prominence resulted from a combination of changing fashions and technology and a deliberate effort on the part of Jewish groups. Jewish organizations continued to ignore Smith's publications except for occasionally refuting an essay or tract; most of Smith's writings were so obviously fraudulent that they required no refutation. Smith was no longer gaining converts but only sustaining his flock.

In 1969 Smith briefly returned to the public eye in the role of evangelical monument-builder. He constructed a seven-story, ivory-white, cross-shaped statue of Christ in the mountain hamlet of Eureka Springs, Arkansas, and later added an outdoor passion play, a Bible museum, and a Christ-only art gallery. In addition, he planned a Disney-like replica of the shrines of the Holy Land. Smith rejuvenated tourism in the village and made it Arkansas's largest tourist attraction.[38]

By this time, however, Smith was no longer a serious threat to the Jewish community. His message was so bombastic and so trite that it was generally ignored. Convinced that he had provided momentum for his movement to flourish after his death in 1976, he had himself buried at the foot of his immense statue. Instead, within a year *The Cross and the Flag* had ceased publication and his lieutenants were fighting among themselves. Recriminations and lawsuits were now rendering the blatantly anti-Semitic aspects of his operations mute.[39]

Although Fineberg's strategy of limiting publicity about Smith's activities crippled his movement, Smith's fate was not inevitable. Realistically, all bigotry will not vanish if simply ignored, since there may be a hard core of bigots in our society that can never be totally uprooted. Silence may be less successful today than in Smith's time. Electronic media have revolutionized the news industry since Rabbi Fineberg conceived the strategy of silence; the time has passed when any organization can impose a blanket silence upon all the media. Nonetheless, one lesson to be learned from Rabbi Fineberg's approach is to avoid excessive reaction.

Anti-Semitism can be combated best by a variety of tactics designed to fit different situations. Militance has its place, but special care should be taken to avoid the violation of free speech and the creation of martyrs. Militance is more effective in improving morale among opponents of anti-Semitism than it is in nullifying vicious oratory or hate publications. The silent treatment is a more reliable tactic which may limit the impact of bigots to their own immediate audiences. These audiences themselves will decline if unprovoked by passionate confrontations. In Smith's case the silent treatment was more effective than were counter-demonstrations, for Smith's decline was primarily the result of an application of disciplined inattention. Most of Smith's sympathizers finally forgot about him and found other ways to invest their energies in causes that seemed more relevant.

Notes

1. Isabel B. Price, "Gerald L. K. Smith and Anti-Semitism" (unpublished Master's thesis, University of New Mexico, 1965), p. 31. For a general account of the evolution of Smith's views see his autobiographical reflections, *Besieged Patriot: Autobiographical Episodes Exposing Communism, Traitorism and Zionism from the Life of Gerald L. K. Smith,* ed. Elna M. Smith and Charles F. Robertson (Eureka Springs, Ark., 1978). The statement about Smith's increasing anti-Semitism after his defeat in the senatorial election is based upon an analysis of *The Cross and the Flag* before and after his defeat.

2. Mencken wrote: "Gerald is the greatest of them all, not the greatest by an inch or a foot or a yard or a mile, but the greatest by at least two light years. He begins where the next best leaves off. He is the master of masters, the champion boob-bumper of all epochs, the Aristotle and Johann Sebastian Bach of all known earsplitters, dead or alive." See John Fergus Ryan, "Twilight Years of a Kindly Old Hatesmith," *Esquire* 70 (Aug. 1968): 89.

3. See Smith, *Besieged Patriot,* pp. 7–8; Price, "Gerald L. K. Smith and Anti-Semitism," p. 31; "Gerald L. K. Smith," *Current Biography* (1943), pp. 707–8. Smith is mentioned in T. Harry Williams, *Huey Long* (New York, 1969) but little detail is provided. The most complete account is Glen Jeansonne, "Preacher, Populist, Propagandist: The Early Career of Gerald L. K. Smith," *Biography* 2 (Fall 1979): 303–27.

4. Huey Long's associates were nearly unanimous in their condemnation of Smith. Mrs. Mary B. Wall, one of Long's secretaries, said, "Huey's friends didn't like him." See Mrs. Mary B. Wall, taped interview with T. Harry Williams, Feb. 20, 1961, New Orleans, La., Box 3, Folder 40, Williams Papers, Louisiana State University Archives. Also see Harnett T. Kane, *Louisiana Hayride: The American Rehearsal for Dictatorship, 1928–1940* (Gretna, La., 1971), pp. 196–97.

5. Herbert Harris, "That Third Party," *Current History* 45 (Oct. 1936): 85; "Smith," *Current Biography* (1943), p. 7. For a general account of Smith's associations with Townsend and Coughlin see David H. Bennett, *Demagogues in the Depression: American Radicals and the Union Party, 1932–1936* (New Brunswick, N.J., 1969).

6. The best account is in Price, "Gerald L. K. Smith and Anti-Semitism," pp. 85–88. See also Ralph Lord Roy, *Apostles of Discord* (Boston, 1953), pp. 43–44; Albert Lee, *Henry Ford and the Jews* (New York, 1980), pp. 110–11; Studs Terkel, *Hard Times: An Oral History of the Great Depression* (New

York, 1971), p. 74. For Smith's own account, see *The Cross and the Flag* 10 (Dec. 1952): 5, and Smith's tract, *Gerald L. K. Smith and the Jews: A Significant Summary*, (n.d., n.p.), copy given by Smith to author.

7. Smith quoted his father as cautioning him about reading a book: "If it is more than the Bible it is too much; if it is less than the Bible, it is not enough; if it is the same as the Bible we don't need it." See *The Cross and the Flag* 11 (Dec. 1952): p. 2.

8. Smith tract, *The Dangerous and Glorious Search for Truth* (n.d., n.p.), pp. 1–6, copy given by Smith to author; Smith, *Gerald L. K. Smith and the Jews;* Smith, interview with Leo P. Ribuffo, Eureka Springs, Ark., Jan. 8, 1973, copy given by Ribuffo to author.

9. *The Cross and the Flag* 11 (Dec. 1952): 3–4.

10. Ibid.; *The Cross and the Flag* 16 (May 1957): 10. For a discussion of the psychological origins of anti-Semitism see Gordon W. Allport, *The Nature of Prejudice* (New York, 1958).

11. *The Cross and the Flag* 11 (Dec. 1952): 3–6, and 16 (May 1957): 10; Gerald L. K. Smith, taped interview with the author, Eureka Springs, Ark., Aug. 10, 1974. I also taped interviews with Smith on Aug. 11 and Dec. 28, 1974, and Jan. 21, 1975. Most administrators of the New York office of the Anti-Defamation League of B'nai B'rith with whom I talked in June 1979 considered Smith a racketeer. Jerome Bakst in a telephone conversation (Dec. 30, 1977) described him as part cynic and part genuine zealot.

12. Price, "Gerald L. K. Smith and Anti-Semitism," pp. 143–44; S. A. Fineberg to Erwin Oreck, Nov. 23, 1945; Dorothy M. Nathan to G. Raymond Booth, Dec. 21, 1945, both in files of American Jewish Committee, New York City.

13. *New York World-Telegram,* July 19, 20, 21, 1945.

14. *St. Louis Post-Dispatch,* Apr. 2, 1946.

15. *Terminiello v. Chicago,* 337 U.S. 1, 4–5 (1949). See also Glendon Schubert, *Dispassionate Justice: A Synthesis of the Judicial Opinions of Robert H. Jackson* (Indianapolis, 1969), p. 88–89. There is extensive coverage of the Terminiello case in the *New York Times* and the Chicago newspapers.

16. In a speech delivered while he was running for the United States Senate in Michigan, Smith said, "There are people who would commit murder to prevent me from going to the Senate—do it as quick as you would snap your finger." See *Tulsa Daily World,* Sept. 15, 1942. In his autobiography Smith wrote: "The conspiracy of my enemies in the City of Chicago was to lock me in the County Jail on some trumped up charge, and then hire some savage criminal, preferably a black, to slaughter me while I was waiting trial. Failing in that, they attempted to kill me by burning the hotel in which I was registered." See Smith, *Besieged Patriot,* pp. 113–14. There are many other examples.

17. The national office of the American Civil Liberties Union, for example, supported Smith's position in the Terminiello case. For the role of the ACLU see Charles L. Markmann, *The Noblest Cry: A History of the American Civil Liberties Union* (New York, n.d.), pp. 66, 79, 138. Many respectable and responsible people rallied to Smith's defense. After a Smith meeting in Minneapolis had been broken up on Aug. 21, 1946, the *Minneapolis Star* said, "A mob is a mob

whether the target of its abuse is Gerald L. K. Smith or an Alabama Negro." Mayor Hubert Humphrey, certainly no friend of Smith, said, "I personally advised against any picketing because I think the silent treatment is more effective in combating Smith's ideology." Both of the above quotations are found in S. A. Fineberg, "Checkmate for Rabble-Rousers," *Commentary* 2 (Nov. 1946): 223.

18. *Detroit News* Jan. 4, 1945; *Washington Post,* July 29, 1946; *St. Louis Post-Dispatch,* July 29, 1946; *The Cross and the Flag* 10 (Sept. 1951): 18; Leo Lowenthal and Norbert Guterman, *Prophets of Deceit* (Palo Alto, Calif., 1970), p. 127; Price, "Gerald L. K. Smith and Anti-Semitism," p. 145.

19. S. A. Fineberg to David Jacobson, Dec. 26, 1945; Fineberg to staff members of the American Jewish Committee, n.d., 1947, in American Jewish Committee files.

20. Broadcast by Mayor Fletcher Bowron, radio station KMPC, Sept. 16, 1946 at 6:45 P.M., Reel 12, File "B," microfilm copy of Smith Papers, Bentley Historical Library, University of Michigan, Ann Arbor. Hereafter cited as Smith Microfilm, BHL.

21. A. Robert Remke, Chairman, Board of Governors of The Society of World Equiteers, Inc., to Smith, Aug. 21, 1946, Reel 13, File "B," Smith Microfilm, BHL.

22. Smith to Mrs. John H. Brown, Mar. 25, 1947, Reel 14, File "Mrs. Catherine Brown," Smith Microfilm, BHL.

23. Ibid.

24. Smith to Joseph H. Stoffel, Mar. 30, 1943, Reel 3, File "S," Smith Microfilm, BHL.

25. S. A. Fineberg to David Jacobson, Dec. 26, 1945; Finebereg to I. Arthur Kamien, July 31, 1946; Confidential Memorandum from Arthur Engel to American Jewish Committee and other organizations, Apr. 20, 1951; all in American Jewish Committee files, New York City.

26. S. A. Fineberg to Editor, New York *National Jewish Post,* Apr. 25, 1947.

27. S. A. Fineberg, *Overcoming Anti-Semitism* (New York and London, 1943).

28. S. A. Fineberg, "Checkmate for Rabble-Rousers," *Commentary* 2 (Sept. 1946): 220–26.

29. Irwin Lee Glaustein and Irving Howe, "How Fight Rabble-Rousers?" *Commentary* 2 (Nov. 1946): 460–66.

30. Ibid.

31. Ibid.

32. Fineberg to David Jacobson, Dec. 26, 1945, American Jewish Committee files, New York City.

33. Memo, George Kellman to Isaiah Termain, "An Appraisal of the Silent Treatment," May 27, 1947; S. A. Fineberg to Will Maslow, July 18, 1950, both in American Jewish Committee files, New York City; *American Jewish Year Book* 49 (1947–48): 192; *American Jewish Year Book* 50 (1948–49): 213–15.

34. Gerald L. K. Smith, *Quarantined by the Anti-Christ,* pamphlet reprinted from *The Cross and the Flag* 15 (June 1956): 2, 27–28.

35. The papers examined were the *New York Times, Boston Christian Science Monitor, Detroit Free Press, St. Louis Post-Dispatch, Washington Post,* and *Los Angeles Times.*

36. Some of the insights in this paragraph were provided by Edd Jeffords, taped interview with the author, Eureka Springs, Ark., June 1, 1979.

37. See yearly statements of ownership and circulation printed on the inside cover of *The Cross and the Flag.* See also *American Jewish Yearbook* for annual summations of circulation.

38. Calvin Trillin, "U.S. Journal: Eureka Springs, Ark.," *New Yorker* 45 (July 26, 1969): 70; John B. Starr, "Gerald L. K. Smith Draws Tourists to Ozark Town," *Baton Rouge Morning Advocate,* Nov. 26, 1971; *Little Rock Arkansas Democrat,* Sept. 20, 1975; Gerald L. K. Smith to Editor, *Little Rock Arkansas Gazette,* July 16, 1975; *Eureka Springs Times-Echo,* June 29, 1972.

39. Charles F. Robertson, taped interview with the author, Eureka Springs, Ark., June 1, 1979; Roland Lee Morgan, taped interview with the author, Eureka Springs, Ark., June 1, 1979; *Little Rock Arkansas Gazette,* Dec. 24, 1977; *Eureka Springs Times-Echo,* Sept. 6, 1979.

Alan M. Kraut and Richard D. Breitman

Anti-Semitism in the State Department, 1933–44: Four Case Studies

Half a century after Adolf Hitler's rise to power in Germany, scholars and laypeople still seek to assign responsibility for the inadequacy of American efforts to save the Holocaust's victims.[1] To some observers, U.S. insensitivity to the Nazi slaughter of European Jews remains puzzling and oddly inconsistent with America's traditional self-image as the sanctuary for the oppressed people of Europe. Until the creation of the War Refugee Board in January 1944, Franklin D. Roosevelt's administration and the Department of State were loathe to acknowledge that the Jews were suffering in greater proportion than other persecuted groups in Nazi-occupied Europe. By that time the Final Solution was near completion, and earlier avenues of escape for European Jews had been choked off.

A memo by a Treasury Department official written in January 1944 carefully raised the possibility that the State Department's hostility toward rescue efforts for European Jews was influenced by anti-Semitism: "However, there is a growing number of responsible people and organizations today who have ceased to view our failure as the product of simple incompetence on the part of those officials in the State Department charged with handling this problem. They see plain anti-Semitism motivating the actions of these State Department officials and rightly or wrongly, it will require little more in the way of proof for this suspicion to explode into a nasty scandal."[2] Some scholars have since raised the suspicion that anti-Semitism in the State Department decisively shaped American reaction to Nazi persecution of Jews from 1933 on. The literature is laced with a variety of veiled and not-so-veiled accusations against the department and specific individuals within it.[3]

These allegations are consistent with a pervasive perception of State Department officers as aloof in posture and elitist in preference. In fact, Foreign Service officers and their Washington superiors were disproportionately recruited from America's upper crust prior to World War I, the graduates of its most prestigious universities and the scions of its wealthiest families. Even the Rogers Act of 1924 that created the modern State Department bureaucracy did not totally destroy the "club" atmosphere of the department. The reviewer of one recent book on the history of the State Department, himself an expert on the subject, writes, "What emerges from these sketches is an impression of an embattled elite, a club, suspicious of outsiders and motivated by desires for self-promotion and deep anti-Semitism."[4]

Historian Phillip J. Baram contends that anti-Zionism more than a vulgar anti-Semitism inspired State Department attitudes toward Jews before and during World War II. This anti-Zionism was born of U.S. desires to accommodate our British allies who governed Palestine, as well as to pacify the Arabs whom we hoped would favor ARAMCO (Arabian American Oil Company) over British oil interests after the war and steer clear of involvement with the Russians. Baram also observes, however, that "the general [State] Department antipathy to Jewish immigration was a home-grown rather than an imported [from Britain] attitude." According to Baram, Secretary of State Cordell Hull felt that "on moral grounds . . . no country should be asked or expected to change its laws to receive refugees—lest dictatorships be encouraged to expel minorities onto the Western Hemisphere and create instability. Dictatorships . . . must be forced to keep these minorities and behave in a civilized manner." Rather than being an anti-Semite colluding with colleagues to discriminate against Jewish refugees, Hull believed it discriminatory to "single out Jews" for special leniency in entrance requirements, Baram contends. He extends to Breckinridge Long, George Messersmith, William Dodd, and others at State Hull's disapproval of distinctions or preferences among refugees on the basis of race or religion, even as a means of counteracting Hitler's own special policies toward Jews.[5]

That anti-Semitism existed in the State Department during the 1930s and 1940s is incontrovertible, but it is far less clear that anti-Semitism was the primary motivation behind State Department policies affecting Jewish refugees. Emotionally charged generalizations about the pervasiveness of State's bigotry remain speculative; what is needed is an operational definition of anti-Semitism and an assessment of individual policymakers measured against that yardstick of prejudice.

Gordon Allport defines ethnic prejudice as "an antipathy based upon a faulty and inflexible generalization. It may be felt or expressed. It may be directed toward a group as a whole, or toward an individual because he is a member of that group."[6] Norman Podhoretz has recently suggested that the essence of anti-Semitism is the application of a double standard to Jews and non-Jews, where "certain vices and failings" are labeled "specifically Jewish when they are in fact common to all humanity."[7] John Higham, however, has observed, "Unfavorable attitudes about an ethnic group do not necessarily comprise our practical responses to individuals."[8] Modern social scientific literature confirms that an individual's personality, his relationship to the social structure of his society, all his other values, attitudes, and beliefs, and the components of the specific situation he confronts must be taken into account to understand fully how and why a prejudice is translated into behavior.[9] Even negative stereotypes of a particular ethnic group, such as the Shylock stereotype of the Jew in the nineteenth century, need not necessarily cause a particular individual or group of individuals to engage in anti-Semitic behavior.[10] Higham's distinction between attitude and response suggests the necessity of determining whether individuals prejudiced against Jews translate their biases into anti-Semitic behavior.

The following four case studies demonstrate that some State Department officials often perceived Jews in stereotypical patterns; however, their policies and behavior often lacked a double standard. One might say that their attitude toward refugees was influenced by their anti-Semitism, but other motives, often ones even more powerful than ethnic prejudice, were primarily responsible for State Department policies that hampered the immigration of Jews imperiled by Nazi Germany.

Wilbur J. Carr has been called by one historian the "epitome of the bureaucrat."[11] Certainly it would not be an exaggeration to describe Carr as the architect of the foreign service as it existed during the 1930s. The son of a poor Ohio farmer, Carr attended a commerical college where he mastered bookkeeping and short-hand. In 1892 he passed his civil service exams and was hired by the State Department as a clerk. Diligent and meticulous about detail, Carr was promoted through the ranks to the directorship of the Consular Service in 1909. "Punctual, methodical, prudent and disciplined," Carr was a proficient bureaucrat who viewed government as a machine that must be made to run efficiently.[12] The cog in that machine for which he bore specific responsibility was the Consular Service, which he described in 1924 "as near perfection as possible."[13]

Carr lacked the Ivy League education possessed by many of his colleagues. Sensitive to this fact, he nonetheless took it as a challenge, confiding to his diary that he was "conscious always of an inferiority of preparation and of mind, lacking in information, but by determination and endless hours of labor . . . [he would do] what better educated and more highly placed men had failed to do."[14] He earned a law degree in the evenings, often returning to his office after class to get in several hours more work. He frequently took instruction in literature and music solely for the purpose of self-improvement. As director of the Consular Service, he made consuls feel personally responsible to him, thus solidifying his influence throughout the Foreign Service. He also shouldered fiscal and budgetary responsibilities on Capitol Hill. By 1920 Secretary of State Bainbridge Colby could describe Carr as the "backbone" of the department.[15]

Carr was a fervent restrictionist. In 1920 he argued before the House Committee on Immigration and Naturalization against continued immigration, testifying that "the unassimilability of these classes . . . is a fact too often proved in the past to bear any argument."[16] Carr's first experience in restricting immigration by limiting the number of visas issued had occurred immediately after World War I when he temporarily suspended the issuance of visas to immigrants to ensure that there would be sufficient Atlantic shipping to accommodate the thousands of American soldiers eager to return home. He personally authorized this expression of gratitude to America's fighting men, and it later

became a mechanism for more serious and comprehensive restrictions. There is no direct evidence that Wilbur J. Carr wrote
the text of the 1924 Johnson-Reed Immigration Act that made
permanent a national quota system; however, his office was instrumental in facilitating its application. His subordinates carefully
prepared tables of statistics with explanations and definitions,
including elaborate estimates of the distribution of foreign nationalities in the U.S. at different times calculated by different
schemes. The purpose was to ensure the maximum restrictive
impact of the new law.[17]

Entries sprinkled throughout Carr's diary suggest that he
harbored anti-Semitic feelings. Social contact with Jews often
aroused these feelings to the point of expression. In early August
1924 Carr took a boat trip to Albany and confided to his diary,
"Most of the passengers were Jews of one kind or another." His
own enjoyment of the scenery was even affected by their presence.
He found it "appalling to observe the lack of appreciation of the
privilege they are having."[18] Later that month he found Detroit
laden with "dust, smoke, dirt, Jews. . . ."[19] Often, Carr distinguished
between poorer Jews, whom he despised, and those more prosperous
who had mastered the social graces. These he could tolerate. Carr
disliked the boardwalk at Atlantic City because there were more
of the former than the latter: "Jews everywhere and of the com-
monest kind. Yet most of them were well dressed. . . . The Claridge
is filled with them and few presented a good appearance. Only
two others besides myself in dinner jacket. Very careless atmosphere
in the dining room." His discomfort led him to change hotels
where he again found "mostly Jewish guests, but of the higher
type than at the Claridge."[20] Nouveau riche Jews may have reminded
Carr uncomfortably of the social inferiority he felt when in the
company of State Department Brahmins. These feelings may have
generated Carr's anti-Semitic diary entries. It would be fair to
conclude that Carr's negative view of Jewish immigrants had
much to do with his support for immigration restriction during
the 1920s, yet Carr, like many Americans in the postwar era, felt
the need for a general immigration restriction. Other groups besides
Jews were objectionable and, in any case, the country could no
longer afford to absorb an unlimited stream of immigrants.

By 1930 the impact of the Depression had created public
demand for even greater curtailment of immigration than the 1924

legislation could provide. Unable to surmount congressional opposition to further restrictionist legislation, President Hoover asked the State Department to use administrative prerogatives based upon existing legislation to accomplish the task.[21] Conveniently, a provision of the 1917 Immigration Act excluded any potential immigrant likely to become a public charge. In 1930 it was possible to regard almost any immigrant either as an illegal contract laborer or as a potential public charge. If an individual claimed to have a promise of employment, he or she could be barred as a contract laborer. If, however, he or she had no reasonable likelihood of being self-supporting, consuls could decide that he or she was likely to become a public charge (LPC) and was, therefore, inadmissible under the 1917 law.[22]

In a White House press release Hoover publicly proclaimed a new policy of rigorous enforcement of the LPC clause, which would curb the entry of foreign laborers from Europe into America's reeling economy. The consuls, responsible for visa decisions under the guidelines and procedures governing the State Department, were to enforce the LPC provision. The new procedure was consistent with Wilbur Carr's own restrictionism and, as assistant secretary of state, he, along with Visa Division chief A. Dana Hodgdon, shouldered the burden of instructing American consuls in Europe on the new LPC interpretation.[23]

The Depression and the new interpretation of the LPC clause, which Carr championed, reduced immigration to the United States from much of the world. Table 1 illustrates some aspects of the change. Although the immigration decline was general, Jewish

TABLE 1

*Decline in Quota Immigration to the United States, 1929–33
(Years Represent Fiscal Year July–June)*[24]

	1929	1931	1933
Eastern hemisphere	146,918	54,118	8,220
Germany (including Jews)	48,468	10,100	1,324
Jews (worldwide)	12,479	5,692	2,372
Jewish immigration as percent of eastern hemisphere immigration	8.5	10.5	28.9

immigration as a percentage of total immigration actually rose, suggesting that the motive behind the new LPC interpretation was restriction rather than anti-Semitism. Thus, Carr's own attitude toward the admission of German Jewish refugees after Hitler's ascension to power in 1933 appears more a consequence of his general restrictionism and an "author's pride" in his own regulations than of calculated bigotry.

Although Carr had initially been wary of Franklin Roosevelt— "I like him, but doubt his capacity and I fear his party more"— Carr did not refuse when FDR asked him to remain at his post after the change in administration.[25] When conflict erupted between Secretary of State Cordell Hull and Secretary of Labor Frances Perkins over the Jewish refugee issue, Carr was quick to defend his department and to oppose any exemption of refugees from the LPC clause. Carr cited a precedent in which President Wilson had stated that to require American consular officials to determine whether or not persecution existed abroad would require them to pass judgments on the acts of friendly countries and would create terrible complications.[26] Pressure from Jewish spokesmen and the Labor Department caused Carr to alert Consul General George Messersmith in Berlin of the American anxiety about German Jews and instructed him to be courteous, provide the necessary advice, but insist upon compliance with existing American laws. Indeed, before sending his letter Carr checked with Hodgdon. "As nearly as you can determine will this letter be understood by the men in the field to mean precisely what it says and not be construed as an invitation to relax enforcement of the law?"[27]

The enthusiasm with which Carr resisted special considerations for Jewish refugees was inspired partly by his sincere belief that he was the appointed steward of America's restrictive immigration laws and bore the responsibility for their enforcement. He and other State Department officials also resented what they perceived to be Labor's jurisdictional incursions. Carr, therefore, resisted with particular energy a bonding scheme under which Labor Secretary Perkins would possess the authority to accept bonds posted by visa applicants as a guarantee that they would not become public charges, a procedure that, if approved, would effectively eliminate rejection on LPC grounds. After consultation with the Visa Division, Carr rejected the bonding scheme and denied that German Jews had been placed at a disadvantage by the stricter enforcement of the LPC clause. He argued that abandonment of enforcement procedures would swamp the country with alien workers just as hints of economic recovery were beginning to appear.[28] Carr was content with the LPC clause as a regulator of immigration and wished to avoid the politically riskier course of advocating permanent reductions in the quotas, later saying: "We have achieved administratively what is proposed, and it is for Congress to say whether that should be permanent."[29]

Although Carr was satisfied to permit his visa officers to sustain restrictionism, a new political climate in early 1936 altered the course of immigration policy in favor of refugees. During the months before the presidential election, Roosevelt gave more personal attention to matters such as Jewish refugees and Palestine. After a number of unsuccessful attempts to meet with the president, Rabbi Stephen Wise, head of the American Jewish Congress, finally conferred with him in January 1936. Shortly thereafter, Wise passed word through FDR's friend Felix Frankfurter that the State Department had been uncooperative, and that the Republicans might make political capital out of FDR's alleged inaction with regard to Nazism. Wise suggested that the president act to make himself "absolutely invulnerable" with American Jews.[30] In July 1936 Governor Lehman followed up his letters about German Jewish immigration by speaking personally to FDR about the situation. Lehman concluded that "he [FDR] feels great sympathetic concern . . . and will do everything in his power to be helpful."[31] In August Roosevelt issued a public statement favoring the rebuilding of the ancient Jewish homeland in Palestine, and after a cabinet discussion on September 2, the United States temporarily persuaded Great Britain not to curtail Jewish immigration to Palestine, a step then under consideration in London.[32] There is no evidence that Roosevelt issued any instructions to the State Department about German Jewish immigration,[33] but careful observers could see which way he was leaning.

Anxious to retain his position at State, Carr now also switched course to keep step with the administration. He suggested that new instructions be issued to visa officers "to bring to their attention the unusual features present in the case of German Jewish refugees." Since July 1933 consuls had been accepting affidavits from relatives of visa applicants pledging to support the immigrant should that be necessary to prevent him or her from becoming a public charge.

It was left to the consul to judge not only the financial capability of the U.S. resident signing the affidavit but also the credibility, based on past conduct, of his or her acknowledgment of responsibility for and interest in the alien relative. Those not closely related to an alien often had difficulty persuading consuls of their concern and commitment. Now Eliot B. Coulter of the Visa Division recommended the acceptance of affidavits from distant relatives because "the Jewish people often have a high sense of responsibility toward their relatives, including distant relatives whom they may not have seen, and . . . they feel keenly the difficult lot of their kin in Germany. . . ."[34] Other Visa officials expressed varying degrees of concurrence. The president's behavior, combined with new currents in the department, swayed the old guard.

Increasingly during the 1930s Carr expressed his dissatisfaction with the Roosevelt administration and the non-hierarchical style that the president encouraged. He objected that the other assistant secretaries, Judge Walton Moore and Sumner Welles, "not only have access to the president but discuss all manner of foreign service personnel things with him. Many of them are not reported to me. Hence I can hardly see how I can go on with this work. . . . I do not want to be a figurehead, and have the real power exercised by others. I do not want to continue in a position if I am not wanted there, and the failure of the president to have any relations with me would seem to indicate that I am not very welcome. I am the only Ass't Sec'y who does not have access to him."[35]

When his confidant William Phillips was appointed ambassador to Rome in 1936, Carr felt even more isolated. Still, he did not relish the thought of being replaced at the end of a long and distinguished career.[36] In 1937 Carr was indeed replaced, but was offered and accepted the face-saving option of a ministership rather than return to private life. Carr served in Prague, Czechoslovakia, from September 9, 1937, until the government of that country was disbanded by the Nazis in the spring of 1939. On July 31 he retired.

Wilbur J. Carr harbored anti-Semitic feelings, but his restrictionism exceeded in intensity and scope the narrower prejudices confided to his diary. Carr's behavior prior to the 1930s suggests a restrictionist predilection that required the exclusion of more than just Jews. Between 1933 and 1936 he tenaciously pursued policies consistent with his belief that increased immigration—of non-Jews as well as Jews—posed social and economic problems for Americans that strict enforcement of existing restrictionist laws could preclude. His personal dislike of Jews aside, Carr did not exercise a double standard of behavior in enforcing the law; perhaps only a bureaucrat's zeal for regulations uniformly applied stood in the way. Whatever his inhibitions, he also understood that a bureaucrat's success is measured by his longevity in his post; therefore, he did not hesitate to moderate his stance when the domestic political exigencies of 1936 caused FDR to demand leniency in the administration of immigration policy. Even if the president were misguided, Wilbur Carr would not violate the chain of command in the organization that had given him a status neither family nor wealth could bestow.

All the pedigree and education that Carr coveted belonged to William Phillips, who was the scion of a family that had included the antislavery reformer Wendell Phillips and, even earlier, the American revolutionary John Jay. During the Wilson administration Phillips had met fellow Harvard alumnus Franklin Roosevelt, who in 1933 called upon Phillips to serve as undersecretary to the diplomatically inexperienced Cordell Hull. It was an unfortunate choice for Jewish refugees from Hitler's Reich because Phillips, even more than Carr, was an immigration restrictionist. Unlike Carr, however, Phillips's attitude was grounded almost exclusively in anti-Semitism rather than in a passion for administrative precision in the enforcement of a legislative mandate.

Phillips hated Jews. His diary contains a number of strongly worded anti-Semitic comments. Like Carr, Phillips was appalled by the Jewish presence in a favorite vacation spot, Atlantic City. He complained that it was "infested with Jews," and that on the weekend the beach had disappeared under a swarm of "slightly clothed Jews and Jewesses."[37] Jewish business associates were also privately ridiculed in the pages of Phillips's diary: "Bernard Morrison, my little Jewish friend from Boston, who has a habit of butting into my affairs, called me to suggest that the estate should sell to some Jewish friend of his in New York the Phillips building."[38] Phillips was also known by contemporaries for his anti-Jewish comments. James G. McDonald, who became League of Nations high commissioner for refugees in 1933, reported to prominent

American Jewish leaders that Phillips entertained very unfavorable attitudes toward Jews.[39] Supreme Court Justice Louis D. Brandeis sensed Phillips's views fairly early and correctly predicted that "Phillips's wrong action on Germany's Jews will not end until he leaves the State Department."[40] Phillips's closeness to FDR ensured both his influence and access to the White House from 1933 to 1936.

Along with Wilbur Carr, William Phillips had successfully resisted Frances Perkins's attempt in 1933 to gain an exemption for German Jewish refugees from the LPC clause. As Jewish leaders requested the State Department to be lenient, Phillips urged that the refugees' advocates be ignored. He also advised Hull against American participation in the League of Nations High Commission for Refugees from Germany because he feared that American Jews might use the commission "as a wedge to break down U.S. immigration policy."[41]

Phillips was not unaware of the political heat generated by the State Department's hard line. To deflect criticism, Phillips suggested to the president that FDR appoint Judge Julian W. Mack of Philadelphia to act as liaison between Jewish groups and the State Department. Meanwhile, he and Carr would work with the Labor Department to devise "some new scheme which while not opening the doors to an influx of Jews, will satisfy them that we are doing everything possible within the law."[42]

In mid-1936, Phillips's appointment as ambassador to Italy removed a key anti-Semite from State Department policymaking circles. In his personal account of his career, *Ventures in Diplomacy* (1952), Phillips says little about the Jews or refugees; however, from his few references it is clear that he regarded their plight as little more than a variable in American diplomacy with domestic political implications. Phillips recalled delivering a letter from FDR to Mussolini in 1939 asking that southern Ethiopia and Kenya be made available for Jewish colonization. He explained to Il Duce that the strained relations between the U.S. and Germany were "partly the result of the methods which have been and are continuing to be employed by the German Government in forcing Jews to leave the country. These methods [having] greatly shocked public opinion in America."[43] When Mussolini spewed forth an anti-Semitic tirade in response, Phillips's only rejoinder was to remind him that "this forced emigration from Europe had created an international problem with which we in the United States were vitally concerned. It was not a question solely for those states from which the emigrants departed, but it was also a question of finding them a suitable home."[44] To Phillips that "suitable home" must never be America.

In sharp contrast to Carr and Phillips, George Messersmith's diary and personal papers offer no hint of personal animosity toward Jews in the United States, or toward those seeking refuge from Nazi oppression. In fact, Messersmith frequently condemned the barbaric behavior of the Nazi regime and showed some sympathy for the plight of German Jews. Like the other two, however, Messersmith believed that through its immigration legislation Congress had mandated a restrictive policy and that the State Department must administer it fairly.

George Messersmith's professional career began in a Delaware classroom rather than along the marble corridors of the State Department. He was born in Fleetwood, Pennsylvania, in 1883 and was educated at the Keystone State Normal School and Delaware State College. He taught high school civics and eventually became a principal in Fulton, Delaware. At the advice of Dr. John Bassett Moore, an authority on international law in whose home he boarded, Messersmith took the entrance examination and entered the Foreign Service as a consul in 1914. Between 1914 and 1930 Messersmith served in American consulates in Ft. Erie, Ontario, Curaçao, Antwerp, and Buenos Aires. Having been promoted to the rank of consul general in Antwerp in 1923, Messersmith became consul general in Berlin in 1930.

Upon his arrival in Germany, Messersmith quickly dispelled the casual climate of the office, reforming procedures and instituting new rules. Of German background and fluent in German, he became known in Washington for long, ponderous dispatches. His insistence upon not sacrificing thoroughness to conciseness earned him the nickname "Forty Page George."[45] If lacking in brevity and literary elegance, his dispatches were, nevertheless, models of analysis.

Messersmith responded promptly and efficiently to State's initiative in using the LPC clause to choke off immigration not already impeded by the national origins quota system. By January 1931 he could report that consular officials in Germany were carrying out this new policy "intelligently and with discretion." He noted that they had held visas issued against the German quota under 10 percent of the monthly quota since October 1930 and would probably not exceed 8 percent for the year. Even this figure would have been lower but for visas granted to Germans at American consulates outside of Germany.[46] At the consulates in Germany 98.78 percent of all immigrant visa applicants in December 1930 were denied visas. In January 1931 the figure was 99.02 percent. The reason for the high rejection rate was Messersmith's very strict interpretation of the LPC clause:

It is this Consulate General's practice (which is thought to be in accordance with the Department's view) to grant visas to non-preference applicants only when they are in possession of funds or property sufficient to support themselves during the probable indefinite period of the present economic crisis without their having to resort to labor or to the assistance of others, i.e. funds or property yielding an income sufficient to provide for their support. The fact that an alien may be going to relatives or friends, or even to a fiancé willing and able to provide support should not relieve . . . the alien of the necessity of being in possession of such funds. . . .

The department promptly commended Messersmith for his interpretation and enforcement of the LPC clause, which antedated the refugee problem created by the Nazi regime from 1933 on.[47]

Although Hitler's appointment as chancellor in January 1933 abruptly transformed the situation in Germany, Messersmith was well aware that the restrictionist climate in Washington had changed but little. Faced by a potential flood of Jewish refugees, he indicated to Wilbut Carr that it might be necessary for the U.S. to adopt barriers more secure than the LPC clause.[48] This is not to say that Messersmith approved of Nazi anti-Semitism. Indeed, with an openness and forcefulness unusual in the Foreign Service, Messersmith condemned the barbaric behavior of the Nazis. He endeared himself to American Jewish leaders by telling one American Jewish visitor in 1933: "There is no greater crime in history than that which the German government is committing against the Jews."[49]

Messersmith reconciled his anti-Nazism and his restrictionism partly through his naive view that the German people would not tolerate the Nazi regime very long. Thus, Messersmith in effect agreed with many German Jews who believed that they could and should outlast a brief period of Nazi persecution. In a moment of irritation he refused to hear the account of a Jewish physician who came to the American consulate to report " 'atrocities' against Jews in a municipal hospital in Berlin." Instead, the physician testified that Messersmith had blustered: "You Jews are always afraid of your own skins. The important thing for us is to preserve friendly relations between the two countries." Messersmith's emotional outburst was uncharacteristic. It was probably the result of the intense pressure under which American consular officials worked as every day hundreds of visa-seekers descended upon their understaffed, overworked offices.[50] Messersmith usually sympathized with those seeking to escape persecution, even as he dutifully enforced laws that kept all but a few from finding their refuge in America.

After Messersmith visited with Jewish leaders during a brief stay in the U.S., Rabbi Stephen Wise sang Messersmith's praises.[51] Sharing an intense dislike of the Nazi regime and rejecting any kind of American economic concessions to Germany, American Jewish leaders and Messersmith had much in common during the mid-1930s. Moreover, Messersmith's frequent prediction that the Nazi regime could not survive long must have fallen upon welcome ears. Finally, when Messersmith left Berlin for Vienna to serve as American minister there, he became friendly with Judge Julian Mack's daughter and son-in-law, which could only have bolstered his standing in the American Jewish establishment.[52]

After two years in Vienna Messersmith took it upon himself to report to Washington about deficiencies in the American visa process. In one rather pointed section of a long memo he observed: "The object of the U.S. immigration laws is not, as some people interpret it, to maintain the United States as an asylum or refuge for dissatisfied and oppressed people in other parts of the world irrespective of their capacity to become good and self-supporting citizens of our country. Their object is also not, as some interpret it, to keep out certain classes of persons on account of their race, religion, or political ideas."[53] Combined with changes in the political climate in Washington during 1936 and with changes in personnel within the State Department, Messersmith's influence helped to establish a new and more realistic interpretation of who was likely to become a public charge, which directly benefited German Jews seeking American visas.[54] Soon after the new policy went into effect, Messersmith returned to Washington to become assistant secretary of state in charge of administration, a position which included supervision of the visa section. When his former subordinate Raymond Geist wrote from Berlin that the new policy had increased the supply of visas, Messersmith wrote back that he was pleased.[55] Whereas 6,978 individuals had been admitted to the U.S. under the German quota in fiscal 1936 (24.3 percent of the quota), some 12,532 were admitted in fiscal 1937 (48.3 percent of the quota).[56]

Whatever his personal feelings toward Jews, Messersmith's behavior leads us to conclude that he was not anti-Semitic; his policy decisions were not bound by a double standard. This does not mean, however, that Messersmith was generous toward Jewish refugees. Because of his strong conviction that the public and Congress would not welcome an influx of Jewish refugees,[57] he became disturbed when events in 1938 led to the filling of immigration quotas with refugees.

The German annexation of Austria, the Munich Agreement, and the barbaric Nazi behavior on November 9–10 (*Kristallnacht*) magnified the refugee problem several times over. President Roosevelt publicly supported efforts to find havens for refugees from Germany, calling for an international conference (held at Evian-les-Bains, France, in July) and the establishment of an Intergovernmental Committee on Refugees. He also formed the President's Advisory Committee on Political Refugees (PACPR), whose task it was to provide liaison between the government and private agencies concerned with immigration to the United States. At the same time, however, FDR committed himself to the preservation of quotas, which meant that the overwhelming numbers of Germans, Austrians, Poles, and Czechs seeking new homes would have to find them outside the United States. This policy allowed approximately 100,000 persons from these central European states to enter the U.S. as quota immigrants during fiscal 1938–40.[58]

Messersmith found it necessary to argue with those members of PACPR who advocated various devices to stretch the quotas; he contended that a higher level of immigration would fuel anti-Semitism within the U.S. and lead to pressure for reduction of the quotas by Congress. He privately opposed the Wagner-Rogers Bill in early 1939, which proposed to exempt 20,000 German Jewish children from the quotas.[59] He sent Visa Division chief Avra Warren to Europe in November 1939 to admonish those consuls issuing visitors' visas to refugees who had no intention of returning to their native lands.[60] Messersmith's stance was not sympathetic to the victims of persecution, for he did not wish to be diverted by humanitarian considerations. Instead, he sought to protect the essential interests of the United States as well as the political position of the administration. In December 1938 he had written to his former subordinate Geist in Berlin:

Fundamental issues are at stake. These issues are greater than any individual or any individual suffering. . . . What we must do is maintain our principle in every field and one cannot maintain principle of so fundamental a character by making concessions in individual cases or by soft-pedalling our adhesion to these principles. . . Human ingenuity and the capacity of governments for action are not up to taking care of a refugee movement such as that which is being created by the German government and which may only be in its beginnings if the present movement continues.[61]

This was in effect a rejection of responsibility for the refugee problem. Moreover, Messersmith's belief that the American public opposed any expansion of the quotas seems to be sustained by polling data. Gallup polls conducted shortly after the *Kristallnacht* showed that although 94 percent of the sample disapproved of Nazi treatment of German Jews, 77 percent opposed permitting a larger number of Jewish exiles to come to the United States to live.[62] Messersmith's position (and Roosevelt's) was justified politically.

In 1940 Messersmith was appointed American ambassador to Cuba. From his new post, Messersmith's perspective became more, not less, restrictionist. In June 1940 he reported rumors that some German Jewish refugees had retained their loyalty to their fatherland despite their own need to escape it. Some Jewish refugees allegedly celebrated the fall of Paris to the German army, while a naval attaché reported that he heard Ursula Einstein, the scientist's grandniece, herself a refugee in Port-au-Prince, express similar sentiments. Messersmith's conclusion was to endorse restrictionism for the additional reason of protecting national security. He hoped that Congress would pass legislation permitting consular officials to assess whether the newcomers' presence in the U.S. would be "in the public interest." For national security reasons, Messersmith argued, "our government can no longer delay giving very specific instructions to consular officers with respect to the degree to which they must go into the character and opinions of aliens desiring to secure immigration visas and visas for a temporary stay in the United States."[63] Mcssersmith's advice reached sympathetic ears in the State Department, including those of his replacement, Breckinridge Long.

Unlike Carr, Phillips, and Messersmith, Breckinridge Long was not a career State Department officer. He was a politician, whose support of Woodrow Wilson in Missouri earned him the patronage post of third assistant secretary of state. Born in St. Louis in 1881, Long was descended from southern aristocratic stock—the Long family of North Carolina and the Breckinridge family of Kentucky— and like others of such breeding attended Princeton University. Later he studied law at Washington University in St. Louis and entered the Missouri bar in 1906. In 1912 he married another descendant of southern wealth and Democratic heritage: Christine Graham, the granddaughter of Francis Preston Blair, Democratic nominee for vice-president in 1868.

Although he enjoyed his uneventful tenure at State, Long resigned in 1920 and ran unsuccessfully for the Senate. He never again ran for political office, but he did remain an active participant of some influence in Missouri politics. He practiced international law throughout the 1920s, but with considerably less enthusiasm than he mustered in working for Franklin Roosevelt's presidential candidacy in 1932. For serving as floor manager at the Democratic convention and a large contribution to the Democratic war chest, Long was rewarded with the ambassadorship to Italy.

At first, Long was enamored of the Fascists and Mussolini. He saw Fascist rule as a powerful force enacting badly needed modernization and reform. However, by 1935 Long was becoming disillusioned. He described Italian Fascists as "deliberate, determined, obdurate, ruthless and vicious."[64] He reported pointedly on Mussolini's militarism and the dangerous implications of the Ethiopian invasion. Severe stomach ulcers and perhaps a falling-out with State Department officials caused Long's resignation in 1935. Without consulting Cordell Hull, he had presented to Mussolini a plan for ending the Ethiopian war. Because the plan would have strengthened Germany's position among the European powers, Long's initiative was repudiated by State.[65] Franklin Roosevelt accepted Long's resignation with regret, assuring him that "after

November I shall want you again to be part of the Administration."[66] Nevertheless, Long remained in semi-retirement for the next three years. But with the outbreak of World War II in 1939, FDR appointed Long to the position of special assistant secretary of state in charge of emergency war matters. In 1940 Long succeeded George Messersmith as assistant secretary and found the issue of visas for Jewish refugees prominent on his desk.

Long perceived himself as the "policy making officer and executive agent of the Government" on the subject of refugees, a perspective that brought him into confrontation with the attorney general's office as well as with those individuals within government and the private sector who championed the refugees' cause.[67] Long opposed a liberalization of America's restrictive policies because he believed that the newcomers would contribute to a fifth-column threat, a belief shared by FDR. Apart from taking in a relatively small number of highly talented individuals, the United States, Long felt, would not gain by involving itself directly with Europe's disorders.[68]

The fear of subversion by foreign agents among the refugees heightened as war in Europe erupted. William C. Bullitt, former ambassador to France, had fueled concern by telling a Philadelphia audience in August 1940 that "more than one half the spies captured doing actual military spy work against the French Army were refugees from Germany."[69] Though Bullitt's contention was unconfirmed and contradicted by others,[70] it added to a general concern. Even before Bullitt's speech, the State Department had initiated preventive measures. In July, Avra Warren of the Visa Division was sent abroad to explain to consuls "in detail" a telegram ordering consuls to grant visas "only when there was no doubt whatsoever concerning the alien."[71] The difficulty in obtaining proper documents caused many visa applicants to be turned down, leading to claims by American advocates of the refugees, including the president's Advisory Committee on Political Refugees, that the State Department was operating in an unfair and prejudicial manner.

When James G. McDonald of PACPR could get no satisfaction from Long, who defended the conscientiousness of his consuls in their protection of national security, McDonald sought and was granted an audience with FDR. The immediate occasion for the dispute was a list of 567 names submitted by the Department of

Justice and PACPR to State for issuance of visas. Fewer than twenty were granted visas by consuls who regarded the refugees' documentation as inadequate. FDR agreed to speak with McDonald at the behest of Eleanor Roosevelt.[72]

Entries in Long's diary suggest that he was well aware that McDonald viewed him as an "obstructionist,"[73] but his recollection of a meeting with Roosevelt shortly after McDonald's suggests that the president was supportive of State's position:

> He [Roosevelt] said . . . when he [McDonald] started condemning and criticizing me the president told him not to "pull any sob stuff" on him and said that he knew enough about the situation to know that the Consuls abroad were not in sympathy with the policy [McDonald's position] and that he as president could not agree with any plan which would allow any organization in this country, whether it be Rabbi Wise, or McDonald, or William Green, to recommend finally that any person abroad whom they had not seen be admitted to this country. He said that he was sure the Consuls had to have and he would insist upon their having jurisdiction in these cases and that they should be passed upon individually.[74]

Clearly, FDR did not take Long to the woodshed, though other notes suggest that the president, in his fashion, may also have been less hard on McDonald than he intimated to Long.[75] FDR was doubtlessly concerned by the security issue and was more sympathetic to Long and the State Department than he was inclined to capitulate to refugee advocates.

Long was no advocate of lenient regulations, but neither was he a supporter of regulations and procedures that were not uniformly applied. He resisted pressures from within the Visa Division to approve instructions which would discriminate against refugees from Germany or Eastern Europe. In a memo Long stated that "nonimmigrants" could be limited in their entry into the United States by making it "depend upon prior authorization by the Department," but, he insisted, "This must be done for universal application and could not be done as regards Germany, for instance, or Russia, for instance, or any other one government because it would first, invite retaliation and second, would probably be a violation of some of our treaty arrangements."[76] Immigration, he argued, could be temporarily stopped by "simply advising our consuls to put every obstacle in the way and to require additional evidence to resort to various administrative advices [*sic*] which would postpone and postpone and postpone granting of visas."[77] In both cases, though, Long insisted, "that discrimination must not be practiced." The instructions would apply to the British as well as the Germans, and even the Canadians could only be handled through a special "exception to the general rule."[78]

Although Long adamantly refused to reverse the new restrictions, he did make some exceptions, perhaps as political concessions, in individual cases. On December 23, Long instructed Avra Warren of the Visa Division to begin expediting the issuance of visas to one group of rabbis and rabbinical students from Lithuania, adding, "I want to do everything we legitimately can to help these people out of the predicaments they find themselves in, at the same time observing the requirements of our law."[79] As the Nazi pressure upon European Jewry escalated, however, so did Jewish requests for visas.

By July 1941 the problem seemed overwhelming. After visits from several Hasidic leaders, Long noted how many rabbis had been to the State Department "time and again during the last twelve months. In all, they have submitted to the department in the neighborhood of 10,000 names. In many instances, the name of the individual does not include the persons of his household who desire to accompany him and for whom application is automatically made. Relatives include wife, children, children-in-law, brothers and sisters-in-law and persons of varying other degrees of consanguinity or relationship by marriage."[80] As charges and countercharges were hurled at Long and his department for not doing enough, he remained consistent in his insistence upon adherence to existing laws. "No single group of these persons [refugees]," he insisted, "can be segregated from another group and made an exception without extending the exception to each member of each other group."[81]

The Bermuda Conference between Great Britain and the United States in late April 1943 produced no tangible movement by either country to facilitate the rescue of Jews. Long's diary entries suggest that he feared Britain's enthusiasm for a meeting derived largely from the desire of British officials to dump "responsibility and embarrassment" for the refugee problem "in our laps."[82] To counter these perceived British machinations and protect the U.S. from the danger of German spies who might be sprinkled among the refugees, Long assumed a highly defensive posture. He also expressed concern that Jewish pressure, especially that under "the leadership of Rabbi Stephen Wise," might produce a "reaction against their interest," an anti-Semitic backlash. Long suspected that this anti-Semitism could even damage the war effort if Hitler's charges that the U.S. had gone to war "at the instigation and direction of our Jewish citizens" were believed.[83]

Long did not go to Bermuda, but he handpicked delegates, most of whom shared his reticence to commit the U.S. to anything more than "rescue through victory," an increasingly popular slogan among those who opposed more aggressive rescue efforts.[84] The final report of the conference reflects much of the assistant secretary's own preferred approach. His advocacy of an already bankrupt international approach to refugee assistance suggests Long's unwillingness to abandon restrictionism. Though later critics blamed the results at Bermuda on Long's anti-Semitism, the foundering of the conference was as much a joint venture as was the meeting itself.

The controversy over Long's behavior in the State Department reached a peak in late 1943 after his November 26 testimony before the House Foreign Affairs Committee was released. The committee was considering a resolution "urging the creation by the President of a commission of diplomatic, economic, and military experts to formulate and effectuate a plan for immediate action designed to save the surviving Jewish people of Europe from extinction at the hands of Nazi Germany." Long denied the need for such a body because the State Department was already engaged in such rescue work, including the resuscitation of the Intergovernmental Committee. He claimed that the U.S. alone had accepted approximately 580,000 refugees "since the beginning of the Hitler regime [1933]."[85]

Long's data were grossly distorted. First, he had confused the total number of visas issued to all categories of aliens (quota immigrants, visitors, etc.) with the number of refugees. Then he confused the number of visas issued and the number of refugees who actually arrived in the United States. In contrast to the 580,000 figure cited by Long, data extracted from reports by the Labor Department and the Immigration and Naturalization Service indicated that 476,930 immigrants (quota immigrants, non-quota immigrants, and visitors) had arrived from all countries, including 296,032 from Europe. The estimated number of refugees from all countries numbered only 218,069, most of them (201,664) from Europe. As for Jews, an estimated 165,756 came from all the European nations combined; 138,089 of them were refugees. Long's statistics offered a greatly exaggerated profile of America's generosity toward refugees.[86]

Long was unaware of his error, but even before his testimony was made public on December 10, Congressman Emanuel Celler circulated it as an example of State's dishonesty on the refugee issue. Upon its release, the Jewish community raised its voice in protest. Congressman Celler accused Long of shedding "crocodile tears" and blamed him for the "tragic" visa "bottleneck." The American Jewish Conference drafted a point-by-point refutation of Long's testimony.[87]

Long never completely understood what had happened or how negative an impression he had made. He blamed "a serious internal pressure based on humanitarian impulses and surrounded with doubts, uncertainty and suspicion on the part of high officials and large part of the public including groups naturally interested on account of race and religion."[88] He well knew that Jews had been his harshest critics, but he never believed that their criticisms were justified. When Roosevelt announced the formation of the War Refugee Board on January 24, 1944, Long wrote that it "is good news for me." When the new director was selected, he would take over, which Long wrote "insures me of staying out." In a tone of hurt pride, he wondered, "What they can do that I have not done I cannot imagine. However, they can try." He concluded, "In my opinion, the Board will not save any persecuted people I could not save under my recent and long suffering administration."[89]

Breckinridge Long has inspired considerable controversy among historians. Henry Feingold has been the most unequivocal accuser, contending that "although Long's anti-Semitism was not as crude as that of the Nazis, it held many of their assumptions."[90] Feingold's evidence is largely the anti-Semitic comments that pepper Long's diary, especially those that link Jews with radicalism and, in particular, "communism and Jewish internationalism." At the opposite pole is Saul Friedman who has observed that "far from being the anti-Semite . . . Long was extremely cordial to the Jews and opened his office on repeated occasions to spokesmen from every faction."[91]

Our own measure of Long is closest to those of Arthur Morse and David Wyman, both of whom acknowledge Long's anti-Semitic rhetoric and prejudices but emphasize that Long was more fearful of internal subversion by Nazi spies and communist agents among the refugees than he was of Jews per se.[92] Long's restrictionism was steeped in anti-radicalism. His policies and behavior were derived from his belief that he must rigorously enforce America's restrictive immigration laws in defense of national security. Long persisted in believing it unfair for Jews to ask for special favors which could only come at a cost to other refugees; he was equally adamant, though, in rejecting special favors for other groups as well. Long's stubborn embrace of law and regulation in the light of the Holocaust's reality was at times modified by his desire to relieve the suffering of those he was convinced would not harm the U.S. By expending extra effort occasionally to save a handful of rabbis or talmudic students, Long was doing the maximum he believed fair to relieve misery that neither he nor the United States had created.

Different in their personal attitudes toward Jews and in their personal motives, all four individuals—Carr, Phillips, Messersmith, and Long—shared in the general State Department consensus that favored restriction, but neither these individuals nor the State Department functioned in a vacuum. The presence of Franklin Roosevelt and the obscurity of the president's own posture on the issue of Jewish refugees looms large and sphinx-like on the historical landscape. The chief executive had the power and resources to impose his policy preferences upon the State Department, had he wished to. Precisely what those preferences were and why he did not exercise his influence remain hazy.

There is no evidence, despite the contention of some contemporary critics, that Roosevelt's attitude toward American Jews affected his behavior toward refugees. Roosevelt was surrounded by Jewish friends and supporters, Samuel Rosenman, Benjamin Cohen, Felix Frankfurter, and Henry Morgenthau among others. There can be little doubt that Roosevelt heard from other prominent Jews such as Julian Mack, Irving Lehman, and Joseph Proskauer in their pleas for leniency toward Jewish refugees. Roosevelt rarely refused these petitions a hearing, but when he acted at all—as in the Evian initiative, the formation of the IGCR, and the establishment of PACPR—he still refrained from direct American commitments. Not until the establishment of the War Refugee Board in 1944 did FDR take dramatic, unilateral action to rescue Jews, and then political pressures virtually forced him to act.[93] Never did Roosevelt call for a change in American immigration laws that would have fundamentally altered restrictionism. A detailed analysis, insofar as sources permit, of his awareness of the Jews' plight and the motives for his own behavior must await further research. From the behavior that Roosevelt undertook or failed to undertake, however, one must conclude that the president accepted the restrictionist legislation of the 1920s and its application by American consuls abroad.

Restrictionism was not a euphemism for anti-Semitism. Because the Jews were Hitler's earliest and most tormented victims, most refugees seeking sanctuary in the United States were Jewish. It is not surprising, then, that many have characterized restrictionists as anti-Semites in disguise. We contend, however, that more than camouflage is involved. Restrictionists believed that lenient immigration and refugee policies were not in the national interest, and that in times of economic depression and war, national interests must take precedence over humanitarian considerations. State Department officials and the president considered that their primary obligation was to American nationals. With the world in upheaval, the western democracies and their policymakers shunned the altruism that their restrictive laws made difficult anyway. Humanitarianism was postponed to a time more convenient.

From the perspective of Jewish refugees being victimized by Nazi madness, and from that of many who remember them today, America's niggardly gesture at rescue suggests either a shocking ebb of human sympathy or a stream of malice that could only be traceable to ancient wellsprings. Morally objectionable and incompatible with America's democratic traditions, anti-Semitism in the United States has proven an all too convenient deus ex machina for some scholars. Our study demonstrates, however, that it is hazardous for the historian to lean too heavily upon personal bias as an explanation of policy unless the individual is very powerful and the prejudice is intense. The recognition of anti-Semitism must not become a substitute for the intricate and difficult work of analyzing the political and bureaucratic processes of government during the Holocaust and the preceding decade.

Notes

Research for this essay was supported in part by a National Endowment for the Humanities Basic Research grant.

1. "Leading U.S. Jews to Explore Painful Holocaust Questions," *New York Times,* Sept. 27, 1981. Lucy S. Dawidowicz, "American Jews and the Holocaust," *New York Times Magazine,* Apr. 8, 1982.

2. "Personal Report to the President," Jan. 16, 1944, in Morgenthau Diaries, Book 694, pp. 194–202, in Franklin D. Roosevelt Library (hereafter FDRL), Hyde Park, N.Y. Also reprinted in Michael Mashberg, "Documents Concerning the American State Department and the Stateless European Jews, 1942–1944," *Jewish Social Studies* 39 (1977): 163–82.

3. The most blatant accusation of anti-Semitism in the State Department is Henry L. Feingold's in *The Politics of Rescue: The Roosevelt Administration and the Holocaust, 1938–1945* (New Brunswick, N.J., 1970), pp. 15, 131–37, 158. Feingold singles out Assistant Secretary of State Breckinridge Long as the engineer of various plans to halt the influx of Jewish refugees during the 1940s and attributes anti-Semitic motives to him. Later, Feingold claims that there was "widespread anti-Semitism in the foreign service." In his more recent publications, however, Feingold has retreated somewhat from his blanket bigotry indictment of the State Department. Instead he writes that "the model of conspiratorial indifference hardly encompasses the complexity of motives behind the inaction of the witness" (a category in which Feingold includes the Roosevelt administration). On Long's anti-Semitism Feingold now concludes that despite "revealing passages in his diary, it is difficult to answer this question with certainty." This time claiming that Long's prejudices were "a matter of gentility and class," Feingold "rarely sees evidence of strident anti-Semitism." Unfortunately, Feingold's change of mind is not accompanied by a fresh discussion on precisely the role that anti-Semitism did play in State Department decision-making. Other than observing that Roosevelt "never trusted" the State Department and "bypassed" it "at every opportunity," using it as a "foil to absorb the ire of the Jews as well as other components of the liberal urban ethnic coalition which sometimes helped to amplify the Jewish voice," Feingold offers little new. See Henry L. Feingold, "The Government Response," in *The Holocaust: Ideology, Bureaucracy and Genocide,* ed. Henry Friedlander and Sybil Milton, The San Jose Papers, (Millwood, N.Y., 1980), pp. 248, 252. Earlier, Arthur D. Morse, *While Six Million Died: A Chronicle of American Apathy* (New York, 1967), pp. 38–42, found anti-Semitism in the State Department but did not label Long an anti-Semite. David S. Wyman, *Paper Walls: America and the Refugee Crisis, 1938–1941* (Amherst, 1968), pp. 155–83, places less emphasis on Long personally and more on the State Department as a whole. Wyman especially emphasizes the constraining influence of anti-Semitism in American society generally, pp. 210–13. In a recent sequel on the 1941–45 period, Wyman sees the influence of State Department anti-Semitism on refugee policy as "problematic," although he does believe that there was a "generally anti-Semitic atmosphere" there. Instead, he finds that State's apathy toward the Jews' plight was conditioned by "the personal anti-alien, anti-immigrant attitudes that prevailed among those involved in refugee

affairs." He describes Breckinridge Long as "an extreme nativist," whose subordinates shared his "anti-alienism." See *The Abandonment of the Jews: America and the Holocaust, 1941–1945* (New York, 1984), p. 190. In *No Haven for the Oppressed, United States Policy Toward Jewish Refugees, 1938–1945* (Detroit, 1973), Saul S. Friedman denies that Long was an anti-Semite at all, pp. 116–21. He is not clear, however, on precisely what role anti-Semitism did play, if any, in State's approach to the refugee issue.

4. Waldo H. Heinrichs, Jr., "Bureaucracy and Professionalism in the Development of American Career Diplomacy," in *Twentieth Century American Foreign Policy,* ed. John Braeman, Robert H. Bremner, and David Brody (Columbus, Ohio, 1971), pp. 119–206; Robert D. Schulzinger, *The Making of the Diplomatic Mind: The Training, Outlook and Style of United States Foreign Service Officers, 1908–1931* (Middletown, Conn., 1975), pp. 52–78; Richard Hume Werking, *The Master Architects, Building the United States Foreign Service, 1890–1913* (Lexington, Ky., 1977), esp. pp. 88–120; Martin Weil, *A Pretty Good Club: The Founding Fathers of the U.S. Foreign Service* (New York, 1978), pp. 46–49; Robert D. Schulzinger, review of *"A Pretty Good Club,"* by Martin Weil, *American Historical Review* 84 (Apr. 1979): 577.

5. Philip J. Baram, *The Department of State in the Middle East, 1919–1945* (Philadelphia, 1978), pp. 260–61, 282–83, 323.

6. Gordon Allport, *The Nature of Prejudice,* abridged ed. (Garden City, N.Y. 1958), p. 10.

7. Norman Podhoretz, "J'Accuse," *Commentary* 74 (Sept. 1982): 28.

8. John Higham, *Send These to Me: Jews and Other Immigrants in Urban America* (New York, 1975), p. 165.

9. For a sampling of rapidly expanding literature on the interaction of attitudes and behavior, see Allport, *Nature of Prejudice,* pp. 463–80; Allen Liska, ed., *The Impact of Attitudes on Behavior* (New York, 1975); Walter Mischel, *Personality and Assessment* (New York, 1968); Philip Zimbardo and Ebbe E. Ebbeson, *Influencing Attitudes and Changing Behavior* (Reading, Mass., 1969); Alan C. Acock and Melvin L. DeFleur, "A Configurational Approach to Contingent Consistency in the Attitude-Behavior Relationship," *American Sociological Review* 37 (1972): 714–26; Richard D. Alba, "Ethnic Networks and Tolerant Attitudes," *Public Opinion Quarterly* 35 (1971): 327–34; A. G. Davey, "Attitudes and the Prediction of Social Conduct," *British Journal of Social and Clinical Psychology* 15 (1976): 11–22; Norman S. Endler, "The Person Versus the Situation," *Journal of Personality* 41 (1973): 287–303; Steven Jay Gross and C. Michael Niman, "Attitude-Behavior Consistency," *Public Opinion Quarterly* 39 (1975): 358–68; Thomas A. Heberlein and J. Stanley Black, "Attitudinal Specificity and the Prediction of Behavior in a Field Setting," *Journal of Personality and Social Psychology* 33 (1976): 474–79; Stanley H. Jones and Stuart W. Cook, "The Influence of Attitude on Judgments of the Effectiveness of Alternative Social Policies," *Journal of Personality and Social Psychology* 32 (1975): 762–73; Russell Middleton, "Regional Differences in Prejudice," *American Sociological Review* 41 (1976): 94–117; Dennis T. Regan and Russell H. Fazio, "On the Consistency between Attitudes and Behavior," *Journal of Experimental Social Psychology* 13 (1977): 28–45; Irwin G. Sarason, Ronald E. Smith, and Edward

Diener, "Personality Research," *Journal of Personality and Social Psychology* 32 (1975): 199–204; Mark Snyder and Elizabeth Decker Tanke, "Behavior and Attitude," *Journal of Personality* 44 (1976): 501–17; Mark Snyder and William B. Swann, "When Actions Reflect Attitudes," *Journal of Personality and Social Psychology* 34 (1976): 1034–42; Alan G. Weinstein, "Predicting Behavior from Attitudes," *Public Opinion Quarterly* 36 (1972): 355–60; Alan W. Wicker, "An Examination of the 'Other Variables' Explanation of Attitude-Behavior Inconsistency," *Journal of Personality and Social Psychology* 19 (1971): 18–30.

10. An excellent critique of the recent literature on American anti-Semitism is Jonathan D. Sarna, "Anti-Semitism and American History," *Commentary* 71 (Mar. 1981): 42–47.

11. Heinrichs, "Bureaucracy and Professionalism," p. 132.

12. Ibid.

13. Joseph G. Grew, as quoted by Heinrichs, "Bureaucracy and Professionalism," p. 133.

14. Wilbur J. Carr Diary, Nov. 7, 1900, Manuscript Division, Library of Congress. Carr's desire for self-improvement and feelings of inadequacy are discussed by Katherine Elizabeth Crane, *Mr. Carr of State: Forty-Seven Years in the Department of State* (New York, 1960), pp. 6–7.

15. Carr Diary, Mar. 23, 1920.

16. U.S. Congress, House, "Temporary Suspension of Immigration," House Report No. 1109, 66th Cong., 3rd sess., Dec. 6, 1920, p. 10.

17. Crane, *Mr. Carr*, pp. 269–70.

18. Carr Diary, Aug. 9, 1924.

19. Ibid., Aug. 15, 1924.

20. Ibid., Feb. 22, 1934.

21. HSC Memorandum for Mr. Hodgdon, Sept. 8, 1930, 150.062 PC/3; Carr to Colonel D. W. MacCormack, June 15, 1933, 150.062 PC/586 1/2; White House Press Release, Sept. 8, 1930, Copy in 150.626 J/no number; all in National Archives and Washington National Records Center (hereafter NA-WNRC).

22. Robert A. Divine, *American Immigration Policy, 1924–1952* (New Haven, Conn., 1957), pp. 62–63.

23. White House Press Release, Sept. 8, 1930; Hodgdon to Undersecretary of State Cotton, Sept. 11, 1930, 150.062 PC/8; Cotton to Hodgdon, Sept. 12, 1930, 150.062 PC/9; Secretary of State Henry L. Stimson to Secretary of Labor James J. Davis, Nov. 21, 1930, 150.062 PC/44; Wilbur J. Carr to Cotton, Nov. 15, 1930, 150.062 PC/45; all in NA-WNRC. These documents indicate that the State Department was concerned about possible criticism of its new interpretation of the LPC clause.

24. This table was compiled from various sources: first row from *The Statistical History of the United States, from Colonial Times to the Present,* intro. by Ben J. Wattenberg (New York, 1976), p. 105; second and third rows from monthly and annual reports of the Immigration and Naturalization Service found in American Jewish Committee Archives, RG 1, EXO-29, Waldman Files, Immigration 1940–44; also Cecilia Razovsky Papers, Box 3 Relief Work 1941–45, American Jewish Historical Society (hereafter AJHS); also National Refugee Service statistics on Hebrew Immigration to the United States, Dec. 1942, copy

in Joseph Chamberlain Papers, YIVO Institute for Jewish Research. In cases of disagreement between primary and secondary sources, we have chosen the primary data.

These statistics measure the number of quota immigrants actually admitted into the United States. They do not include the relatively small number of very close relatives (e.g., wives and children of U.S. citizens) plus certain professionals who were entitled to non-quota status. The immigration figures vary slightly from State Department statistics on the number of visas issued. One other comment is necessary: the number of Jews is almost certainly too low in each year. Some Jews refused to declare themselves as of the "Hebrew" race. Still the number of self-declared "Hebrews" provides some measure of the number of Jews.

25. Carr Diary, Nov. 8, 1932.

26. Ibid., Apr. 20, 1933; Hodgdon to Carr, Apr. 24, 1933, and attachment, "The Problem of Aliens Seeking Relief from Persecution in Germany," Apr. 20, 1933, written by Carr, 150.01/2110, all in NA-WNRC.

27. Carr to Messersmith, June 1, 1933, and Carr to Hodgdon, June 6, 1933, 150.626 J/92, NA-WNRC.

28. Carr's "Memorandum in Regard to the Requests of the Delegation Headed by Judge Lehman Representing Various Jewish Organizations in Relation to Facilitating the Immigration to the United States of Jewish Refugees from Germany," Oct. 13, 1933, 150.626 J/31 1/2, NA-WNRC.

29. Carr's handwritten comment on John Farr Simmons's letter, Feb. 19, 1936, 150.01/2385, NA-WNRC.

30. Wise to Brandeis, Jan. 26, 1936, Wise Papers, Box 106, AJHS; Wise to Frankfurter, Mar. 2, 1936, Brandeis Papers, Louisville Microfilm Series, Section VI, Reel 103.

31. Lehman to Felix Warburg, July 14, 1936, Lehman Papers, Special File, Felix Warburg Folder, Columbia University School of International Affairs.

32. Unidentified newspaper clipping, Aug. 14, 1936; Mack to Brandeis, Sept. 17, 1936; both in Brandeis Papers, Louisville Microfilm Series, Section 6, Reel 103.

33. Feingold, *Politics of Rescue,* p. 16, claims that FDR ordered the State Department to extend to the refugees "the most humane treatment possible under the law," but Feingold's source, FDR's letter to Lehman of July 2, 1936 (OF 133A, FDRL), was drafted in the State Department, apparently by John Farr Simmons of the Visa Division. Roosevelt had simply asked the State Department to prepare a reply. FDR Memorandum for the State Department, June 17, 1936; Carr to the President, with attached draft, June 27, 1936, 150.626 J/208, NA-WNRC. The State Department issued no new instructions to consuls until December 1936.

34. Coulter to Carr, Nov. 30, 1936, 150.626 J/242, NA-WNRC.

35. Carr Diary, June 6, 1934.

36. Ibid., Apr. 23, July 2, July 3, 1936, June 24, 1937.

37. William Phillips Diary, Aug. 10, 1936, William Phillips Papers, Houghton Library, Harvard University.

38. Phillips Diary, Apr. 20, 1935, quoted in Shlomo Shafir, "The Impact

of the Jewish Crisis on American-German Relations" (unpublished Ph.D. diss., Georgetown, 1971), p. 162 n. 23.

39. Julian W. Mack to Rabbi Stephen S. Wise, Oct. 17, 1933, Wise Papers, Box 105, AJHS.

40. Brandeis to Mack, Jan. 24, 1934, Mack Papers, Section XVI/93, Zionist Archives and Library.

41. Barbara McDonald Stewart, "United States Government Policy on Refugees from Nazism, 1933–1940" (unpublished Ph.D. diss., Columbia, 1969), p. 107.

42. Phillips Diary, Oct. 30, 1933.

43. William Phillips, *Ventures in Diplomacy* (North Beverly, Mass., 1952), p. 224.

44. Ibid.

45. Kenneth Moss, "George S. Messersmith and Nazi Germany: The Diplomacy of Limits in Central Europe," in *U.S. Diplomats in Europe, 1919–1941*, ed. Kenneth Paul Jones (Santa Barbara, 1981), pp. 114–15. See also, Moss, "George S. Messersmith: An American Diplomat and Nazi Germany," *Delaware History* 16 (1977): 236-49; Shlomo Shafir, "George S. Messersmith: An Anti-Nazi Diplomat's View of the German-Jewish Crisis," *Jewish Social Studies* 35 (1973): 32–41; Robert Dallek, "Beyond Tradition: The Diplomatic Careers of William E. Dodd and George S. Messersmith, 1933–38," *South Atlantic Quarterly* 66 (1967): 233–44.

46. Messersmith to Secretary of State, Jan. 7, 1931, 811.111 Quota 62/319, NA-WNRC.

47. Messersmith to Secretary of State, Feb. 18, 1931, 811.111 Quota 62/326, NA-WNRC, commendation noted on document.

48. Messersmith to Carr, July 27, 1933, 150.626 J/25 (filed under Nov. 14, 1933), NA-WNRC.

49. Jacob Billikopf to Judge Julian W. Mack, Sept. 14, 1933, in George S. Messersmith Papers, Folder 298, University of Delaware.

50. Max Kohler to Joseph Proskauer, July 12, 1933, American Jewish Committee Archives, New York City, RG1, EXO-29, Germany/State Department Efforts, Waldman File. For an explanation of the pressure the American consular office was under, see Messersmith to Carr, July 27, 1933 (attached to Early to Secretary, Sept. 14, 1933), 150.626 Jews/25, NA-WNRC.

51. Wise to Billikopf, Jan. 15, 1934, Stephen S. Wise Papers, Box 105, AJHS.

52. Julian W. Mack to Louis D. Brandeis, Apr. 17, 1935, Brandeis Papers, Louisville Microfilm Series 6, Reel 102. Mack explains that his children, Mark and Ruth, like Messersmith, though they think him a bit naive. See Mark (to JWM), Oct. 15, 1934; Ruth (to JWM), Mar. 16, 1935; Mark (to JWM), Mar. 16, 1935; Ruth (to JWM) Mar. 20, 1935; all in Brandeis Papers, Louisville Microfilm Series 6, Reel 102.

53. "Some Observations on Visa Practice" (written by Messersmith for the guidance of his staff in Vienna and transmitted to Washington with the suggestion that it be circulated to the Foreign Service), Nov. 30, 1936, 150.01/2458, NA-WNRC.

54. Messersmith's position seemed especially timely when Inspector Jerome Klahr Huddle reported, after a visit to the consulates in Germany, that a great many applicants came from better-class families, and that their relatives in the U.S. were both sincere and capable of supporting them. Stewart, "United States," p. 260.

55. Geist to Messersmith, Nov. 1, 1937, and Messersmith to Geist, Nov. 27, 1937, Messersmith Papers, Folders 906 and 907, University of Delaware.

56. Jenkins to Secretary of State, Aug. 3, 1937, 811.111 Quota 62/555, NA-WNRC.

57. Minutes of President's Advisory Committee on Political Refugees, May 16, 1938, Wise Papers, Box 65, AJHS.

58. Stewart, "United States," pp. 407–8; Shafir, "The Impact," pp. 835–36; *Monthly Review,* Immigration and Naturalization Service, Department of Justice, Quota Immigration, 1925–44.

59. Messersmith to Hull, Welles, Moffat, Achilles, Jan. 23, 1939, 150.01 Bills/99, NA-WNRC. Clarence Pickett Journal, Jan. 21, 1939, Pickett Papers, American Friends Service Committee.

60. Messersmith to Geist, Nov. 30, 1938, Messersmith Papers, Folder 1084.

61. Ibid.

62. George Gallup, ed. *The Gallup Poll: Public Opinion 1935–1971,* vol. 1, 1935–48 (New York, 1972), p. 12; *Public Opinion 1935–1946,* ed. Hadley Cantril (Princeton, 1951), p. 385.

63. Messersmith to Secretary of State, June 21, 1940, 150.626 J/798, NA-WNRC.

64. Breckinridge Long to Franklin D. Roosevelt, Sept. 6, 1935, Box 115, Breckinridge Long Papers, Library of Congress.

65. Fred L. Israel, ed., *The War Diary of Breckinridge Long, Selections from the Years 1939–1944* (Lincoln, Neb. 1966), p. xxiv; see also Phillips Diary, Aug. 1, 1935, Houghton Library, Harvard.

66. FDR to Long, June 18, Feb. 22, 1936, Box 117, Long Papers, Library of Congress.

67. Long Diary, Dec. 29, 1940.

68. Long Diary, June 17, 1940, Nov. 20, 1940; Long to FDR, Sept. 18, 1940, 811.111 Refugees/260, NA-WNRC. Presidential Press Conference, June 5, 1940, *Complete Presidential Press Conferences of Franklin D. Roosevelt,* vols. 13–14 (New York, 1972). Roosevelt and Hull were receiving information that Soviet subversives were among the refugees. Steinhardt to Secretary of State, Oct. 2, 1940, 811.111 Refugees/397, NA-WNRC, and Welles to FDR, Nov. 22, 1940, attached to Steinhardt to Secretary of State, Nov. 5, 1940, PSF Box 68, Russia 1937–40 Folder, FDRL.

69. *New York Times,* Aug. 2, 19, 1940, cited in Feingold, *Politics of Rescue,* p. 129.

70. See editorial and article in the same issue, Henry Pol, "Spies Among Refugees?" *Nation,* Aug. 31, 1940.

71. Circular Telegram to all Diplomatic and Consular Offices, June 29, 1940, 811.111 W.R./108A, NA-WNRC.

72. FDR, Memorandum for the Undersecretary of State, Oct. 2, 1940, and attachments concerning McDonald's charges, OF 3186, FDRL; Minutes of Forty-

First Meeting of the President's Advisory Committee on Political Refugees, Oct. 30, 1940, Box 65, Wise Papers, AJHS.

73. Long Diary, Sept. 24, 1940.

74. Ibid., Oct. 10, 1940, quoted in Wyman, *Paper Walls*, p. 147.

75. James G. McDonald to Mrs. Franklin D. Roosevelt, Oct. 10, 1940, McDonald Papers, General Correspondence, Eleanor Roosevelt File, Columbia School of International Affairs; McDonald to Frankfurter, Oct. 10, 1940, McDonald Papers, General Correspondence, Frankfurter Folder.

76. Long to Adolf Berle and James C. Dunn, June 26, 1940, 811.111, W.R./ 107, NA-WNRC, copy also in Breckinridge Long Papers, Visa Division File.

77. Ibid.

78. Ibid.

79. Long to Warren, Dec. 23, 1940, Visa Division File, Long Papers, Library of Congress.

80. Memorandum, Long to Welles, July 1, 1941, Visa Division File, Long Papers, Library of Congress.

81. Ibid.

82. Long Diary, Mar. 19, 1943.

83. Ibid., Apr. 20, 1943.

84. The delegation consisted of its head, Supreme Court Justice Owen J. Roberts, Senator Scott Lucas, Democrat of Illinois, and Sol Bloom, Chairman of the House Foreign Affairs Committee. Bloom, the only Jew on the committee, had the reputation of being the "State Department's Jew" in Jewish organizational circles. Long sent three members of the Visa Division personally loyal to him: Robert Borden Reams, Avra Warren, and Robert Alexander.

85. U.S. Congress, House, Committee on Foreign Affairs, *Hearings on Resolutions Providing for the Establishment by the Executive of a Commission to Effectuate the Rescue of the Jewish People of Europe on H. Res. 350 and H. Res. 352,* 78th Cong., 1st sess., 1943, p. 23.

86. Memo, Dr. Slawson to M. Gottschalk, Dec. 21, 1943, American Jewish Committee, New York City RG1, EXO-29 Immigration/Refugees/Rescue, pp. 42–48, Waldman File; see also, Proskauer to Long, Dec. 28, 1943, ibid.

87. *New York Times,* Dec. 8, 1943, cited in Feingold, *Politics of Rescue,* p. 236.

88. *Foreign Relations of the United States, Diplomatic Papers, 1943* (FRUS), vol. 1 (Washington, 1955), p. 226.

89. Long Diary, Jan. 24, 1944.

90. Feingold, *Politics of Rescue,* p. 135.

91. Friedman, *No Haven,* p. 116.

92. Morse, *While Six Million Died,* pp. 38–42; Wyman, *Paper Walls,* pp. 155–83.

93. See n. 2. This report to the president was written by Josiah DuBois and presented to FDR by Henry Morgenthau. DuBois informed Morgenthau that if he needed to use further pressure, Morgenthau could tell FDR that DuBois was prepared to resign from his Treasury Department post and publicize the whole story of State Department obstructionism. DuBois does not know whether Morgenthau passed along this threat to FDR. Interview with Josiah DuBois, Oct. 12, 1982.

Social
Discrimination

David A. Gerber

Cutting Out Shylock:
Elite Anti-Semitism and
the Quest for Moral Order in
the Mid-Nineteenth-Century
American Marketplace

"... One could invent reality, so that it became real;
for example, one could invent Jews oneself in order
to hate them ...."

Gregor von Rezzori
Memoirs of An Anti-Semite

The nineteenth-century northern city was increasingly a society
of strangers who were learning, from the perspective of various
ethnic cultures, to live with one another, while at the same time
having to come to terms with ever-accelerating urban growth and
economic development. That much is certainly well known, but
the relationships among these processes of change, as they were
interpreted in the lived experience of contemporaries, are less well
known. To some extent, this is because the complex ways in
which values appropriate to the emerging social order were created
continue to remain in need of explanation. This essay asserts that
a significant relationship exists between two problems in American
historiography that have not yet been juxtaposed. If brought together, however, these problems may well illuminate an aspect
of the reorientation of values at one social level in the mid-
nineteenth century. The two problems are the social functions of

American anti-Semitism and the cultural changes prompted by the antebellum expansion of commercial capitalism that dramatically increased the scope and scale of markets.

In particular, we are interested here in the relation between the anti-Semitism of American Protestant elites and the evolution of perceptions underlying standards of ethical—and unethical— business behavior. While the origins of American anti-Semitism remain obscure, after years of scholarly concentration on the Populist-Progressive period the formative period of American hostility toward Jews has recently, though tentatively, been pushed further back into the early nineteenth century.[1] It is wholly appropriate, then, that an effort be made to place elite anti-Semitism, a specific aspect of the problem of the origins of anti-Semitism, in that earlier era. Typically, elite anti-Semitism has been interpreted as a late nineteenth-century phenomenon. Its origins are said to be found both in resentment of the social ambitions of upwardly mobile, bourgeois Jews and in displaced hostility toward all of the forces, conveniently symbolized by Jews, that were challenging the cultural authority and power of older, American-born, Protestant elites.[2] This interpretation is troublesome to the extent that so few nineteenth-century American Jews, most of whom were poor immigrants, were in a social position to have significant contacts, premised upon the presumption of equality, with higher status Americans.[3] Of course, social attitudes need not mirror social realities, and under any circumstance a small number of contacts breeding hostility and resentment may well have an influence considerably out of proportion to their narrow origins. Nonetheless, it may prove useful to refocus the discussion. Not only may we choose to shift it back into an earlier era, but we may profit, too, from moving it away from the amorphous realm of leisure and recreational contacts to the one sphere of society in which large numbers of Jews and Gentiles did have sustained interaction prior to the mid-twentieth century. This is economc life, broadly construed here to mean not only economic behavior and the social relations created by production and exchange, but also the standards and values attached by culture and ideology to such relations and behavior. In this arena of social interaction, anti-Semitism has frequently found expression in the notion that, in the name of profit and advancement, Jews will grasp every unfair advantage and break legal and moral codes.[4] The reformulation of this view of Jews to serve social and cultural functions in mid-nineteenth-century America is our focus.

On the basis of research in both local sources and the credit-reporting documents on businesses owned by immigrant Jews in mid-nineteenth-century Buffalo, New York, a significant formative force in elite anti-Semitism can be seen to exist in the commercial relations between credit-starved Jews, newly and perilously embarked upon careers in petty enterprise, and powerful, native white Protestant commercial and professional men who controlled the flow of commercial credit. The circumstances of mid-nineteenth-century society and commerce prompted a desire to establish clear boundaries between social good and evil. This activity, when combined with American perceptions of the commercial ethics and behavior of immigrant Jews, served to give new meanings to traditional anti-Semitic prejudices, which were a part of the cultural inheritance of native-born American Protestants. The result was not only a deepening hostility toward Jews, but a systematic discrimination against Jewish enterprises in recommendations concerning commercial credit. To be sure, the experience of one city hardly provides us with confident generalizations, yet, while the analysis offered here should be considered tentative, it remains the case that the processes of ethnocultural diversification, urbanization, and capitalist economic development at the heart of the developments in mid-nineteenth-century Buffalo were present throughout the northern urban United States.[5]

Between 1830 and 1860 Buffalo grew from a quiet backwater to the nation's tenth most populous city, with a population of 81,000. This impressive growth was attributable to closely related developments in transportation and in the structures of the American economy. The city's strategic location made it a natural site for the placement of a lake port and for the terminus of the Erie Canal; soon after the canal opened, Buffalo emerged as the principal transshipment point in the commerce and passenger traffic which tied the Upper Northwest to the Northeast. This commerce grew at previously unimaginable rates in the 1840s and 1850s, as grain from rich wheat lands around the lakes went east to feed the burgeoning industrial and commercial cities of the seaboard which, in exchange, sent back finished goods. In the 1840s, too, severe grain shortages in the British Isles, prompting the repeal of the Corn Laws, also expanded this trade. Grain shipment was indeed the city's economic lifeblood—25 million bushels passed through in 1856 alone. It was the source of much of its growth, prosperity, and vitality, providing the initial impetus to the rise of Buffalo's other economy, a domestic one, geared to supplying food, clothing, and shelter to an expanding population.[6]

From their offices not far from the docks, Buffalo's commercial elite, which was comprised in the 1840s and 1850s of several dozen Yankee and Yorker Protestants, commanded the city's interregional trade and directly supported a vast network of attorneys, insurance brokers, bankers, clerks, bookkeepers, ship provisioners, and shipbuilders of their own ethnic groups. These commercial men grew rich in the business of commissioning and forwarding grain and produce; a number also bought and sold outright the same commodities. Most of their profit was reinvested into the local forwarding business in the form of new lake ships, canal packets, grain elevators, warehouses, and slips along the canal terminus and the various manmade, ancillary basins. This pattern of capital use was a product not only of a desire to make more money, but also of the familiar civic ethos which identified the progress of the city with the growth and prosperity of its principal industry. Buffalo's commercial men were proud of the role they played in facilitating the city's remarkable growth. Not until the late 1850s when railroads—with no particular reason to stop at Buffalo—began to carry produce and to dominate passenger traffic west, did they come to realize that the city's excessive reliance on waterborn commerce, and the consequent retardation of local manufacturing, destined the local economy to stagnation.[7]

Buffalo's commercial men of this era were also proud of the financial prudence and high standards of business and personal ethics they believed governed their group. But the maintenance of these standards proved an anxious struggle. Two influences caused particular uneasiness. First, as Methodists, Presbyterians, Baptists, and Episcopalians influenced to different degrees by conservative variants of contemporary evangelicalism, many of the commercial men and their professional and white-collar allies were deeply troubled by the rampant materialism and speculation which they saw around them or saw lurking as a constant temptation, and which were frequently themes of the jeremiads of their preachers. Second, and intimately related, many were deeply scarred by the memory of the city's financial collapse in the mid-1830s. Even before the Panic of 1837 decimated the business community, Buffalo had reeled under the impact of the fall of Benjamin Rathbun, a tragic, protean bourgeois figure of the type depicted vividly later in the century by Ibsen. A former tavernkeeper with a dubious financial history, who was straining to bury the past amidst poses of rectitude, this self-styled "Master Builder and Architect" had singlehandedly designed and constructed most of the city's central business section and become western New York's largest employer. In the face of mounting debts and his creditors' growing suspicions, Rathbun failed in August 1836, only to be arrested soon after when it was discovered he had forged the signatures of the area's most prominent men as endorsers of his otherwise worthless commercial paper. Sentenced eventually to five years at hard labor, Rathbun's disgrace was chilling enough, but his fall left 2,500 employees, some 40 percent of the Buffalo work force, without work and owed back wages. Further, it sent shock waves throughout banking and commercial circles. To this extent, the panic began a year early at Buffalo, but when the national cataclysm did reach Buffalo, it left in its wake more bankruptcies, ruining many respectable entrepreneurs who had recklessly plunged into land speculation.[8]

Memories and moral concerns aside, however, those Buffalo merchants dealing in agricultural commodities were engaged in a business which was speculative by its very nature. Whether buying outright or earning percentages through commissions, these merchants were dependent on making contracts in the spring to deal in crops, the selling price of which because of weather and other market factors might be quite different by the fall harvest. Although this web of moral and business dilemmas could never be resolved, the commercial men took steps both to commit themselves to standards of business ethics tailored to an era of intensive capitalist development and to institutionalize these. Doubtless in so doing, through the force of their example, they also influenced the American professional men and white-collar employees with whom they had close business and personal relations. The creation in 1844, in the wake of the depression, of the Buffalo Board of Trade was intended to curb reckless speculation and competition by standardizing price schedules and weights in grain shipping and to provide a setting for the establishment of models of business probity and for the arbitration of disputes among members of the merchant community. But the process of finding business ethics appropriate to the era was multi-layered. On a deeper level, in which group culture and individual psychology intermingled, it involved the desire not only to assert positive standards but to define negative ones, and this process would deeply influence the attitudes of Buffalo's powerful Americans toward immigrant Jews.[9]

Also troublesome to these commercial men was the difficulty they and their American allies experienced exerting leadership and control over the city's vast immigrant population. This problem merged in their minds with both their reluctant dependence on unpredictable foreign labor and the inchoate nature of urban growth, which seemed to spawn endless neighborhoods populated by foreigners. Numbering approximately 77 percent of the 1855 population, immigrants, the large majority of whom were Germans and Irish, sorted themselves out distinctively in Buffalo's neighborhoods and in its domestic and interregional economies. Some 18 percent of the population, the Irish were poor and unskilled, comprising a large portion of the dockworkers, teamsters, and others facilitating water-borne commerce, and of those living in the congested slums around the docks. Approximately 45 percent or 50 percent of the 1855 population,[10] Germans worked almost exclusively in traditional crafts and as building laborers and small shop proprietors, and resided on the vast east side, far from the docks. In the 1840s and 1850s, as Irish and German settlement accelerated, all the familiar, controversial issues of antebellum pluralism (i.e. immigrant political power, mobilized by the new mechanisms of mass politics; temperance and prohibition; Sabbath observation; the role of the Catholic Church) agitated the American commercial men and their allies. Separated by a vast abyss of culture as well as by residence (most higher status Americans lived on the west side), the American elite seemed unable to transform wealth and authority into the power necessary to set Buffalo's cultural standards and civic priorities.[11]

The commercial men developed two related responses. First, the majority of the commodity dealers and their professional and mercantile allies turned to nativist politics. In doing so, they hoped to use local government to impose behavioral conformity, modeled closely after their own habits, on the foreign majority, whom the Americans judged harshly through depersonalized stereotypes. Second, through their own institutions (the New England Society, the City Temperance Society, the Buffalo Historical Society, the Society of Natural Science, the Board of Trade, the American Party, and the Protestant churches, charities, and revivals—all but the latter founded in the 1840s and 1850s), they forged an ethnocultural unity and identity of their own as Americans which eroded the divisiveness of long-standing denominational loyalties. In doing so, they were afforded the means for continuously re-committing themselves to the bourgeois values they revered: order, temperance, civic pride, self-reliance, and business ethics. It is essential to see the two responses as different sides of the same coin. Occurring simultaneously, nativism and ethnogenesis informed one another: the positive identity provided by the latter was rein-forced by the rejection of the foreigner upon which the former was based. Again, the problems the Americans had encountered—here, in obtaining cultural hegemony in relations with the masses of Germans and Irish—led them to seek to draw boundaries around emergent definitions of social morality and immorality. Here, too, the process would influence their response to the Jews.[12]

The presence of Jews in Buffalo began to be commented on locally in the early 1850s, by which time a settled Jewish community, including two recently founded synagogues, had begun to take root.[13] There were very probably no more than 200 or 300 Jews in the city in 1855. The origin of this new community may well be found in the interaction between distinctive Jewish career paths and Buffalo's strategic location. In contrast to the Germans and the Irish, who were largely manual workers, data gathered for a large (relative to the city's total Jewish population) sample of Jewish household heads confirm the traditional image of Jewish immigrants as petty entrepreneurs, the calling followed by many Jews in Europe.[14] In 1855, three-quarters of the Jews in the sample were owners of small businesses, principally shops in the wholesale or retail garment trade. The remaining quarter of the sample was composed of artisans, most of whom were garment workers. These data may somewhat exaggerate the commercial concentration of the Jews. Many of those whom the census listed as "merchant tailors" were probably not much different in the scale of their enterprise, nor in the return it brought them, than those said to be merely "tailors." Many of the latter, however, whom we number among artisans, were by the same criteria petty entrepreneurs. Under any definition, the garment sector of Buffalo's economy was dominated by Jews and Germans, with little native-born American presence. (This ethnic job segregation implies that commercial relations between Jews and native-born Americans were not competitive ones, disposing at the outset of one of the most common formulations of the social origins of anti-Semitism.)[15]

Though 96 percent (twenty-three) of the Jewish sample for whom nativity data was found were foreign-born, most probably had not come to Buffalo directly upon immigration.[16] Some had come to the city to form branch stores for small operations owned by relatives in New York City, where they had worked for a time after coming to America. Others, probably a larger number, who became sedentary merchants in Buffalo might previously have been peddlers, a common first occupation of many Jewish immigrants of the era. Emanating initially from an immigrant-receiving port in the East, these peddlers are known to have worked their way further west each year, settling their families at some convenient point while they traveled into surrounding areas. Eventually peddlers might have chosen to settle permanently in Buffalo, which, with its extensive wholesale markets and excellent location, was a particularly convenient spot for beginning peddling journeys into the wealthy farm districts of western New York, Ohio, and Michigan. Having saved enough to begin a small business or, as was often the case with Jews, merged one's capital with a partner's, the peddler turned "merchant prince" had a vast, expanding market in Buffalo to tap, with convenient lines of transportation linking him to New York City garment and textile suppliers.[17]

Historians arguing that antebellum Jewish populations were too small and scattered to be highly visible, and hence intrusive, need to investigate more closely the spatial arrangements of Jewish communities in cities like Buffalo.[18] Here, a relatively small number of Jews, though not legally ghettoized, nonetheless quickly came to be visible because they were concentrated in one area. Most Jewish garment stores (and Buffalo's small garment manufacturing district itself) were located in a neighborhood but seven blocks long and six blocks wide, south of the central business district and just north of the canal terminus. Here second-hand dealer, clothier, and merchant tailor alike had access to the traveling public, the Irish working class (at the western end, around squalid Commercial Street), and some affluent Protestants (at the opposite end, around Seneca Street, the one elite enclave east of Main Street, the city's principal thoroughfare). By 1854, the first block of Commercial Street had at least eight Jewish clothing stores, while the first four blocks of Main had at least fifteen. Most of these shops were at consecutive addresses. Residential patterns and Jewish family size and household organization may well have increased the visual and psychological impact of concentrated location. Thirty-seven percent (thirty-two) of the owners of these businesses and their families for whom data on residence were found resided in back of their stores, while a majority of the rest lived close by. Moreover, Jewish families were likely to be larger, and Jewish households more likely to be extended, than those of other ethnic groups.[19] Thus, a local Gentile walking through the lower end of town, and possessed of a sensitivity for making ethnic identifications from names on shop doors or physiognomy, might have easily gotten the impression that Buffalo had a good many Jews. Certainly the association of Jews with this one neighborhood was becoming fixed: it would not be long before "Commercial Street Jew"—i.e., a shrewd operator almost as shabby as the slum environs of his shop—needed no explanation for many Buffalonians.[20]

This sort of stereotype, to which we shall soon return, was not the *public* face, as revealed in the daily press, of the Protestant elite's response to the increasing visibility of the new Jewish community. The public response was actually quite limited, perhaps because Jewish participation in civic life was very limited. The Jewish vote was too small to merit ethnic appeals, and Jewish organizations never participated alongside other ethnic organizations in Fourth of July festivities or the public funerals of notables. No newspaper sought to comment on this absence or encourage participation. Some may call this neglect. If it were, the city's Irish and Germans might well have wished for the same treatment. After all, at the very time a Jewish community emerged in Buffalo in the mid-1850s, the city was convulsed by interethnic conflict. Irish Catholics and American Protestants fought in the streets. The local American party campaigned on platforms calling for a curbing of immigrant political rights. The city's leading daily and organ of the commercial elite, the American party-affiliated *Com-*

mercial-Advertiser, regularly excoriated the Catholic clergy and characterized the Irish, and less frequently the Germans, in the crudest manner. Even the Democratic *Courier* seemed hard-pressed to defend the Irish and the Catholic church, and did little more than make bland statements on the need for fairness for "our adopted citizens."[21]

None of this public controversy touched the Jews, whom both newspapers treated, on the few occasions when the Jews were mentioned at all, either matter-of-factly or positively. Both papers occasionally printed news of preparations for Jewish holy days, with respectful explanations of relevant rituals, and the *Courier* carried a description of the consecration of the second synagogue. Only once before 1860 did the *Commercial-Advertiser* indulge in the sort of sensationalistic, stereotypical portrayal of crime by Jews which it daily allowed itself in the case of the Irish. It never singled out Jews, again in contrast to the Irish, as a burden to the Republic, priest-ridden, or hopelessly enveloped in clouds of religious superstitution. An 1854 *Courier* editorial, on the other hand, went out of its way, prompted by no public controversy, to praise Jews *as a group,* not simply as members of some amorphous "adopted citizenry." The Jews, the *Courier* said, were useful, hardworking citizens, who never begged, went to prison, committed violent crime or asked for even temporary relief: "Though by most regarded as a close and cold-hearted race, none can deny that they take care of their poor, comfort their afflicted, and relieve their distressed." In a city in which harsh winters brought unemployment to thousands of already poor outdoor workers, throwing many of them on grudgingly offered, paltry Protestant charity, this was no mean judgment. It might well have struck readers how sharply Jews differed in these matters from the usual notions of Irish and newer, German peasant immigrant behavior. In concluding, the *Courier* felt confident that the Jews, with their unexpectedly Calvinist habits, were exemplary citizens: "They set an example worthy of all imitiation. They are among the best, most orderly, well-disposed citizens."[22]

Though not without its ambivalent elements and very probably based more on vague images than actual contact with Jews, the praise recorded on this one occasion is noteworthy. It seems to suggest that, from their own ethnic and class perspectives, some Americans may have recognized that the immigrant Jews possessed resources capable of facilitating their integration into American life on terms which need not produce social disorder and assaults on revered standards. One suspects, though, that this praise may have been prompted less by philo-Semitism than by an unconscious endowing of the Jews with virtues in direct proportion to the presumed inadequacies of the more numerous, more troublesome Irish and Germans.

This explanation is prompted by the sharply contrasting *private* face of Jewish-Gentile relations, as it was revealed in commerce, the only social arena in which the two groups had regular contacts. Here, shaped by the central economic processes of the time, the negative evaluation of the Jews formed one cutting edge in the effort to reformulate commercial morality, an effort which had taken a concrete, institutional form in the creation of the Buffalo Board of Trade. The direct root of this emerging, troubled relationship was the coincidence in the mid-nineteenth century of Jewish immigration and the advent in America of large-scale commercial capitalism, which expanded markets and undermined traditional relations between the links of the mercantile distribution chain. Consequently, since so many mid-nineteenth-century Jews knew nothing but petty enterprise when they sought a livelihood, Jewish-Gentile relations were freighted from the beginning of the era of mass migration with a dual burden: the historic legacy of religious and social prejudice and the more general problem of business relations, across vast cultural and physical distance, between strangers in a changing economy. The implications of these large economic changes for Jewish-gentile relations may best be understood if two relevant and interrelated contexts are first briefly established: the problem of debt in the new mercantile economy and the related rise of credit-reporting.

Because all mercantile business at mid-century was ultimately rooted in the seasonal movement of crops, seasonal shortages of operating capital were universal. As a consequence, temporary debt was a common experience among merchants purchasing finished goods from suppliers. This situation was exacerbated by a decentralized, conservative banking system which circulated dozens of competing currencies, had no standardized rates for discounting merchants' notes, and proved wary of lending to any but familiar customers. Further complicating matters were periodic depressions, in which the entire structure of credit, encompassing financial institutions, manufacturers, wholesalers, jobbers, and local shops collapsed. In circumstances in which even prudent men became hopelessly indebted, it was not surprising that the perception of insolvency began to change from moral failure to simple misfortune. This evolution was mirrored in law. In many states imprisonment for debt was abolished and a more lenient system of bankruptcy began to develop. With a relaxation of insolvency laws usually came creditor complaints, particularly frequent, as Peter Coleman has noted, throughout New York state, which had one of the nation's most liberal laws. Creditors charged that the new laws encouraged irresponsible levels of indebtedness and the acceptance of bankruptcy as a convenient way to avoid paying obligations.[23]

While merchants recognized that credit was a necessity in the American economy, conditions such as these naturally gave rise to a psychology of caution, which worked its way among businessmen throughout the trading system and spread both high interest rates and hesitation in granting seasonal credit on goods purchased for eventual sale in distant cities. After the Panic of 1837 many businessmen recognized the need for reliable credit information to replace the now inadequate reliance on face-to-face relations between debtor and creditor or word-of-mouth among peers. To fill the vacuum, in 1841 the New York City merchants and social reformers, Arthur and Lewis Tappan, founded the Mercantile Agency, parent of the R. G. Dun Company. Run as a subscription service for eastern wholesalers doing business with inland merchants, the agency provided up-to-date information based on reports from the field. Information was prepared twice a year by unpaid local attorneys, though some got fees for collecting debts owed subscribers. The local businesses investigated were by no means only the large and successful ones. Any business—even the lowly peddler—desiring to order goods such as cloth or ready-to-wear clothing on credit, pending sale, from outside the local mercantile community was likely to be investigated. Occasionally, however, businesses within the same community as their wholesalers were also investigated.[24]

Although begun solely to serve eastern markets, by 1860 the agency had become a national organization capable of gathering and organizing data on thousands of individuals. It acquired great power over the informal, social selection of those individuals who were to profit, through the enhanced position commercial credit afforded, from national economic expansion. This gatekeeping function was reinforced by the fact that although subscribers were sworn to secrecy about the reports they received, inevitably a great deal of gossip circulated throughout various mercantile networks about those who had been investigated.[25]

This power highlights the influential position of the local credit-reporter, who for our purposes must be seen as the central intermediary in commercial relations between Jew and gentile. The reporter's task was to determine the creditworthiness of individuals, necessitating often a good deal of snooping about into the private and business lives of local merchants. Worthiness (i.e., the ability to repay debts) was conceived of not only in terms of business prowess, market and personal savings, and real estate holdings, but also in terms of such moral conditions as marital status and drinking or gambling habits. The resulting tendency to make *ad hominem,* as opposed to strictly commercial, judgments was reinforced by the nonspecific nature of the data collected; not until 1864 did systematic *rating* by objective criteria replace more impressionistic *reporting.*[26]

Ethnic stereotypes often provided a basis for assumptions about moral character and business ability, but the matter is complex. While there may be no doubt that bigotry played its role, cultural and socioeconomic differences between reporter and businessman were also relevant. The requirements of the job (legal training; knowledge of local markets, local neighborhoods, and English; and wealth sufficient to pursue a nonpaying task) dictated that reporters would be recruited out of the ranks of American Protestant attorneys who served and were—or aspired to be—members of commercial elites like Buffalo's. Given the influence of nativism upon this class, one would certainly expect demeaning stereotypes, based on overt prejudice, in their judgments about ethnic businessmen. American commercial and professional men were also possessed, however, of deeply held ideological commitments and personal and business values, which may have frequently been ethnocentric but need not necessarily always have been mean-spirited or bigoted. Yet, ideology and values did, in turn, provide one cultural lens through which objective ethnic differences were to be interpreted to the detriment of people unlike themselves.

While, practically speaking, it is difficult to sort out where objective differences left off and prejudicial stereotyping began, both influences were at work in the credit-reports I have examined for samples of Buffalo's German, Irish, and Jewish merchants doing business during 1845–65.[27] To a large extent, this is true because, although exaggerated and cruel, stereotypes are often based on some fragments of reality. The local stereotype of Buffalo's Germans— phlegmatic, staid, cheap, and unambitious—had its complement in the most common pattern of German retailing, one perhaps brought from the small emigrant towns of south and west Germany, as revealed in the reports. Typically, the German shopkeeper was a grocer who, without a partner, kept a very small inventory of a wide variety of groceries and dry goods and sold beer in a back room. What little money he made was not spent on improving the business, which remained at the same address and in the same condition throughout the owner's tenure; instead, he spent his profit on purchasing a house, or the store, or a small parcel of real estate. From an American entrepreneur's viewpoint, this lack of dynamism was typically German. But if not worthy of commercial emulation, it was not entirely lacking in merit: the German grocer was unlikely to go into debt he couldn't handle. Seldom, in fact, did a German business fail. German real estate holdings were not only testimony to the German's permanence but allowed for mortgaging of property to pay debts. Thus, the German grocer was said to be "safe"—worthy of small extension of credit. The Irish story was much different. The Irish, who were less likely to have even small amounts of capital and lacked an entrepreneurial tradition in Europe, were seldom in retailing. When they were, usually as grocer-saloonkeepers, their businesses were poor in inventory, ill housed, and dependent on the ethnic patronage of the city's poorest people. Irish businesses had a high rate of attrition. Such patterns confirmed the American view of the Irish as passionate but purposeless, ignorant, ineffectual and morally deficient because of intemperance and lack of discipline. ("Grog-shop—himself as the best customer," said the report on one Irish grocer.) The presumption was that the Irish grocers would fail, and they frequently did. Thus, they were deemed poor risks, a situation which doubtless exacerbated the problem Irish immigrants encountered in breaking out of the most stultifying poverty.[28]

The same mix of prejudice and perception of actual ethnic differences informed the reports on those businesses identified as owned by Jews. Buffalo investigators were often intrigued—as well as appalled—by the distinctive patterns of Jewish enterprise they observed. Doubtless these patterns were derived from several sources: Jewish adjustments to resettlement in America; the specific context of the garment business; and long centuries of petty commercial involvement, to which proscription in many crafts and in land ownership in many parts of Europe had relegated the Jews.[29]

If we were to attempt the admittedly difficult exercise of sorting out fact from fancy in these reports, three interrelated characteristics of Jewish enterprise would repeatedly emerge. To the American reporter, the impression they created was one of instability, risk, and a high probability of failure. First, the typical Jewish businessman—a garment dealer—was a marginal operator who entered business with minimal capital. This marginality is suggested by the greater likelihood of Jews having partners: in the samples generated from credit reports, there were 2.12 Jewish owners per business, compared to 1.37 and 1.23 for the Germans and Irish respectively. Also, while failure to pay debts may have a number of causes, this marginality may, too, have been suggested by the persistent existence of a sizeable (27 percent—nine) portion of Jewish businesses which were said to be slow or fail completely to pay creditors; (61 percent—twenty—were reported to pay promptly). From the credit reporters' perspective, central to this marginality was the fact that Jews were less likely to own real estate that could be sold or mortgaged to pay debts. While 61 percent (seventy-four) of the individual German businessmen owned real estate and only 2 percent (three) were known not to, the comparable figures for individual Jewish entrepreneurs are 23 percent (sixteen) and 20 percent (fourteen). When profit was not put into personal savings or consumption, typically the Jewish entrepreneur used it to expand inventory or, in the case of 37 percent (twelve) of the Jewish firms, open a branch store in another local neighborhood, an option almost never exercised by the Germans. In turn, such a commercial use of profit made the Jews more defenseless in the face of depressions and individual reversals. Second, Jewish enterprises do appear to have been more likely to fail. While 12 percent (eleven) of the German businesses were recorded as having failed, a very high 57.5 percent (nineteen) of the Jewish businesses did. Third, as the lack of Jewish real estate holdings implied for investigators many Jewish entrepreneurs lacked deep roots in Buffalo. As the reports indicate, many had come to the city with complex American business histories, including prior failures and insolvencies, and some continued to have commercial ties elsewhere which regularly took them away for extended periods of time and which threatened to drain off funds from their Buffalo enterprise. Seventeen percent (twelve) of the individual Jews were known to have eventually left the city altogether, some for destinations unknown. In contrast, only 9 percent (eleven) of the individual Germans did so, and a quarter of them simply settled on farm land around Buffalo, a pattern entirely unknown among the Jews.[30]

The credit investigators' interpretation of these characteristics carried grave consequences for Jewish-gentile relations. As we have seen, both Irish and German business patterns complemented the prevailing stereotypes of these groups. The same could be said for the Jews, but with a vital difference. The Irish and German stereotypes were general images, lacking any particular historical foundation in commercial behavior and morality. In the case of the Jews, however, a specific historical image, deeply rooted in European and American consciousness and forming what Michael Dobkowski has called "the most persistent theme in anti-Semitism since the Middle Ages," had special relevance for interpreting Jewish business behavior. This was the image of Shylock, but a Shylock, as Dobkowski has said, "stripped of the dignity Shakespeare gave him." This was Shylock as economic parasite and predator. He was heartless and greedy, a cynical materialist ever-calculating the main chance. He was utterly untrustworthy. Capable only of morality in relations with members of his own "tribe," he flew in the face of Christian morality and cheated Gentiles at every turn. Thus, in one guise he was a criminal: the fraudulent bankrupt; the arsonist cheating his insurers; the shrewd peddler selling trinkets at outrageous prices to the lonely farmwife while her husband labored unknowingly in a distant field.[31]

As John Higham has noted, in all of the arsenal of anti-

Semitic images, this one had particular relevance for Americans.[32] Both non-producer and predator assaulted the individualistic, independent yeomen ethic of American culture. To be sure, just as the *Courier* saw Jewish commitment to ethnic self-help commendable in the terms of that same ethic, as the mark of exemplary American citizenship, credit investigators might have chosen to judge Buffalo's Jews exemplary American capitalists: risk-takers, bent on achieving personal fortunes and accepting the possibility of frequent failure and relocation, who were increasing the sum-total of American capital. But investigators very seldom revealed such a belief,[33] nor did they allow themselves to be convinced that the substantial number of Jewish business failures were simply evidence, as it was thought to be for the Irish, of incompetence. To have chosen either of these explanations would have required members of the American Protestant commercial and professional group to overcome both the traditional image of the Jew as Shylock, which was a part of their own cultural inheritance, and the pressures of their contemporary crisis of leadership and confidence, which seemed to require that boundaries be drawn, in the relevant contexts of daily life, separating ethical from unethical business behavior. We should not lose sight of the fact that Jewish enterprises were different enough in structure and organization to constitute a genuine cultural puzzle for American Protestants. The problem was that *differences* were interpreted and embellished so that they became evidence of *defects*. Hence the failure of Jewish businesses provided evidence not of ineptitude or foolhardy risk-taking, but of deception. Of course, these American Protestants were probably not the only people in Buffalo whose cultural background prepared them to bring negative imagery and expectations to their puzzling, daily interactions with foreign Jews of different habits and beliefs. They were, however, the only ones with power enough, in this case through control of the processes of commercial credit, to mobilize prejudice to serve the purposes of discrimination and hence to establish new and broadly ramifying social patterns.[34]

What the credit reports reveal is the refurbishing of the historic image of Shylock to create a new image applicable to American commercial and social realities, and thus able to mediate the experience of American credit investigators dealing with Jews for the first time. This was the image of *Jewish business,* a mental construct with a dual function. This construct provided a baseline for judging the businesses of individual Jews, thereby helping to solve the cultural puzzle which Jewish enterprises did indeed constitute. More generally—this was to be its chief social function for the mid-nineteenth-century American—it provided an additional standard for reinforcing efforts to redefine "good" and "bad" business. *Jewish business* had two characteristics. First, in contrast to the open and consultative practices encouraged by the board of trade, it was secretive, conducted in a communal world closed to Gentiles. Though investigators actually had little difficulty establishing Jewish identity, even when Jews had names such as "Black" and "Alexander", they often complained that they could find out little about Jewish merchants: ". . . are called good [i.e., responsible] by other Jews, but a Christian can't learn anything with certainty"; "No one knows as the pecuniary affairs of Jews are usually in the dark"; "One of those Jews it is impossible to tell anything about"; ". . . are Jews, and therefore, cannot be well-estimated." This situation was doubtless reinforced by the Jews themselves, for either out of ethnic solidarity or simple distrust of prying Gentiles, they refused to speak about each other. One investigator complained that when a Jew was asked about a former partner, he replied with finality, "Dat be none of dis business." Sighed the investigator, "So say most of the Jews."[35]

Under such circumstances, those resourceful investigators who were willing to be inconvenienced had to conduct unusually wide-ranging inquiries: talking to neighbors, snooping around residences, or addressing questions to contacts in distant cities. Such research did pay off to the extent that, though with less frequency than among the Germans, the nature of Jewish real estate ownership was determined in 43 percent of the investigations, and other aspects of entrepreneurial profiles were discovered. But the relative difficulty involved and the common front of silence the Jews established before these outsiders reinforced the investigators' habit, revealed in the very constancy with which they felt the need to identify Jews as such, of seeing Jews as a people apart.[36]

Doubtless closely connected with the view that Jewish business was secretive was its second putative characteristic, its deception. *Jewish business* was possessed of its own morality, which was not only not Christian, but sanctioned cheating Christians; therefore, there was always a presumption of the likelihood of dishonesty among Jewish merchants. Credit reports revealed that the fact of

Jewish identity alone signaled caution: "Prudence in large transactions with all Jews should be used"; "We can learn nothing—it is enough to say that they are Jews"; "A Jew of the hardest mold; don't trust him." Since Jews were deceptive, any honesty they manifested had to be qualified by their own Jewishness: "If you trust him, it must be on the strength of his Jew worth"; "Good, but Hebrew good"; "No more than Jewish honesty." Moreover, since Jews had their own morality, predictable only in its own strange terms, gentiles had to be warned of the likelihood they would change suddenly, becoming dishonest without warning: "An Israelite in pretty fair standing, but have no confidence in him"; "Is a Jew, and will pay or not as he pleases"; "Responsible now, but is a Jew; there is no telling how long he will remain so"; "Are Jews and should not be allowed to get behind. . . ." Of course, the change most feared was a sudden refusal to pay debts or a fraudulent bankruptcy, and most investigators appear to have accepted the premise that every Jew was capable of such capricious changes of behavior. Summing up this attitude, one investigator wrote of a merchant, "He is a Jew and although in point of fact he may now be perfectly responsible, yet Jews have a wonderful faculty of becoming at almost any moment they choose entirely irresponsible."[37]

As is the case with stereotypes generally, views such as these were applied to those about whom nothing negative was known. Wrestling unsuccessfully with his conscience, one investigator became mired in contradiction as he tried to balance individual reality and cultural expectation: "The more we know of this man, the less we think of him. But we don't know anything of him that will do us any good or him any harm." Others resolved the problem reluctantly in favor of an individual, but in a manner preserving the stereotype for Jews in general: "Is a son of ——— Jew, but is deserving"; "Jews but responsible"; "Rank among the better class of Israelites." Even when a positive judgment was made, lingering doubts, stirred by some barely comprehended disgust at things thought Jewish, could prompt remarks such as "May be safe, but not desirable." This statement is eloquent testimony to the boundary-drawing function of contemporary anti-Semitism; so, too, is the use of the idea of *Jewish business* to castigate a suspicious *Gentile.* Thus, when it got back to one merchant that he had not only received a bad report but had been falsely identified as a Jew, he protested. Replied his investigator, "If not a Jew, he has all the tricks of the Jew trade."[38]

For all of the credit investigators' culturally predetermined fears, however, their experience, as revealed in their own reports, was that the large majority of Jews turned out to be—whatever the expectations continually brought to dealings with them over many years—"responsible." After all, of the thirty-three businesses in the sample, twenty (61 percent) were said to pay promptly, while only nine (27 percent) were said to be slow to pay, or in a small number of cases never to pay. Moreover, though there were many business failures among Jews, Jews very often seem to have reached honorable settlements with creditors. Of nineteen failures, only four were *suspected* of fraud; of twelve Jewish merchants who left town, only two were *suspected* by investigators of running from creditors. Under any circumstance, taking time to pay debts, or defrauding creditors, was hardly a "Jewish problem" in nineteenth-century New York. It had been a source of creditor complaints long before there were many Jews in the state, echoed in areas where there were few, if any, Jews.

In the end, therefore, the investigators' fears were irrational, testimonies to the tyranny that prejudice, fueled by sudden contact with entrepreneurs of a different culture in a period of rapid and disorienting change, exercised over experience. The effects were real enough. So well did the investigators succeed in creating a negative image of Jewish merchants that on the one occasion when a Jew was lauded by a local investigator as "one of the best men in his line here," his report was returned from the New York office for confirmation. Seemingly confident, he replied, "I do not know that I want to alter my first report of him." But then: "Still he is a Jew . . ."; and he finished by explicitly accepting, against his own evidence,[39] a negative judgment based on the stereotype. It is not surprising that Jews were rarely recommended for anything other than small advances of commercial credit. More than a few in the course of the careers recorded in the log books of the Mercantile Agency and its successors were often recommended for none at all. Since small retail enterprises historically have been more dependent on commercial than bank credit in achieving even modest prosperity, the impact of this discrimination may well have been significant for many Jewish businessmen.

Unfortunately, one predictable reaction of Jewish merchants to the credit investigators and to the discrimination inadvertently eventuating from their judgments may well have exacerbated the situation. It was a source of continuous anxiety to credit investigating agencies that those seeking credit were frequently informed by gossip or by creditors of the judgments made about them by local investigators. We can imagine that Jewish entrepreneurs, too, learned of the ratings they received. In only one case, however, did a Buffalo Jew challenge an investigator's report.[40] Accustomed in Europe, particularly before the late nineteenth century, not to challenging power but to living shrewdly within the boundaries it imposed on them, many Jews thus developed elaborate financial and other strategies for dealing with the discrimination credit reporting agencies were instrumental in imposing on them. Among these was doubtless a strengthened resolve not to cooperate with the investigators, who must have been seen at some point as a particularly menacing example of the various groups of Christians bent on harassing Jews. But a passive retreat into silence merely reinforced the view that the "tribe" was going about its dishonest business in communal secrecy, a situation that the credit reporters and their class could, in turn, only see as contributing to the further decay of an already precarious social morality. Hence, the presence of Jews involved in *Jewish business* required the creation of boundaries separating unacceptable, Jewish ways from acceptable, Christian ones. In a similar manner, the presence of other ethnic sources of instability, located in the Irish and German working classes, necessitated the creation of other types of moral boundaries to be achieved through temperance, Sabbatarianism, or nativist politics. In the long run, however, anti-Semitism had greater vitality. Its roots were ancient and deep, and they would be nourished everywhere in the Western world throughout the late nineteenth and early twentieth centuries. And it has passed the test of time: it is still with us.

It is not possible to elaborate here upon the issues suggested by the reconceptualization of elite anti-Semitism through analysis of the mechanisms by which one local elite sought internal coherence and a commercial morality appropriate to new economic circumstances. Based on the assumption that both the social processes and the forms of Jewish-Christian relations present in Buffalo are, at some general level, representative of the experience of other northern commercial cities, it is possible to address briefly two sets of implications. The first involves an opportunity for increased understanding of the processes by which an elite is formed and comes to contend for social dominance and cultural hegemony in a modernizing, mid-nineteenth-century American city. The second involves implications for the analysis of the interaction among family, domestic economy, social mobility, aspiration, and group and individual self-image in the history of American Jews and quite possibly that of other ethnic minorities.

Thanks principally to the work of Eugene Genovese, the processes of cultural hegemony, by which an elite strives to gain legitimacy and dominance less through overt force than through the dissemination of its values, morality, and social vision, have been much on the minds of American social historians in the last decade. The analysis presented in this essay suggests that, particularly in periods of transforming economic change which give rise to new elites, the processes of cultural hegemony are themselves premised upon processes by which an elite comes to self-awareness and gains its own social identity. Genovese clearly reveals this understanding in his analysis of nineteenth-century southern slave masters. Similarly, in the analysis of antebellum northern commercial cities, the process of elite formation must be understood from the perspective of both class and ethnic group formation. In fact, the two seem to have been inextricably linked together. In a society characterized by increasing cultural diversity, it would hardly have been possible for higher status American Protestants to have avoided developing an enhanced understanding of themselves as ethnics. Even brief contacts with Germans, Irish, Jews, and others in such impersonal settings as the streets, the polls, or the post office constantly made manifest such ethnic criteria as religion, dress, and language, and called ethnic comparisons to mind. At the level of group self-awareness and identity, such ethnic understanding reinforced and was, in turn, reinforced by the material interests and ideologies to which economic development gave rise. To take the example presented here, we have the evaluation of the activities of a small number of struggling Jewish merchants, members of a group to which an ancient, aversive, Christian folklore was attached, aiding in both of the simultaneous processes by which an American elite came to understand itself in ethnic terms and to formulate the boundaries of an economically functional commercial morality. Apparently, there may well be no end to the roles played by that elusive "other," who, even in such small numbers as the Buffalo Jews, has been so functional and so constant a companion of our problematic pluralism. If this analysis proves to be a useful guide, it suggests that even the wealthy and powerful, those most insulated from the daily asperities of interethnic competition and cultural misunderstanding, seem nonetheless to have been deeply influenced by the opportunities and perils presented by a increasingly fragmented pluralism.[41]

The implications for Jewish, and perhaps more generally, minority history are more directly evident. We face the necessity of reconstructing the strategies used to circumvent economic discrimination. Most immigrant Jews lacked both American banking experience and the capital to create banks.[42] Furthermore, they probably dedicated the economic programs of their ethnic associations *(landsmanschaftn)* to personal needs (home purchases or family emergencies) as much, if not more than, to business loans.[43] Under any circumstances, the use of such financial institutions for the creation or expansion of businesses by young men beginning careers and new immigrants lacking communal ties seems problematic. More accessible, therefore, seem alternatives based upon borrowing from within immediate personal networks.

Money could be obtained from family or friends, a common practice for most petty proprietors, whatever their ethnicity, in the past, but obviously less common as one worked one's way up the commercial ladder and needed more substantial sums of capital.[44] Money might also be raised indirectly, within families, through a merging of domestic and commercial economies, principally through ruthless family underconsumption and the employment of unpaid family members.[45] Both strategies based on personal relations might be supplemented by the formation of partnerships, these frequently within family and kin lines, thus possibly reinforcing the "tribal" image of the Jews. Apparently many Jews used these mechanisms with skill; after all, Jewish social mobility is not merely enshrined in our fiction and popular culture but established by our recent social mobility literature.[46] But what were the costs when those eager to improve themselves mixed family, business, and friendship? What deformations of personal and family relations may have developed? Jewish children were more frequently educated than their peers in other ethnic groups. What burdens did they bear as they sought to combine schooling with long hours of work in a family store? What of Jewish women, who carried the dual burdens of home and children and work in a family business? Until we know more about these matters, and about the emotional context of anxiety and frustration blocked ambition may have produced, we lack a full understanding not only of the impact of anti-Semitism upon Jewish lives, but of Jewish participation in the American economy.[47]

These considerations suggest another issue of interest: the effects upon the self-perception and culture of American Jews of the curiously contradictory evaluation of Jewish social and economic behavior observed here. On the one hand, in praising Jewish self-help, as the *Buffalo Courier* did, American Gentiles appeared to encourage assimilation, suggesting that Jews were quite like— perhaps even as good as—"real" Americans, and therefore acceptable to them. Yet through criticism, and ultimate rejection of Jewish economic behavior as corrupt and excessively materialistic, and subsequent discrimination, gentiles seemed to draw back from encouraging Jewish assimilation—and at the very point at which Jews may have predicted the most heartfelt praise. For anti-Semites, the situation was ideal. They might damn Jews, when appropriate, not only for poverty and failure but also for success and prosperity. Doubtless, too, the views of the Jews as corrupt and materialistic made more likely the late nineteenth-century discrimination against those upwardly mobile bourgeois Jews who sought acceptance in the resorts, clubs, and social circles of wealthy gentiles from prestigious, old families. Rejecting the ways parvenu Jews made their money was surely a sound basis upon which to reject the ways they sought to profit from it.

Jews, however, might be excused for finding the situation confusing and lamenting the "double-bind" in which they were placed. Did the national success ethic apply to everyone but them? Was one to be looked down upon for seeking self-improvement with the only talents one had? If Jews aspired to live like and be accepted by affluent Gentiles, and worked deliberately to those ends, was this not admirable? In America must a Jew feel guilt for the desire to make money and shame at the prospect of delighting in spending it? What Jews had stumbled upon was a problem larger than American anti-Semitism: the ambivalence of the national culture toward materialism and success, an ambivalence that, in part, accounted for the anxieties of Buffalo's commercial men as they confronted changing, capitalist markets.[48] But the Jews seemed somehow to be uniquely victimized by that ambivalence. The influence of such tensions upon Jewish culture and psychology needs historical analysis as much as the literary treatment it has more frequently received at the hands of writers from Abraham Cahan to Philip Roth.[49] Such analysis may help us to understand a curious fact of our contemporary cultural history: it has remained for Norman Podhoretz, a Jew of immigrant parents, to give us our most trenchant recent discussion of the perilously divided consciousness Americans bring to judging the fulfillment of aspirations they enthusiastically encourage.[50]

Notes

© 1982 Organization of American Historians (appeared in the *Journal of American History* 69 [Dec. 1982]). Reprinted with permission of the editors.

1. On anti-semitism in the nineteenth century, see Jonathan D. Sarna, "Anti-Semitism and American History," *Commentary* 71 (Mar. 1981): 42–47; Sarna, *Jacksonian Jew: The Two Worlds of Mordecai Noah* (New York, 1981); Michael N. Dobkowski, *The Tarnished Dream: The Basis of American Anti-Semitism* (Westport, Conn, 1979); John Higham, "Social Discrimination against Jews, 1830–1930," in his *Send These to Me: Jews and Other Immigrants in Urban America* (New York, 1975), pp. 141–43. Higham's position is somewhat confusing: he finds evidence of a changing situation in the antebellum period characterized by an increase in "disparaging comment" against Jews, prompted by a growing Jewish population; conversely, however, he finds little social discrimination against Jews, and hence, it would seem, little anti-Semitism. In his "Anti-Semitism and American Culture," ibid., pp. 177–84, Higham also finds evidence for, but downplays the importance of, antebellum anti-Semitism.

On the origins of anti-Semitism in the Populist-Progressive period, see Oscar Handlin, "American Views of the Jew at the Opening of the Twentieth Century," *Publications of the American Jewish Historical Society* 40 (June 1951): 323–44, and "How U.S. Anti-Semitism Really Began: Its Grass Roots Source in the '90's," *Commentary* 2 (June 1951): 542–43; John Higham, "Anti-Semitism in the Gilded Age: A Reinterpretation," *Mississippi Valley Historical Review* 43 (Mar. 1957): 559–78; Higham, "Ideological Anti-Semitism in the Gilded Age," "Social Discrimination against Jews, 1830–1930," and "Anti-Semitism and American Culture," in his *Send These to Me*, pp. 116–37, 138–73, 174–95, respectively; Richard Hofstadter, *The Age of Reform: From Bryan to F.D.R.* (New York, 1956), pp. 77–81; Cary McWilliams, *A Mask for Privilege: Anti-Semitism in America* (Boston, 1948). While Michael N. Dobkowski's *Tarnished*

Dream occasionally looks back to earlier decades, most of its analysis relates to the period 1890 to 1920.

2. Barbara Miller Solomon, *Ancestors and Immigrants: A Changing New England Tradition* (Cambridge, Mass., 1956), pp. 17–19, 37–41, 167–74, 201; Edward N. Saveth, *American Historians and European Immigrants, 1875–1925* (New York, 1948), pp. 65–89; Dobkowski, *Tarnished Dream,* pp. 113–38.

3. For suggestive remarks on the scope and scale of American Jewish-Gentile contacts historically, see Nathan Glazer, *American Judaism,* 2nd ed. (Chicago, 1972), pp. 81–89, 99–102, 116–20; Sidney Goldstein and Calvin Goldscheider, *Jewish Americans: Three Generations in a Jewish Community* (Englewood Cliffs, N.J., 1968), pp. 152–61, 169–70; Marshall Sklare, *America's Jews* (New York, 1971), pp. 66–68, 180–206; Seymour Levantman, "From Shtetl to Suburb," in *The Ghetto and Beyond: Essays on Jewish Life in America,* ed. Peter I. Rose (New York, 1969), pp. 33–56; Benjamin Ringer, *The Edge of Friendliness: A Study of Jewish-Gentile Relations* (New York, 1967).

4. For analysis of expressions of this constellation of perceptions in three distinct periods of the nineteenth and twentieth centuries, see Higham, "Ideological Anti-Semitism in the Gilded Age," in his *Send These to Me,* pp. 123–26, 129–33; Louis Harap, *The Image of The Jew in American Literature: From Early Republic to Mass Immigration* (Philadelphia, 1974), pp. 48–57, 70–71, 77–79, 83, 200–238; Gertrude J. Selznick and Stephen Steinberg, *The Tenacity of Prejudice: Anti-Semitism in Contemporary America* (New York, 1969), pp. 3–21.

5. For examples see Kathleen Neils Conzen, *Immigrant Milwaukee, 1836–1860: Accommodation and Community in a Frontier City* (Cambridge, Mass., 1976); Allen Dawley, *Class and Community: The Industrial Revolution in Lynn* (Cambridge, Mass., 1976); Oscar Handlin, *Boston's Immigrants, 1790–1880* (Cambridge, Mass., 1951); Theodore Hershberg, ed., *Philadelphia: Work, Space, Family, and Group Experience in the Nineteenth Century* (New York, 1981), pp. 43–92, 93–120, 128–73, 174–203, 351–67.

6. John G. Clark, *The Grain Trade of the Old Northwest* (Urbana, Ill., 1966), pp. 9–123, 179; Marvin Rapp, "The Port of Buffalo, 1825–1860," (unpublished Ph.D. diss., Duke University, 1948), pp. 45–113; Arthur Markowitz, "Joseph Dart and the Emergence of Buffalo as a Grain Port, 1820–1860," *Inland Seas* 25 (Fall 1969): 179–97; Laurence A. Glasco, *Ethnicity and Social Structure: Irish, Germans, and Native-Born of Buffalo, New York, 1850–1860* (New York, 1980), pp. 84–140.

7. Clark, *Grain Trade of the Old Northwest,* pp. 278–81; Rapp, "The Port of Buffalo, 1825–1860," pp. 124–88; Glasco, *Ethnicity and Social Structure,* pp. 89–97; Patricia T. Harris, "The Rise of the Grain Trade and the Grain Merchant in Buffalo, New York in the Mid-Nineteenth Century," seminar paper (1981), Archives, Buffalo and Erie County Historical Society, Buffalo, N.Y.

8. *Buffalo Christian Advocate,* Mar. 14, Apr. 11, 1850, July 2, 1851, Mar. 4, 1852, Mar. 3, 1853, May 11, 1854, Sept. 19, 1854, Mar. 6, 1856; Rev. John Chase Lord, *Pride, Fullness of Bread, and Abundance of Idleness: The Prominent Causes of the Present Pecuniary Distress of the Country* (Buffalo, 1839); Roger Whitman, *Queen's Epic: Benjamin Rathbun and His Times,* unpublished typescript (1942), Archives, Buffalo and Erie County Historical Society, Buffalo, N.Y.;

Samuel Welch, *Home History: Recollections of Buffalo during the Decades of 1830–1840, or 50 Years' Since* (Buffalo, 1891); John T. Horton et al., *History of Northwestern New York: Erie, Niagara, Wyoming, Genesee, and Orleans Counties*, 3 vols. (New York 1947), 1: 56–78.

9. Clark, *Grain Trade of the Old Northwest*, pp. 117–23; Rapp, "Port of Buffalo, 1825–1880," pp. 124–44, 167–88; Harris, "Rise of the Grain Trade and the Grain Merchant in Buffalo," pp. 38–58; Frank Severance, "Historical Sketch of the Board of Trade," *Buffalo Historical Society Publications* 13 (1909): 237–45.

10. Calculation of the percentage of Germans in the Buffalo population depends on how one counts Alsatians, German-speaking natives of France, who constituted some 5 percent of the local population.

11. Glasco, *Ethnicity and Social Structure*, pp. 84–140, 226–322; Horton et al., *History of Northwestern New York* 1: 143–72; David A. Gerber, "Modernity in the Service of Tradition: Ante-Bellum Catholic Lay Trustees at Buffalo's St. Louis Church, 1829–1854," *Journal of Social History* 15 (June 1982): 655–84; Gerber, "Ethnics, Enterprise, and Middle Class Formation: Using the Dun and Bradstreet Collection for Research in Ethnic History," *Immigration History Newsletter* 12 (May 1980): 1–7. (The correct name of the collection is "The R. G. Dun and Company Collection."); Gerber, "Ambivalent Anti-Catholicism: Buffalo's American Protestant Elite Faces the Challenge of the Catholic Church, 1850–1860," *Civil War History* 30 (June 1984): 120–43; Gerber, "Language Maintenance, Ethnic Group Formation, and Public Schools: Changing Patterns of German Concern, Buffalo, 1837–1874," *Journal of American Ethnic History* 4 (Fall 1984): 31–61.

12. Glasco, *Ethnicity and Social Structure*, pp. 226–318; Horton et al., *History of Northwestern New York* 1: 117–72; Gerber, "Ethnics, Enterprise, and Middle Class Formation," pp. 3–7; Welch, *Home History*, pp. 340–47; *Buffalo Christian Advocate*, May 4, 1854; *Semi-Centennial Celebration, The Buffalo Orphan Asylum, April 26, 1887* (Buffalo, 1887); *Seventy-fifth Anniversary of the Founding of the Buffalo Historical Society* (Buffalo, 1837); New England Society of Buffalo, *Constitution and Members* (1853), in Archives, Buffalo and Erie County Historical Society, Buffalo, N.Y.

13. The history of the early Buffalo Jewish community is contained in Selig Adler and Thomas Connolly, *From Ararat to Suburbia: The History of the Jewish Community of Buffalo* (Philadelphia, 1960), pp. 3–76. This excellent study, which is limited only by defining its purposes according to the paradigm of traditional American-Jewish community histories (social mobility, social acceptance, and institution building), finds little anti-Semitism before the later nineteenth century and only some thereafter.

14. Although many Buffalo Jews were from the German states, Jews will be separated from Germans here. This is not merely an analytical convenience. In spite of common nativity and language, Jews and Germans created different religious and institutional worlds and, as demonstrated here, were often characterized by greatly different social patterns.

15. The sample is composed of eighty-five male and one female household heads. The sample is derived from the names of all early Jewish settlers identified

in Adler and Connolly, *From Ararat to Suburbia*, pp. 3–76, and from shopkeepers and other entrepreneurs identified as Jews by credit investigators in Buffalo during the period 1845 to 1865; these credit reports are found in the R. G. Dun and Company Collection, Baker Library, Harvard University School of Business, Boston. The names were then traced through Buffalo city directories and an alphabetized print-out of the names of all Buffalonians who apeared in the 1855 New York state census. The print-out is found at the University Archives, Capen Hall, State University of New York at Buffalo, Amherst, New York. Information could not be found for every individual for every category of analysis. I believe the sample is quite representative of Jewish heads of household. The Adler and Connolly lists are composed of those engaged in the relatively democratically organized work of religious observance and synagogue organization, as well as of those known to have been in business or artisan work. The credit reports, which are discussed at length below, probably contain a significant proportion of the city's Jewish small businessmen, the major trade of Buffalo Jews. Given Jewish concentration in the garment business and the nature of that business, credit investigations were a routine occurrence; see also n. 27.

16. National origins: German states, twelve (52 percent); Poland, four (17 percent); Russia, two (9 percent); England, two (9 percent); Holland, two (9 percent); USA, one (4 percent).

17. On Jewish peddling, see Rudolf Glanz, "Notes on Early Jewish Peddling in America," *Jewish Social Studies* 7 (Apr. 1945): 119–36; Herbert L. Feingold, *Zion in America: The Jewish Experience from Colonial Times to the Present* (New York, 1974), pp. 73–79.

18. For example, see Higham, "Social Discrimination against Jews, 1830–1930," pp. 141–42.

19. Mean number of children: Jews, 3.125; Germans, 2.12; Irish, 2.37; native-born Americans, 2.06. Extended households (i.e., one or more relatives co-resident): Jews, 16.6 percent; Germans, 6 percent; Irish, 12 percent; native-born Americans, 20 percent. Sources: sample of eighty-six Jewish household heads in Buffalo; Glasco, *Ethnicity and Social Structure*, pp. 149–57, 160–65.

20. This term is found in credit reports on Buffalo's Jewish entrepreneurs; see "Abrahams and Sylvester," Credit Report Ledger 80, p. 274, R. G. Dun and Company Collection. The author gratefully acknowledges permission of the Dun and Bradstreet Company to quote from the records of the R. G. Dun and Company here and in subsequent notes.

21. Horton et al., *History of Northwestern New York,* 1: 143–72; Glasco, *Ethnicity and Social Structure,* pp. 226–318.

22. *Buffalo Courier,* July 23, 27, 1850, June 13, 1854, Sept. 23, 1857; *Buffalo Commercial Advertiser,* Apr. 2, 22, 1856.

23. Glenn Porter and Harold Livesay, *Mercants and Manufacturers: Studies in the Changing Structure of Nineteenth Century Marketing* (Baltimore, 1971), pp. 2–74; Peter J. Coleman, *Debtors and Creditors in America: Insolvency, Imprisonment for Debt, and Bankruptcy, 1607–1900* (Madison, Wis., 1974), pp. 105–6, 119, 122–29, 269–93; John Duer et al., preparers, *Revised Statutes of the State of New York as Altered by Subsequent Enactments: Together with*

Statutory Provisions of a General Nature, Passed between the Years 1828–1845, 3rd ed., 3 vols. (Albany, 1846–1848) 2: 63–114.

24. James D. Norris, *R. G. Dun and Company, 1841–1900: The Development of Credit Reporting in the Nineteenth Century* (Westport, Conn. 1978), pp. 3–23; Bertram Wyatt-Brown, "God and Dun and Bradstreet," *Business History Review* 40 (1966): 432–50; James H. Madison, "The Credit Reports of R. G. Dun and Company as Historical Sources," *Historical Methods Newsletter,* 8 (Sept. 1975): 128–31; Stephen G. Mostov, "Dun and Bradstreet Reports As A Source of Jewish Economic History: Cincinnati, 1845–1875," *American Jewish History,* 72 (Mar. 1983), 333–39.

25. Norris, *R. G. Dunn and Company, 1841–1900,* pp. 25–83.

26. Ibid., pp. 84–87; Gerber, "Ethnics, Enterprise, and Middle Class Formation," p. 3.

27. Sample sizes: Germans (122 individuals; 89 firms); Irish (26; 21); and Jews 70; 33). Irish and Jewish samples represent the totals of all businessmen/firms identified with those groups by investigators. See Credit Report Ledgers 80 and 81, covering 1845–85 and 1858–88, respectively, R. G. Dun and Company Collection. It is quite possible this sample represents a very significant proportion of Jewish businessmen, and indeed of the total male Jewish head of household population. One must consider three factors in evaluating this claim: the small size of the city's Jewish population; the very pronounced over-representation of mid-nineteenth-century American Jews in petty enterprise; and the over-representation of American Jews in the garment trade. Moreover, the garment trade, in the case of Buffalo, was a business dependent on cloth and accessories not produced in the city; as a consequence, Buffalo Jews in the garment trade were likely to have had to seek credit from distant, principally New York City, suppliers who probably would require credit investigations. It could certainly not be said that these samples represented a substantial percentage of the total German and Irish populations, even if they were representative samples of German and Irish business. The majority of Irish were unskilled laborers, and the majority of Germans were artisans and laborers.

28. Gerber, "Ethnics, Enterprise, and Middle Class Formation," pp. 4–6. On the Germans, see *Buffalo Commercial Advertiser,* Mar. 13, 1846, July 7, 1847, May 21, 1850, Jan. 28, 1856, June 15, 1857, July 24, 1860; Mack Walker, *German Hometowns: Community, State, and General Estate, 1648–1871* (Ithaca, N.Y., 1971), p. 329 n. 38. On the Irish, see *Buffalo Commercial Advertiser,* Dec. 9, 1844, A. 21, 1856; *Buffalo Courier,* Jan. 13, 1844, Jan. 27, 1847, Jan. 1, 1852, May 12, 1857; Oliver MacDonagh, "The Irish Famine Emigration to the United States," *Perspectives in American History* 10 (1976): 361–72, 426, 435, 440; "Robert Coveny," Credit Report Ledger 80, p. 13, R. G. Dun and Company Collection.

29. Jacob Katz, *Out of the Ghetto: The Social Background to Jewish Emancipation* (Cambridge, Mass., 1973), pp. 9–27, 176–90; Simon Kuznets, "Economic Structure and the Life of the Jews," in *The Jews,* ed. Louis Finkelstein, 2 vols. (Philadelphia, 1960) 2: 1497–1666; Glanz, "Notes on Early Jewish Peddling," pp. 119–36.

30. The likelihood of prior residence in the U. S. before settlement in Buffalo has already been noted. In addition, in the mid-1850s, the Jews were more likely to be relative newcomers than was the balance of the city's population. In 1855, the mean years of residence of all Buffalo heads of household was 8.8 years, while for Jewish heads of household in the sample for whom data were found (N = 23), the figure is 6.78 years. Nonetheless, Jews were not much more likely to be strangers to Buffalo than, for example, Germans. The mean years for Jews aged twenty-five to fifty-four is 6.82; for age fifty-five and over is 10; for Germans, 6.15 and 10.6 respectively. Data on Germans are from Michael B. Katz et al., "Migration and the Social Order in Erie County, New York: 1855," *Journal of Interdisciplinary History* 8 (Spring, 1978): 684.

31. Michael N. Dobkowski, "American Anti-Semitism: A Reinterpretation," *American Quarterly* 29 (Summer 1977), 171, 172, and *Tarnished Dream,* pp. 41–112. On the European origin and development of Shylock, see Hermann Sinsheimer, *Shylock: The History of A Character,* paperback edition (New York, 1963).

32. John Higham, "American Anti-Semitism, Historically Reconsidered," in *Jews in the Mind of America,* ed. Charles H. Stember, et al. (New York, 1966), pp. 247–48.

33. Higham, "Ideological Anti-Semitism in the Gilded Age," in his *Send Them to Me,* pp. 121–22, and Dobkowski, *Tarnished Dream,* p. 79, find greater ambivalence in the view of Jewish commercial acumen than I do in my sources.

34. For anti-Semitism in the cultural heritage (i.e. myth, oral tradition, and iconographic representation) of nineteenth-century American Protestants, see Dobkowski, *Tarnished Dream* and Harap, *Image of the Jew in American Literature.* One must also go back to Britain and to Europe. See, for example, Sinsheimer, *Shylock: The History of A Character;* Rudolf Glanz, *Jew and Irish* (New York, 1966); Edgar Rosenberg, *From Shylock to Svengali: Jewish Stereotypes in English Fiction* (Stanford, 1960); Bernard Glussman, *Anti-Semitic Stereotypes without Jews: Images of the Jews in England, 1200–1700* (Detroit, 1972). More general works include Cecil Roth, *Ritual Murder and the Jews* (London, 1935); Joshua Trachtenberg, *The Devil and the Jews* (New Haven, Conn., 1943); George K. Anderson, *The Legend of the Wandering Jew* (Providence, R.I., 1965).

35. "M. and L. Gitsky," Credit Report Ledger 80, p. 294, "Samuel Lowi: Abraham Geiershofer," p. 119, "Nicholas Hyman," p. 233, "Nathan Bosberg," p. 241, and "Jacob Romberg," p. 97, R. G. Dun and Company Collection. For an analysis, largely agreeing with this one, of the image of Jews in the reports, see Mostov, "Dun and Bradstreet Reports as A Source of Jewish Economic History," pp. 348–52.

36. "M. Mansfield," Credit Report Ledger 80, p. 248, "Abrahams and Sylvester," p. 274, and "Bergman and Romberg," p. 97, R. G. Dun and Company Collection.

37. "Samuel Lowi; Abraham Geiershofer," Credit Report Ledger 80, p. 119, "Abrahams and Sylvester," p. 274, "M. Freidenberg," p. 203, "Israel Boaz," p. 214, "Nicholas Hyman," p. 232, "Louis Dahlmann and Company," p. 5, "Henry Cone," p. 78, "Abraham Levi," p. 39, "Samuel Lichenstein," p. 169, "J. B. Manning," p. 341, "Seligman, Hirsh, and Company," p. 336, and "Warner

Brothers (John and Joseph)," p. 277, R. G. Dun and Company Collection. Another Jewish shopkeeper was alternately deemed "responsible" and questioned on the basis of the assumed unpredictability of Jews over the course of *three* decades; see, "Nathan Boasberg," Credit Report Ledger 80, p. 241, R. G. Dun and Company Collection.

38. "Samuel Hirsh," Credit Report Ledger 80, p. 120, "Lemuel H. Flersheim," p. 34, "Samuel Loewi; Abraham Beiershofer," p. 119, "Nicholas Hyman," p. 233, and "J. B. Manning," p. 341, R. G. Dun and Company Collection. Manning had been considered a Jew, based on a neighbor's statement, for over a year before he protested the identification.

39. "Henry Cone," Credit Report Ledger 80, p. 93, R. G. Dun and Company Collection.

40. "Hiram Block," Credit Report Ledger 80, p. 257, R. G. Dun and Company Collection.

41. On hegemony, see Thomas R. Bates, "Gramsci and the Theory of Hegemony," *Journal of the History of Ideas* 36 (Apr.–June 1975): 351–66; Walter L. Adamson, *Hegemony and Revolution: Antonio Gramsci's Political and Cultural Theory* (Berkeley, 1980); and the most thoroughgoing application in American historiography, Eugene Genovese, *Roll, Jordan, Roll: The World the Slaves Made* (New York, 1974). On ethnic group formation, see William Yancey et al., "Emergent Ethnicity: A Review and Reformulation, *American Sociological Review* 41 (June 1976): 399–409; Jonathan Sarna, "From Immigrant to Ethnic: Toward A New Theory of 'Ethnicization,' " *Ethnicity* 5 (Dec. 1978): 370–78; and, for the case most apposite here, Charles H. Anderson, *White Protestant Americans: From National Origins to Religious Group* (Englewood Cliffs, N.J., 1980).

42. On early Jewish banking in the U.S., see Feingold, *Zion in America,* pp. 79–82; in Buffalo, where two banks owned by Jews had a precarious existence at different times in the late nineteenth and early twentieth centuries, see Adler and Connolly, *From Ararat to Suburbia,* pp. 107, 175–76, and "Abraham Altman," Credit Report Ledger 81, pp. 305–7, R. G. Dun and Company Collection.

43. Oscar Handlin, *Adventure in Freedom: 300 Years of Jewish Life in America* (New York, 1951), pp. 114–15; Irving Howe, *World of our Fathers* (New York, 1976), pp. 183–90.

44. Ivan Light, *Ethnic Enterprise in America: Business and Welfare among Chinese, Japanese, and Blacks* (Berkeley, 1972), pp. 19–23.

45. "Ruthless underconsumption" is Stephan Thernstrom's phrase, which is used in connection with a similar problem: the strategies for property accumulation among mid-nineteenth-century Irish working class immigrants. Stephan Thernstrom, *Poverty and Progress: Social Mobility in a Nineteenth Century City* (Cambridge, Mass., 1964), pp. 136, 115–37.

46. Peter Decker, *Fortunes and Failures: White Collar Mobility in Nineteenth Century San Francisco* (Cambridge, Mass. 1978), pp. 25, 80–85, 96–99, 114–15, 187, 205; Clyde Griffen and Sally Griffen, *Natives and Newcomers: The Ordering of Opportunity in Mid-Nineteenth-Century Poughkeepsie* (Cambridge, Mass. 1978), pp. 74–75, 121–23, 171; Thomas Kessner, *The Golden Door: Italian and Jewish Immigrant Mobility in New York City, 1880–1915* (New

York, 1977), pp. 44–160; Stephan Thernstrom, *The Other Bostonians: Poverty and Progress in the American Metropolis,* 1880–1970 (Cambridge, Mass. 1973), pp. 145–75.

47. We might also wish to inquire into the relationship between anti-Semitic conceptions of Jewish business behavior and the discrimination Jews have encountered historically in competition for higher-strata managerial positions in those sectors of the industrial and commercial economies where Jews have lacked representation. Among the sectors in question are commercial banking, automobiles, shipping and transport, steel (except for scrap), coal, rubber, oil, and insurance. See "Jews in America," *Fortune* 13 (Feb. 1936): 130, 133–36; Ferdinand Lundberg, *The Rich and the Super-Rich* (New York, 1968), pp. 290–306; relatedly, Digby Bultzell, *The Protestant Establishment* (New York, 1964), pp. 81–108, 111–40, 206–9, 315–34, and G. William Domhoff, *Who Rules America?* (New York, 1968), pp. 14–15, 19, 25, 29–30, 52.

48. On the tensions within the success ethic, see John Cawelti, *Apostles of the Self-Made Man* (Chicago, 1965), pp. 4–6, 35–36, 48–50, 201–36; Richard Huber, *The American Idea of Success* (New York, 1971), pp. 357–79, 448–57.

49. Abraham Cahan, *The Rise of David Levinsky* (New York, 1917; Philip Roth, "Eli the Fanatic," in *Goodbye, Columbus* (New York, 1959), pp. 180–216. In the intervening years, see the work of, among others, Arthur Miller, Jerome Weidman, Budd Schulberg, and Myron S. Kaufman.

50. Norman Podhoretz, *Making It* (New York, 1967), esp. xi–xvii.

Marcia Graham Synnott

Anti-Semitism and American Universities: Did Quotas Follow the Jews?

"Lowell Tells Jews Limit At Colleges Might Help Them," reported the *New York Times* on its front page of June 17, 1922. Never before had an American university president stated so frankly his reasons for limiting various national and racial groups, especially Jews, to certain percentages within the college population. Unless their numbers were reduced, he feared that anti-Semitism might become so strong that Jewish students would be excluded altogether from colleges, a process that had already occurred at clubs, hotels, and private preparatory schools. "If every college in the country would take a limited proportion of Jews"—Harvard had then almost 22 percent but could "effectively educate" only about 15 percent—"we should go a long way," he insisted, "toward eliminating race feeling among the students, and, as these students passed out into the world, eliminating it in the community." Quotas, openly worked out in cooperation with Jews, were preferable to the "indirect methods" already adopted by private colleges in New York City.[1]

President A. Lawrence Lowell's candor backfired. After thoroughly investigating the records of Jewish students in selected classes from 1900 to 1922, the special university Committee on Methods of Sifting Candidates for Admission recommended, in April 1923, that "Harvard College maintain its traditional [admissions] policy of freedom from discrimination on grounds of race or religion." Their other recommendations—to raise admissions standards and to attract more students from the South and the West—did not reduce the percentage of Jewish freshmen, which rose to 27.6 percent (243 out of 880) in 1925. The next year, Lowell achieved with minimal controversy the objective which had previously eluded him: Harvard limited the freshman class to 1,000 students, who would be selected not only for scholarship but also for "character and fitness and the promise of the greatest usefulness in the future as a result of a Harvard education." Using its discretion, the Committee on Admission began "to reduce their 25% Hebrew total to 15% or less by simply rejecting without detailed explanation."[2]

Harvard's ultimate adoption of a Jewish quota indicated what took place behind-the-scenes, between the late 1910s and the mid-1940s, at most eastern private liberal arts colleges for men and women and nationally at such professional schools as medicine, dentistry, and law. Though few presidents were as candid as Lowell, admissions officers at private and some public institutions followed instructions of administrators and trustees that they select only a certain percentage of Jews each year, usually under 10 to 15 percent. The limitation of Jewish students was an essential function of those colleges, universities, and professional schools that sought to perpetuate the economic and social position of middle- and upper-middle-class, white, native-born Protestants. Academic anti-Semitism had a reciprocal relationship, moreover, with discrimination in employment. Few manufacturing companies, corporate law firms, private hospitals, or such governmental bureaucracies as the State Department welcomed Jews as businessmen, lawyers, doctors, or career diplomats. This pattern of exclusion, begun in college and extended to business and professional life, did not change significantly until after World War II.

From its origins through its crystallization and extension to its breakdown, the history of Jewish quotas, from the 1870s to the 1970s, falls into three periods of approximately thirty years each: 1870–1917 (pattern of anti-Semitic discriminations established and then intensified by large-scale Jewish immigration from eastern Europe and Russia); 1918–1947 (adoption of quotas in eastern liberal arts colleges and professional schools and their extension to other parts of the nation); and 1948 to the 1970s (decline of quotas as a result of their exposure in reports on educational discrimination and civil rights, the consequent enactment of fair educational practices laws, and a brief period of "meritocratic" admissions, followed by the adoption of "benign" quotas to increase the representation of racial minorities, perhaps, as some have claimed, at the expense of Jews and other white ethnic groups).

Enrollment statistics from 1908 to 1947, from the earliest evidence of significant first- and second-generation Jewish representation in higher education to postwar studies of anti-Semitic admissions policies, suggest that quotas did follow the Jews. Institutional and regional variations related to the size of the Jewish population occurred in the extent of their adoption and in the severity with which they were imposed. Without question, New York City and New England institutions, which received the most applications from Jews, discriminated the most against Jewish applicants. During the 1920s, in reaction to quotas in the Northeast, Jews applied in increasing numbers to colleges and universities in the East North Central, East South Central, and South Atlantic states. Then, between 1925 and 1946, as Jews encountered geographic restrictions outside their home area, more began to apply "to their own state-supported institutions" in the Middle Atlantic and Pacific Coast states, which "increased their facilites to meet the growing demands for college training." On the whole, Jewish applicants to midwestern, Pacific Coast, and southern universities experienced only slight or moderate discrimination, except at some private colleges and professional schools, where it was frequently severe until after World War II.[3]

The social discrimination against German Jews on the East Coast, which began in the 1870s as they joined the "middle-class scramble for prestige" by seeking entrance to summer resorts, professional associations, city and country clubs, college fraternities, and desirable residential housing, intensified with the influx of hundred of thousands of Jewish immigrants from eastern Europe and Russia. Prior to the Russian pogroms of the 1880s, the American Jewish community had numbered around 250,000 out of 50,189,209, about one-half of 1 percent of the national population. In New York City, the number of Jewish residents rose from an estimated 80,000 (under 9 percent) in 1870 to almost 1,400,000 (close to 28 percent) by 1915. The timing and rapidity of this Jewish immigration and its concentration in a few geographical areas of the United States, principally in and around New York City, were major factors in the origin of the "Jewish problem" and the subsequent decision to "solve" it by quotas. These new immigrants entered the United States and then American colleges and universities at a time when both were adjusting to the demands of an expanding industrial economy and the social aspirations of a ballooning new white-collar middle class. To accommodate the growing applicant pool, colleges and universities increased their undergraduate enrollments from about 44,000 in 1890 to about 82,000 or 2.4 percent of college-aged students in 1900. By 1930–31, enrollments had climbed to 1,101,000 or about 7.2 percent of 18-to-24-year-olds. By 1946–47, including veterans, 2,078,000 or 12.5 percent of 18-to-24-year-olds would be enrolled in all degree programs out of a total population of 141,389,000.[4]

Jews were the most educationally mobile of all first-generation immigrants, despite the fact that their parents were usually manual workers. In the 1908 Immigration Commission survey of eighty-five higher educational institutions, first generation male and female Jewish students (1,207 or 3.7 percent of all the college students tabulated), most of whom (900) had been born in Russia, outnumbered the other foreign-born groups. Together, first and second generation Jewish males were 8.44 percent (2,177) of the 25,779 males in the survey. When 315 Jewish women were included, the 2,492 native-born of foreign father and the foreign-born Jews were 7.57 percent of the total 32,882 students surveyed. Although first and second generation Germans (2,669 or 8.11 percent of the total) outnumbered Jews, only 346 of them were foreign-born. The Irish also entered college in the second generation (1,408), rather than in the first (133). By 1918, Jewish enrollment in the nine largest higher educational institutions in the New York area reached 38.5 percent (7,148) of the 18,552 students; at the College of Dental and Oral Surgery, Jewish students were 80.9 percent of the enrollment.[5]

Their conspicuous academic success made Jews potential economic competitors of the white, native-born, Protestant middle class. Competition increased with the transformation of the college from "a cloister" for schooling gentlemen to a "workshop" for preparing middle-class sons (and occasionally, daughters) to enter the marketplace. "Our modern industrial professions," commented Edwin E. Slosson in 1909–10, were "assuming the arrogance of the old clerical professions. As education has become more vocational, the trades union idea has come in. An engineer who has invested $5000 or $10,000 in an education as a capital or his life work . . . is . . . in favor of the limitation of apprentices. Raising fees and admission requirements is now not always looked upon as a disagreeable necessity, but rather welcomed as a good thing because it 'keeps out the muckers.' " Led by medicine, the professional schools and vocationally oriented academic departments were becoming guilds, in which membership was granted to those who shared not only common aims, but also common backgrounds. Following the publication of Abraham Flexner's 1910 report on "Medical Education in the United States and Canada," that exposed the "enormous over-production of uneducated and ill-trained medical practitioners," inferior commercial medical schools were eliminated, thereby reducing from 162 to 76 the number of those accredited. In order to ensure places for native-born, white, Protestant applicants, medical school admissions officers added religious and social criteria to academic qualifications. The obvious targets of restriction or exclusion were Jews, Catholics, Negroes, and women.[6]

Concurrently with the development of the "guild spirit" came the intensification of the "caste spirit" on campus. Imitating the social snobbery of city and country clubs, Greek letter societies excluded Jews (at City College of New York as early as 1878), although in the past they had occasionally admitted Sephardic and German Jews to membership. By the turn of the century, a well-developed social system, averaging about a dozen chapters of national fraternities, existed at both private colleges and state universities. In response, Jews began, in 1898, to form parallel social organizations; Zeta Beta Tau, the first, established chapters at CCNY (1903) and Columbia University (1904). By 1923, ZBT had founded over thirty permanent chapters in all regions of the country: for example, University of Pennsylvania and Cornell (1907); Boston University (1908); Tulane (1909); Louisiana State University, Massachusetts Institute of Technology, and Ohio State (1911); Harvard and the universities of Illinois and Michigan (1912); universities of Virginia and Alabama (1915 and 1916); universities of Chicago, Southern California, and Vanderbilt (1918); Washington and Lee (1920); University of California and Yale (1921). Whereas ZBT recruited sons of Sephardic and German families, the next largest fraternity, Sigma Alpha Mu, founded at

CCNY in 1909, pledged the newer Jews of eastern European origin. By 1927, there were twenty-two national Greek letter Jewish fraternities and three sororities, with 401 chapters serving almost 25,000 students in 114 out of 139 universities.[7]

Many Jews seeking higher education and professional positions experienced double exclusion from both caste and guild systems. Ludwig Lewisohn, who in 1890 had emigrated with his parents from Berlin to South Carolina, wrote poignantly about his yearning to be accepted as classmate and colleague. He had not been invited to join the Greek letter fraternity at the College of Charleston and, after graduate work at Columbia University, had been denied a position as an English instructor by the universities of Minnesota and Virginia. Teaching German at Ohio State University, Lewisohn found that native-born American students came "not to find truth, but to be engineers or farmers, doctors or teachers. They did not want to be different men and women." College reinforced, rather than modified, ethnic stereotypes and social prejudices, because faculty members, alumni, and public opinion held that Anglo-Saxon or Nordic "races" and their "American" offspring set the standards of achievement and behavior against which all other "races" should be judged.[8]

Although American educators saw themselves as standing above the crude prejudices of the common people, they, too, were deeply influenced by ideas of "superior" and "inferior" races, ranked according to mental abilities, morals, and physical features. During the years 1918 to 1947, pervasive social snobbery and professional exclusiveness fused with quasi-scientific assumptions about "survival of the fittest" races and with "One Hundred Percent Americanism" to justify the almost simultaneous adoption of national immigration and college admission quotas. This fusion occurred in President Lowell of Harvard, who also served as national vice-president of the Immigration Restriction League. Identifying democracy with a homogeneous population, he believed that only races capable of being assimilated within a few generations—northern Europeans—should be admitted to the United States and to Harvard. Both the country and the college had to protect themselves from the ethnic and religious antagonisms caused by Gentile anti-Semitism and Jewish "clannishness." Noting the post–World War I revival of anti-Semitism in Europe, Lowell saw it as "a new problem" in the United States, one which "did not originate here, but has been brought over from Europe—especially from those counties where it has existed for centuries."[9]

Indeed, Russia and eastern European countries imposed quotas on Jewish students as a means of controlling social tensions. Beginning in 1882, Tsar Alexander III had restricted the admission of Jewish students to 5 to 10 percent at universities and to 3 percent at engineering and technical schools. In September, in reaction to the large migration of Jews to the state universities of eastern Europe, the Hungarian Parliament enacted a 10 percent quota on Jewish university students. Two years later, anti-Semitic outbursts erupted at the four large Polish state universities of Cracow, Lemberg, Vilna, and Warsaw, and at the universities of Vienna and Bucharest.[10]

Anti-Semitism took a more virulent form in the state universities of central and eastern Europe than it did in American colleges and universities, yet striking parallels existed between its occurrences in both places. The catalyst was similar. In eastern Europe, it was refugee Jewish students displaced by World War I and its revolutionary aftermath; in the United States, it was first- and second-generation Russian Jewish immigrants. The earliest public signs of efforts to limit their enrollment occurred in both eastern Europe and the United States between 1919 and 1923. Although anti-Semitism never gained in the United States the political currency (a legislated *numerus clausus*), even respectability, it attained in Europe, American university administrators sought a similar solution to the "Jewish problem": a percentage limitation on their admission, albeit quietly implemented.

An early documented discussion showing official concern that American colleges might soon be overrun by Jews took place among representatives of Bowdoin, Brown, MIT, Tufts, and Yale at the May 1918 meeting of the Association of New England Deans at Princeton University. The following year, led by President Nicholas Murray Butler, Columbia University became the first of the elite private institutions to adopt a psychological test and new admissions form for the specific purpose of reducing Jewish enrollment. Based on the Army Alpha Tests used during World War I and improved by E. L. Thorndike of Columbia Teachers College, the psychological test measured innate ability—and middle-class home environment. The new application blank asked religious affiliation, father's name and birthplace, and required a photograph and a personal interview for local candidates. During the next three years, as the percentage of New York area residents at Columbia College (the undergraduate college of Columbia University) dropped, Jewish enrollment in the freshman class correspondingly fell from 40 to 20 percent. So that its student body would regain an "American" quality, in September 1919 New York University also required all incoming freshmen to the University Heights campus to take "a personnel and psychological examination" measuring "moral values."[11]

Within a few years, private liberal arts colleges in New England followed suit and cut Jewish admissions. In 1922–23, while Harvard debated whether it had a "Jewish problem," Yale discovered one with its New Haven applicants. When the adoption of a proposal to limit the freshman class size to 850 students failed to reduce significantly the number of Jews, Yale entrusted to its Board of Admissions discretionary authority to decide which ones and how many should be admitted annually. The class of 1927 had reached a high of 13.3 percent Jews; the class of 1928 had just 10 percent (88 out of 880). During the next decade, Jewish enrollment at Yale fluctuated between 8.2 and 12.7 percent (see Table 1).[12]

Of the eight Ivy League colleges, Cornell, Brown, and the University of Pennsylvania remained relatively open to Jewish students. Although Jewish enrollment may ultimately have been limited at all three, it did not drop sharply, as it did at Columbia and Harvard. Instead, Jewish representation seemed to level off in the early 1930s: about 12 percent at Cornell, 14 percent at Brown, and 20 percent at the University of Pennsylvania. Institutional leadership, land-grant origin, and urban location were factors that could lessen anti-Semitism. For example, as partly a land-grant college, Cornell was more in tune with the spirit of the state universities. Opened in 1869, it was the youngest of the Ivy League colleges, the other seven having been founded between 1636 (Harvard) and 1769 (Dartmouth). Attracting foreign students, Cornell's campus was fairly cosmopolitan, although separate gentile and Jewish fraternities had developed. Both presidents Livingston Farrand (1921–37) and Edmund Ezra Day (1937–49), moreover, had opposed quotas.[13]

Liberal elements ultimately prevailed at Pennsylvania and at Brown. A close connection existed between the city of Philadelphia and the University of Pennsylvania in terms of student clientele

TABLE 1
Number and Percentage of Jewish Students at Selected Colleges and Universities, 1908–35

	1908–9	1915–16	1918–19	1920–30	1934–35
		I. Elite Eastern Private Colleges and Universities			
Amherst		14/430 3.25%	8/421 1.9%		45/770 5.84%
Barnard	20/455 4.39%	.....[a]	249/3,194[a] 7.79%		.....[a]
Bowdoin			14/774 1.8%		37/580 6.37%
Brown	20/880[b] 2.27%	44/1,114 3.95%	34/1,140 2.98%		286/2,016 14.18%
Bryn Mawr		18/455 3.95%	13/454 2.86%		30/486 6.17%
Colgate			5/137 3.64%		10/971 1.02%
Columbia	146/1,283 11.37%	1,204/7,652[a] 15.73%	1,226/3,749[a] 32.7%	18–22%[c]	2,598/17,751[a] 14.63%
Cornell		435/5,416 8.03%	317/3,505 9.04%	650/5,500[d] 11.81%	737/5,910 12.47%
Dartmouth		48/1,468 3.26%	33/1,173 2.81%		140/2,422 5.78%
Harvard	99/2,273[e] 4.35%	402/5,228 7.68%	385/3,843 10.01%	243/880[f] 27.61%	1,322/7,729 17.1% 165/1,028[f] 16.05%
Mt. Holyoke		9/1,171 .007%			15/929 1.61%
Pennsylvania	7/233[e] 3%	564/8,069 6.98%	596/4,072 14.63%	(Wharton)[g] 27%	1,813/9,126 19.86%
Princeton	11/362[h] 3.03%	39/1,615 2.41%	30/1,142 2.62%	25/635[h] 3.93%	51/2,295 2.22%
Radcliffe	12/445 2.69%			12%[i]	135/990 13.63%
Smith		56/1,725 3.24%	99/2,103 4.7%		208/1,896 10.97%
Vassar		24/1,125 2.13%	37/1,122 3.29%	4.5%[j]	66/1,216 5.42%

Table 1 *(Continued)*

	1908–9	*1915–16*	*1918–19*	*1920–30*	*1934–35*
Wellesley		49/1,512 3.24%			197/1,541 12.78%
Wesleyan		9/504 1.78%			30/620 4.83%
Williams			7/481 1.45%		37/792 4.67%
Yale	70/1,314[k] 5.32%	165/3,260 5.06%	113/1,487[k] 7.59%	115/863[k] 13.32%	525/5,362 9.79%

II. New York City Area Colleges and Universities (except Barnard and Columbia)

	1908–9	*1915–16*	*1918–19*	*1920–30*	*1934–35*
Adelphi	7/121 5.78%		42/309 13.59%		140/431 32.48%
Brooklyn (opened 1932)					6,856/9,162 74.83%
Brooklyn Polytechnic Institute	55/344 15.98%	209/758 27.57%	97/329 29.48%		
College of the City of New York	503/676 74.4%	8,061/9,484 84.99%	1,544/1,961 78.73%		17,752/22,175 80.05%
Cooper Union					534/1,417 37.68%
Fordham	1/104		290/1,247 23.25%		726/5,966 12.16%
Hunter		457/1,590 28.74%	502/1,295 38.76%	85%[j]	7,920/11,892 66.59%
Long Island University					840/1,331 63.11%
New School for Social Research					3,000/5,000 60%
New York University	13/36 36.11%	1,768/8,428 20.97%	2,532/5,536 45.73%		12,709/28,291 44.92%
St. John's University					2,897/6,156 47.05%

III. Other Eastern Colleges and Universities (New England and Middle Atlantic States)

	1908–9	*1915–16*	*1918–19*	*1920–30*	*1934–35*
Boston University	2/266 .0075%		169/1,714 9.85%		1,258/10,031 12.54%

Table 1 *(Continued)*

	1908–9	*1915–16*	*1918–19*	*1920–30*	*1934–35*
Carnegie Institute of Technology					281/3,786 7.42%
Clark University	5/107 4.67%		17/233 7.29%		57/572 9.96%
Colby College					50/600 8.33%
Connecticut State College					130/728 17.85%
Dana College					371/1,605 23.11%
Duquesne University					232/2,358 9.83%
Lehigh University		28/775 3.61%	48/1,511 3.17%		85/1,541 5.51%
Massachusetts Institute of Technology	29/973 2.98%				258/2,525 10.21%
New Jersey Normal School at Newark					108/509 21.21%
Northeastern University					562/3,794 14.81%
Pennsylvania State College		50/3,555 1.4%			346/5,238 6.6%
Pittsburgh		195/3,951 4.93%	443/3,627 12.21%		897/6,362 14.09%
Rhode Island State College			9/255 3.52%		81/1,048 7.72%
Rochester			27/561 4.81%		108/1,271 8.49%
Rutgers		39/460 8.47%	43/512 8.39%		468/2,550 18.35%
Sarah Lawrence					27/271 9.96%
Simmons	1/508 .0019%		52/1,251 4.15%		183/1,613 11.34%
Skidmore School of Arts			2/197 1.01%		42/635 6.61%

243

Table 1 *(Continued)*

	1908–9	1915–16	1918–19	1920–30	1934–35
Syracuse		333/4,020 8.28%	199/3,317 5.99%		527/6,726 7.83%
Temple	4/89 4.49%	684/3,696 18.5%	266/1,854 14.34%		2,170/9,960 21.78%
Tufts	4/392[l] 1.02%	213/1,541 13.82%	310/1,635 18.96%	15%[j]	402/2,043 19.67%
Vermont		14/602 2.32%	22/658 3.34%		120/1,270 9.44%
U.S. Military Academy			22/994 2.21%		17/1,560 1.08%
Worcester Polytechnic Institute	0/473	9/543 1.65%	22/473 4.65%		40/593 6.74%

IV. Middle Western Colleges and Universities
(East and West North Central States)

	1908–9	1915–16	1918–19	1920–30	1934–35
Armour Institute of Technology	39/548 7.11%		95/605 15.7%		92/837 10.99%
Chicago	52/1,194 4.35%		761/4,106 18.53%	15–20%[m]	1,082/6,158 17.65%
Cincinnati	22/462[b] 4.76%	154/2,635 5.84%	167/1,987 8.4%		944/9,570 9.86%
Detroit Institute of Technology					300/1,539 19.49%
Illinois, Urbana		379/6,427 5.89%	264/6,207 4.25%		855/9,433 9.06%
Illinois, Chicago (professional)					475/1,059 44.85%
Lewis Institute					519/3,036 17.09%
Marquette					282/3,092 9.12%
Michigan		437/6,284 6.95%	297/7,311 4.06%		1,392/11,638 11.96%
Minnesota	4/998 .004%				1,125/14,022 8.02%

Table 1 (*Continued*)

	1908–9	1915–16	1918–19	1920–30	1934–35
Missouri		162/4,349 3.72%	103/3,510 2.93%		238/3,801 6.26%
Northwestern	2/336[b] .0059%	273/5,293 5.15%	221/3,194 6.91%		652/6,300 10.34%
Oberlin		59/1,749 3.37%	12/1,129 1.06%		50/1,696 2.94%
Ohio State		106/5,822 1.82%	234/5,188 4.51%		1,013/13,505 7.5%
Purdue		12/2,473 .0048%	24/2,553 .0094%	2%[i]	88/4,534 1.94%
Washington University					642/3,400 18.88%
Wayne State					1,019/6,015 16.94%
Western Reserve	10/528[b] 1.89%		269/1,838 14.63%		899/9,077 9.9%
Wisconsin			143/4,314 3.31%		872/8,657 10.07%

V. Southern Colleges and Universities
(South Atlantic, East and West South Central States)

	1908–9	1915–16	1918–19	1920–30	1934–35
Alabama					375/4,700 7.97%
Arkansas					148/2,119 6.98%
Baltimore, University of					250/1,200 20.83%
College of Charleston					34/414 8.21%
Delaware			5/301 1.66%		59/760 7.76%
Duke					79/3,214 2.45%
Emory					101/1,646 6.13%
Florida					153/2,982 5.13%

Table 1 *(Continued)*

	1908–9	*1915–16*	*1918–19*	*1920–30*	*1934–35*
Georgia		19/1,873 1.01%	21/854 2.45%		129/2,584 4.99%
Georgetown					135/2,096 6.44%
George Washington		160/1,767 9.05%			321/4,631 6.93%

Goucher
  (Women's College
  of Baltimore)
	2/291
	.0068%
					164/630
					21.26%

Johns Hopkins	9/132 6.81%	100/649 15.4%	322/1,983 16.23%		709/4,031 17.58%
Louisiana State		19/842 2.25%			128/5,901 2.16%
Louisville				8-9%[j]	160/2,982 5.36%
Kentucky		34/1,445 2.35%	25/1,204 2.07%		46/3,270 1.4%
Maryland, College Park		18/612 2.94%		under 10%[j]	223/2,002 11.13%
Maryland, Baltimore					457/1,410 32.41%
National University					161/1,155 13.93%
North Carolina, Chapel Hill		8/1,158 .0069%			261/4,063 6.42% 14%[n]
Randolph-Macon College for Women			2/610 .0032%		13/607 2.14%
Rice Institute					75/1,282 5.85%
Sophie Newcomb					100/650 15.38%
Texas		66/2,434 2.71%	42/3,216 1.3%		346/7,662 4.51%
Tulane		54/2,708 1.99%	133/1,880 7.07%	7%[j]	250/2,527 9.89%
Vanderbilt			12/477 2.51%	7%[j]	94/1,443 6.51%

Table 1 *(Continued)*

	1908–9	1915–16	1918–19	1920–30	1934–35
Virginia			51/1,399 3.64%		201/2,435 8.25%
U.S. Naval Academy					32/1,977 1.61%
Washington and Lee			12/504 2.38%		47/874 5.37%
William and Mary					78/1,205 6.47%

VI. Far Western Colleges and Universities
(Mountain and Pacific States)

	1908–9	1915–16	1918–19	1920–30	1934–35
Arizona				2%[i]	85/2,640 3.21%
California Institute of Technology					24/753 3.18%
California, Berkeley	18/2,225[b] .008%		268/7,286 3.67%		983/13,251 7.41%
California, Los Angeles					775/6,896 11.23%
Colorado		32/1,402 2.28%	50/1,651 3.02%		51/3,479 1.46%
Denver		62/1,456 4.25%	36/856 4.2%	12.5%[i]	166/2,670 6.21%
Los Angeles Junior College					227/4,739 4.79%
Mills					22/471 4.67%
Reed			10/338 2.95%		45/448 10.04%
Southern California			61/3,636 1.67%		325/4,000 8.12%
Stanford					125/4,346 2.87%
Washington					338/9,954 3.39%

Source: For 1908–9, see U.S. Congress, Senate, Reports of the Immigration Commission, *Children of Immigrants in Schools,* 61st Cong., 3d sess., 1910–11, S. Doc. 749, vol. 5, *Students in Higher Educational*

Institutions, Table 1, Number of students within each specified age group, by institution and by general nativity and race of student, Academic and Engineering and technological, pp. 715–23, 725–26, 728, 730, 732–38, 740–42, 744, 746, 748–53. For 1915–16, see Table Showing Enrollment of Jewish Students in American Colleges and Universities in 1915–16 (From the *Menorah Journal*, Oct. 1916), *American Jewish Year Book, 5678* 19 (Sept. 17, 1917–Sept. 6, 1918): 407–8. In the fifty-seven leading institutions surveyed, Jewish students numbered 17,653 or 11.9 percent of 147,352. For 1918–19, see Table 1, Number and Proportion of Jewish Students Enrolled in 106 Colleges, Universities and Professional Schools in the U.S. for Scholastic Year 1918–19, *American Jewish Year Book, 5681* 22 (Sept. 13, 1920–Oct. 2, 1921): 387–89. Jews numbered 14,837 or 9.7 percent of the 153,084 students enrolled. Discrepancies exist between the 1915–16 and 1918–19 figures for certain institutions because some were estimates and the 1918–19 table divided enrollments into male and female; World War 1 caused a decline in male students. For 1934–35, see Table A, Detailed List of 1319 colleges with Number of Jewish Students, accompanying Dr. Lee J. Levinger, *The Jewish Student in America: A Study Made By The Research Bureau Of The B'nai B'rith Hillel Foundations* (Cincinnati, 1937), and Dan W. Dodson, "Religious Prejudice in Colleges," *American Mercury* 63 (July 1946): 11–12.

a See Columbia University, whose enrollment figures included women students.
b Cincinnati and Northwestern included male and female academic and engineering and technological students; Brown and California (Berkeley), male and female academic and male engineering; Western Reserve, male and female academic and female technological students.
c Approximate percentages from 1921 to 1940s; see Harold S. Wechsler, *The Qualified Student: A History of Selective College Admission in America* (New York, 1977), pp. 163–64.
d Saul R. Kelson, "Jewish Students on the Cornell Campus, A Revealing Survey of their Academic and Extra-Curricular Participation," *American Hebrew* 128 (Dec. 19, 1930): 160.
e Harvard and Pennsylvania (one female academic) male academic and engineering students.
f Freshmen only entering in fall of 1925 and 1938; see Marcia Graham Synnott, *The Half-Opened Door: Discrimination and Admissions at Harvard, Yale, and Princeton, 1900–1970* (Westport, Conn., 1979), pp. 107, 112, 115 (table), and 261 n. 59.
g "May Jews Go to College?" The Nation 114 (June 14, 1922): 708.
h For classes entering in 1908 and 1922, see *Princeton University, President's Annual Report, January 1st, 1909* and tables in Synnott, *The Half-Opened Door*, pp. 181–82, 195.
i Estimated by Rabbi Leon Spitz, as cited in Heywood Broun and George Britt, *Christians Only: A Study in Prejudice* (New York, 1931), p. 59.
j *Jewish Daily Bulletin* Spring 1930, survey of thirty-six institutions, in Broun and Britt, *Christians Only*, pp. 94–95.
k For classes of 1911–14, 1919–22, and class of 1927, see tables in Synnott, *The Half-Opened Door*, pp. 143, 158.
l Tufts male and female engineering and technological students.
m Wechsler, *The Qualified Student*, pp. 221, 230, 235–36 n. 48: Floyd W. Reeves and John Dale Russell, *The Alumni of the Colleges*, University of Chicago Survey no. 6 (1933), p. 15.
n Over 14 percent of the 1936 freshman class was Jewish; see n. 33, Kemp D. Battle to Frank P. Graham, Nov. 17, Dec. 3, 1936, President's Papers, University of North Carolina, no. 9033, file 494.

seeking admission to its vocationally oriented schools. Together, the Wharton School of Finance and Commerce and the Evening School of Accounts and Finance enrolled more than twice as many students as the liberal arts division. Despite strong efforts during the 1920s to turn the university into a "country college," which would be "an oasis of quietude" and reflection, conservative alumni could not stop "the democracy of the street car," which brought to campus "the more ambitious boys of the city masses." In 1925, Brown yielded to Rhode Island's tradition of religious toleration and to alumni pressure and petitioned the state legislature to delete from its charter the restriction that its president must be a Baptist. (The administration also denied recognition, for a time, to a Jewish fraternity, because it was organized along "religious" lines.)[14]

In contrast to city institutions, which politically could not afford to be too exclusive, small liberal arts colleges located in country towns usually had the tightest restrictions on Jews. Princeton and Dartmouth, like Amherst, Bowdoin, Colgate, and Williams, had no local "Jewish problem" but wanted to preserve their social homogeneity. Princeton relied on the reputation of its upper-class eating clubs, which virtually excluded Jews, to discourage their application. As a reinforcement, in 1922–23, it inaugurated a "selective admission" policy: the number of Jewish students declined from 25 out of 635 in the class of 1926 to 5 out of 635 in the class of 1935. Until 1950, when Princeton dropped the question on religious preference from its application form, Jewish enrollment averaged around 3 to 4 percent, roughly the proportion of Jews in the national population. Dartmouth used its alumni as a screening device in the admissions process by requiring every applicant to secure a written reference from an alumnus or an undergraduate. In the spring of 1930, 7 percent of the freshman class was Jewish; by 1936, only 25 to 30 Jews were accepted or 5 percent of the 500 or so Jewish applicants. Just before leaving the presidency which he had held for thirty years, Ernest M. Hopkins defended Dartmouth's limitation on Jewish enrollment as the only way to prevent anti-Semitism from increasing in the United States as it had in Nazi Germany. Echoing Lowell, he insisted that Dartmouth " 'would lose its racial tolerance' " were it " 'to accept unexamined the great blocs of Jewish applications which come in, for instance, from the New York high schools and other great metropolitan centers.' " Dartmouth was, moreover, a " 'Christian college founded for the Christianization of its students.' "[15]

Catering to the same middle- and upper-class, native-born Protestant clientele as the Ivy League colleges, the "Seven Sister" colleges of Barnard, Bryn Mawr, Mount Holyoke, Radcliffe, Smith, Vassar, and Wellesley carefully watched their Jewish enrollments. By the 1940s, they collectively had the reputation for "flagrant discrimination," although the percentage of Jews admitted varied considerably among them. From 1916 to 1934, for example, Vassar admitted only between 2 and 5 percent (66 out of 1,216 Jewish students. It had used "two admission lists," one for the early registration of alumnae daughters and the other for the "competitive honor group" of about 100 students. In selecting the latter, the Committee on Admission gave preference, when records were equal, to "a girl from a small high school in Nevada or Georgia."[16]

In the 1930s, Mount Holyoke and Bryn Mawr admitted few Jews, respectively 2 and 6 percent. As president of Bryn Mawr (1894–1922), M. Carey Thomas had collected data on the ancestries of entering freshmen and embraced the Anglo-Saxon racism of Lothrop Stoddard and immigration restriction. She also blocked both the admission of black students and the promotion of Jewish instructors. When Columbia College cut its Jewish enrollment in half, Barnard, too, probably limited their admission (and, at the same time, endeavored to exclude blacks). The three women's colleges with the highest percentages of Jewish students—Radcliffe (13.6), Smith (11), and Wellesley (12.8)—were also the ones, according to W. E. B. Du Bois, which received Negro students "with tolerance and even cordiality."[17]

Even though discrimination against Jewish applicants by the elite private men's and women's colleges affected a relatively small percentage of the total number of Jewish students, the admission policies of these schools set the course for those of another 700 or so liberal arts colleges. They made the aura of exclusivity a desirable commodity for the college-seeking clientele. They also justified, if not made quite respectable, the "right" of a college to use various devices "to prevent itself from becoming a Jewish institution, as it would become if everything were competitive." The most common device, which would be employed by 90 percent of American colleges and universities, was the inclusion on the application form of a question on religious preference, and, for additional checks, questions on nationality and race. Some devices, such as restrictions on scholarship aid and placement on a waiting list, obviously discriminated against Jews, while others were more subtle: enrollment limitation, required campus residency and chapel attendance, rejection of transfer students, and preference for alumni sons and daughters. A combination of devices usually achieved the desired limitation on the number of Jews, which might fluctuate a few percentage points from year to year to blunt charges of discrimination.[18]

Discrimination by private liberal arts colleges effected a shift in enrollment patterns: in 1935, Jews were 10.2 percent of the students in men's colleges and 11.8 percent in women's colleges; by 1946, their percentages had dropped, respectively, to 4.7 and 8.4. Concurrently, the percentage of Jewish students attending co-educational schools, mostly public institutions, rose from 7.2 to 9.5 percent. Overall, by 1946, 90.2 percent of all Jewish students were in co-educational schools, while 5.3 and 4.5 percent, respectively, were in women's and men's schools. Because over two-thirds of Jewish high school seniors applied to college, compared to somewhat over one-third of Protestants and one-fourth of Catholics, Jewish students were represented in higher educational institutions above their proportion in the population. In 1934–35, for example, Jews were 9.13 percent (104,906) of 1,148,393 students enrolled in 1,319 colleges and universities and 3.5 percent (4,500,000) of the national population of 128,053,000. Because of multiple applications, 87 percent of Jews, as opposed to 88 percent of Protestants and 81 percent of Catholics, were admitted to some college; but only 56 percent of all Jewish applications were successful, in contrast to 77 percent of Protestant and 67 percent of Catholic ones.[19]

"If discrimination in the colleges is an ugly inconvenience for Jews," wrote historian Edward N. Saveth in 1950, "discrimination in admission to medical schools is a constantly burning wound." Not until the 1930s, however, did the national percentage of Jewish medical students begin to decline, despite the sharp reduction in the number of accredited schools following the Flexner report. In 1908, Jews were 7 percent (302) of the 4,322 students in the thirty medical schools surveyed by the Immigration Commission. By 1918, their numbers had climbed to 16.4 percent; between 1935 and 1946, their numbers dropped from 15.9 to 12.7 percent in sixty-seven out of eighty-nine schools. In reaction to declining income during the Depression, in 1933 the Council on Medical Education of the American Medical Association urged a drastic reduction in the number of physicians trained. Nationally, the number of Jewish medical students fell from 912 in the 1933 freshman class to 617 three years later. The class of 1940 had only 477 Jews.[20]

The first restrictions on the number of Jewish medical students began when Columbia's College of Physicians and Surgeons cut its Jewish enrollment, which had exceeded 50 percent in the class of 1923, to under 20 percent in the class of 1928. By 1940, it was down to 6.4 percent. Cornell's Medical School also imposed a "rigid" quota, which reduced Jewish admissions from about 40 percent in 1920 to 5 percent in 1940. The New York Homeopathic Medical College and the Long Island Hospital Medical College introduced quotas more slowly: between 1929 and 1934, the former reduced its Jewish representation from 68.82 to 33.65 percent; the latter began in 1932 to reduce its 42.24 percent Jewish population to 14.14 percent by 1940. New York University School of Medicine was the only one of the five that approached a policy of non-discrimination: between 1929 and 1934, Jews numbered over 69 percent of its medical students; by 1940, they numbered 40 to 50 percent.[21]

New York City Jewish applicants had only one chance in four of being admitted to one of the five medical schools. From 1929 to 1946, their representation in these schools had dropped from 43 percent to 30 percent, although Jews were frequently three-fourths of the applicants. Concurrently, Jewish medical enrollment declined at four Philadelphia schools, from 103 in 1934 to 58 two years later. Indeed, between 1935 and 1946, Jewish enrollment fell in most regions: in New England, from 15.2 to 8.8 percent; in the East North Central states, from 31.3 to 17.9 percent; in the South Atlantic states, from 14.5 to 5.8 percent; and in the Mountain states, from 11.9 to 5.6 percent. Many Jews were among the 1,471 Americans who enrolled, in 1934–35, in Canadian and foreign medical schools. More than 10 percent of the enrollment at six of Canada's ten medical schools was Jewish, ranging from 32.57 percent (57 out of 175) at Dalhousie and 26.73 percent (54 out of 202) at the University of Manitoba to 10.71 percent (54 out of 504) at McGill. By 1943, however, the medical demands of World War II began significantly to raise Jewish admissions at American schools; for example, to the class of 1946, Columbia admitted about 30 Jews out of 119 students (see Table 2).[22]

Candid comments by medical school administrators supported the "overwhelming" discriminatory data. Concerned with Jewish "overrepresentation," but not with the "underrepresentation" of Negroes, Dean Willard C. Rappleye of the College of Physicians and Surgeons argued " 'that the representation of the various social, religious and racial groups in medicine ought to be kept

TABLE 2
Number and Percentage of Jewish Students at Selected Medical Schools, 1908–46

	1908–9	1918–22	1929–30	1934–35	1940–41	1945–46
I. New York City Area Medical Schools						
Columbia University College of Physicians and Surgeons	58/322 18.01%	48–52/98[a] 49–53%	25–30/115[a] 22–26%	48/421 11.4%	8/124 6.45%	30–36/111[a] 27–32%
Cornell University School of Medicine	41/169 24.26%	40%[b]	30/219[c] 13.69%	25/284 8.8%	3/84[b] 3.57%	5%[b]
Long Island Hospital Medical College		189/343 55.1%	54/120[d] 45%	108/431 25.05%	14.14%	
New York Homeopathic Medical College	4/76 5.26%		245/356[d] 68.82%	52/328 15.85%	35/104[d] 33.65%	
New York University-Bellevue Hospital Medical College			69.7%[d]	410/592 69.25%		40-50%
II. New England Medical Schools						
Boston University	788 7.95%		200/413 48.42%	32/257 12.45%	20%	
Dartmouth				1/23 4.34%		
Harvard	10/289 3.46%	29/108[e] 26.85%	46/510 9.01%	22/529 4.15%	9.5%[f]	
Tufts			189/486 38.88%	125/473 26.42%	15%	
Vermont				46/173 26.58%		
Yale			42/215 19.53%	28/218 12.84%	12%	
III. Middle Atlantic (New York State and Pennsylvania) Medical Schools						
Buffalo				47/287 16.37%	10.91%	
Hahneman Medical College			49/455 10.76%	59/498 11.84%	9%	

253

Table 2 *(Continued)*

	1908–9	*1918–22*	*1929–30*	*1934–35*	*1940–41*	*1945–46*
Jefferson Medical College	31/331 9.36%		116/592 19.59%	151/557 27.1%		
Pennsylvania	34/542 6.27%		70/469 14.92%	91/524 17.36%		
Pittsburgh			20/260 11.53%	28/264 10.6%		
Rochester				16/167 9.58%	6%	
Syracuse			40/182 21.97%	37/197 18.78%	12.7%	3/50[g] 6%
Temple	18/60 30%		95/290 32.75%	85/448 18.97%		
Union				16/112 14.28%		
Women's Medical College of Pennsylvania	9/84 10.71%			30/132 22.72%	31%	

IV. Middle Western Medical Schools
(East and West North Central States)

	1908–9	*1918–22*	*1929–30*	*1934–35*	*1940–41*	*1945–46*
Chicago Medical				100/280 35.71%		
Chicago, University of Rush Medical College	4/80 5%		75/305 24.59%	(Division of Biology) 220/662 33.23%		
Cincinnati	4/112 3.57%		46/245 18.77%	47/291 16.15%		
Creighton			18/240 7.5%	34/298 11.4%	4%	
Detroit College of Medical Surgery	4/129 3.1%			144/401 35.91%		
Illinois	22/351 6.26%		198/575 34.43%	277/625 44.32%	41.8%	
Indiana			24/420 5.71%	40/413 9.68%		
Iowa				25/255 9.8%		

Table 2 *(Continued)*

	1908–9	1918–22	1929–30	1934–35	1940–41	1945–46
Kansas	1/53 1.88%		16/233 6.86%	9/304 2.96%		
Loyola				38/487 7.8%		
Marquette			44/345 12.75%	52/358 14.52%		
Michigan			88/636 13.83%	56/455 12.3%		
Minnesota	7/285 2.45%			76/502 15.13%		
Nebraska				20/340 5.88%		
North Dakota				4/60 6.66%		
Northwestern	4/65 6.15%			51/725 7.03%		
Ohio State			48/324 14.81%	63/371 16.98%		
South Dakota				2/56 3.57%		
Washington University	6/120 5%			52/351 14.81%		
Western Reserve	2/97 2.06%		41/241 17.01%	35/275 12.72%		
Wisconsin	2/59 3.38%			50/318 15.72%		

V. Southern Medical Schools
(South Atlantic, East and West South Central States)

	1908–9	1918–22	1929–30	1934–35	1940–41	1945–46
Alabama				14/123 11.38%		
Arkansas				29/229 12.66%		
Baylor			14/345 4.05%	52/376 13.82%		
Bowman Gray School of Medicine, Wake Forest					1.5%	

Table 2 *(Continued)*

	1908–9	1918–22	1929–30	1934–35	1940–41	1945–46
Duke				25/210 11.9%		
Emory				32/225 14.22%		
Georgetown				23/556 4.13%	8%	
George Washington			79/290 27.24%	62/295 21%		
Georgia			14/139 10.07%	20/144 13.88%		
Howard				7/203 3.44%		
Johns Hopkins	8/220 3.63%		7–11/75[d] 10–15%	45/276 16.3%		
Louisiana State				42/317 13.24%		
Louisville			52/350 14.85%	36/347 10.37%		
Maryland			200/413 48.42%	167/443 37.69%		
Medical College of South Carolina				9/181 4.97%		
Medical College of Virginia				46/332 13.85%		
Mississippi				2/49 4.08%		
North Carolina				7/66 10.6%		
Oklahoma			4/200 2%	5/243 2.05%		
Tennessee			23/405 5.67%	30/429 6.99%		
Texas			10/310 3.22%	23/362 6.35%		
Tulane				46/465 9.89%		
Vanderbilt				15/204 7.35%		

Table 2 *(Continued)*

	1908–9	1918–22	1929–30	1934–35	1940–41	1945–46
Virginia, University of			16/245 6.53%	17/245 6.93%		

VI. Far Western Medical Schools
(Mountain and Pacific States)

	1908–9	1918–22	1929–30	1934–35	1940–41	1945–46
California, Berkeley	1/31 3.22%			71/230 30.86%		
Colorado				29/224 12.94%		
Oregon				21/242 8.67%		
Southern California			(two years) 16/92 17.39%	26/176 14.77%		
Stanford				15/220 6.81%		
Utah				5/60 8.33%		

Source: For 1908–9, see Reports of the Immigration Commission, 1910-11, vol. 5, *Students in Higher Educational Institutions*, Table 1, Number of Students within each specified age group, by institution and by general nativity and race of student, Medicine, pp. 757–60, 762–75. For 1918–19, see Table 1, Number and Proportion of Jewish Students Enrolled in 106 Colleges, Universities and Professional Schools in the U.S. for Scholastic Year 1918–19, *American Jewish Year Book, 5681* 22 (Sept. 13, 1920– Oct. 2, 1921): 387–89. For 1929–30, see Jewish enrollment in thirty-one medical schools outside New York City, compiled by Dr. A. J. Rongy from questionnaire, as cited in Broun and Britt, *Christians Only*, pp. 147–50. For 1934–35, see Table C, Medical Schools, accompanying Levinger, *The Jewish Student in America*. At seventy-three American (Missouri, St. Louis, Wake Forest, and West Virginia not reporting) and ten Canadian medical schools, Jews numbered about 4,200 or 16.28 percent out of 25,784 students. For 1940–41 and 1945–46, see Frank Kingdon, "Discrimination in Medical Colleges," *American Mercury* 61 (Oct. 1945): 395–99.

[a] Classes entering in 1919, 1929, and 1946, table in Wechsler, *The Qualified Student*, p. 170.

[b] For 1920, 1941, and 1945, see Kingdon, "Discrimination in Medical Colleges," p. 395. American Jewish Congress gave higher percentages for Cornell's classes: 9.52 (1944), 8.97 (1945), and 12.94 (later in 1945), *New York Times*, Dec. 24, 1946, pp. 1, 18.

[c] Kelson, "Jewish Students on the Cornell Campus," *American Hebrew* (Dec. 19, 1930): 160.

[d] Long Island Hospital Medical College class entering in 1928, New York Homeopathic Medical College total enrollment in 1929–30 and class of 1934, New York University-Bellevue Hospital percentage of total enrollment in 1929–30 (about 125 in each entering class), and Johns Hopkins class entering in 1929–30, in Broun and Britt, *Christians Only*, pp. 137–42.

[e] For class admitted in 1918, see table in Synnott, *The Half-Opened Door*, p. 97.

[f] Henry K. Beecher and Mark D. Altschule, *Medicine at Harvard: The First Three Hundred Years* (Hanover, N.H., 1977), pp. 484–85, counted "patently Jewish names" in fourth-year classes and obtained these percentages: 5.5 (1910), 8 (1932), 9.5 (1939), 22.3 (1953), and 20 (1972).

[g] Jewish percentage dropped from 19.44 (1936) to 6 (1942), Kingdon, "Discrimination in Medical Colleges," p. 395.

fairly parallel with the population makeup.' " Intellectually rationalizing the use of a quota to explain Cornell Medical School's rejection of a particular applicant, Dean W. S. Ladd stated, in a letter of April 25, 1940, that " 'we take in from 10–15 percent Jews,' " in each class of eighty, which was " 'roughly the proportion of Jews in the population in this State.' " Jews, like Gentiles, were judged on character and personality as well as scholarship; hence the rejected Jewish applicant was simply " 'surpassed . . . in desirability' " by other Jews admitted under the quota. He did not say whether this particular Jewish applicant would have been admitted had he been a Gentile.[23]

In the December 1944 *Journal of Dental Education,* Dr. Harlan H. Horner, secretary of the Council on Dental Education of the American Dental Association, advocated that all dental schools impose quotas on " 'one racial group' " from the New York City area, which provided about 24 percent of all the students. His report recommended that the federal government help subsidize a national effort to reverse " 'the trend toward marked racial and geographical imbalance' " among dental students by elevating qualifications. Because of public opposition, especially from Jewish groups, the Council on Dental Education denounced racial quotas but did not censure Horner. Between 1935 and 1946, the percentage of Jewish dental students dropped from 26.4 to 17.1 percent. Subsequently, both Columbia and New York universities removed questions on religious preference from their application forms.[24]

Since law students did not cost universities as much as medical and dental students, the pressure to restrict Jews did not mount until the Depression. Jewish enrollment had grown rapidly since 1908, when they constituted the largest ethnic group with 13 percent (496) of the 3,828 students in the 19 law schools surveyed by the Immigration Commission. By 1918, Jews were 21.6 percent (1,194) of the 5,515 law students counted by the Bureau of Jewish Social Research in their study of 106 leading institutions. In 1934–35, they were almost 24 percent (7,138) of the 30,110 students in 111 of 130 law schools. As to be expected, their heaviest concentration was in New York City's six law schools, in which they numbered over 56 percent (3,827) of 6,816 students. Columbia enrolled almost 35 percent Jews (206 out of 592); New York University, 59 percent (735 out of 1,244); and Fordham, almost 24 percent (240 out of 1,003).[25]

Reacting to possible loss of status and income from so many new practitioners, state bar associations began adding "character" tests and put pressure on law schools, especially in New York City and the East North Central states, to be more "selective." In 1928, for example, Columbia had limited law enrollment and included among its admissions criteria scores on "capacity" tests and geographical distribution. By 1946, Jewish enrollment had decreased by 2,800 in forty-six private law schools, while their total enrollment dropped by 600; and in thirty-one public law schools, there were 200 fewer Jewish students, although their total enrollment had risen 3,600. Only in the Pacific states did the number of Jewish law students increase. By 1946, the number of Jewish students in the same seventy-seven law schools surveyed in 1935 had fallen from 5,884 to 2,862 or to 11.1 percent of the 25,796 total. Even the best Jewish students, those who had been law review editors at Columbia and Harvard, observed H. Louis Jacobson, found that " 'the doors of most New York law offices were closed, with rare exceptions, to a young Jewish lawyer.' "[26]

Jewish students denied admission to medical, dental, and law schools (also to engineering, pharmacy, and veterinary schools, whose Jewish representation between 1935 and 1946 declined, respectively, 24, 45, and 70 percent) may have shifted into education, library science, military science, music, nursing, osteopathy, and theology, all of which registered increases in Jewish enrollment ranging from 52 percent (education) to 318 percent (music). While their overall representation in higher education remained almost unchanged between 1935 and 1946 at about 9 percent (192,476 out of 2,140,331 students enumerated), total Jewish enrollment in professional schools declined from 8.8 to 7 percent.[27]

By the 1930s, quotas seemed indeed to be following Jews in private liberal arts colleges and in half a dozen professional fields. Since "overcrowding" was the most common reason given for rejecting applicants, New York City residents constituted "half of all migratory students in the United States." As of 1942, New York City (over 41 percent Jewish) and state had an out-migration of 31,639 students or 26 percent of its total 123,361 college enrollment; its in-migration was only 17,453 or 16 percent of enrollment. While Jewish enrollment declined in New York City from 52.6 to 50.2 percent between 1935 and 1946, it increased in the Mid-Atlantic states (from 11.2 to 14.5 percent), in the Pacific states (from 3.5 to 4.8 percent), and in Canada (up .4 to 1.9 percent). As the "New York Jew," who was "a minority in a double sense," appeared "in large numbers in every part of the country, in sections as far removed as the University of Alabama, Ohio State University, and the University of Wisconsin," he occasionally sparked discrimination against all Jewish students. Out-of-state Jewish applicants to southern, midwestern, and western universities encountered "hurriedly" erected "barricades" in the form of "regional quotas." These prevented any mass exodus of Jewish students from the East Coast. Moreover, for financial reasons, many chose to attend such free public institutions as CCNY and Hunter College, which admitted a high percentage of Jews, 80 and 66 percent, respectively, in 1934–35.[28]

Despite growing opposition to out-of-state Jewish students, four factors mitigated anti-Semitism in the Midwest, South, and Far West: first, in contrast to the Northeast, Jews who settled west of the Appalachians were in many communities among the pioneer families and from the beginning were able to participate in the development of civic, educational, and political institutions. Second, the fact that Jewish settlements were smaller and tended to be stable put less pressure on the economic and social structures of these communities. Third, eastern European and Russian Jews generally arrived in the West a decade or so later than in the East, so that existing Jewish settlements were in a better position to absorb them; very few immigrant Jews went South. Finally, both the South and the West had to struggle "to uphold white supremacy in the face of a colored race, the Negro in one, the Oriental in the other." Given the availability of other targets, prejudice against Jews softened; they were more often viewed as white allies than as economic competitors or social intruders. For their part, Jews acquiesced to each region's consensus on racial minorities.[29]

Of the four main sections of the country, Jews encountered the least social discrimination in the Far West. In contrast to the Northeast and such midwestern cities as Detroit, German Gentiles in the Far West welcomed Jewish settlers, who were predominantly German Jews and Germanized Polish Jews from Posen, into their cultural, political, and social organizations. As a result, Jews won governorships in western states—in California, 1886–87, and in Idaho, Utah, New Mexico, and Oregon between 1914 and 1931—

before they did in New York and Illinois. The influx of eastern European and Russian Jews around 1900 did not jeopardize, moreover, the position of western Jewish communities, which was well established in San Francisco (the largest, with 30,000 in 1906) and in Los Angeles. In San Francisco, Jews "were not newcomers, did not suffer discrimination and could, therefore, give of themselves without hesitation—it was *their* City and they were proud of it." In New York, wealthy German Jews were "intruders" when they attempted to join social clubs or patronize summer resorts, while the masses of Russian Jewish immigrants were "invaders." Prior to World War II, prominent New York Jews usually moved within their own circle, nicknamed "our crowd," exercising limited influence over the city's civic, cultural, and political institutions. Until recently, southern Jews were country cousins, the "provincials" described by Eli N. Evans, the token Jewish families in small towns or the members of a "highly structured, non-assimilated ethnic group" in a city like Charleston. To survive, they became "southern" in almost every way, except religious conversion, although that, too, occurred.[30]

Regional variations in the number and position of Jews within both the communities and colleges prevented the quota system from fulfilling President Lowell's objective of an enforced proportional distribution of Jewish students throughout the country. In the Midwest, South, and Far West, as contributors to the founding of new colleges and universities or to the rebuilding of older ones, Jews gained some voice, including trusteeships. While Jacob Schiff, a major benefactor of Columbia Teachers and Barnard colleges, knew he had been rebuffed by the " 'tacit understanding, [which] excludes the Hebrews from the Trustee-room of Columbia College, of the public museums, the public library, and many similar institutions,' " Jews found a warmer welcome at the University of Chicago. Members of the all-Jewish Standard Club had raised $25,000 in 1890 toward its founding, and Jewish students soon exceeded the percentage of Baptists, the denomination of chief benefactor, John D. Rockefeller. Between 1893 and 1930, Jews comprised 11 percent of enrollment at the University of Chicago; in 1934–35, they numbered 17.6 percent. The University of Illinois was also quite open to Jews, admitting 9 percent to its Urbana campus and 44.85 percent to its professional division in Chicago, while its medical school was second only to New York

University in Jewish admissions—41.8 percent in 1940 (its Catholic enrollment was then 20 percent). Northwestern had 10.34 percent Jewish students, but its medical school's "rigid quota system" limited them to about 7 percent. In the small denominational colleges of the Midwest and South, few Jewish students were represented and virtually no Jewish faculty hired until the 1960s or even the 1970s.[31]

Religion could be a barrier, nevertheless, even at some state universities. August Kohn, who served effectively as a trustee of the University of South Carolina for two dozen years, failed to be re-elected in 1924, because of "religious intolerance" on the part of some legislators. In times of economic dislocation and social unrest, nativist passions, aroused by the Ku Klux Klan, overcame the positive image of Jews as descendants of Old Testament prophets, which most Protestant fundamentalists held. The lynching of Leo Frank in 1915 had also revealed the vulnerability of southern Jews as "an almost invisible minority" of less than 1 percent (under 250,000) on the fringes of white Protestant culture.[32]

As long as Jews on southern campuses were both a tiny minority and southern-born (children of one of "our Jews," for example, the owner of a small-town dry goods store and president of the Rotary), they experienced insignificant prejudice. By the mid-1930s, however, the influx of northern Jews began to arouse resentment. Jews were only .86 percent of the population in the South Atlantic states, but Jewish college enrollment (3.98 percent) was four-and-one-half time greater. Although just over 6 percent of the student body at the University of North Carolina at Chapel Hill was Jewish, their representation had climbed to about 14 percent in the freshman class. Rather than excluding "undesirable" Jews by covert administrative policies, as one concerned trustee proposed, President Frank Porter Graham, one of the most liberal North Carolinians, suggested instead that out-of-state students pay higher tuition fees and that "geographical diversity" be considered in their admission. Upon learning that Jewish students had been segregated in campus housing, Graham explained to the cashier that university policy required all rooms to be assigned, without discrimination, according to the order of application.[33]

President Graham also had to veto a proposal of Dean I. H. Manning of the Medical School to limit the number of Jews to only four out of thirty-five in each entering class. The dean resigned, and the controversy was publicized and debated. While North Carolina during President Graham's administration did not impose an obvious quota—about 10 percent of its medical students were Jewish—the community's " 'provincialism' " limited their welcome, as Dean M. T. Van Hecke of the law school recognized. In 1932, for example, he doubted "the wisdom of hiring" a *Harvard Law Review* editor who was Jewish.[34]

Jews who were state residents usually had an easier time being admitted to state medical schools. The University of West Virginia, for example, " 'never refused to accept a Jewish student whose home [was] in West Virginia.' " If all qualified Jews from the Northeast were accepted, however, the president of the University of Alabama said, there would be no room for the state's " 'native sons.' " The University of Virginia, which asked applicants to identify ethnic origin ("English, French, Hebrew, Italian, etc."), had a "rigid quota system," under 7 percent, for Jews. At Baptist-controlled medical schools, the percentages of Jews ranged from under 5 percent at Wake Forest College to about 14 percent at Baylor. Methodist-supported Duke admitted almost 12 percent and Emory about 14 percent[35]

Probably the most glaring example of anti-Semitic discrimination in a southern professional school occurred at the Dental College of Emory University. Its dean (1948–61), John E. Buhler, who served on the executive committee of the American Association of Dental Schools and on the Council of Dental Education, evidently was influenced by Dr. Horner's 1944 report. To counteract the trend which brought to Georgia and other South Atlantic states a percentage of Jewish dentistry students that was five times higher than that for all Jewish students, the Emory Dental College stopped admitting Jewish, but not gentile, applicants from New York, New Jersey, and Connecticut. From 1948 to 1958, moreover, Jewish students experienced a repeat and fail rate of 64.6 percent, which was over four times that for gentile students (15.4 percent). On the 1961 dental school admissions blank, the applicant was asked to indicate whether his "race" was "Caucasian, Jew, Other." After the Atlanta Anti-Defamation League exposed these practices, Buhler resigned; later he served as dean of the College of Dental Medicine at the Medical University of South Carolina, in Charleston, 1964–71.[36]

By the late 1930s, as increasing numbers of Jews sought

admission to major western universities, they had difficulties getting into medical schools. The privately controlled University of Southern California, for example, took into consideration ethnic origin: "Anglo-Saxon, French, Germanic, Italian, Negro, Oriental, Scandinavian, Slavonic or Spanish." The public University of California School of Medicine was reported to have a mildly discriminatory policy; its percentage of Jewish students had risen from 3.22 (1 out of 31) in 1908 to 30.86 (71 out of 230) by 1934–35. In undergraduate admissions, the university did "not discriminate either for or against men of another race or color." (In its first four-year academic class of 1873, two Jews—Nathan Newmark, first valedictorian, and Jacob B. Reinstein, later a regent—were among the twelve graduates, nicknamed the "Apostles.") In 1934–35, 983 (7.41 percent) of its 13,251 students were Jewish.[37]

Of all major western private universities, Stanford probably imposed the strictest quota on Jews when, in the 1920s, it limited enrollment and counted character evaluation 40 percent, with school record and aptitude test each being weighted 30 percent. In 1934–35, Jewish enrollment (125 out of 4,346) was under 3 percent. Racism and snobbery existed on campus. President David Starr Jordan (1891–1931), who believed in an alleged international conspiracy of Jewish bankers, described " 'the Irish, the Greeks, the South Italians and the Polish Jews' " as having " 'largely elements permanently deficient in the best traits we hope for in America.' " Imitating the prejudices of their elders, the Stanford "Cardinals" defaulted matches to the University of California, rather than box with Negroes on the "Bears' " squad. Student life had also been divided between "Greeks and barbarians," between fraternity members and outsiders. Since there were no Jewish fraternities on campus and no Jews in Palo Alto, Jewish students went to San Francisco for both religious and social activities. After World War II, however, Stanford liberalized its attitudes just as the elite eastern private colleges did. Stanford also received generous gifts from Jewish alumni and philanthropists. In 1974, President Richard W. Lyman thanked Walter A. Haas, board chairman of Levi Strauss and Company and trustee for the estate of his aunt, Lucie Stern, for their many benefactions—student loans, research funds, and buildings—which were exceeded in generosity only by the grant of the founders, Senator and Mrs. Leland Stanford.[38]

By the 1940s, racial and religious quotas came under increasing attack, as various committees and organizations investigated and exposed the difficulties that Jews had in gaining admission to medical and other academic and professional programs. For example, the Mayor's Committee on Unity in New York City (1946) denounced discrimination by higher educational institutions in the metropolitan area, while both President Truman's Commission on Higher Education (1947) and Committee on Civil Rights (1947) outlined the problem's scope nationally. The May 1947 Elmo Roper survey and interviews of more than 10,000 white high school seniors and of an additional 5,500 seniors in big cities indicated that while college admissions practices did discriminate against Jewish applicants, the extent was less than had been assumed, perhaps suggesting a decline in discrimination since World War II. These and other reports underscored, nevertheless, the seriousness of discrimination and led to the enactment of state fair educational practices laws in New York, New Jersey, and Massachusetts. Although most colleges and professional schools deleted questions on nationality, race, and religion from application forms, such devices as regional or out-of-state quotas, which had initially been adopted to limit Jewish enrollment, continued to be applied by both private and public institutions seeking to maintain either "geographical balance" or "student diversity." Occasionally, the devices were aimed at East Coast Jews.[39]

When and if all discriminatory quotas ended cannot be determined. Some medical schools, notably Cornell, continued to restrict Jewish admissions by limiting to one or two applicants the number it would accept from any one undergraduate college, which hurt the heavily Jewish pre-medical group in New York area colleges. In 1950, for example, Cornell Medical School accepted only twenty applicants from Cornell University—five Jews (out of twenty-nine) and fifteen Gentiles (out of thirty-five). Jewish applicants had 10 percent higher grades but less positive personality evaluations from faculty advisers. These practices began to decline after the AMA stated in 1951 that it did not intend to limit the training of qualified physicians. By 1952, Jewish enrollment had definitely increased at elite private colleges: Harvard had one of the larger percentages (25), followed by Cornell (23), Dartmouth (15), Yale (13), and Wesleyan (12).

Thus, as a result of public exposure and denunciation, the

second major period in the history of Jewish quotas, in which discriminatory admissions policies were adopted by colleges, universities, and professional schools in all sections of the United States, had ended. The third period saw a marked rise in Jewish student enrollment at the academically best—and at even the socially prestigious—private and public institutions. Indeed, about 80 percent of college-aged Jews attended college, in contrast to only 40 percent of all youths. The 1960s and 1970s introduced, however, another debate over admissions policies: should they be based primarily on academic qualifications—"meritocratic"—and seek to recruit an intellectual elite, or should they consider ethnic and racial backgrounds—admit minorities under "benign" quotas— in order to make universities proportionately representative of the national population? In resolving this debate and weighing competing claims, universities must not forget the lessons of past quotas.[40]

Notes

1. *New York Times,* June 17, 1922, pp. 1, 3. For a detailed discussion, see Marcia Graham Synnott, *The Half-Opened Door: Discrimination and Admissions at Harvard, Yale, and Princeton, 1900–1970* (Westport, Conn.; 1979), p. 60, chaps. 3, 4, and 7.

2. Synnott, *The Half-Opened Door,* pp. 93–110.

3. Robert Shosteck, *Two Hundred Thousand Jewish Collegians, Report of the Decennial Census of Jewish College Students for 1946,* in consultation with Max F. Baer (Washington, D.C., 1948), pp. 16 (table), 17.

4. Ibid., pp. 13–14, 110–11; John Higham, *Send These To Me: Jews and Other Immigrants In Urban America* (New York, 1975), p. 110; Irving Howe, with the assistance of Kenneth Libo, *World of Our Fathers* (New York, 1976), pp. 280–83; Moses Rischin, *The Promised City: New York's Jews 1870–1914* (Cambridge, Mass., 1962), pp. 94, 261–63; Colin B. Burke, *American Collegiate Populations: A Test of the Traditional View* (New York, 1982), pp. 215–22; U.S. Bureau of the Census, *Historical Statistics of the United States, Colonial Times to 1970,* Bicentennial Edition, pt. 1 (Washington, D.C., 1975, pp. 8–9, 383.

5. U.S. Congress, Senate, Reports of the Immigration Commission, *Children of Immigrants in Schools,* 5 vols., 61st Cong., 3rd sess., 1910–1911, S. Doc. 749, vol. 1, pt. 5, Students in Higher Educational Institutions, pp. 154–64; vol. 5, tables on nativity of students in various departments: Academic, Engineering and Technological, Medical, Law, Postgraduate, Pharmaceutical, Theological, Dentistry, and Veterinary, pp. 715–866; "Professional Tendencies Among Jewish Students in Colleges, Universities, and Professional Schools" (Memoir of the

Bureau of Jewish Social Research) *American Jewish Year Book, 5681,* vol. 22 (Sept. 13, 1920–Oct. 2, 1921), pp. 384, [381]–89; Selma C. Berrol, "Education and Economic Mobility: the Jewish Experience in New York City, 1880–1920," *American Jewish Historical Quarterly* 65 (Mar. 1976): 257–71; Sherry Gorelick, *City College and the Jewish Poor: Education in New York, 1880–1924* (New Brunswick, N.J., 1981), pp. 122–23.

6. Edwin E. Slosson, *Great American Universities* (New York, 1910), pp. 329–32; Laurence R. Veysey, *The Emergence of the American University* (Chicago, 1970), p. 61; Henry S. Pritchett, "Introduction" to Abraham Flexner, "Medical Education in the United States and Canada," Carnegie Foundation for the Advancement of Teaching, Bulletin no. 4 (New York, 1910), pp. vii–xvii; David Otis, "Discrimination in Medical Schools: An Examination, *Jewish Forum* 15 (Jan. 1932): 4–8, 32.

7. Slosson, *Great American Universities,* pp. 331–32; Joseph R. Demartini, "Student Culture as a Change Agent in American Higher Education: An Illustration from the Nineteenth Century," *Journal of Social History* 9 (June 1976): 536; *Z.B.T., 1898–1923: The First Twenty-five Years* [New York, 1923], pp. 82–83; *American Jewish Year Book, 5690,* vol. 31 (Oct. 5, 1929–Sept. 22, 1930), pp. 141–43, 243–46, 354–58.

8. Ludwig Lewisohn, *Up Stream: An American Chronicle* (New York, 1922), pp. 89, 123–26, 146–47, 155–57, 160; Lewis S. Feuer, "The Stages in the Social History of Jewish Professors in American Colleges and Universities," *American Jewish History* 71 (June 1982): 447–48, 454–65.

9. *New York Times,* June 17, 1922, p. 3; Barbara Miller Solomon, *Ancestors and Immigrants: A Changing New England Tradition* (Cambridge, Mass.: 1956), pp. 101–6, 118–51, 204–7; John Higham, *Strangers in the Land: Patterns of American Nativism, 1860–1925,* corrected and with a new preface (New York, 1968), pp. 264–99.

10. Frazier Hunt, "Strangling the Jewish Student in Europe," *Hearst's International* 43 (June 1923): 53–55, 129–30.

11. Synnott, *The Half-Opened Door,* pp. 15–20; Harold S. Wechsler, *The Qualified Student: A History of Selective College Admission in America* (New York, 1977), pp. 155–59, chap. 7; Theodore Francis Jones, ed. *History of New York University, 1832–1932* (New York, 1933), pp. 234–35; Stephen Steinberg, "How Jewish Quotas Began," *Commentary* 52 (Sept. 1971): 67–76.

12. Synnott, *The Half-Opened Door,* pp. 151–59; Norman Hapgood, "Jews and College Life," (Jan. 15, 1916): 53–55, "Schools, Colleges and Jews," (Jan. 22, 1916): 77–79, and "How Should Jews Be Treated?" (Jan. 29, 1916): 104–6, in vol. 62, *Harper's Weekly;* "May Jews Go To College?" *The Nation* 114 (June 14, 1922): 708; Arthur Gleason's three-part series on "Jews in American Colleges," *Hearst's International* 43 (Mar. 1923): 14–17, 144, (Apr. 1923: 32–35, 110, and (May 1923): 38–39, 149–50; Stuart Baskin, "Raising the Ivy Covered Walls: Jews and the Universities, 1910–23," *Stanford Quarterly Review* (Winter 1972): 20–29.

13. Saul R. Kelson, "Jewish Students on the Cornell Campus, A Revealing Survey of their Academic and Extra-Curricular Participation," *American Hebrew* 128 (Dec. 19, 1930): 160–64; Frederick Rudolph, *The American College and*

University: A History (New York, 1962), pp. 252–53, 265–68; Slosson, *Great American Universities*, pp. 329–41; Synnott, *The Half-Opened Door*, pp. 64–65, 252 n. 33.

14. Slosson, *Great American Universities*, pp. 351–66; Edward Potts Cheyney, *History of the University of Pennsylvania 1740–1940* (Philadelphia, 1940), pp. 378–90; Everett Colby to Charles W. Eliot, July 3, 1925, Charles William Eliot Papers, Box 390, 1924, folder A-C, Harvard University Archives; Heywood Broun and George Britt, *Christians Only: A Study in Prejudice* (New York, 1931), pp. 122–23.

15. Dan W. Dodson, "Religious Prejudice in Colleges," *American Mercury* 63 (July 1946): 6–12; President Hopkins' letter in *New York Post*, Aug. 7, 1945, as quoted in Dodson, "College Quotas and American Democracy," *American Scholar* 15 (Summer 1946): 270–71; "Anti-Semitism at Dartmouth," *New Republic* 113 (Aug. 20, 1945): 208–9; "Dartmouth College, The Selective Process for Admission, 1921–22" (brochure); Synnott, *The Half-Opened Door*, pp. 160, 192–96, 221–24; Carey McWilliams, *A Mask for Privilege: Anti-Semitism in America* (Boston, 1948), pp. 132–41.

16. Dodson, "Religious Prejudice in Colleges," pp. 7, 11–12; Table Showing Enrollment of Jewish Students in American Colleges and Universities in 1915–16 (from the *Menorah Journal*, Oct. 1916), *American Jewish Year Book, 5678,* vol. 19 (Sept. 17, 1917–Sept. 6, 1918), pp. 407–8; C. Mildred Thompson to Robert N. W. Corwin, Oct. 17 and Sept. 1, 1922, "Registration for Admission prior to 1929," Freshman Office Records, file Com. on Limitation of Numbers 1922, Yale University Archives.

17. Table A, Detailed List of 1319 Colleges, with Number of Jewish Students, accompanying Dr. Lee J. Levinger, *The Jewish Student in America: A Study Made By The Research Bureau Of The B'nai B'rith Hillel Foundations* (Cincinnati, 1937); Laurence R. Veysey, "Martha Carey Thomas," in *Notable American Women, 1607–1950, A Biographical Dictionary,* ed. Edward T. James, Janet Wilson James, and Paul S. Boyer, vol. 3, P-Z (Cambridge, Mass., 1971), p. 448; W. E. B. DuBois, "Negroes in College," *Nation* 122 (Mar. 3, 1926): 228–30; Stanley Feldstein, *The Land That I Show You: Three Centuries of Jewish Life in America* (Garden City, N.Y., 1978), p. 248.

18. Dodson, "Religious Prejudice in Colleges," pp. 6–7; Hapgood, "Schools, Colleges, and Jews," p. 79.

19. Shosteck, *Two Hundred Thousand Jewish Collegians*, pp. 13, 38–39 (table), 111–13; A. C. Ivy and Irwin Ross, *Religion and Race: Barriers to College?* Public Affairs Pamphlet no. 153, published in cooperation with the Anti-Defamation League of B'nai B'rith (New York, 1949), pp. 7–14.

20. Edward N. Saveth, "Discrimination in the Colleges Dies Hard," 9 (Feb. 1950): 119–21, and Lawrence Bloomgarden, "Medical School Quotas and National Health: Discrimination That Hurts Us All," 15 (Jan. 1953): 30–31, 29–37, *Commentary;* Frank Kingdon, "Discrimination in Medical Colleges," *American Mercury* 61 (Oct. 1945): 393, 391–99; *Children of Immigrants in Schools,* vol. 1, pp. 154–57, and vol. 5, pp. 754–75; Shosteck, *Two Hundred Thousand Jewish Collegians,* pp. 54–55 (tables), 69–73.

21. Wechsler, *The Qualified Student,* Table 7.2, School of Medicine, Columbia University, Jewish Student Enrollment, 1908–46, p. 170; Kingdon, "Discrimination

in Medical Colleges," pp. 395–99; Broun and Britt, *Christians Only,* pp. 106–8, 137–53; Harold Rypins, "The Jewish Medical Student, Unjustified Claims of Discrimination—Analysis of Factors that Prevail," *American Hebrew,* 128 (Dec. 26, 1930): 181; Alfred L. Shapiro, "Racial Discrimination in Medicine (With Special Reference to Medical and Specialty Education and Practice)" 10 (Apr. 1948): 103–34, and Jacob A. Goldberg, "Jews in the Medical Profession—A National Survey" 1 (July 1939): 327–36, *Jewish Social Studies.*

22. Bloomgarden, "Medical School Quotas and National Health," pp. 30–33; Shosteck, *Two Hundred Thousand Jewish Collegians,* pp. 71–72; Saveth, "Discrimination in the Colleges Dies Hard," pp. 120–21; Levinger, *The Jewish Student in America,* pp. 73–75, and Table C-Medical Schools, in accompanying volume; Wechsler, *The Qualified Student,* pp. 169–70.

23. Dean Rappleye, as quoted in Kingdon, "Discrimination in Medical Colleges," p. 397; Dean Ladd, as quoted in Walter R. Hart, "Anti-Semitism in N.Y. Medical Schools," *American Mercury* 65, no. 283 (July 1947): 62, 53–63.

24. Shosteck, *Two Hundred Thousand Jewish Collegians,* pp. 54–55 (tables), 77–81; Dr. Horner's report, as quoted in the *American Jewish Year Book, 5706,* vol. 47 (1945): 278; Dodson, "College Quotas and American Democracy," p. 269. Upon complaint of the American Jewish Congress, the *Journal of Clinical Psychology* retracted its proposal, in the January 1945 issue, implicitly to limit the number of Jews admitted to professional psychological training.

25. *Children of Immigrants in Schools,* vol. 1, pp. 154–57, and vol. 5, pp. 776–89; "Professional Tendencies Among Jewish Students . . . ," *American Jewish Year Book, 5681,* vol. 22, p. 392; and Table C, accompanying Levinger, *The Jewish Student in America.*

26. H. Louis Jacobson to Louis Marshall, Sept. 4, 1900, as quoted in Jerold S. Auerbach, "From Rags to Robes: The Legal Profession, Social Mobility and the American Jewish Experience," *American Jewish Historical Quarterly,* 66 (Dec. 1976): 251, 259–66, 249–84; Wechsler, *The Qualified Student,* pp. 171–73, 184–85 n. 135; Shosteck, *Two Hundred Thousand Jewish Collegians,* pp. 54–55 (tables), 67–69; Broun and Britt, *Christians Only,* pp. 125, 162–74.

27. Shosteck, *Two Hundred Thousand Jewish Collegians,* pp. 11, 54–55 (tables), 56.

28. Ibid., pp. 15, 16 (table), 17–18, 48–51, 104–7; Levinger, *The Jewish Student in America,* pp. 16 (tables), 17–18, 91–95; Broun and Britt, *Christians Only,* pp. 65, 83, 126–27, 144.

29. Higham, *Send These to Me,* pp. 162–64.

30. Irena Narell, *Our City: The Jews of San Francisco* (San Diego, Calif., 1981), p. 12; Earl Raab, " 'There's No City Like San Francisco,' " *Commentary* 10 (July–Dec. 1950): 371, 369–78; issue on "The Jews of the West," *American Jewish History,* 68 (June 1979). In *Western States Jewish Historical Quarterly,* see Norton B. Stern and William M. Kramer, "Anti-Semitism and the Jewish Image in the Early West" (Jan. 1974): 129–40; Stern, "California's Jewish Governor" 5 (July 1973): 285–87; "Periodical Reflections" 7 (Apr. 1975): 274–75; Stern and Kramer, "The Major Role of Polish Jews in the Pioneer West" 8 (July 1976): 326–44; and Daniel K. Oxman, "California Reactions to the Leo Frank Case" 10 (April 1978): 216–24. See also Stephen Birmingham, *"Our Crowd": The Great Jewish Families of New York* (New York, 1967), pp. 20, 26, 171–

74, 177; Eli N. Evans, *The Provincials: A Personal History of Jews in the South* (New York, 1973), pp. viii, 330; Frank Petrusak and Steven Steinert, "The Jews of Charleston: Some Old Wine in New Bottles," *Jewish Social Studies* 38 (Summer–Fall 1976): 341–46.

31. Jacob Schiff, 1898 letter to Episcopal Bishop Henry Codman Potter, as quoted in Howe, *World of Our Fathers,* p. 410; Wechsler, *The Qualified Student,* pp. 136–40, 188–89, 221–23, 230, 235–36 n. 48 (a 20 percent limitation on Jewish students, roughly in proportion to Jews in Chicago's population, may have been imposed but did not survive World War II); Thomas Wakefield Goodspeed, *A History of the University of Chicago: The First Quarter-Century* (Chicago, 1916), pp. 86–89; Floyd W. Reeves and John Dale Russell, *The Alumni of the Colleges,* University of Chicago Survey no. 6 (Chicago, 1933), table 6, Percentage Distribution of Graduates of Each Period According to Religious Preference, p. 15; Kingdon, "Discrimination in Medical Colleges," pp. 397–99; Levinger, *The Jewish Student in America,* tables A and C; Arnold Shankman, "Ronald Linden Loses a Job, Academic Anti-Semitism 1977," *Jewish Currents* 31, no. 7 (July–August 1977): 5–7 (Davidson College's religious requirement for tenure); Broun and Britt, *Christians Only,* pp. 89–95.

32. Helen Kohn Hennig, in collaboration with Alice Blanton Carter, *August Kohn, Versatile South Carolinian* (Columbia, S.C., 1949), pp. 158–62; August Kohn to David R. Coker, Mar. 27, 1924, David R. Coker Papers, South Caroliniana Library, Columbia; Leonard Dinnerstein, "A Neglected Aspect of Southern Jewish History," *American Jewish Historical Quarterly* 61 (Sept. 1971): 61–62, 52–68; Dinnerstein, "A Note on Southern Attitudes Toward Jews," *Jewish Social Studies,* 32 (Jan. 1970): 43–49; Nathan M. Kagonoff and Melvin I. Urofsky, eds., *"Turn to the South," Essays on Southern Jewry* (Charlottesville, Va., 1979), p. xii; Marcia G. Synnott, "Anti-Semitism on Southern University Campuses," presented at the annual meeting of the Southern Jewish Historical Society, Mobile, Ala., Nov. 7, 1981.

33. Harry L. Golden, *Jewish Roots in the Carolinas: A Pattern of American Philo-Semitism* (Charlotte, N.C., 1955), pp. 55–57; Levinger, *The Jewish Student in America,* pp. 16–18, and tables A and C; Kemp D. Battle to Frank Porter Graham, Nov. 17, and Dec. 3, 1936, and data on out-of-state enrollment (1936); Graham to Ben Husbands, Nov. 30, 1936; Graham to Rabbi Bernard Zieger, Nov. 30, 1936; Francis F. Bradshaw to Dean R. B. House, Dec. 23, 1936, Jan. 1, 1937, President's Papers no. 9033, 1936/37, file 494 Discussion of Admissions Policy (out-of-state, Jewish students, etc.), Southern Historical Collection, University of North Carolina, Chapel Hill.

34. Louis R. Wilson, *The University of North Carolina Under Consolidation, 1931–1963, History and Appraisal* (Chapel Hill, N.C., 1964), p. 83; M. T. Van Hecke to James Landis, Dec. 2, 1932, as quoted in Auerbach, "From Rags to Robes," pp. 267–68.

35. Statement from West Virginia University School of Medicine, as quoted in Broun and Britt, *Christians Only,* pp. 147–53 (Dr. A. J. Rongy's spring 1930 questionnaire revealed that Jews were 18.42 percent [2,018] of 10,950 students in thirty-one medical schools outside New York City); Kingdon, "Discrimination in Medical Colleges," pp. 396–99; and Levinger, *The Jewish Student in America,* Table C.

36. Benjamin R. Epstein and Arnold Forster, "Some of My Best Friends . . ." (New York, 1962), pp. 169–82; Levinger, *The Jewish Student in America,* pp. 84 and 107 (table).

37. Levinger, *The Jewish Student in America,* tables A and C; Kingdon, "Discrimination in Medical Colleges," pp. 395–99; editorial, "Fair and Open Competition," *Daily Californian,* Mar. 9, 1923, p. 2; William M. Kramer and Norton B. Stern, "Nathan Newmark: First Valedictorian of the University of California," *Western States Jewish Historical Quarterly* 9 (July 1977): 341–49.

38. J. Pearce Mitchell, *Stanford University 1916–1941* (Stanford, Calif., 1958), pp. 52, 47–56; Levinger, *The Jewish Student in America,* tables A, C, and D; Michael Dobkowski, *The Tarnished Dream: The Basis of American Anti-Semitism* (Westport, Conn., 1979), pp. 189–90; David Starr Jordan to H. Ben Humphrey, Jan. 29, 1924, quoted in Edward McNoll Burns, *David Starr Jordan: Prophet of Freedom* (Stanford, Calif., 1953), pp. 74, 61–77; "Stanford Cancels Boxing Matches with California, Cardinals' Action is Taken Because of Presence of Two Colored Men as Members of Bear Squad," *Daily Californian,* Mar. 9, 1923, p. 1; Veysey, *The Emergence of the American University,* p. 293; "Walter A. Haas, Sr.: Civic, Philanthropic and Business Leadership," Interview conducted by Harriet Nathan, with an introduction by Clark Kerr, Bancroft Library Regional Oral History Office, 1975, University of California at Berkeley. In the 1960s, Stanford was reported as having quotas of 22 percent for Jewish and 50 percent for out-of-state students.

39. Benjamin Fine, "Bias in Colleges Against City Youth Charged in Report," Jan. 23, 1946, pp. 1, 20, and Fine, "Curb Is Demanded on Bias in Colleges," Jan. 24, 1946, p. 18, *New York Times;* Leonard Dinnerstein, "Anti-Semitism Exposed and Attacked, 1945–1950," *American Jewish History,* 71 (Sept. 1981): 134–49; Dinnerstein, "Education and the Advancement of American Jews," in *American Education and the European Immigrant: 1840–1940,* ed. Bernard J. Weiss (Urbana, Ill., 1982), pp. 44–60; President's Commission on Higher Education, *Higher Education for American Democracy,* vol. 2, *Equalizing and Expanding Individual Opportunity* (Washington, D.C., 1947), Chap. 3; Morton Clurman, "How Discriminatory Are College Admissions? The Evidence of Recent Studies," *Commentary,* 15 (June 1953): 618–23. Three years after the University of Wisconsin began to reduce out-of-state admissions to 15 percent—state legislators disliked campus activists who were New York Jews—Jewish enrollment dropped by two-thirds; Dorothy Rabinowitz, "Are Jewish Students Different?" *Change, the Magazine of Higher Learning* 3 (Summer 1971): 47–50.

40. "Race Bias Charged At Cornell School," Oct. 23, 1946, p. 24, "Curbs on Bias Backed by Council After Inquiry Into Colleges of City," Dec. 24, 1946, pp. 1, 18, "Jewish Students Reported Curbed," Sept. 29, 1947, p. 8, and "Decline in Bigotry in 1949 Reported," Apr. 10, 1950, p. 21, all in *New York Times;* Bloomgarden, "Medical School Quotas and National Health," pp. 34–36; Seymour Martin Lipset and David Riesman, *Education and Politics at Harvard,* Two Essays Prepared for the Carnegie Commission on Higher Education (New York, 1975), pp. 179, 307–9; Stephen Steinberg, *The Academic Melting Pot: Catholics and Jews in American Higher Education,* a report prepared for the Carnegie Commission on Higher Education (New York, 1974), pp. 130, xvii–xviii, 88–115.

Intergroup
Relations
in the City

Leonard Dinnerstein

The Funeral of
Rabbi Jacob Joseph

The funeral of Rabbi Jacob Joseph on New York City's Lower
East Side on July 30, 1902, culminated in the worst anti-Semitic
police riot witnessed in America. Neither before nor since has
any organized group of public officials displayed such animosity
and wanton cruelty toward Jews in this country. Under the guise
of maintaining order, the police went berserk. Thus, the riot
highlighted not only the ineptness of the force in handling disturbances among large crowds but it underscored, as well, the
severely antagonistic relationship that existed between the new
Jewish immigrants and the officers of the law. Furthermore, it
reflected the tensions extant in the city between the Jews and the
Irish. Although the history of the police in the United States is
replete with incidents of brutality and disrespect for the rights of
minorities, laborers, strikers, civil rights advocates, and students,
the anti-Semitic component in this one makes it stand out from
all the rest.[1]

The turn-of-the-century influx of immigrants to the United
States threatened many New Yorkers ensconced in their own
communities, especially the Irish.[2] Since the early decades of the
nineteenth century, the city never had the opportunity to achieve
social stability or to assimilate its newcomers. There were always
more economic changes, additional technological innovations, and
flocks of people to be absorbed. "The institutional structure of
the city," James Richardson has informed us, "had great difficulty

meeting the challenge put upon it by the rapid rate of social change." In May 1902, the *New York Times* observed, "So far the year of 1902 has broken the record of the past decade for immigrants landing at this port." In August it commented, "the volume of immigration pouring into this country is larger than it has ever been before, with the exception of two years—1881 and 1882." The following January, however, the paper noted that 551,645 immigrants landed at Ellis Island in 1902, and that total broke all records since the government began keeping them in 1819.[3]

The figures for Jews came to about 10 percent of the total. Although the peak year for Jewish immigration had been 1892, when 73,636 peopled arrived in the United States, the numbers for 1900 (60,764), 1901 (58,098), and 1902 (57,688) ranked just below the all-time high to that date, and the three year combination exceeded the total for any other three consecutive years to that point. At least 75 percent of these Jewish newcomers moved into the Lower East Side ghetto.[4]

The Irish, and this included the police, resented the Jewish tenement dwellers crowding into the ghetto and, for several years, had been attacking them. Along with the Germans, the Irish felt intruded upon by these newcomers. The Germans had started to move out of the Lower East Side and up the social ladder more quickly than the Irish had, so their hostility toward Jews possessed a lesser intensity than did that of the Irish. Moreover, Germans never entered the police force in numbers as great as the Irish, thereby precluding another area of daily friction. During the 1890s Jewish publications commented upon the accumulation of insults and assaults against their brethren in the larger urban areas throughout the country. Irish and German gangs preyed upon Jews but the police rarely intervened to protect the victims.[5]

The source of this hostility is difficult to pinpoint. One historian, Gerald Kurland, concluded that the "pervasive intergroup conflict seems less traceable to circumstances in the United States than to attitudes or traditions going back to their history in Ireland." Kurland also noted that in the old country, "those whom an Irishman encountered in centuries past could be readily categorized as either (1) another Irishman or (2) a bitter enemy. . . ." As Christians, of course, the Irish had imbibed the tale of the Jew as Judas and Christ-killer from religious teachings, and they knew, too, about the image of Shylock, or the Jew as the representative of money and power. Anti-Jewish outbreaks occurred in Ireland from 1884 through the end of the century as the exodus from Russia began to make an impact on that nation's largest cities. If humorist Finley Peter Dunne accurately captured the essence of Irish-American views in his fictional essays about "Mr. Dooley," they were instinctively, and without reason, anti-Semitic. For example, in 1899 during the retrial for treason of the French captain, Alfred Dreyfus, one of Dunne's characters, "Mr. Hennessy," reached his verdict before hearing the evidence. "I don't know anything about it [the Dreyfus affair], but I think he's guilty. He's a Jew."[6]

Intergroup tensions and hostilities arose frequently, not only between Jews and Irish, but among the Irish and several other peoples as neighborhoods engaged in the process of transition. "Most of the immigrants who arrived after the Civil War," historian James Richardson noted, "moved into slums formerly dominated by the Irish. Italians, Jews, Chinese, and Negroes found that to the Irish beating up newcomers was a kind of sport. Too often the predominantly Irish police force arrested the victim rather than the aggressor or joined in on the Irish side."[7] Why the Irish, in particular, had such conflict with so many others is perplexing. Throughout much of the period between their arrival in America before the Civil War and the end of World War II, group antagonisms, rather than cooperation, seem to have been the norm for them even though the leading Irish-American politicians had the facility for getting on with members of practically all other ethnic groups.[8]

Irishmen represented a significant percentage of the members of the police forces in the urban northeastern quadrant of the nation, and a majority of those in New York City. As police officers, they displayed little of the politicians' finesse in dealing with other peoples. The cops routinely dispensed "curbside justice," using their clubs indiscriminately on peddlers and other lower-class immigrants who offended their sensibilities or challenged their authority.[9] As police officers, the Irish behaved in a manner similar to those in the same occupation nationally so it is difficult to distinguish on many occasions whether their behavior stemmed from ethnic association or occupational ethos. When their professional interests coincided with Irish prejudices, as they did during the riot that occurred during Rabbi Joseph's funeral, they positively exploded.

The Irish police looked down upon the Jews because of their immigrant status and low-class position, but they also harbored other resentments. The East European Jews tended to be more socialistically inclined than were the Irish and favored reforms in society to uplift the working classes. The Irish had been brought up to oppose socialism and to accept the status quo while the police were trained to uphold law and order. "The rank and file of the police department," Richardson tells us, "were every bit as anti-labor and anti-radical as the department's civilian heads."[10] Police officers, as well as devout Irish Catholics, lived in an authoritarian world with a multiplicity of rules that governed their lives. Order was a key word for both of them. The endless labor disputes on the Lower East Side between Jewish laborers and Jewish entrepreneurs exasperated the officers in blue. Thus, during strikes and labor conflicts, the police invariably supported the employers, which heightened the tensions between them and the Jewish immigrants.[11]

In 1901, the Jews on the Lower East Side rebelled against police harassment and general corruption, and voted "en masse" for the Reform administration promised by patrician Seth Low. The Reform ticket won and the police had another reason for opposing the ghetto Jews. The accumulated venom of the Irish officers and patrolmen toward the Jews then erupted at the most unexpected time—during the course of a rabbi's funeral.

Jacob Joseph, born in Krozh, province of Kovno, Russia, in 1840, studied Talmud his entire life. His intellectual gifts were recognized early and the local Jewish community supported him while he steeped himself in Talmudic lore. As an adult, he lived in Vilna, then known as the "Jerusalem of Lithuania and the greatest center of Talmudic scholarship in the world," and his fame spread throughout the Jewish quarters of eastern Europe and reached as far west as the orthodox circles of American Jews. In 1888, when prominent Jews on the Lower East Side sought to enhance the prestige of their community, a federation of several local synagogues asked the renowned spiritual leader to come to American as "chief rabbi" and to preside over the inauguration of what was hoped would be a new era in the history of American Jewry. Leaping at the opportunity presented by the challenge in the New World, "the greatest Rabbi that ever came to this country" accepted the offer and arrived in New York City on July 7, 1888.[12]

Joseph's career in America proved a terrible disappointment both to him and to the people who brought him. The most serious problem stemmed from the fact that Orthodox Jewry has no formal procedure for recognizing a "chief rabbi"; other rabbis in America saw no need to subordinate their views to his authority despite his superior erudition. His Old World sermons and customs seemed quaint in New York where people dressed and behaved differently than they had in Europe, and where they tried desperately to adapt to life in the United States. American Jews read secular newspapers, attended theaters and public schools, and strove for success. The learned rabbi never could accept the changes he saw about him. To Abraham Cahan, editor of the popular Yiddish newspaper, the *Forward,* Joseph always seemed "the man of the third century." "The very notion of a man and his wife taking a walk together, like a Gentile couple," Cahan continued, "would have shocked [the rabbi's] sense of decency." He also opposed labor unions, which infuriated the Jewish workers. His views, his manner, his dress, almost everything about him, in fact, showed the gulf between him and other American Jews. Soon people drifted away from this antiquated scholar and the rabbi found increasing solace in reading his Holy Books.[13]

For several years before his death on July 28, 1902, Rabbi Joseph dwelt quietly with his wife, practically ignored by the community. Bedridden with paralysis, his last years were as bleak as his early ones were brilliant. When the eminent Talmudist died, "like a flower transplanted to uncongenial soil," a wave of remorse spread over the ghetto. Perhaps feeling guilty over having rejected traditional Judaism and/or because they wanted to make up for all of the years that they had ignored and humiliated the great rabbi, thousands of people who had never laid eyes upon Joseph, but who knew of his reputation for scholarship and piety, gathered in front of his house at 263 Henry Street and "wept and moaned at his door." His portrait, which had not been seen on the streets for six or seven years, appeared in store windows "heavily draped in mourning." The East Side teemed with stories of his erudition, his greatness, and his philanthropy. The *Jewish Messenger* commented, "The irony of fate has again been illustrated in the case of Rabbi Joseph. The neglect to which he was subjected in his lifetime has been followed by a kind of apotheosis; and while a few weeks ago the great mass of American people were in absolute ignorance of his existence, now his name has appeared in every newspaper."[14]

Plans were made to conduct the most solemn and impressive Jewish funeral yet seen in America. Several congregations vied for the honor of burying the rabbi. Since the great man left no estate, the "prize" fell to congregation Beth Hamedrash Hadol which offered the widow $1,500 in cash and $15 a week for life. This act, called "buying a mitzva," or good deed, was supposed especially to please God and to help smooth the path to eternal happiness for all who contributed. At the same time, the synagogue lost no money. A Canal Street merchant offered $5,000 to purchase the burial plot next to the rabbi's grave and several families indicated their willingness to pay huge sums for the privilege of lying nearby in the cemetery.[15]

On the morning of July 30, 1902, sixty-two persons, including prominent rabbis from as far away as Boston and Philadelphia along with members of the family, gathered in the Joseph apartment to wash the body and dress it in the traditional shroud and prayer shawl before putting it, according to Orthodox tradition, in a plain pine box. Before removing the casket to the hearse, the men present conducted religious services and chanted the prayer for the dead. As the police and pallbearers carried the box out of the building, shortly after 11 A.M., they had to struggle against crowds of mourners who surged forward trying to touch the coffin and pay homage to the dead man.[16]

Once the bier was securely placed, Captain William Thompson of the 7th Precinct (who had already called ahead to the police in Brooklyn to warn them that this was no ordinary procession and advised that they be adequately prepared when the Grand Street ferry carrying the cortege docked early in the afternoon) moved to the front while a solid line of officers framed the hearse on all sides. Two hundred carriages carrying members of the family, distinguished mourners, and those wealthy enough to ride, attempted to follow, but the crowds rushed in between and the carriages made their way to the ferry as best they could. Directly in front of the horses and wagon pulling the hearse, hundreds of beardless youths from the religious schools in Manhattan, the Bronx, and Brooklyn, walked slowly while solemnly chanting the *Thillim,* or "Promise of David." Tears filled their eyes.[17]

The police had not anticipated the huge throngs that observers estimated at between 50,000 and 100,000 people. Mourners stood shoulder to shoulder across most of the Manhattan streets upon which the funeral cortege would proceed on its journey to the rabbi's final resting place. Hundreds of stores on the Lower East Side closed for the funeral and thousands of mechanics, laborers, peddlers, pushcartmen, and shop keepers gave up a day's wages to pay homage to the memory of Rabbi Jacob Joseph. "No Orthodox Jew was too old or too feeble to join" the throng, the *Sun* informed readers the next day.[18]

The previous night one of the men who had arranged the funeral sought a police permit allowing the hearse and attendant mourners to parade through the streets. He suggested that perhaps 20,000 persons would be present and he thought that an escort of twenty to twenty-five policemen would be enough to handle the crowds. The sergeant on duty at the station granted the permit. Later in the evening the police received a telephone call from a reporter at one of the Yiddish newspapers stating that the crowds would be enormous and that twenty-five police officers could not handle them. No attention was paid to the reporter's warning.[19] Police procedures dictated that the inspector in charge be informed when large public demonstrations were scheduled to occur. In this case Adam A. Cross, the responsible official, was not told by the sergeant who received the petition. Cross, temporarily in command because of another officer's leave, was also the key deputy to Police Commissioner John N. Partridge.[20]

Before the procession left the dead man's home, the police on duty that morning knew that they would need reinforcements and called for assistance. Although the exact number of police in the streets and protecting the cortege at first was not ascertained, there were at least fifty men on the job. Ten more were sent at 10:15 A.M.; then at 10:40 reserves were called out from four additional precincts; ten minutes later a call for more officers brought forth police from the 2nd, 6th, 9th, 10th, 15th, 16th, 17th, 18th, 19th, 20th, 21st, 22nd, 24th, and 25th precincts, along with increased supervisory personnel. In all, between 10 and 11 A.M. two sergeants, four roundsmen (supervisors of the foot patrol), and 102 patrolmen were dispatched. As events later proved, this was still not enough.[21]

The funeral cortege proceeded slowly from Joseph's home to synagogues on Madison, Pike, Eldridge, Forsyth, and Norfolk streets. In front of each building rabbis recited the prayer for the dead. The intention had been to remove the casket at each synagogue, but with people wailing, sobbing, and chanting from curb-to-curb, all waiting to pay final respects and most hoping to touch the bier, the plan was altered. Unceasing lamentations were pierced by wails and screeches as the funeral procession meandered through the Lower East Side.[22]

Fortunately, at first no major disturbances arose to tax the energies of the police. To be sure, there had been some difficulty getting the procession reorganized again after the prayers had been finished in front of the last synagogue stop on Norfolk Street. The sergeant in charge, however, ordered his men to clear the block and admonished them, "But don't forget that this is a funeral and not a riot. No clubs." The patrolmen did as ordered, and many of the Jews present were astonished at the gentleness of police treatment. Within five minutes the street was cleared and the hearse began moving toward the Grand Street ferry, its final destination in Manhattan.[23]

As the procession turned east from Norfolk onto Grand Street shortly before 1:00 P.M., one could see the Hoe and Company printing press manufacturing factory, a massive building which occupied the block bound by Grand, Sheriff, Cannon, and Broome streets. More than 1,800 people, mostly of Irish descent, worked there. Very few Jews were on the payroll. (Estimates ran from one to fifty Jewish employees, but even if one accepts the highest figure it still meant that over 97% of the workers were non-Jews.) On several occasions in the past few years male factory employees had insulted, terrorized, and assaulted neighborhood Jews, especially during the noon lunch break. The police and the Hoe management had received several complaints about the behavior of the young men but little had been done to curb their actions; nor had much newspaper publicity been given to the unpleasant incidents. Robert Hoe, Jr., the owner, later admitted that "some of the boys" disliked Jews and had harassed them in the past but he also indicated that he had asked them to discontinue such activities. In fact, management posted a notice in February 1901 ordering "boys throwing snowballs and other missiles at passersby on the street" to stop; the message was neither observed nor enforced. After the funeral Hoe would speculate that perhaps he had not been as strict with about 300 of these "mischievous boys" as he should have been.[24]

The police knew about the hostility that existed between the Hoe workers and the Jews (several officers admitted afterwards that the strained relations between the two groups was "common knowledge") but law enforcers sympathized with, and engaged in actions remarkably similar to, those of the Irish workers. Most policemen were of Irish descent and they had, as John Higham has written, "a reputation for brutal treatment of East Side Jews." Their rough and uncivil handling of the neighborhood people was "inexcusably common," the mayor's investigating committee later reported. Complaints about their behavior often resulted in only slight fines or reprimands from their superior officers, also usually of Irish ancestry. The *New York Times* editorialized after the mayor's investigating committee report appeared, that "the police, or a considerable portion of them, regard the Jews of the Lower East Side not as claimants for protection but as fit objects of persecution. These unhappy Jews are not only not protected by the police, they are in need of protection against the police."[25]

It is not surprising, therefore, that the advance warnings of a Jewish undertaker to Captain Thompson of the 7th Precinct went unheeded. The undertaker informed the police captain that he had never taken a Jewish funeral procession past the Hoe factory without trouble occurring. Only three weeks earlier, the undertaker explained, a driver of his had been struck in the face by an apple core thrown from one of the factory windows.[26]

As the procession made its way down Grand Street toward the ferry, one heard more clearly the shouting and jeering of the Hoe workers; as soon as the hearse passed in front of the factory, the assaults began. A stale loaf of bread hit the coachman of the wagon carrying the bier while pieces of iron and screws showered down upon the casket. An oil-soaked rag fell into the carriage behind the coffin, shocking four of the rabbis who had participated in the services that morning. Then, in a sequence which observers found difficult to recall exactly, iron bolts, blocks of wood, screws, melon rinds, and sheets of water from buckets and hoses rained out of the windows, pummeling and dousing the people in the streets. The mourners had not anticipated such a torrent of debris or such disrespectful behavior and they lost their composure. Some hurled back the same objects that had been thrown at them. Others ran into the downstairs offices of the factory to protest the demonstration.[27]

The office workers below, unaware of the happenings on the upper floors and in the streets, panicked when a mob of people, many babbling hysterically in Yiddish, surged through the front doors. Hoe officials immediately telephoned the police station requesting protection while at the same time telling the protestors, "in no doubtful language," to get out of the building. (One individual later testified that when he ran into the office and asked to have the hoses turned off he heard the response, "Get out, you sheenies, we'll soak you.") As the first committee of mourners turned to leave, another group of complainants entered. Some of the outsiders even tried to rush the stairs but were repelled when the factory superintendent, after first glancing at Mr. Hoe and getting a nod of approval, pulled the fire hose off of the wall and set forth a four-inch stream of water upon those trying to reach the upper floors. This force of water along with concerted efforts of Hoe employees chased the protestors out of the building. According to the later report of the mayor's investigating committee:

either during the struggle before the closing of the gates or immediately thereafter, the first hose on the office floor was run out and a stream of water was discharged therefrom, not only on those just ejected, but indiscriminately on the spectators in street cars and in the street, on the mourners in the procession and into the house on the opposite side of the street. Some people in the street in their resentment thrust their umbrellas through windows on the ground floor, and a fusillade of missiles sprang up on both sides, the people in the street supplying themselves from the heaps of stones and broken brick under the new East River Bridge Structure, a block and a half away, while the occupants of the building used whatever came to hand, particularly a number of large iron bolts and nuts. . . . At an early stage of the difficulty water was thrown out to the streets from the upper windows of the Hoe factory and also from the Sheriff Street entrance of the office floor and used in a reckless manner. Large numbers of people in the adjoining streets were drenched with this water, which penetrated a house across the street, and the water was cast in all directions.[28]

When the riot began observers saw four policemen stationed

in front of the Hoe factory. None of them attempted to halt the disruption or curb the assailants. Had even one of the policemen "cared to perform his duty," the Yiddish newspaper, the *Jewish Gazette* noted, "this outrage could have been stopped."[29]

The rioting at the factory and in the streets apparently peaked when the hearse reached the Grand Street ferry. Those people and carriages immediately behind also remained part of the cortege. Captain Thompson had deployed about 100 men to the ferry, and they smoothed the path for a quick boarding and departure across the East River.

Three hundred policemen and another 15,000 mourners awaited the boat in Brooklyn. To avoid further demonstrations the police altered the planned route, but an altercation developed anyway at Kent Avenue and South 6th Street where some factory workers hooted, jeered, and threw things from the window. The police in Brooklyn ended the demonstration swiftly. The cortege then moved slowly on its way to the cemetery where, according to the *New York Times,* crowds "trampled over graves, jumped fences, hung to the horses' heads, and rushed past the few policemen who had been sent out with the procession." Under a fierce sun, sixty-two rabbis took more than an hour chanting the appropriate prayers. Then the men began digging the grave; when ready, they deposited the coffin and covered it over with the earth they had just removed. It was almost night when the last of the mourners left the cemetery.[30]

Meanwhile, by 1:20 P.M. when the police arrived at the Hoe factory, the melee in Manhattan had begun to subside. Responding to the call from factory officials, and perhaps from others as well, about 200 addition policemen and six patrol wagons, under the command of Inspector Cross, came upon the scene. "Without a word of warning or any request to disburse," the mayor's committee wrote afterwards, the reserves "rushed upon the remnant of the gathering, some of them with great roughness of language and violence of manner." As the *New York Times* observed, "It was evident from the actions of the officers that they considered the mourners in the wrong."[31] Given the values and expectations of the police, their conclusions were, in retrospect, understandable. "Usually contemptuous of civil liberties unless the people they were dealing with were of sufficient social and political status to make trouble for them,"[32] the police had been called by a representative of the neighborhood's largest employer to complain about an unruly Jewish mob about whom the men in blue were prepared to believe any accusation. Further inquiry as to what had happened seemed unnecessary. The police viewed their responsibility as one in which they had to disperse the gathering and restore order.

Leading the way, Inspector Cross charged the crowd yelling as he slashed his club this way and that, "Kill those Sheenies! Club them right and left! Get them out of the way!" Since, as a later police commissioner wrote, the inspector "sets the pace and gives the tone" to the activities of his subordinates, it is not difficult to imagine what occurred next. The patrolmen also ran into the assemblage swinging their sticks with abandon, "shouting as they waded through the dense gathering, and shoving roughly against men and women alike. . . ." Heads were bloodied and eyes slashed as people tried to run from uniformed officers who had apparently gone crazy. Owners of carriages could not control their horses that, along with people scurrying for cover, trampled over the weaker and smaller members of the crowd as they tried to escape the scene.[33]

In the thirty minutes it took to disperse the gathering, hundreds of Jews were injured. An insurance man who witnessed the riot from his office half a block away saw policemen pursue those trying to get away, clubbing them on their heads, shoulders, and backs. Some of the Hoe employees who had started the trouble poured into the streets to aid the police. One Jew testified that as he tried to get out of the way an officer knocked him senseless. A second claimed that after being beaten without cause and thrown into a patrol wagon, he was choked by several other patrolmen. Another accused a cop of knocking his head against the wagon and then choking him. "As the man told the story," the *New York Times* reported, "his face looked as though he had been the loser in a prizefight." Doctors worked on the scene for over an hour. More than 200 people required medical attention while others ministered to their own wounds. The *Sun* reported that "several hundred" Jews had been clubbed by the police. Three of the detectives also needed medical aid. One had been hit by a stone and lost consciousness.[34]

On the afternoon of the riot, the police tried to bring the alleged culprits to justice. They arrested eleven Jews and one Hoe employee and took them to the Essex Market Court. The Jews, despite the protests of their attorneys—who included Congressman Henry Goldfolgle—that they were the victims and not the offenders, were fined $5 or $10 each for their activities that afternoon. The magistrate ordered two of the Jews held for $1,000 bail and charged them with inciting others to riot. The Hoe employee had, unfortunately, sprayed a policemen with his hose. In court he claimed that he had acted upon orders from his foreman and had not meant to douse the officer.[35]

The Hoe company and its employees also suffered from the riot. More than 200 glass window panes had been shattered, offices had been soaked, and office furniture destroyed. The factory damage totaled about $1,200. The sidewalks in front of the building on Grand Street were cluttered with sticks, stones, bits of scrap iron, bolts, barrels, and other debris. Policemen patrolled the factory during the rest of the afternoon and at 5 P.M. ordered the employees to leave in a single file. They then escorted the workers out of the neighborhood.[36]

The entire incident shocked the Lower East Side Jewish community. One Jew could not believe that after being victimized by the factory workers, the police "who should have protected us, clubbed us into insensibility." Another reflected that "it was a thing that even a Russian, with all his dislike of our people, would have been ashamed of." That evening and during the next few days protest meetings were held throughout the Jewish quarter and in other areas of the city. Resolutions were passed criticizing Hoe employees, demanding Inspector Cross's removal, denouncing police brutality, and calling for a thorough investigation of the events.[37]

East Side Jews considered the behavior of the police during the riot not as an ephemeral outburst but as part of a systematic and persistent persecution. In fact, one of the resolutions adopted at a protest meeting specifically attributed the occurrences during the rabbi's funeral to a "smoldering anti-Semitism which, if uncrushed, will lead to anarchy." Hostilities between the police and the Jews had been the norm for several years. The ghetto residents firmly believed that they would not get adequate protection from the men in blue and that they had to be wary of them.[38]

Inspector Cross received the most severe vilification. One protester characterized him as "not fit to be a butcher, much less to command 200 policemen," and others made equally harsh evaluations. Delegations of Jews went both to the mayor and the police commissioner requesting that the inspector be relieved immediately of his duties and brought up on charges. The next day Cross was transferred to the Bronx. That exile did not satisfy the ghetto residents. Cahan of the *Forward* told an enthusiastic gathering that the inspector should have been sent to Siberia.[39]

Mayor Seth Low assured the Jews that a full investigation would be made. Low campaigned for office in 1901 under the banner of reform and primarily on the issue of police corruption. He had promised to clean up the department and rid it of its "rapacity and inefficiency." The police actions during the funeral obviously embarrassed City Hall.[40]

During the previous administration, dominated by Tammany Hall, Bill Devery ran the police department. Although newspapers clamored for his removal, Mayor Robert A. Van Wyck, a stooge of Tammany boss Richard Croker, refused to do so. He even proclaimed Devery "the best Chief of Police New York ever had," despite the fact that Devery openly associated with known gamblers and conducted business on a street corner in front of a saloon which remained open long after its legal closing time. (When reporters questioned Devery about allowing the saloon to remain open after it should have been shut, the police chief responded that although he saw men going in and coming out of the building, he did not know whether it was a saloon.)[41]

Van Wyck's refusal to discharge Devery, despite his open flouting of the law, so infuriated the Republican state legislators in Albany that they abolished the position of New York City chief of police. The mayor consulted Tammany boss Croker, then living in England but still managing Democratic politics in New York City, about how to handle the situation. Croker wired back that a new post, "Deputy Police Commissioner," should be created with Devery named to it. Van Wyck did as he was told.[42]

When the municipal election of 1901 approached, Richard Croker and several of his associates realized that Devery's antics served them ill and that the police chief's mingling with known criminals reflected poorly upon the city's Democratic party. Seth Low, formerly mayor of Brooklyn, led a coalition of reformers, which included William Travers Jerome as candidate for district attorney, against the incumbents. Low spoke softly but Jerome struck the theme for the election by railing against existing prostitution and political graft. The Reform ticket won the election and was committed to end the corruption that existed in the police department.[43]

As his first move, Low chose Colonel John N. Partridge, his Brooklyn police commissioner twenty years earlier, as New York City's chief of police. Partridge knew little about what had been going on in the police department before his arrival and showed this ignorance almost immediately by selecting as "his principal uniformed advisor Inspector Cross . . . whose reputation among policemen and others familiar with the affairs of the force was the worst." Five months into the new city administration, complaints about lax discipline and unchecked police blackmailing activities continued as if nothing had changed.[44]

Thus the charges made against the police, and especially against Inspector Cross, after their discreditable performances on the day of Rabbi Joseph's funeral, came before a mayor sensitive to the misdeeds of the force. Even without a background of police bumbling and corruption, an investigation would have been expected, but in light of the suspicions that press and public already had of Partridge's operations and Cross's activities, a thorough police department inquiry was ordered by the mayor. A few days later Low expanded the investigation by asking a distinguished group of citizens of conduct their own investigation and report directly to him.[45]

The result of the police inquiry was presaged on the very day of the riot when, after the funeral, Colonel Partridge requested an immediate report from Cross. That afternoon the inspector, having spoken only with Hoe officials about the causes, quickly summarized his findings for the chief. When newspapermen queried Cross about whether he would also seek information from "East Side Hebrews," the following exchange occurred:

Cross: "No, I am not sending out invitations to people to come here and tell me their troubles. If anyone has a grievance I expect him to call on me. I have never found people bashful under those circumstances."

Reporters: "Then you do not intend to solicit such complaints?"

Cross: "No, why should I?"

Reporters: "How, then, do you expect to get at the facts?"

Cross: "Never you mind. Leave that to me."[46]

The police department released Cross's report to the public.

The document stunned both participants in, and spectators at, the riot. According to the police inspector, huge crowds had not been anticipated and therefore a smaller number of policemen were assigned than might otherwise have been the case. He also claimed that "no clubbing was done in front of the Hoe factory after I got there, and the men told me that they had not seen any previous to that time. . . . If there were isolated instances of clubbing, however, I was in no way responsible for them." Then Cross made what the *Sun* called a "remarkable assertion." He stated that the mourners came armed with stones, nuts, and bolts, and had deliberately flung them at the factory windows thereby precipitating the riot. "Those who broke the windows and destroyed the property of Hoe and Co.," the report read, "came there prepared to do what they did, showing at the time that the attack on Hoe and Co. was premeditated."[47]

The police department's investigation of the riot was obviously a travesty. "The inherent belief of all the police force from top to bottom," a later commissioner wrote, is "that the press and public are prejudiced against them, and that the courts are their enemies instead of their friends. . . ." In times of crisis, the police of 1902, just as those in other eras, shielded each other.[48] Accordingly, no officer could be found to make incriminating remarks about another or break ranks when confronted by outsiders. William McAdoo, the police commissioner who made the assertions, attributed these characteristics to the strong Irish heritage of the police. An Irish mother would rather see her child dead than see him "inform." McAdoo then quoted a policeman of Irish ancestry who told him, "I would be ashamed to look my children in the face if I turned informer." In a broader study of the Irish and their cultural ethos, Daniel Levine wrote, "The Irish policemen exercised wide discretion in apprehending violators—and upholders—of the law. They interpreted the law with the latitude and flexibility appropriate to their interests. . . ." Mutually reinforcing occupational and cultural traditions ensured that the police inquiry into their own behavior vis-à-vis a local outgroup—the Jews—would not lead to the exposure or punishment of any of the culprits.[49]

The independent citizens committee that the mayor appointed, however, included individuals more distinguished and impartial than the members of the police force. Low chose five men renowned for their independence and public service. They included William H. Baldwin, president of the Long Island Railroad and chairman of a former citizens committee which had unearthed previous maladministration in the police department when Tammany Hall had controlled the city government; Thomas Mulry, a well-known Catholic banker and philanthropist; Edward B. Whitney, a prominent attorney and former member of the New York state Tenement House Commission; and two highly regarded Jews, Louis Marshall and Nathan Bijur. The members elected Whitney as chairman, and a Jew, Bernhard Rabbino, vice-president of the East Side Civic Club, as clerk. The composition of the committee pleased the Lower East Side ghetto residents. The *Jewish Gazette* observed, "If the Mayor had carefully scrutinized every Jew in New York City, he could not have secured two more representative men" than Marshall and Bijur. The Christians on the committee, the editorial continued, "are men who are known throughout the city as possessing rare culture and education and men possessing a high sense of American fairness. We feel that if this committee really has power it will do the East Side justice."[50]

The committee possessed few legal powers. It could not subpoena witnesses nor penalize those who refused to cooperate, but its members had prestige as well as the respect of a large majority of the Lower East Side Jews. This meant that the committee's report would probably be received by the Jews, the mayor and his associates, and others in the city with appropriate recognition and appreciation. The *Jewish Gazette* even engaged in some wishful thinking and speculated that the committee investigation might lead to "the relief from the petty persecutions and picayune tyrannies to which the East Side has been subjected for so long."[51]

The group met for the first time on August 12, 1902, at 61 Rivingston Street in the heart of the ghetto. Through August 20 the members heard testimony that, for the most part, unearthed no information about the riot that had not already been published. One of the committee's functions, it seems, was to provide a forum for the expressions of accumulated grievances that the Jews had been harboring toward the police. Most of the witnesses related their own horrible experiences and repeated stories about long-time police brutality in the neighborhood. People told of a boy being beaten by a policeman for loudly reciting poetry in the park, of Jews and Jewish funerals being regularly attacked in front of the Hoe premises, and of the police shutting their eyes when the victims happened to be Jewish. Furthermore, many of the people spoke of the inability of a Jew to get justice in the station house or in the local magistrate's court. One man explained to the committee that until "5 or 6 years ago" there had been few Jews in the area of the Hoe factory, but that recent immigration had changed the composition of the neighborhood. The man continued, "There has been a certain amount of race feeling in that locality for years." A physician claimed that he had been a resident of the area for 26 years and had seen many outrages perpetrated by the Gentiles and the police upon the Jews but had not bothered to complain because experience had taught him that such protests "would do no good."[52]

The mayor's committee also invited Hoe workers and supervisors to appear. Their testimony contradicted that given by the Jews. One foreman claimed that the riot had been planned in advance and began when a fracas developed in the street between cigarmakers and cloakmakers. He also asserted that no water could have emanated from the factory windows because the hoses stopped ten feet in front of them. More than twenty Hoe workers stated that no iron bolts like those found in the streets were used in the factory; therefore they must have been thrown first from the outside before being hurled back. A foreman even asserted that he had observed a woman with an apron full of stones supplying the men with missiles used to bombard the factory. Hoe employees also told the committee members that no hot water existed in the building and therefore they could not have scalded anyone outside. (Committee members Marshall and Mulry later toured the factory and found hundreds of bolts such as those that had been flung from the windows and also tested the water and discovered that it was hot.) The attorney for the Hoe firm told committee members on the last day of the hearings that the owners of the factory would not testify because they had nothing to add to the declarations that had already been made.[53]

Several policemen also had an opportunity to speak before the committee. They confirmed the tensions that existed between Hoe workers and Jewish area residents. Inspector Cross reiterated his belief that the mourners had come armed and had determined beforehand to attack the factory. He also admitted that he had obtained the information for his report primarily from the people at the Hoe factory and had not even spoken to one Jew until more than two hours after he had arrived at the scene of the riot. In addition to the public hearings, the members heard some witnesses in private and had access to the records of the police commissioner as well as to affidavits given to the district attorney.[54]

Less than three weeks after the hearings the committee delivered its unanimous report. Although temperate and even understated, the findings devastated the police and Hoe workers alike. The document asserted, "It is universally conceded that those who actually took part in the funeral procession are entirely without fault." Inspector Cross's attempt to put blame upon the bystanders was "without any basis of justification." The primary responsibility for the disturbances rested with the Hoe employees. Although the factory employers were not held responsible for the riot, they were censured for failing to identify or reprimand the perpetrators. "To us," the report read, "there seems to be every indication of a concerted effort to hush up the affair and to protect all the inmates of the factory from discharge or prosecution." Several Hoe executives refused to speak with the committee and also prohibited those who had been assaulted from going into the building to identify the culprits. Simply because few Hoe workers chose to come before the committee did not mean that they were in the wrong, the report noted, "though we cannot but be affected in our judgment of the whole affair by the fact that so many desisted from inquiry into its cause where the temptation to inquire would naturally be so strong."[55]

Another section of the conclusions addressed itself to the negligence of the police. The committee members reprimanded those at police headquarters who accepted a layman's analysis of how many patrolmen would be needed for the funeral and for rejecting the advice of a late-evening caller telling them that the anticipated crowds would demand a huge patrol. In private conversation with the committee members, police authorities actually acknowledged that 400 patrolmen should have been assigned along with a suitable number of ranking officers. Those police officers charged with escorting the funeral procession and controlling the crowds, committee members concluded, did not conduct themselves in a professional manner. "Through the day," the findings stated, "the mourners and spectators were treated by the police with marked incivility and roughness." The committee members also commented on the general relations between the police and the ghetto dwellers. For a period of years, they observed, there seems to have been "a complete lack of sympathy between the policemen and the residents of the East Side."[56]

The leading daily and Jewish newspapers applauded the committee's conclusions. The *Tribune* editorialized that not only did the report confirm the impression that the police "failed disgracefully" in their duty to protect the mourners but observed as well that since the riot "the police authorities have been most lenient to policemen charged with ill treating the abused mourners." The editorial sharply depicted the attitudes that existed among the Irish toward other groups in the city: "It is evident that a great number of rank and file of the force, as well as many of the sergeants and captains, sympathize with the rowdies and are rather glad to see them give vent to race prejudices. The fact is the 'tough' spirit is strongly intrenched in the police force. The rowdies who think it smart to pummel 'niggers,' stone poor Russian Jews, kick over Syrians' fruit stands, annoy industrious 'Dagos,' pull the pigtails of the 'Chinks,' and trample under foot plain citizens of American blood are generally the friends of the policemen." The *New York Times* called for the "very sternest administration of justice . . . upon such policemen as are proved to have persecuted the people they were bound to protect." The *Jewish Messenger* approvingly admitted that "it was rare" for the police department to have been so "vigorously condemned," while London's *Jewish Chronicle* stated: "The report forms the most telling arraignment of the police administration made since Mr. Low came into office. . . ."[57]

Mayor Low, after being told by District Attorney Jerome that the committee's conclusions coincided with reports made to him by subordinates, ordered those culpable for malfeasance brought to trial. The mayor's immediate and forthright response brought praise from the *Jewish Messenger*. Low "has done his full duty," the paper wrote; "we don't have enough words of praise for him." Then it added, prophetically, that Colonel Partridge had "very few" days left as police commissioner.[58]

In the time allotted, Partridge further demonstrated his inadequacies. He followed the mayor's orders in having charges brought against Inspector Cross for failing to assign an adequate number of officers to the procession, for permitting patrolmen to use their clubs on the crowds, and for conduct unbecoming an officer in making a misleading and untrue report of the riot; against Captain John D. Herlihy for failing to provide an adequate escort for the funeral and for permitting a sergeant to disregard a warning that there would be at least 100,000 persons at the funeral; and against Captain Charles Albertson for going out to lunch while the procession was passing in front of the Hoe factory and for not informing him of the needs for preserving order during the course of the funeral. Two others charged resigned from the force before the trial while those indicted by the district attorney's office later won acquittal in the courts. The officers tried by the police department also escaped without punishment. Commissioner Partridge judged all of the accusations against his men to be "without foundation" and concluded that the evidence produced did not sustain the charges.[59]

Partridge's decision was not surprising. Historically, both before and after 1902, policemen throughout the country have generally closed ranks and protected one another when attacked by persons outside of the department. The literature on this subject indicates that it is neither an "Irish" nor a "New York" phenomenon. "To maintain the morale of their organization," Richardson wrote in his study of the New York police, "commissioners tended to accept the policeman's word against that of a civilian complainant unless the civilian had social or political influence." Moveover, since there were no institutional sanctions against it, "police perjury was commonplace."[60] The policemen simply lied to protect themselves and their superiors chose to believe them.[61]

The exoneration of those officers tried for their culpability for the riot came in late December, two weeks after Partridge submitted his resignation, effective January 1, 1903. The attacks made upon him personally, as well as in his professional capacity, left no doubt that he did not accomplish what the mayor had originally promised. One of Low's biographers later wrote that Partridge's "customary inactivity in the wake of the Rabbi Joseph riot sealed his fate as Police Commissioner." The City Club, a good government organization, investigated the police department and found that "the connection of the members of the police force with illicit business that characterized the last administration have not been adequately diminished." On December 12, 1902, the day that the City Club intended to send a delegation to the mayor requesting him to dismiss the police commissioner, Partridge resigned.[62]

Neither the commissioner's departure, the report of the mayor's committee, nor the riot led to any significant changes. Low's next appointee, Francis V. Greene, tried to improve the quality of police work, and, in fact, had charges of neglect of duty and conduct unbecoming an officer brought against Cross. The accusations were sustained in a department trial, and after the conviction Green dismissed Cross from the force.[63] Police harassment of Jews continued, commissioners came and went at the Police Department, and Tammany Hall unseated Low at the next election thereby regaining control of the city government, which it held onto for the better part of the next thirty years.

In September 1908, only six years after the riot at Rabbi Joseph's funeral, New York City Police Commissioner Theodore A. Bingham announced that Jews constituted 50 percent of the city's criminals. The furor that arose by this assertion forced Bingham, who could not factually substantiate his remarks, to retract them two weeks after they appeared in print.[64] The original assertion indicated that police prejudices towards Jews continued unabated and that whatever impact the report of the mayor's investigating committee might have made in 1902, its effect had been entirely dissipated by 1908.

In retrospect, it seems that the outstanding significance of the riot was not to unveil police brutality—which was and remained a fairly common occurrence in most cities of America throughout the century—but to highlight the friction that existed between minority groups in the growing cities of industrial America. The Irish resented the Jews, and those feelings reflected themselves in the policemen's attitudes. As William McAdoo, who succeeded Greene as police commissioner, wrote, "Irish traditions and feelings have been incorporated into the very organization of the police."[65] Thus one must consider the ways of the policemen and their actions not only as those of officers of the law but as expressions of group feeling.

A specific example, commented upon by contemporaries, of the differing attitudes of the New York City police toward one of their own in contrast with an outsider was the comparison of their performances after the deaths of two religious figures. Archbishop Michael A. Corrigan, son of Irish immigrants, died in May 1902. He had been the reigning prelate in the city's Roman Catholic Church since his consecration in 1885. For the archbishop's ceremonies at St. Patrick's Cathedral, where more than 100,000 people passed by the bier in two days, about 500 policemen were assigned. No unseemly behavior occurred. The police arrangements were even singled out by the *New York Times* for being "excellent both in plan and execution." The corresponding lack of respect for a Jewish leader, however, was striking. Despite the fact that Corrigan, a major ecclesiastical figure in the community, had, unlike Joseph, maintained his dominant position and the respect of his congregants throughout the seventeen-year period that he headed the Roman Catholic Church in New York City, the *Jewish Messenger* asserted, "The contrast between the funerals of Archbishop Corrigan and Rabbi Joseph could not be glossed over." The *New York Times* echoed the Jewish journal's conclusions: "The contrast" between the two funerals "explains the whole business. . . ."[66]

Thus the riot at the funeral resulted not only because of inadequate police protection, nor because of Inspector Cross's viciousness, but because of the total insensitivity of the police to minority rights as well as to the intense interethnic animosity which had developed in the city with the huge influx of Jews (there were about 600,000 of them in New York in 1902, with about two-thirds of these people having arrived during the previous decade).[67] The funeral of Rabbi Jacob Joseph, therefore, must be seen in the context of developing antagonisms caused by an older and established ethnic group—the Irish—feeling overwhelmed and encroached upon by a newer one—the Jews—whose numbers appeared unlimited. The Jews did change the character of the Lower East Side just as the Irish feared they would, and the continued and expanded immigration during the next two decades precluded any peaceful resolution of conflict between the two groups. Not until well into the twentieth century, when both the Jews and the Irish ceased competing with one another for a secure place in American society, did their animosity begin to subside. By that time there were other ethnics in the city experiencing the same tensions that the Jews and Irish had overcome, and charges of "police brutality" and insensitivity to minority needs were hurled by blacks and Hispanics who replaced the former groups at the bottom of society.

Notes

Financial assistance to do this research was provided by grants from the American Philosophical Society and the University of Arizona Humanities Fund.

1. Moses Rischin, *The Promised City: New York's Jews, 1870–1914* (New York, 1970), p. 91; John Hingham, *Send These to Me* (New York, 1975), p. 136; see also Robert M. Fogelson, *Big City Police* (Cambridge, Mass., 1977), p. 34; Samuel Walker, *A Critical History of Police Reform* (Lexington, Mass., 1977), p. 17.

2. Ronald H. Bayor, *Neighbors In Conflict* (Baltimore, 1978), p. 3.

3. James F. Richardson, *The New York Police: Colonial Times to 1901* (New York, 1970), pp. 165–66; *New York Times*, May 4, 1902, p. 6, Aug. 17, 1902, p. 6, Jan. 1, 1903, p. 5.

4. Edward A. Steiner, "The Russian and Polish Jew in New York," *Outlook* 72 (1902): 532; Leonard Dinnerstein and David M. Reimers, *Ethnic Americans*, 2nd ed. (New York, 1982), p. 163.

5. Rischin, *The Promised City*, p. 91; Higham, *Send These to Me*, pp. 134–35; Philip Cowen, *Memories of an American Jew* (New York, 1932), p. 289; *American Israelite* (Cincinnati), July 13, 1899, p. 4; *B'nai B'rith Messenger*, May 20, 1899, p. 4; Morris D. Waldman, *Nor By Power* (New York, 1953), pp. 297–98; Rose A. Halpern, "The American Reaction to the Dreyfus Case" (unpublished Master's thesis, Columbia University, 1941), pp. 85, 88–89.

6. Gerald Kurland, *Seth Low: The Reformer in an Urban and Industrial Age* (New York, 1971), p. 41; Rudolf Glanz, *Jew and Irish* (New York, 1966), pp. 12–13, 22, 106, 128–29; Finley Peter Dunne, *Mr. Dooley At His Best* (New York, 1938), p. 136.

7. Richardson, *New York Police*, p, 167.

8. Kurland, *Seth Low*, pp. 39, 40, 41, 118.

9. "Hard On The Jews," *Life* 40 (Sept. 25, 1902): 266; Richardson, *New York Police*, pp. 158, 189, 193, 201; Higham, *Send These to Me*, p. 136; Walker, *A Critical History of Police Reform*, pp. 15, 17.

10. Richardson, *New York Police*, p. 200; see also Fogelson, *Big City Police*, p. 34.

11. Walker, *A Critical History of Police Reform*, p. 17; Richardson, *New York Police*, pp. 172, 199, 200, 201.

12. Abraham Cahan, "The Late Rabbi Joseph, Hebrew Patriarch of New York," *American Review of Reviews* 26 (Sept. 1902), 312–13, 316; Stanley Feldstein, *The Land That I Show You* (Garden City, N.Y., 1978), p. 179; Paul Masserman and Max Baker, *The Jews Come to America* (New York, 1932), pp. 253–54; Peter Wiernik, *History of the Jews in America* (New York, 1912),

p. 278; Abraham Cahan, "The Late Rabbi Joseph," *American Hebrew* 71 (Aug. 1, 1902): 302; see also Abraham J. Karp, "New York Chooses a Chief Rabbi," *Publications of the American Jewish Historical Society* 44 (Mar. 1955).

13. Masserman and Baker, *The Jews Come To America*, pp. 253–54; Cahan "The Late Rabbi Joseph," p. 313.

14. Cahan, "The Late Rabbi Joseph," pp. 311, 314; *American Hebrew* 71: 302; *New York Times*, Aug. 10, 1902, p. 25; *Jewish Messenger* (New York), Aug. 15, 1902, p. 6.

15. *American Israelite*, Aug. 7, 1902, p. 4; *New York Times*, July 31, 1902, p. 2; Harry Simonhoff, *Sage of American Jewry, 1865–1914* (New York, 1959), p. 199.

16. *New York Sun*, July 31, 1902, p. 2; *New York Times*, July 31, 1902, p. 2; Cahan, "The Late Rabbi Joseph," p. 312.

17. *New York Times*, July 31, 1902, p. 2; *New York Sun*, July 31, 1902, p. 2; Cahan, "The Late Rabbi Joseph," p. 312.

18. *New York Sun*, July 31, 1902, p. 2.

19. *New York Times*, July 31, 1902, p. 2; *New York Tribune*, July 31, 1902, p. 3; Cahan, "The Late Rabbi Joseph," p. 312; *Jewish Messenger*, Aug. 8, 1902, p. 6.

20. "The Report of the Mayor's Committee," *American Hebrew* 71 (Sept. 19, 1902): 497; *New York Times*, Oct. 21, 1902, p. 16; letter from John N. Partridge to Seth Low, July 31, 1902, in "Scrapbook, 1902," p. 116, in Seth Low MSS., New York City Municipal Archives.

21. Partridge to Low, July 31, 1902, Low MSS.; "Report of the Mayor's Committee," p. 497.

22. *New York Times*, July 31, 1902, pp. 1, 2; *New York Sun*, July 31, 1902, p. 2; *New York Tribune*, July 31, 1902, p. 1.

23. *New York Sun*, July 31, 1902, p. 2.

24. *New York Sun*, July 31, 1902, p. 1, Aug. 1, 1902, p. 1, Aug. 3, 1902, p. 4; *New York Times*, July 31, 1902, p. 1, Aug. 1, 1902, p. 4, Aug. 3,, 1902, p. 3, Aug. 14, 1902, p. 9, Sept. 16, 1902, p. 2; *New York Tribune*, July 31, 1902, p. 1, Aug. 1, 1902, p. 3; *American Israelite*, Aug. 7, 1902, p. 7.

25. *New York Times*, Aug. 26, 1902, p. 14, Sept. 16, 1902, p. 8; Higham, *Send These to Me*, p. 136; "Report of the Mayor's Committee," p. 498; see also William McAdoo, *Guarding a Great City* (New York, 1906), p. 262; *Life* 40 (Sept. 25, 1902): 266.

26. *New York Times*, Aug. 1, 1902, p. 4, Aug. 19, 1902, p. 7; see also Higham, *Send These to Me*, pp. 135–136.

27. *Jewish Gazette* (New York), Aug. 15, 1902, p. 1 (English Supplement; all references to this newspaper are to its English Supplement); *New York Sun*, July 31, 1902, p. 1; *New York Times*, July 31, 1902, p. 1, Aug. 19, 1902, p. 7.

28. *New York Times*, July 31, 1902, p. 1; *New York Tribune*, July 31, 1902, p. 1, Aug. 6, 1902, p. 4; *New York Sun*, July 31, 1902, p. 1; "Report of the Mayor's Committee," p. 497.

29. *Jewish Gazette*, Aug. 15, 1902, p. 2.

30. *New York Sun*, July 31, 1902, p. 2; *New York Times*, July 31, 1902, pp. 1, 2.

31. "Report of the Mayor's Committee," pp. 497–98; *New York Times,* July 31, 1902, p. 1.

32. Richardson, *New York Police,* p. 194.

33. McAdoo, *Guarding a Great City,* p. 22; *New York Times,* July 31, 1902, p. 1, Aug. 1, 1902, pp. 1, 14, Aug. 2, 1902, p. 2, Aug. 3, 1902, p. 3; *New York Sun,* Aug. 1, 1902, pp. 1, 14; *American Israelite,* Aug. 7, 1902, p. 7.

34. *New York Times,* July 31, p. 2, Aug. 2, 1902, p. 2, Aug. 14, 1902, p. 9; *New York Sun,* July 31, 1902, Aug. 2, 1902, p. 10; *New York Tribune,* Aug. 5, 1902, p. 3; *Jewish Gazette,* Aug. 15, 1902, p. 1; *American Israelite,* Aug. 14, 1902, p. 7.

35. *New York Tribune,* July 31, 1902, p. 3; *New York Times,* July 31, 1902, p. 2, Aug. 1, 1902, p. 14.

36. *New York Times,* July 31, 1902, pp. 1, 2; *New York Tribune,* July 31, 1902, pp. 1, 3; *New York Sun,* July 31, 1902, p. 2.

37. *New York Times,* July 31, 1902, p. 2, Aug. 1, 1902, p. 14, Aug. 2, 1902, p. 2, Aug. 7, 1902, p. 14; *New York Sun,* Aug. 1, 1902, p. 1; *New York Tribune,* Aug. 1, 1902, p. 3, Aug. 6, 1902, p. 4.

38. *New York Times,* Aug. 2, 1902, p. 2, Aug. 3, 1902, p. 3, Aug. 7, 1902, p. 4; *Jewish Chronicle* (London), Aug. 8, 1902, p. 17; *New York Sun,* July 31, 1902, p. 2; *New York Tribune,* Aug. 1, 1902, p. 3.

39. *New York Times,* Aug. 1, 1902, p. 14, Aug. 2, 1902, p. 2; *New York Sun,* Aug. 2, 1902, p. 10.

40. *New York Tribune,* Aug. 1, 1902, p. 3; *New York Sun,* Aug. 5, 1902, p. 10; *Jewish Messenger,* Aug. 8, 1902, p. 6.

41. "A Serious Matter," *American Hebrew* 71 (Aug. 1, 1902), 92.

42. Ibid.

43. Gustavus Myers, *The History of Tammany Hall* (New York, 1917), pp. 473, 487.

44. Kurland, *Seth Low,* p. 145; Myers, *History of Tammany Hall,* p. 303; *New York Times,* Mar. 1, 1903, p. 2; Francis Vinton Greene, *The Police Department of the City of New York* (New York), 1903), pp. 50, 52, 53–54; "The Police Failure," *Nation* 74 (May 29, 1902): 420; Steven C. Swett, "The Test of a Reformer: A Study of Seth Low, New York City Mayor, 1902–1903," *New York Historical Society Quarterly* 44 (Jan. 1960), 35.

45. *New York Sun,* Aug. 1, 1902, p. 1; *New York Times,* Aug. 1, 1902, p. 1, Aug. 7, 1902, pp. 2, 14; *New York Tribune,* Aug. 1, 1902, p. 3; *Jewish Gazette,* Aug. 15, 1902, p. 1.

46. *Jewish Gazette,* Aug. 22, 1902, p. 5; *New York Times,* Aug. 1, 1902, p. 14.

47. *New York Tribune,* July 31, 1902, p. 2, Aug. 1, 1902, p. 3; *New York Times,* Aug. 1, 1902, p. 14, Aug. 2, 1902, p. 2; *New York Sun,* July 31, 1902, p. 2.

48. Mark H. Haller, "Historical Roots of Police Behavior: Chicago, 1890–1925," *Law and Society Review* 10 (Winter 1976): 320, 321; Harlan Hahn, "A Profile of Urban Police," in *The Police Community,* ed. Jack Goldsmith and Sharon S. Goldsmith (Pacific Palisades, Calif., 1974), pp. 19, 20; Egon Bittner,

"Espirit De Corps and the Code of Secrecy," in *The Police Community*, ed. Goldsmith and Goldsmith, pp. 237, 238.

49. McAdoo, *Guarding a Great City*, pp. 268, 271–272; Edward M. Levine, *The Irish and Irish Politicians* (Notre Dame, Ind., 1966), pp. 122–23.

50. *New York Times*, Aug. 7, 1902, p. 14; Jan. 6, 1911, p. 9; Mar. 11, 1916, p. 11.

51. *Jewish Gazette*, Aug. 22, 1902, p. 5.

52. *New York Times*, Aug. 13, 1902, p. 4, Aug. 21, 1902, p. 5; *New York Tribune*, Aug. 13, 1902, p. 2.

53. *Jewish Gazette*, Aug. 29, 1902, p. 4; *New York Times*, Aug. 19, 1902, p. 7, Aug. 21, 1902, p. 5, Aug. 26, 1902, p. 14.

54. *Jewish Gazette*, Aug. 19, 1902, p. 4; *New York Times*, Aug. 26, 1902, p. 14; "Report of the Mayor's Committee," p. 497.

55. "Report of the Mayor's Committee," p. 497.

56. Ibid., pp. 497–99.

57. *New York Tribune*, Sept. 17, 1902, p. 10; *New York Times*, Sept. 16, 1902, p. 8; *Jewish Messenger*, Sept. 19, 1902, p. 5; *Jewish Chronicle*, Sept. 19, 1902, p. 8; see also n.54.

58. Kurland, *Seth Low*, p. 159. *New York Times*, Sept. 18, 1902, p. 1; *Jewish Gazette*, Sept. 26, 1902, p. 1.

59. *New York Times*, Oct. 1, 1902, p. 16, Dec. 25, 1902, p. 2; *New York Tribune*, Oct. 21, 1902, p. 4; Louis Marshall to the editor of the *Jewish Gazette*, Dec. 29, 1902, in *Louis Marshall: Champion of Liberty*, ed. Charles Reznikoff, 2 vols. (Philadelphia, 1957), I, 11.

60. Richardson, *New York Police*, p. 203.

61. See Haller, "Historical Roots of Police Behavior," *Law and Society Review* 10:320, 321; Hahn, "Urban Police," p. 19, and Bittner, "Espirit de Corps," p. 237, both in *The Police Community*, ed. Goldsmith and Goldsmith.

62. *New York Times*, Nov. 21, 1902, p. 2, Dec. 13, 1902, p. 1; Kurland, *Seth Low*, p. 159; *Nation* 75 (Dec. 18, 1902): 473.

63. *New York Times*, Mar. 1, 1903, p. 1, Mar. 7, 1903, p. 3, Mar. 21, 1903, p. 16, Apr. 10, 1903, p. 5, Apr. 18, 1903, p. 2, May 7, 1903, p. 1.

64. Arthur A. Goren, *New York Jews and the Quest for Community* (New York, 1970), pp. 24, 34.

65. McAdoo, *Guarding a Great City*, p. 261.

66. *New York Times*, May 9, 1902, p. 3, May 10, 1902, p. 3, Aug. 3, 1902, p. 3, Sept. 16, 1902, p. 8; *Jewish Messenger*, Sept. 19, 1902, p. 6.

67. Isaac Max Rubinow, "The Jewish Question in New York City (1902–1903)," *Publications of the American Jewish Historical Society* 44 (Sept. 1959): 92; Dinnerstein and Reimers, *Ethnic Americans*, p. 63.

Radicals and
Reformers

Elinor Lerner

American Feminism and the Jewish Question, 1890–1940

Jews have been associated with and held responsible for almost every American reform and radical movement for the last one hundred years. Jews have been accused of leading, financing, and being disproportionately represented in an array of diverse movements such as union organizing, anarchism, socialism, communism, the 1960s civil rights movement, anti-Vietnam war protests, the New Left, and internationalist and peace movements.[1] Feminism is a notable exception. Writers on the American women's movement have been conspicuously silent about Jews. Breaking with this tradition in the late 1970s, some feminists raised the issue of anti-Semitism within the movement and the relationship of feminism to Jewish issues. Most of this discussion focuses on current concerns and lacks grounding in the history of the interaction between American Jews and American feminism.[2] It is important to examine this interaction and to explain why Jews have been essentially discounted in the history of American feminism.

At the beginning of the twentieth century, as organized feminism was gathering force, so was anti-Semitism; although the former was constantly, potentially, faced with the latter, the liberalism of mainstream American feminism largely enabled it to avoid the issue by practicing an anti-Semitism by neglect. Indeed, the relationship between American Jews and native-born, white American feminists was as obvious and also as complicated as that of Jews to American society as a whole. Unquestionably, Jews are considered different, a minority group subject to discrimination, yet the major difficulty in pursuing this topic is, in some sense, the unifying theme. In the context of American liberalism, Jews are often the unspoken minority and anti-Semitism takes the form of neglect and refusal to acknowledge. Perhaps an appropriate title for this study would be: How to acknowledge Jewish support while refusing to recognize that Jews exist. American liberalism conflicts with pluralism in that liberalism is based on the non-legitimacy of differences (we are all alike under the law and no one is to be treated differently because of individual differences), and on the possibility and desirability of assimilation. Thus liberal, Gentile America defines the Jew as "other" yet treats Jews under a liberalism which denies the validity of recognizing this otherness. Liberal reform movements, with their emphasis on equality, have had particular trouble dealing specifically with Jewish involvement. The apparent desire of many Jews to assimilate and the lack of a Jewish public identity taken by many politically active Jews have added to the silence about Jewish participation. So critics of movements point to a few Jews and cry domination, while liberal Gentile participants seem not to notice any Jews around them at all. Supposed assimilation, religious freedom, and a liberal refusal to acknowledge differences help to conceal from Gentile members the existence and importance of Jews in their social movements and provide a means by which they can avoid facing the reality of Jewish involvement—a recognition which would thus necessitate the admitting of anti-Semitism, and in particular, their own anti-Semitism. American feminists' silence on Jewish involvement in feminism was related to their inability to acknowledge, and lack of desire to combat, American anti-Semitism. To borrow an ironic term, a traditional "gentleman's agreement" held in American feminism, an agreement not to discuss explicitly American anti-Semitism.[3]

In spite of this silence, the relationship between Jews and feminism was rich and complex. Jews were involved with feminism in several ways: participation of individual Jews in feminist organizations and with feminist causes; connections between Jewish women's groups and the feminist movement; support for feminist issues by the Jewish community. Correspondingly, there was the relationship of women's groups and of individual feminists to Jewish issues, and the stance of feminists and feminist organizations toward Jews in general. Exploring these interconnections will show the importance of ethnic considerations in feminist politics and some mechanisms which perpetuate anti-Semitism in America.

Although the stereotype of American feminists (particularly suffragists) is white, Anglo-Saxon, and Protestant, a remarkable number have been Jewish women; currently, two of the most widely recognized are Betty Freidan and Gloria Steinem. Jewish women have been prominent in all areasof feminist activity from early feminism and the abolition movement through twentieth-century social reform and political movements. Most worked on feminist issues in predominantly gentile women's groups, although some maintained associations with Jewish organizations (both secular and religious), and some worked extensively with a Jewish constituency such as women garment workers. Among these women were Ernestine Rose, Lillian Wald, Maud Nathan, Rose Schneiderman, Emma Goldman, and Rose Pastor Stokes.[4]

Not only were individual Jewish women active feminists, several organizations of Jewish women supported feminist causes, working in coalitions with other women's groups. For example, the National Council of Jewish Women (NCJW), whose activities were mainly concerned with Jewish community civic, cultural, and religious issues, joined the Women's Joint Congressional Committee (WJCC), an umbrella group formed in 1920 to lobby for congressional legislation dealing with women's issues. If at least five member groups backed a particular bill, then a legislative subcommittee was formed to lobby for it. Although supposedly restricted to women-related issues, in practice the committee lobbied for a broad range of social concerns including peace, anti-lynching legislation, racial discrimination in education, internationalism, and home rule for the District of Columbia.[5]

Although the National Council of Jewish Women was an important member, many of its concerns relating primarily to Jewish issues were not supported by enough other members to have legislative subcommittees. In its early years the committee had task forces on various pieces of immigration legislation, opposing immigration restriction. By 1933, the committee still reported on congressional immigration bills, many of which were clearly aimed at easing regulations so that Jewish victims of European anti-Semitism could more easily enter the United States. Although this legislation was consistently supported by the NCJW, it did not receive the endorsement of the four other groups necessary for the formation of a subcommittee to work actively for its passage. This provides an example of how a strong, explicit, organized Jewish presence in an organization does not necessarily imply support for Jewish issues.

There was also enormous Jewish community support for feminist issues. In New York City, Jews were the base of popular support for women's suffrage, with the strongest and most consistent voting support from Jewish neighborhoods, and with Jewish women among the most dedicated, hardest-working suffragists. Involvement of Jewish women in organizing women workers and the large numbers of Jewish women who joined unions have been well documented.

Before World War I, Jewish working women often found their feminist political expression in socialism. The New York Socialist party had several women's groups in Jewish areas. After winning suffrage in New York, one-half of the Socialist party registrations in many Jewish neighborhoods were female. The birth control movement provides another example of the crucial role played by Jewish women. Demand for birth control information and eagerness to use contraception was high in Jewish communities. It is no accident that one of Margaret Sanger's first birth control clinics was opened in 1916 in a Jewish neighborhood in Brownsville, New York.[6]

In spite of this broad-based, strong support for feminist issues, feminist organizations were noticeably reticent about acknowledging Jewish support, in some cases actively downplaying, and even concealing, Jewish participation. For example, Manhattan's suffragists never publicly acknowledged crucial Jewish support in winning the vote. When they announced the 1915 election results, they never mentioned the predominantly Jewish assembly district which was the only Manhattan district to vote in favor of suffrage. Nor did they mention Jewish districts with relatively high pro-suffrage votes. Instead they extolled support from more gentile areas, although the percentage of pro-suffrage votes in these districts was less than in Jewish areas. This, together with blaming immigrants for the defeat of suffrage in the 1915 election, was too much for Lillian Wald and Livinia Dock, suffrage organizers in lower Manhattan. Wald and

Dock protested to the Woman Suffrage party over its neglecting to mention these immigrant districts that supported suffrage. It is important to note that in this interchange between the Woman Suffrage party and Wald and Dock, never was the word "Jewish" mentioned; rather, the discussion centered around whether all immigrants voted against suffrage.[7] This reluctance to talk explicitly about Jews is an important factor both in hiding Jewish support for feminism and in enabling feminists to avoid dealing with anti-Semitism.

Even after the 1917 suffrage victory in New York, suffragists were unwilling to acknowledge publicly the importance of the pro-suffrage Jewish vote. In part, this was because of the association between Jews and socialism. The stereotype of the radical Russian immigrant Jew was very strong in New York. Partly based in fact— Jews did comprise a sizeable percentage of the New York City Socialist party—suffragists feared that admitting Jewish support for suffrage would firmly associate feminism with socialism. Since suffragists were seriously aiming for a federal amendment and thus needed support from conservative state legislatures, they sought at all costs to disassociate themselves from radical politics. Sometimes the costs were too high, as in Manhattan when they did not invite the Socialist party to share the stage, along with other city political parties, during the suffrage victory celebration. Since the Socialist party had been a major supporter and many socialist areas voted heavily for suffrage, the protest at this snub was too great and the Woman Suffrage party was forced to apologize publicly.[8]

While the relationship of individual Jews, some Jewish organizations, and Jewish communities to feminism was fairly straightforward—most supported it and relatively few worked against it—the relationship of individual feminists and feminist organizations to Jews was much more complicated. Two factors tended to obfuscate the relationship: the uncritical use of the term "immigrant" and the liberal refusal to acknowledge differences. In spite of enormous ethnic differences which influenced immigrant political behavior, American feminists tended to use "immigrant" as if it represented a homogeneous group. Coupled with their inability to talk explicitly about Jews, this served to make Jews invisible in their discourse and thus automatically subsumed under the catchall "immigrant" label. Suffragists often blamed defeats on immigrant opposition. Inez Irwin of the National Women's party stated that "everywhere experience had shown that naturalized aliens were less amenable to suffrage arguments than people of the old American stock."[9] This was often repeated in spite of the fact that it simply was not true for American Jews.

The reluctance of feminists to talk about Jews was also the result of feminists' growing internationalism. The emergence of this internationalism can be seen in the political development of Carrie Chapman Catt. As a young suffragist, she started out an isolationist, making speeches in 1887 on "America for Americans" in which, according to a reporter, she described "the evil influence of an unassimilated and unsympathetic foreign element in American society and American politics." By 1914, Catt had become active in the peace movement and had begun to develop an international perspective. In 1923, already an advocate of the League of Nations, she urged the United States to intervene in Europe. By 1936 Catt was espousing anti-colonial views such as attributing the cause of war to racism and imperialism on the part of white nations.[10]

Given this internationalism, it is not surprising that feminists rarely took up nationalist issues, even when it would have been in their interest. Though New York City suffragists badly wanted the Irish vote, they did not endorse Irish nationalism. Internationalism also hindered feminists' ability, before World War II, to talk openly about Jews, since Jews were the nationality without a nation. To discuss Jews meant to acknowledge them as a group and thus as a nationality. To internationalists, bent on breaking down national boundaries, however, the theoretical creation and recognition of Jews as a nationality was full of undesirable political implications. Whenever feminists entered the international political arena, it was usually to endorse internationalist issues such as peace or entry into the League of Nations.

Feminists, therefore, rarely took up issues that were specifically Jewish. Feminists worked for causes which mainly involved Jewish women, such as organizing female garment workers; supported issues that related to immigrant women in general, such as naturalization reform to permit immigrant women to become citizens independently of husbands or fathers; and backed the same liberal, civil rights issues, which neither group defined as "Jewish" issues. When American political matters had clear implications for Jews, though, feminists remained silent. Feminists were distressed by the political repressions between the two world wars. They protested the attacks on advocates of birth control and the arrests of pacifists during World War I. They were upset by the repression of labor radicals during the Red Scare of 1919–20. They did not voice opposition, however, to anti-Semitism evident in immigrant deportations. Even when the anti-Semitic attacks involved feminist and pacifist allies, American feminists did not take public stands against them. Beginning in 1904, for example, the Jewish Hungarian activist Rosika Schwimmer had extensive contacts with American feminists, and in 1921 she settled in the United States. Since she had been one of the main organizers of a peace ship expedition financed by Henry Ford in 1915, Schwimmer became implicated in Ford's vicious attacks on Jews which began in 1920. While American feminists supported Schwimmer in her attempts to become an American citizen, they did not voice opposition to Ford's anti-Semitism.[11]

The unwillingness of American feminist groups to take pro-Jewish stands became clearest in the 1930s when most refused to take formal positions against the persecution of Jews in Europe. The National Consumers' League, although founded by Maud Nathan and extensively involved in assisting Jewish garment workers before World War I, refused to endorse or cooperate in a boycott of German goods when asked to do so by the American Jewish Congress in 1934. After repeated questioning as to whether the league would condemn German persecution of minorities, in 1938 it voted not to on the grounds that "for the League to act as an organization in this regard would be to take it beyond its fixed scope." For many years, however, the league had supported anti-lynching legislation, certainly not more within the league's purpose than anti-Nazi reolutions.[12]

In fact, many organizations such as the Women's Joint Congressional Committee and the National Consumers' League, which refused to take formal stands against European Jewish persecution using the rationale that it would go beyond the scope of the organization, had adopted a wide range of issues that were rather removed from explicit women's concerns, such as peace, the League of Nations, and anti-lynching legislation. For example, in 1936 the National League of Women Voters endorsed neutrality and reciprocal trade legislation; the National Women's Trade Union League endorsed anti-lynching and neutrality legislation; the American Federation of Teachers backed anti-lynching legislation, suffrage for the District of Columbia, and the World

Court.[13] Questions of what is legitimate or within the scope of an organization to support is often decided by practical considerations: How will the issue affect the constituency? How is it related to the base of support and those the organizations need to influence? What stands a group takes are tempered by what is politically convenient and the degree of internal and external pressure backing the issue. Often organizations will endorse an issue if they sense enough moral outrage (on the part of the public, their members, or their political associates), so that the issue becomes one of general decency, rather than a special interest group concern. Apparently this moral imperative to speak out against European anti-Semitism was lacking.

The reluctance of women's groups to condemn European anti-Semitism did not necessarily reflect the beliefs of individual feminists. A large number were sincerely troubled by European events and worked, as individuals, to publicize anti-Semitic attacks in Europe. Several leading feminists, most notably Carrie Chapman Catt and Mary Dreier, were very active in the support of European Jews and many voiced concern over the rise of anti-Semitism in Europe. There were several reasons why some American feminists, however unwilling they were to confront anti-Semitism at home, were able to deal with it abroad. Beginning in 1900, through various international organizations and alliances such as the International Suffrage Alliance and the international peace movement, American feminists had made numerous European feminist friends, many of whom were Jewish women. From 1920 through 1939, American feminists traveled to Europe, seeing anti-Semitism first hand. They also gained information through a correspondence network established by these international organizations. Accounts written by trusted European contacts, often relaying an individual's pain and fear along with concrete information about acts of anti-Semitism, convinced American feminists of the seriousness, immediacy, and danger of the situation. Additionally, repression in Germany had concrete effects on United States feminists in that it curtailed the viability, and even existence, of branches of international women's organizations. Thirdly, international tensions and differences were reflected in problems with management and policy in international women's groups. Lastly, it was simply safer to address anti-Semitism somewhere else. One could admit the existence of European anti-Semitism without having to acknowledge it at home.

American feminists engaged in a surprising amount of intercontinental travel for political purposes. As early as 1922 and 1923 feminists traveling in Europe detailed the rise of fascism and repression of Jews. Often these letters were sent to many organizational and political associates, thus creating the spread of information over a wide network. During the 1930s American feminists knew very well what was happening in Europe, since they continued to visit Europe and receive correspondence from European feminists documenting the growing repression. European women wrote of tragedies which befell their friends and allies: harassment, arrest, and murder. They also wrote of the growing refugee problem.[14]

Of great concern to American feminists was the effect of rising reactionary politics in Europe on international feminist organizations. In 1933 several organizations were forced to disband their German branches rather than comply with Nazi regulations that all Jewish members resign. Americans carefully followed European debates over whether to comply or disband. In 1937 Rosa Manus, a Jewish Dutch feminist, wrote about a public meeting of the International Alliance in Zurich where "a fascist or Nazziman (sic) found it necessary to throw raw eggs at [the speaker] crying out: 'we do not want Jews.'" This woman had been forbidden to address a meeting in Strasbourg several weeks earlier. The alliance had canceled plans to hold a conference in Poland because no Jews would have been allowed to speak. Eventually, Jewish feminists such as Rosa Manus left the alliance and other women's groups to devote themselves full time to helping European Jews.[15]

American feminists' response was largely spontaneous, individualistic, and limited. In 1933, Catt organized a public protest against German anti-Semitism. Forming a new, ad hoc committee rather than working through established organizations, in June she circulated a strongly worded petition, aiming to get signatures of 5,000 non-Jewish feminists. By the middle of August, over 9,000 had signed, including almost every prominent United States feminist. The petition called for an end to persecution of German Jews and for international protection to secure their safety. In private correspondence to friends Catt assured them that facts were even worse than stated in the petition and press, that information received from feminists' European sources was reliable, and that Americans could have no excuse for claiming that they did not know what was happening in Germany.[16] Catt insisted that the signers be non-Jews because she feared that Hitler would retaliate against German Jews if American Jews signed the petition. Catt is usually given credit for originating the petition, but in a letter to Rosa Manus she stated, "I have been asked to make a woman's demonstration of protest against the anti-Jewish Hitlerism of Germany." It is quite possible that the request came from the National Council of Jewish Women since, according to Catt, they did clerical work for the petition and Catt worked closely with them on other projects to aid Jewish refugees. The petition was sent to governments and the League of Nations. It received wide press coverage and the American Jewish community praised feminists for their support. An issue of the *American Hebrew* had Jane Addams and Catt on the cover and contained a long article on the petition. Catt was awarded the American Hebrew medal for "promoting better understanding between Christians and Jews" for 1933, an award of which she was very proud.[17]

Aside from this much publicized petition, gentile American feminists made few public or practical efforts to aid European Jews. It was relatively easy to sign a petition; it was much harder to work for refugee aid or to sponsor Jewish immigrants to America. In fact, like the feminist organizations cited earlier, many refused to take a more active stance or to support actual measures to aid European Jews. There was little sympathy for the boycott of German goods. In a letter to Jane Addams, Catt indicated that she did not think it would be "useful." In the same letter, Catt wrote, "I want to tell you just for amusement that the work done in connection with th protest against the persecution of Jews in Germany has met with quite unexpected returns." Indeed, American Jews asked that the signers of the petition assist in actual measures to aid European Jews: support the boycott of German goods, or help to bring Jewish refugees to the United States (by donating money, lobbying the government to change immigration laws, and sponsoring immigrants, particularly children).[18]

Although most Gentile feminists balked at these requests, a few, along with Catt, continued to work for the cause of European Jews. In December 1933 Catt organized a small committee of ten to pressure the United States government to ease immigration laws, permitting more Jews to enter. A much more modest endeavor than the earlier petition, she sought only one hundred signatures to this letter. The differences between the two gives a clear example of the sentiment concerning European anti-Semitism. It was relatively easy to get thousands of signatures on a public petition asking that someone else do something about it. For a letter asking that the United States do something, Catt aimed for far fewer signatures and, rather than make a public protest, she sent it to the government with a detailed statement, "Asylum for Refugees Under Our Immigration Laws." Although in her seventies, Catt persisted in pressuring the government to aid refugees, often co-operating with the National Council of Jewish Women in this work. She consistently forwarded to the council information from Rosa Manus on the situation of Jews in Europe.[19]

This support for Jewish refugees caused problems in the international women's movement because questions of national loyalty sometimes clashed with pacifist and humanitarian ideals. As American and European feminists began to criticize British restrictions against Jewish refugees in Palestine, British feminists found themselves painfully on the defensive against women with whom they had been friends and political allies, sometimes for twenty to thirty years. Later, when many American feminists supported Zionist aspirations, deplored the British refusal to accept Jewish refugees in Palestine, and raised money for a Jewish state, English feminists found their relations with their old allies even more strained.[20]

Although it is relatively easy to document feminists' relationships to specific Jewish issues, it is more difficult to come to grips with their general attitude toward Jews. Again, contradictory attitudes, reflecting a certain hypocrisy, clouded the actions of feminists with respect to Jews. Pluralism dictated that one should recognize differences and be tolerant; however, liberalism prescribed that everyone ought to be treated the same, since differences were not to be acknowledged. For example, Carrie Chapman Catt wrote that the reason suffrage workers stopped Bible reading and prayers at meetings was that meetings were attended by Protestants, Catholics, and Jews, and "since the prayers were very often in the interests of one of the denominations it was easier to put them all off the program." This solution of treating everyone as if they were the same, i.e., Anglo-Saxon Protestants, often led to a patronizing tolerance of Jews. This was reflected in simple neglect of Jews to overt acts of anti-Semitism.[21]

There were some clear acts of overt anti-Semitism and use of Jewish stereotypes. For years suffrage leader Anna Howard Shaw asserted that Jewish voters in South Dakota in 1890 had defeated woman suffrage, claiming that counties inhabited by Russian Jews voted almost solidly against it. In 1915, an editorial in the *American Hebrew* noted that Shaw had "mistaken" Russians for Jews, pointing out that while there were indeed Russian immigrants in South Dakota, there were not enough Jewish votes in the whole state to carry any county for any issue.[22]

Another instance occurred in the New York Women's Trade Union League, an organization heavily Jewish both in leadership and membership. For many years the league had its major successes organizing Jewish women in the needle trades. It had tried, largely in vain, to unionize native-born American women in millinery, garment, sales, and clerical occupations. By 1910 factions within the league led by Helen Marot challenged the value of concentrating on garment unions, demanding that the League switch priorities to organizing native-born American women. The arguments were often anti-Semitic, and Marot waged a nasty campaign against Rose Schneiderman and her garment union involvement.

In 1911 Marot launched a virulent public attack on the garment unions' leadership and Abraham Cahan, editor of the leading Jewish socialist paper, the *Forward*, stating, "We have always realized for several years that the Russian-Jews had little sense of administration and we have been used to ascribing their failure to their depending solely on emotions and not on constructive work." Marot coupled her attacks on Jewish unions with attacks on socialist and radical politics. Making the stereotypical association of "Jew" with "radical," she blamed the supposed lack of stability in the garment trades unions on utopian socialist politics.[23]

More common than open, anti-Jewish statements was anti-Semitism by neglect: the nonrecognition of Jewish existence. New York City suffragists maintained a double standard with respect to Jewish communities. They recognized that certain aspects of Jewish life needed to be taken into account when organizing in Jewish neighborhoods, so they planned events for Friday afternoon and Sunday, rather than the usual Saturday afternoon. In spite of their knowledge that Jews constituted the strongest support for suffrage, when planning city-wide events, especially those designed to gain the most publicity or attract the broadest appeal, they frequently did not take Jews into account. In 1910 the second annual convention of the Woman Suffrage party in New York City was held on a Friday night, which seriously limited the participation of Jewish women in formal party business. In 1911 the party acknowledged that such scheduling limited Jewish involvement, noting that few Jewish women took part in the large June suffrage parade since it was on Saturday. Although expressing hope that immense numbers of Jews would march in the next parades, the party continued to hold them on Saturday.[24]

The silence in official statements by suffragists about the major part played by Jews in supporting suffrage in New York City has already been noted, yet in internal movement publications the involvement of Jews was frequently mentioned. This double standard—the private acknowledgment with the public disavowal— was also reflected in the use of the term "immigrant." In public statements and analyses, immigrant was used as a catchall for all non-native Americans; however, internal propaganda contained characterizations of various ethnic groups, particularly the Irish, Italians, and Jews. The Irish male was often portrayed as politically corrupt and anti-suffrage, the Irish woman as hesitantly pro-suffrage, and the Jewish woman as very pro-suffrage, politically astute, and ethical. These depictions appear most strongly in political plays with suffrage or labor union themes. These explicit, usually favorable, portrayals of Jews present them as models of Americanization, blending the best of Jewish tradition with American culture. They rarely mention anti-Semitism, either as existing in the United States or as a reason for immigration from Eastern Europe. A notable exception is the play *Some Citizens* by Mary Dreier, a leader in the New York Women's Trade Union League. The first scenes take place in Europe and depict the anti-Semitism which causes the leading characters to flee to America. While not mentioning American anti-Semitism directly, the play equates jail treatment of striking Jewish workers with pogroms in Europe. Dreier also compares sisterhood to Jewish identity, as when the young Jewish woman worker cries: "We've had hard blows because of our Faith, shall we be afraid of hard blows because of our faith in the new sisterhood?" In no fictionalized accounts written by feminists is American anti-Semitism actually presented.[25]

Occasionally feminists would recognize Jewish support for women's issues. Often they had to be directly confronted with it, as when addressing Jewish women's groups or writing articles for or being interviewed by Jewish publications. At these times they might express solidarity with Jewish causes. When Mary Garret Hay, New York feminist, was interviewed by the *American Hebrew* in 1922, she claimed that many of her non-Jewish friends were not sending their sons to Harvard because of the school's anti-Semitic quota. There were infrequent articles in the non-Jewish press in which feminists would praise Jewish women and their support for feminism, as in "Jewish Women in Public Affairs" by the suffragist Alva Belmont; however, most of these appeals for contact and cooperation between Jews and Gentiles, and confirmation of Jewish support for feminism, were class-based. Gentile feminists cited upper-class women, like Maud Nathan, and praised the involvement of Jewish club women, rarely mentioning the thousands of working immigrant women who worked for feminist issues.[26]

Feminists' desire to publicly disassociate from Jews was connected for some to a wish to disassociate from radicalism. Feminists who aspired to a broad-based movement, who consciously sought support from conservative sectors, or who tried to preserve their organizations and causes against right-wing attacks, attempted to break the connection between women's issues and radicalism. From the early 1900s, a standard attack on women's issues (as on practically all American radical and reform movements) was to accuse them of being socialist, un-American, and foreign influenced.

Feminists and birth control advocates were often attacked as being in favor of free love and an end to the family. Suffragists, pacifists, and labor organizers were accused of being subversive, socialist, and foreign dominated. To combat these attacks, women involved in reform movements often found themselves in the odd position of claiming that they were not feminists. This tendency to deny the accusations by disclaiming adherence to political movements served to push feminists further and further toward the center as political attacks against them increased after World

War I. Often these various attacks were tied together in a convenient bundle and hurled at any women's political movement. For example, the National Association Opposed to Woman Suffrage stated: "Pacifist, socialist, feminist, suffragist are all parts of the same movement—a movement which weakens government, corrupts society and threatens the very existence of our great experiment in democracy."[27] A writer to an anti-suffrage paper warned that naturalization drives advocated by feminists and socialists were a threat to American democracy.

These attacks made suffragists increasingly nervous about their connections with socialism. Although they had initially welcomed Socialist party endorsement, and many leading suffragists were active socialists, by World War I many were anxious to break the public connection between suffrage and socialism. Since during World War I suffragists appealed to conservative state legislatures for the federal amendment, they felt very sensitive to accusations of radicalism and un-Americanism. Anti-suffragists continued their attacks on suffrage as socialist and foreign (i.e., immigrant oriented) as in a letter sent to Pennsylvania senators urging them to vote against the federal amendment. The 1918 letter pointed to socialist support for suffrage in New York and warned, "Think of [New York] with hundreds of thousands of poor illiterate foreign women, four-fifths of which will vote" as directed by the Socialists.[28]

Feminists' advocacy of pacifism was another favorite point of attack. Before World War I many leading feminists such as Jane Addams, Carrie Chapman Gatt, Lillian Wald, and Charlotte Perkins Gilman were active in pacifist endeavors and argued against United States involvement in the war. Again, since the Socialist party also took these stands, women involved in the peace movement were accused of being unpatriotic and were even more vulnerable to charges of foreign influence. Again, as in many feminists' disowning of socialism in order to protect their causes, some women's groups actively supported America's involvement in World War I, returning to peace work after the war's end.

As conservative attacks against feminists increased, women's groups became more reluctant to acknowledge Jewish support because of the stereotypes of Jews as socialist, pacifist, and foreign. Americans had long viewed Jews as radicals and as foreigners whose primary allegiance lay outside the United States. These sentiments intensified with Wold War I and the 1917 Russian revolution, culminating during the Red Scare. Many of the immigrants arrested in the Palmer raids and later deported were eastern European Jews. Government investigations in 1919 to determine the degree of socialist infiltration in American society focused on supposed associations between Russian Bolsheviks, Russian Jews, and American Jewish immigrants. Some witnesses before the Senate committee went so far as to claim that the Russian revolution had been led by New York City East Side Jews.[29] Attacks accusing Jews of being behind a world-wide communist movement continued up to World War II. Indeed, American Jews never seemed to have an acceptable position on the United States' involvement in the world wars. Until the Russian revolution, many American Jews were against American participation in the war since they were eager to see Germany defeat tsarist Russia. Although the 1917 revolution changed many American Jews' attitudes on the war, Americans still regarded Jews as pacifists and a hindrance to the war effort. On the other hand, when American Jews urged United States involvement in World War II, they were accused of leading us into a war where we did not belong. Thus, Jews were never a non-controversial ally in a pre-war America.

These formal and public persecutions of Jewish immigrants— the arrests and deportations, the banning of organizations and journals, the government investigation committees—brought attention to the involvement of Jews in many feminist activities. The banning of the magazine the *Masses*, for its socialism and pacifism, also called attention to its support for birth control and Jewish immigrants in the birth control movement. The arrest of anarchist Emma Goldman focused attention on her feminist politics. In particular, many feminists found themselves attacked because of their association with the Jewish, Hungarian, pacifist, and feminist Rosika Schwimmer. Involved in the International Woman Suffrage Alliance, she came to the United States in 1914, sponsored by Carrie Chapman Catt who had connections with Schwimmer from her international peace and suffrage work. Schwimmer toured the United States during 1914 and 1915, giving speeches on international peace and suffrage and becoming a major influence in the formation of American feminist peace organizations. At first, Schwimmer was accused of being a German spy enlisting American feminists to aid the German side during World War I and later a Bolshevik agent recruiting feminists to communism during the 1920s. A typical flyer, by a Massachusetts anti-suffrage association, called "Is Woman Suffrage Pro-German?" stated, "At the very beginning of the war an Austrian Socialist woman, Frau Schwimmer, came to this country to work for suffrage, and through the suffragists, for Germany's interests in the war." Initially, when she arrived in 1914, feminists such as Catt and Jane Addams were thrilled by her presence and, well aware that she was Jewish, made special arrangements for her to speak to Jewish groups. Catt and others continued to defend her against attackers over the years, but they also had to defend their women's groups from attacks based on the connection between Schwimmer and feminism.[30]

Although splits had existed in the feminist movement prior to World War I, the intensity of right-wing attacks on radicalism caused serious divisions among feminists and ended with a definite swing toward more moderate, reformist feminist politics between the wars. Previously, distinctions and tensions between feminists resulted from disagreements over issues and the degree of tactical militancy. Issues of political affiliation, such as socialism, were not crucial, with socialists found among the adherents to all the major feminist causes. With World War I and the Russian revolution, America's relative tolerance for radicalism and socialism ended. Activists had to choose in very significant ways between socialism, which now effectively meant the Communist party, and reform social movements. With elimination of the socialist middle and in the face of continuing attacks on radicals, feminists had few choices: they could join those attacked; they could disassociate as much as possible from those attacked; or they could disassociate from but become defenders of radicals' civil liberties, for example by joining the newly formed American Civil Liberties Union. Some feminists, such as Rose Pastor Stokes, chose socialism and became active in the Communist party, and thereby spent relatively less time on feminist issues. Most individual feminists and the major women's groups chose one of the second or third alternatives, spending the years between the wars not in mass organizing but rather in defending themselves against right-wing attacks and working for legislative reforms.

Because of the association between Jews and radicalism, this turn toward moderation and the perceived necessity of defending feminism against conservative attacks resulted in even more denial of Jewish support for feminism and a reluctance on the part of feminists to protest against the rising anti-Semitism. In contrast to previous protests against harassment of labor leaders and radicals, neither feminists nor women's organizations condemned the Red Scare repressions. They did not speak out against the Palmer raids, deportations, public government accusations against immigrants, and banning of periodicals. Their unwillingness to do so was perhaps related to a sense of vulnerability. Because feminists had so many affiliations—memberships in multiple groups and activity in many causes—it left them open to attacks on several fronts. In addition, the shift from mass-based organizations to working in smaller groups primarily for legislative reform made them more dependent on established authority. During World War I, two primary concerns were the federal suffrage amendment and conditions for women working in war industries. Political considerations thus made it risky for feminists to defend those attacked during the Red Scare. Even more important, feminists were susceptible to the same charges that were made against Jews. Many feminists had been socialists before World War I, including nationally known women such as Mary Beard, Rose Schneiderman, Florence Kelley, Harriet Stanton Blatch and Charlotte Perkins Gilman. Many feminists were also internationalists and pacifists. Sensitive to the implications that conservatives drew from their involvement in international women's groups, American feminists tried to maintain a patriotic image in the twenties and thirties. For all these reasons, they were wary of being identified with Jews or protesting against anti-Semitism.

Indeed, the same attacks, in the same manner and by the same people, were made on feminists as were made on Jews. Henry Ford began his conservative attacks by lashing out at Jews through his *Dearborn Independent* from 1920 to 1924. When Ford began to change his attacks from Jews to radicals, he, and others, began to explicitly include feminists. In 1924 Ford published a series of articles accusing women's organizations of being fronts for communist activity. One, entitled "Are Women's Clubs 'Used' by Bolshevists?" presented interconnections between the membership of various feminist and peace groups. This "interlocking directorate" was held to represent an international Bolshevik conspiracy. The Spider Web Chart, as this diagram of women's multiple affiliations was called, became a major tool in conservative attacks on women's groups. In 1926, the Daughters of the American Revolution (DAR) entered the fray by claiming to have updated the Spider Web Chart and by forming a blacklist which included most prominent American feminists. Among the favorite targets were Jane Addams, Florence Kelley, and Rose Schneiderman (who they called "the Red Rose of Anarchy"). In 1927, the right-wing *Daily Data Sheet,* written by F. R. Marvin, published a series of articles accusing women's groups of communist orientation and connections to the USSR. All of these attacks had a decidedly anti-immigrant tinge, and with a few words altered, read similarly to the corresponding attacks on Jews.[31]

Curiously, not only did feminists avoid referring explicitly to Jews but so did conservatives when attacking them. Marvin, in his anti-feminist articles, spoke of socialists, communists, and reds. He mentioned various Jewish feminists by name; however, he did not explicitly label them as Jewish. (When Marvin was attacking organized labor, he did not show the same restraint. In one article he referred to a female labor leader as "a radical Jewess.")[32] During all of these attacks, feminists tended to remain mute on anti-Semitism even when it was part of the attack on feminists themselves. Rosika Schwimmer provides a case in point. When she began to apply for United States citizenship in 1924, she was subjected to increased harassment and her application underwent several court reviews until her citizenship was denied in 1929, a decision officially based on her pacifism. A reading of the court proceedings makes it clear, however, that she was also being persecuted because she was Jewish. Many feminists rallied to her support, but they did not address the issue of anti-Semitism and the case did not prompt them to speak out against anti-Semitism in general. Symptomatic of some feminists' fear of association with radicalism, Catt urged Schwimmer not to seek help from the American Civil Liberties Union (ACLU) since its radical reputation would only hurt her cause by association; Catt also refused to sign an ACLU petition for Schwimmer, although she provided her with much assistance in other ways. Avoidance of the issue of anti-Semitism is particularly striking in this case since Schwimmer had been a favorite target of anti-Semites in the early twenties; feminists such as Catt must surely have known that anti-Jewish prejudice was the basis of much of the hostility to Schwimmer.[33]

On the whole, feminists' reaction to these attacks was denial: denial that feminists were un-American, and denial that feminists were now communists or had been socialists. Afraid and wary in the midst of repression and growing reactionary politics, they sought to appear as pure as possible. They did have certain problems refuting charges of radicalism since so many feminists had been active socialists for many years before World War I. Catt sought to counter DAR claims that women's groups were communist front organizations by showing that several prominent feminists whom the DAR had especially attacked were innocent. Unfortunately for her, those she selected to defend publicly—Jane Addams, Rose Schneiderman, Florence Kelley—gave her trouble by refusing to deny their socialist past, their present sympathy for socialism, and/or their strong pacifism. Schneiderman wrote to Catt: "I am a Socialist. I am not a member of the party, however, and have not been since 1919 . . . and although I am a Socialist by conviction, I am not that strict that I do not scratch my ticket and vote for candidates who I think will do some immediate good." Nevertheless, Catt managed to construct a suitable statement which got much media coverage as a refutation of the DAR charges.[34]

These attempts to disassociate from radical feminists and radical politics had the effect of denying many Jewish feminists and their past activity in women's organizations. Conveniently "forgotten" were Rose Pastor Stokes and Clara Lemlich, who had become Communist party members. It also had the effect of discouraging protest against the rising anti-Semitism in America. Quite clearly, Jews were dangerous allies for those trying to retain political respectability, and feminists knew well that the label "Jew" could be used to discredit women and their causes. In 1936, Secretary of Labor Frances Perkins was the subject of a rumor campaign asserting that she was a Jew. This was part of the general right-wing claim that Roosevelt was Jewish and the New Deal was communist inspired and controlled. Responding to questions from another feminist, after presenting a long, detailed family history to show that she was, in fact, *not* Jewish, Perkins wrote: "I have written you at length . . . because a number of similar letters of inquiry in recent weeks have led me to the conclusion that some rumor intended to be malicious is in circulation and that for the ease of all interested I should not ignore it. The purpose, although obscure, appears to be political as those who are circulating it do not know me and therefore can have no personal ill will toward me. The utter un-Americanism of such a whispering campaign, the appeal to racial prejudice and the attempt at political propaganda by unworthy innuendo must be repugnant to all honorable men and women."[35] Perkins's reply acknowledges the reality of anti-Semitism and its use as a political weapon.

All of this is not to condemn American feminists for their lack of political work against American anti-Semitism. Many, such as Catt and Mary Dreier, did good, liberal things to aid European Jewish victims of anti-Semitism and became ardent supporters of the state of Israel. The failing of many, like Catt, was in their political opportunism and determination to keep feminism, as they understood it, alive as a viable force, even if it meant discounting radical or inconvenient allies in a time of political repression. Feminists were not the first political group to choose self-preservation over moral correctness, nor was this the first or last time such decisions were made. When it becomes a choice between practical politics versus moral imperatives, Jews tend to lose out since, unfortunately, Jews have never been "safe" political allies in America.[36]

The ultimate failure of American feminism with respect to Jews was its inability to accept American Jewish existence and thereby to recognize the presence of American anti-Semitism. By buying into the myths of liberalism and assimilation, feminists were able to avoid dealing with American Jews as Jews. Thus Jews remained hidden, the unspoken minority. Only with regard to "other" Jews, European Jews, those being persecuted someplace else, by someone else, could American feminists act against anti-Semitism. Catt provides an example of the degree to which American feminists negated the existence of American Jews. Her long association with New York feminism brought her into contact with prominent New York Jewish feminists, such as Maud Nathan. The Nathans were Catt's social equals and they often attended the same political and social functions. Maud Nathan attended European suffrage meetings, traveling with Catt for weeks at a time. Yet, in a letter mourning the death of Rosa Manus while under German arrest, Catt comments that the Manus family was the only Jewish family which she knew well.[37]

Notes

1. Among the numerous such studies are the classic "Jews and Negroes in the Communist Party," in *The Crisis of the Negro Intellectual*, ed. Harold Cruse (New York, 1967), pp. 147–70, and Stanley Rothman and S. Robert Lichter, *Roots of Radicalism: Jews, Christians, and the New Left* (New York, 1982).

2. For example, see Letty Cottin Pogrebin, "Anti-Semitism in the Women's Movement," *Ms.* (June 1982): 45–49, 62–72; Selma Miriam, "Anti-Semitism in the Lesbian Community," *Sinister Wisdom* 19 (1982): 50–60; special issue of *Lilith* 7 (1980); letters in *Sojourner* (Mar. 1982), pp. 2–3, (July 1982), p. 4, (June 1982), pp. 3–4; Melanie Kaye, "Anti-Semitism, Homophobia, and the Good White Knight," *Off Our Backs* 12 (May 1982): 30–31; articles in *Big Mama Rag* (Feb. 1982), pp. 9–19, 3, 8, 6, (July 1982), pp. 8, 10, 11, 17; Ann Leffler, "Feminism and Anti-Semitism" (unpublished paper, 1981).

3. I am indebted to Ann Leffler and Deborah Dash Moore for discussions which led me to the development of this analysis.

4. There is an increasing amount of material on American Jewish women. Among the best sources are Charlotte Baum, Paula Hyman, and Sonya Michel,

The Jewish Woman in America (New York, 1975); Jacob Marcus, *The American Jewish Woman, 1654–1980* (New York, 1981), and *The American Jewish Woman: A Documentary History* (New York, 1981; Rudolf Glanz, *The Jewish Woman in America*, 2 vols. (New York, 1976); Aviva Cantor, *The Jewish Woman: 1900–1980, An Annotated Bibliography* (Fresh Meadows, N.Y., 1981); *Notable American Women*, 4 vols. (Cambridge, Mass., 1980). The biographic information in this article on prominent Jewish women is taken from these sources.

5. Information on the Women's Joint Congressional Committee obtained from the "Minutes of Meetings" in the papers of the Women's Joint Congressional Committee for the years 1920–39, Library of Congress, Washington, D.C., and reports in *The Jewish Woman*, the journal of the National Council of Jewish Women. Other members of the committee included the National Women's Trade Union League, National League of Women Voters, the National Consumers' League, the YWCA, the American Federation of Teachers, and the American Association of University Women.

6. Elinor Lerner, "Jewish Involvement in the New York Woman Suffrage Movement," *American Jewish History* 70 (June 1981): 442–61; Nancy Schrom Dye, "The Woman's Trade Union League of New York 1903–1920" (unpublished Ph.D. diss., University of Wisconsin, 1974); Emma Goldman, *Living My Life* (New York, 1970), vol. 2, p. 569.

7. Lerner, "Jewish Involvement," pp. 459–60.

8. Charles Leinenweber, "The Class and Ethnic Base of New York Socialism,

1904–1915," *Labor History* 22 (Winter 1981): 31–56; Lerner, "Jewish Involvement," pp. 460–61.

9. Inez Irwin, *Angels and Amazons* (Garden City, N.Y., 1933), p. 342; *New York Times*, Nov. 4, 1915.

10. Flyer and *Washington Post* clipping Jan. 1936 in Catt Papers, Library of Congress, Washington, D.C.; *New York Tribune*, June 6, 1923.

11. Albert Lee, *Henry Ford and the Jews* (New York, 1980), pp. 143–47.

12. Board of Directors meeting minutes, National Consumers' League, Nov. 21, 1938, and Apr. 4, 1934; National Consumers' League papers, Library of Congress, Washington, D.C.

13. Yearly Statement (1936–37) of the Women's Joint Congressional Committee, Women's Joint Congressional Committee Papers, Library of Congress, Washington, D.C.

14. Between the world wars large delegations of Americans attended European congresses of the International Woman Suffrage Alliance and peace organizations. American women also toured extensively throughout Europe, Asia, and Latin America. Catt spent much of the years between 1904 and 1914 traveling in Europe, Asia, and the Middle East, and in 1922–23 in South America. She was often accompanied on her travels by Dutch Jewish feminist friends, Aletta Jacobs and Rosa Manus.

A 1923 report from Hungary noted the rise of anti-Semitism, "a sinister anti semetic (*sic*) movement sprung up and sorry vengence has been wreaked on many an innocent Jew." "Hungary report," Feb. 10, 1923, in National American Woman Suffrage Association Papers, Library of Congress.

15. Rosa Manus to Catt, Nov. 29, 1933, Apr. 1, 1937, in Catt Papers, Library of Congress.

16. Catt, "Friend of Human Justice" letter, petition, and list of signatures in Catt Papers, Library of Congress; Catt letter to Mrs. Edward Dreier, Aug. 11, 1933, Catt Papers, Library of Congress.

17. Catt to Manus, June 20, 1933, in Catt Papers, Library of Congress; *American Hebrew* Aug. 18, 1933; Mary Gray Peck, *Carrie Chapman Catt* (New York, 1944), pp. 446–49.

18. Catt to Jane Addams, Sept. 12, 1933, in Catt Papers, Library of Congress.

19. "Asylum for Refugees Under Our Immigration Laws" and Committee of Ten letter; Catt letter to Mrs. Slade, Dec. 13, 1933; Catt to Rosa Manus, June 20, 1933, Oct. 6, 1933, Mar. 6, 1934, in Catt Papers, Library of Congress.

20. Lady Astor to Catt, Dec. 15, 1936, in Catt Papers, Library of Congress.

21. Catt to Charlotte Perkins Gilman, Sept. 16, 1933 in Catt Papers, New York Public Library, New York City.

22. *American Hebrew* (Nov. 12, 1915), p. 15.

23. Secretary Report to New York Women's Trade Union League, May 25, 1911, and Apr. 27, 1911, in New York Women's Trade Union League Papers, New York State Department of Labor Library, New York City.

24. *New York Times*, Oct. 29, 1910, May 6, 1911.

25. Mary Dreier, "Some Citizens," in Mary Dreier Papers, Schlesinger Library, Cambridge, Mass.; Inez Milholand, "If Women Voted," National

American Woman Suffrage Association Papers, Library of Congress, *Life and Labor* (Mar. 1912), p. 91.

26. *American Hebrew* (Sept. 22, 1922); Alva Belmont, "Jewish Women in Public Affairs," *American Citizen* 2 (May 1913): 181–82.

27. *The Woman's Protest* (Apr. 1917), p. 15. For a survey discussion of conservative attacks on feminists between the two world wars, see J. Stanley Lemons, *The Woman Citizen* (Urbana, Ill., 1975), Chapter 8.

28. Mimeographed form letter from W. R. Barnhart, Washington, D.C., Aug. 12, 1918, National American Woman Suffrage Association Papers, New York Public Library, New York.

29. Robert K. Murray, *Red Scare* (Minneapolis, 1955), pp. 91–97; Michael Dobkowski, *The Tarnished Dream: The Basis of American Anti-Semitism* (Westport, Conn., 1979), Chapter 7; Albert Lee, *Henry Ford and the Jews*, p. 92.

30. Catt letter to Jane Addams, Sept. 25, 1914; leaflet, "Is Woman Suffrage Pro-German?"; newspaper clipping, "The Sad Plight of the Antis," Jan. 25, 1919, all in Catt Papers, Library of Congress.

31. *Daily Data Sheet*, Dec. 6, 1927, June 23, 1927, July 27, 1927; *Dearborn Independent*, Mar. 15, 1924; newspaper clipping, July 6, 1927, in Catt Papers, Library of Congress.

32. *Daily Data Sheet*, Dec. 6, 1927.

33. Rosika Schwimmer to Catt, Dec. 27, 1928; Catt to Schwimmer, Jan. 6, 1926, Nov. 6, 1925, Catt Papers, Library of Congress. Fred Marvin, "Bootlegging Mind Poison," Catt Papers, Library of Congress, p. 9.

34. Catt to Jane Addams, May 26, 1927; Catt to Maud Swartz, June 4, 1927; Catt to Ethel Smith, June 4, 1927; Catt to Rose Schneiderman, June 6, 1927; Schneiderman to Catt, June 8, 1927; Catt to Addams, June 11, 1927, all in Catt Papers, Library of Congress; *New York Times*, July 6, 1927; Mary Grey Peck, *Catt*, pp. 424–29.

35. Francis Perkins to Mrs. MacMillan, Apr. 1, 1936, Dreier Papers, Sophia Smith Collection, Smith College, Northampton, Mass.

36. *Off Our Backs* (Nov. 1982) contains a report on the NOW convention and the discussion of the need to moderate support for radical parts of the movement in the face of the growing reactionary political climate.

37. Mimeographed letter from Catt to friends, n.d. Catt Papers, Library of Congress.

Arthur Liebman

Anti-Semitism in the Left?

The Ambivalent European Tradition

In order to arrive at an understanding of the relationship between anti-Semitism and the Left in twentieth-century America, it is first necessary to set the historical stage by a brief consideration of the association between Jews and the Left as it obtained in nineteenth- and early twentieth-century Europe.[1]

The Left has long been perceived by Jews as a friendly force. It was, after all, French revolutionists who first granted Jews civic equality. From that time Leftists often championed the rights of Jews. It was Leftist parties and organizations that opened their doors and leadership positions to Jews, and it was Leftists who most vociferously challenged anti-Semitism.

Conversely, throughout nineteenth- and early twentieth-century Europe, it was the Right that typically promoted anti-Semitism and sought to limit the economic, social, and political rights of Jews. Based as it was on a narrow clericalism, a particularistic nationalism, and/or a rigid hierarchical social order, the Right viewed Jews as outsiders and subversive elements within Christian nation-states. It was the attitudes and actions of this Right that the conservative and Jewish-born prime minister of England, Benjamin Disraeli, contended drove Jews into the arms of radicals.[2]

Coexisting with this history there was another. A closer scrutiny of the relationship between Jews and the Left reveals a darker underside that challenges the tight division between Jews and philo-Semitic Leftists on one side and anti-Semitic Rightists on the other. The evidence reveals that major figures and parties of the European Left expressed sentiments and engaged in actions that bordered on and indeed crossed over the line into anti-Semitism.

Karl Marx, for example, the father of modern scientific socialism, in his private correspondence and his published works expressed anti-Semitic comments and opinions about Jews. Marx's negative feelings about Jews stemmed from his focus on their economic acquisitiveness. In his essay "On the Jewish Question," he wrote of Jews: "What is the worldly cult of the Jew? *Huckstering*. What is his worldly God? *Money*."[3] It should be noted here that the imagery of the stereotypical economic Jew was not confined to Karl Marx or other Leftists but was prevalent among intellectuals and writers of all political leanings in the mid-nineteenth century.[4]

The hostility toward Jews within the Left camp in Europe in the nineteenth and early twentieth centuries was evident in the writings, speeches, and attitudes of this movement. It was revealed in the work of the leading thinkers of the French socialist tradition, Charles Fourier and Pierre Proudhon. In Russia, the anarchist Bakunin had harsh things to say about them. It was in Russia, too, that segments of the late nineteenth-century populists actually encouraged pogromists in their attacks against Jews. Leaders in the Austrian and German Social Democratic movements also expressed their hatred of Jews; some, like the Russian *narodniki*, saw in the expression of mass anti-Semitism in their countries a form of incipient socialism.[5]

It is important to keep the issue of the complex relationship between Jews and the Left in perspective. The European Left was not consistently positive toward Jews and Jewish interests, but while attacks were made on Jews and Jewish concerns, these were rarely, if ever, a central feature of any Leftist movement of consequence. The hatred of Jews where it existed in socialist movements was generally not as virulent, as racist, or as massive as was the case in Rightist movements.

Thus, there existed within European socialism ambivalent and contradictory positions with respect to Jews. On the one hand, the leaders and the movement fought for Jewish rights, while on the other these socialists, often the very same people, expressed anti-Semitic opinions. At this point, a brief consideration of this problem is appropriate because much of this problematic relationship would later be transported to America in the baggage of the European immigrants, Jewish and non-Jewish.

First, it is important to stress that socialist leaders and their supporters lived within Christian societies and thus were exposed to a long and deep tradition of religious anti-Semitism. This was a heritage that was not easy to cast aside, especially for first-generation socialists who had been raised Christian and whose socialist ideology was still in a relatively primitive stage.

Second, the occupational concentrations of European Jews and the pattern of economic interaction between Jews and Christians made their own contributions to anti-Semitism within the ranks of socialism. Long barred by anti-Semitic laws and customs from agriculture, guild occupations, and the professions, in the nineteenth century Jews were largely to be found in middlemen occupations: merchants, hucksters, estate managers, loan and mortgage collectors, and money lenders. These were popularly considered (and by segments of the Jewish community like the labor Zionists as well), to be non-productive or "parasitic" occupations. Christians who met and knew of Jews primarily as hard driving businessmen allowed their economic antagonism to take on a religious or ethnic trappings: anti-Semitism. The publicity given to the few wealthy Jewish bankers like the Rothschilds gave further fire to this eco-nomically based hatred of Jews. It was not until the emergence of a significant Jewish working class that the "Shylock" image of Jews would be challenged, but such a class did not develop until the end of the nineteenth century.

Many late nineteenth- and early twentieth-century Leftists obviously shared this economically rooted hatred of Jews as well as the long-engrained religious prejudice against them. The "Jewish question," as they called it, involved more than their own personal feelings. They were political people acting within movements aimed at changing society. Given this, they had to concern themselves with gaining recruits and developing a constituency—which meant working with anti-Semitic masses and competing for their allegiance with non-Leftist anti-Semites.

The European Left held diverse and ambivalent positions as to how to respond to the anti-Semitism of the masses. There were those like Friedrich Engels who advocated a direct and open assault upon it. Some, as in the French socialist movement at the time of the Dreyfus case, advocated a neutral position. Others like the Russian populists and a segment of the Austrian and German Social Democrats took an indirectly favorable position on the issue. This latter stance was "the socialism of fools" thesis. The prominent German Social Democrat Auguste Bebel articulated the thesis for his party—which it should be noted had already officially condemned anti-Semitism: "Social Democracy opposes anti-Semitism . . . but despite its reactionary character and against its will, it exerts an ultimately revolutionary effect, because the petty-bourgeois and small-farmer strata of society, who are aroused against the Jewish capitalists by the anti-Semitic movement, must finally realize that their enemy is not merely the Jewish capitalist but the capitalist class as a whole, and that only the attainments of Socialism can free them from their misery."[6] The Russian populist position was similar but stated in a cruder fashion. "It is indeed a pity that the peasant beat the Jew—the most innocent of his exploiters. But he beats, and this is the beginning of his struggle for liberation. When . . . his fists have grown strong and hard, he will strike those who are above the Jew."[7]

Friedrich Engels, on the other hand, saw nothing positive for socialism in anti-Semitism. Transcending his own earlier anti-Semitic attitudes, Engels, toward the end of his life, came to view anti-Semitism as a threat to socialism. In an appeal to the Austrian Social Democrats in 1890 whom Engels viewed as flirting with anti-Semitism, he cautioned, "I must ask you to consider whether you will not do more harm than good through anti-Semitism . . . [it] is nothing but a reactionary movement of decaying, medieval social groups against modern society . . . and therefore anti-Semitism serves only reactionary purposes underneath its socialist disguise; it is a variety of feudal socialism from which we must stay away."[8]

The issue of how best to deal with anti-Semitism within strata and classes necessary for socialism's success was not resolved in Europe. It was a problem that the Left faced in America during and after the massive immigration from Europe in the late nineteenth and early twentieth centuries.

Socialism's ambivalent response to Jews was also conditioned by factors internal to it. A central article of socialist faith was— and remains—a unified, class-conscious working class as a vital element in the socialist triumph. Those factors which contributed to this development were positively evaluated and those which detracted from it were negatively assessed. From this perspective, religion and ethnic separatism were considered to be forces that hindered the advance of working-class unity and consciousness and thus of socialism itself. From this perspective, Judaism and Jewish separatism or nationalism were similar to any other group's religion or nationalism: forces to be subdued in the struggle to build socialism.

The socialist attack on Judaism and Jewish nationalism was also fostered by other Marxist concerns. Some Marxists like Lenin, sincerely moved by the plight of Europe's Jews, argued that the basic solution to the problem of anti-Semitism was that proposed by the socialist theorist Karl Kautsky: assimilation. Lacking the socialist criteria to be a nation, the Jews were a religious and social atavism whose isolation and separatism left them open to attacks by various classes. As time progressed, as the working class became more integrated, and as the struggle for socialism strengthened, the structural and psychological bases sustaining Jewish separatism would be worn away. Thus Jews would assimilate or disappear and in so doing eliminate anti-Semitism, too. Indeed, from this perspective, *the best way* of solving the Jewish question was not to give it any special attention but instead to focus all energies on the class struggle. Anti-Semitism would disappear as a byproduct of the victory of the working class.[9]

The socialists who attacked the Jewish religion and Jewish nationalism from these socialist grounds certainly did not regard themselves as anti-Semites. Their behavior was generally motivated by humanistic and socialistic principles. As principled socialists many fought to protect the rights of Jews, but it was the rights of Jews as individuals that were championed. Collective expressions of Jews as Jews, on the other hand, were generally opposed. Such was the legacy that the European Left passed on to its American counterpart in the early twentieth century.

The Left and the Jews in the U.S.: The Early Years

The late nineteenth century in America marked the commencement of three interrelated phenomena affecting Jews. One was the start of mass Jewish—primarily eastern European Jews—immigration; second, the rise of a Left; third, an increase in and greater visibility of anti-Semitism.

Anti-Semitism had existed in America in various forms before the arrival of the great wave of eastern European Jewry. One was legal restrictions on the civic rights of Jews such as voting and the holding of public office. Such legal indignities lasted in several states into the mid-nineteenth century. Anti-Semitism was also to be found in the popular literature of the nineteenth century. In these stories and novels, Jews were often portrayed as pernicious characters devoted to money-making. These attacks were not limited to literature but also could be found in religious tracts and sermons of the day. Despite these and other expressions of anti-Semitism, America from independence through the end of the nineteenth century was, compared to Europe, a uniquely positive environment for Jews. In fact, the major problem that Jews had in this time period was not anti-Semitism but assimilation and intermarriage, factors indicative of a relatively friendly society.[10]

The late nineteenth century marked somewhat of a change in attitude and behavior toward Jews. It was a period of dramatic economic and social unrest. A leading social historian, John Higham, described these years in the following manner: "It was a time of mass strikes, widening social chasms, unstable prices, and a degree of economic hardship unfamiliar in earlier American history. On the same scene a strong upsurge of nationalism expressed itself in jingoist outbursts . . . proliferation of patriotic societies, a powerful tariff agitation, and the birth of a movement for immigration restriction."[11] This was also the same period in history during which many of the German Jews, who had arrived in the 1840s and 1850s, achieved considerable economic success. At roughly the same time, the eastern cities were beginning to host thousands of strange looking, impoverished, Orthodox Jews from eastern Europe seeking as best they could to eke out a living either through low wage salaried employment or peddling.

The conditions appeared ripe for an upsurge in anti-Semitism in this period. Indeed, it did occur but not to the degree that might be expected given the prevailing economic and social conditions. (The presence of other religious and ethnic minorities might have helped deflect antagonism from Jews.) Anti-Semitism increased among various groups including patrician families, the nouveau riche, urban immigrants, and, most important for our purposes, the Populists.[12]

The Populist movement, although not inspired or guided by strictly Marxist or socialist beliefs and concepts, can be considered as Leftist in that it was essentially a mass democratic movement intent upon democratizing an inequitable political economic system. Indeed, Populism at its peak was one of the largest movements for progressive political and economic reform ever to appear in America. It was primarily made up of farmers in the Midwest, West, and South. Hard pressed by declining farm prices, an inequitable railroad rate structure, and an onerous mortgage indebtedness among other economic travails, these farmers and their movement sought out reasons and solutions for their plight. In this search and in the process of building support for the movement, its critics allege, Populist leaders and writers engaged in or fostered anti-Semitism.

The evidence is two-tiered. The first consists of anti-Semitic statements and images in the writings and speeches of Populist leaders and propagandists. The second consists of an assessment of the movement's analysis and response to the economic crisis. The critics charge that the Populists failed to understand properly the dynamics of the capitalist system and in so doing adopted other perspectives that fed directly or indirectly into anti-Semitism. These included anti-industrial, anti-urban, and anti-foreign motifs that reflected the Populists' desire to return to some pre-industrial state of affairs. In addition, lacking a basic understanding of the political economy of capitalism, Populists, it is charged, seized upon a conspiratorial model which simplistically focused on bankers' and international financiers' control and manipulation of the monetary system. In this context, prominent Jewish bankers, such as the Rothschilds, were singled out for opprobrium. This simplistic conspiratorial scenario, the Populists' critics contend, survived the movement's decline and nurtured almost every anti-Semitic personality or movement of consequence in America for decades: Tom Watson, Henry Ford, Father Coughlin, Theodore Bilbo, and the Ku Klux Klan.[13]

The anti-Semitic thesis of Populism has not gone unchallenged. The critics of this thesis have marshaled arguments and evidence to detail its weakness. Given the importance of the issue for our purposes, a consideration of their position is merited.

First, there is no denial of the existence of anti-Semites and anti-Semitic writings and speeches within the corpus of Populism. The issue here is their importance in the movement and not their presence or absence. Those who are most condemnatory of Populism for its anti-Semitism, like the social scientists and historians Peter Viereck, Daniel Bell, Oscar Handlin, and Richard Hofstadter, present little in the way of significant systematic data to support their claims. The historian who amassed the most evidence in support of the anti-Semitic Populist position, Michael Dobkowski, believes that Handlin and Hofstadter overemphasized the importance of anti-Semitism within Populism. Dobkowski's evidence, it should be noted, is primarily garnered from Populist fiction and literary works.[14]

The linking of anti-Semitism to Populism has been vigorously attacked by other historians, most notably Norman Pollack and Walter Nugent. Both claim to have independently examined thousands of Populist documents and found scant evidence or, in Pollack's term, "infinitesimal" proof of anti-Semitism in the Populist movement. They do admit to the presence of some anti-Semites and some anti-Semitic references but strenuously argue that hatred of Jews was not a major ideological focus within Populism. Indeed, they even found positive references to Jews in their investigations.[15] It should also be noted that two of the most important general treatments of the Populist movement, John D. Hick's *The Populist Revolt* and Lawrence Goodwyn's *Democratic Promise*, contain no references to the Populists' treatment of Jews or anti-Semitism.[16]

Second, the Populists do not seem as simplistic with respect to capitalism or as conspiratorially bent as their critics contend. Populist rhetoric and ideology did pay attention to conspiracies, bankers, and usurers, but such phenomena were not wild notions in the minds of ignorant and embittered agrarians. There were financial conspiracies, bankers, and usurers who oppressed and exploited farmers and workers in the late nineteenth century, and some of the conspirators and bankers were indeed Jews. In any event, however, Populism did not dwell solely or primarily on these factors.

Populists were not adept at political and economic analysis. They sometimes crudely groped to understand what was happening in the American political economy. In so doing, they did manage to identify capitalism and capitalists as the root of the problem and the basic enemy of farmers and urban workers alike. In their prescriptions for alleviating the misery of farmers and workers, the Populists demanded not only cheap money but also a graduated income tax, governmental ownership or regulation of the railroads, control of monopoly, the right of labor to organize, increased education, a secret ballot, and direct election of U.S. senators. Populists also arduously campaigned for egalitarian cooperatives as practical alternatives to dealing with rapacious capitalists.

The Populists were certainly more complex and sophisticated about capitalism than their critics would have us believe. If Henry Ford or Father Couglin heard only conspiracy theories or assaults on money-manipulating financiers from Populist leaders and spokesmen, the fault lies not with the Populists but in the selective hearing of these anti-Semites. That they seized upon Populist themes to rationalize their anti-Semitism should not lead to the condemnation of Populism.

In short, anti-Semitism was never a central element in the ideology or politics of the Populist movement. On the contrary, there is a considerable body of evidence which would indicate that it was a minor component. Populism was a movement rooted in a mass base which aimed to significantly reform the American polity and economy. In the mobilization of members and ideas, the Populists were prone periodically to stereotype and engage in rhetorical excesses. Given the anti-Semitic illusions and notions especially with respect to the Jewish relationship to money that existed within the nineteenth-century American public, it would have been incredible if the Populist movement were free of this scourge. What is remarkable is the relative unimportance of anti-Semitism to this indigenous mass leftist movement.

Jews and the Marxist Left: 1900–1967

After the Populists, the next major Leftist movement to develop in the United States was the socialist movement. From the early 1900s through the mid 1960s, it was primarily made up of the Socialist and Communist parties and their offshoots. This Left differed from the Populists in several respects. It was explicitly socialist; it acquired most of its ideas, leaders, and adherents from Europe; it was largely based in the urban working class; and shortly after the turn of the century it contained a disproportionately

337

large number of Jews in its ranks and particularly in its leadership. Indeed, it was this large Jewish population within the socialist movement which made Jewish or Jewish-related issues important to this Left.

The socialist movement in the U.S. was first sensitized to the Jewish question by many of the Jewish intellectuals and activists who were drawn to it in the early 1900s. These were cosmopolitan Jews who had abandoned Judaism, rejected Jewish nationalism or separatism, and denigrated Yiddish and Yiddish culture. They were European Marxists like Morris Hillquit, who accepted the predominant Marxist perspective on the Jewish question—namely that its solution lay in assimilation. For many years, on issues bearing on Jewish matters, cosmopolitan assimilationist Jews influenced their Socialist parties toward positions that could be and indeed were perceived as hostile to Jewish interests and concerns by non-cosmopolitan Jews in and out of the Left movement. Indeed, at times the actions and policies these cosmopolitan Jews took toward things Jewish could have been interpreted as anti-Semitic, if they had not been Jews.[17]

One of the first contests to emerge around the Jewish question in the Socialist party was a largely internecine struggle that pitted the cosmopolitans against non-cosmopolitan Jews. Many of the issues embodied in this contest were to remain within the socialist movement for a long period of time. The contest revolved around the question of a special party organization for Jews.

This particular issue was only in part a Jewish issue. In the early 1900s the leadership of the Socialist party, taking cognizance of the growing number of foreign-born and foreign-language-speaking immigrants in the American working class sought out ways to reach them. One organizational form was the foreign language federation. This was used as a means to bring non-English speakers into the Socialist party and simultaneously allow them to be in a sub-group consisting only of their fellow native speakers. The foreign language federation scheme was approved at the Socialist party convention in 1910, and by 1919 members in these federations constitued 53 percent of the party.[18]

Jewish cosmopolitans vigorously objected to the organization and recognition of a Jewish federation. In their objections, they employed the same arguments about collective Jewish expressions originally framed by European Marxists. A separate Jewish socialist organization, they contended, would divide Jewish from non-Jewish workers and thus weaken the class struggle. Furthermore, they argued, such an organizational form would foster Jewish nationalism and thus weaken Jews' commitment to socialism. And, the cosmopolitans fumed, what was there so special about being Jewish for a non-believing socialist? After all, from their perspective once the Jewish religion was stripped away, assimilation would soon erase other factors like language which made Jews different from non-Jews. Again, they stressed rights for Jews as individuals but nothing for Jews collectively, especially in the ranks of socialism itself.

The cosmopolitans lost on this issue. The flood of Yiddish-speaking Jews, including Bundists from the czarist empire whose Jewish identities had been steeled by years of separate existence and special oppression, inundated the assimilationists. These new Jews were too large a constituency to be kept separate from the Socialist party for the length of time necessary for them to accept the arguments of the sophisticated Marxist cosmopolitan Jews. If these masses of Jews who valued their Jewish identity and language would come to socialism through a special Jewish organization, then the Socialists decided they would have it. The Jewish Socialist Federation was officially recognized by the Socialist party in 1912.

The recognition and organization of separate Jewish entities within the Socialist party and later the Communist party did not lay the Jewish issue to rest either among Jewish or non-Jewish leaders and members. What it did was to facilitate the recruitment of a relatively large number of Jews into the socialist movement in America and sensitize that movement to Jewish issues and concerns. It also had the unintended consequence of heightening the Jewish identities of some leaders and activists who came to view the Jewish membership as their special constituency.

The disproportionate presence of Jews and the foreign born generally in the socialist movement coupled with the relative absence of non-Jews and native Americans troubled many of its leaders, Jews and non-Jews alike. The Communist party, for example, in the 1920s was made up almost entirely of Jews and foreign born, most of whom were in foreign language federations. The Jews alone in the 1930s and 1940s accounted for approximately 40 to 50 percent of the membership of the Communist party. The Jewish and non-Jewish leaders of the Socialist and Communist parties (and the Comintern also) wanted their organizations to move beyond their Jewish and foreign-born bases. This was an eminently reasonable desire given two facts: Jews in the U.S. constituted only 3 to 4 percent of the overall population, and the cessation of mass immigration (and therefore foreign-born recruits) to the U.S. began in the early 1920s.[19]

The problem arose as to the means to accomplish the objective of Americanizing what was an essentially Jewish and European socialist movement. No socialist party handled this well. In the process of dealing with it, the Left was not overly concerned with the sensibilities of its Jewish members or potential members. Indeed, at times the Left in pursuit of Americanization ventured into anti-Semitism, particularly of an institutional variety. This anti-Semitic tendency can be seen most vividly in the issue of leadership, especially visible leadership. In the interwar years there were struggles over who or which faction would hold the offices of power. This phenomenon is not peculiar to the socialist movement. In all cases, Socialist, Communist, and Socialist Workers parties, the struggles divided along predominantly Jewish and predominantly non-Jewish lines, and in all cases the defeated, largely Jewish contenders perceived anti-Semitism at work.

In the Communist party, the contest pitted William Z. Foster and his faction (which included Jews) against Jay Lovestone and his largely Jewish supporters. In the hard fought battle, the Foster camp used the Jewish identities of his opponents as a cudgel against them. In a word-of-mouth campaign, the Fosterites charged that "Lovestone, Bert Wolfe, Willie Weinstone were . . . JEWS . . . and COLLEGE MEN-bourgeois [emphasis in the original]."[20] Such tactics were not unique in Communist power struggles. Stalin had several years earlier employed the same tactics against his Jewish opponents, Trotsky, Zinoviev, and Kamenev.)[21] The Foster faction won and never again did a Jew hold the rank of party chairman or a spot on the party's presidential ticket. (Similarly, in the German Communist party, despite a large proportion of Jews in its ranks and leadership, not one of its one hundred deputies in the Reichstag in 1932 was Jewish.)[22]

The struggle for the American Socialist party chairmanship in 1932 highlighted a similar situation within that organization.

Here, too, there was a battle for leadership pitting a Jew and his primarily Jewish supporters against a non-Jew prominently, although not exclusively, backed by other non-Jews. The contest pitted the incumbent chairman, Morris Hillquit, and his faction against the Socialist party's presidential standard bearer, Norman Thomas, and his supporters.

There were various ironies in the clash between these two men especially as the Jewish issue came to the fore. First, Morris Hillquit, an important socialist theoretician and leader for over thirty years, was a foreign-born, cosmopolitan Jew whose Jewish identity was not very salient. Second, Hillquit and other Jews prominent in the Socialist party had been prime sponsors of Thomas's rapid rise. They had wanted someone like Norman Thomas, a tall and handsome Protestant clergyman, to help the party dilute its Jewish image so as to better reach out to the Gentiles.

In this particular power struggle Hillquit's Jewishness was not an issue for Thomas. Thomas's problem with Hillquit was his moderate politics. The Thomasites wanted a more militant chairman. They also wanted a person who could reach out more effectively to Americans across the land. Here Hillquit's European accent was somewhat of a factor in that radio was becoming more important on the political scene.

The struggle for Socialist party chairman came sharply into focus at the party's 1932 convention. The Thomas faction advanced the nomination of the long-time mayor of Milwaukee, Daniel Hoan—a non-Jew from a non-Jewish power base. The contest became acrimonious and rumors of anti-Semitism spread through the hall. The issue almost burst into the open when a Milwaukee delegate openly proclaimed: "We want to attend to America's problems. We want an American Socialist Party." Morris Hillquit, in turn, brought the unmentionable to the center stage in an emotional speech, declaring, "I 'apologize' for having been born abroad, for being a Jew, and living in New York City."

Hillquit's oblique reference to anti-Semitism assured him victory. As Thomas later commented, "Once the anti-Semitic issue was raised, even though unjustly, I was inclined to think it best that Hillquit won." The Socialist party did not want to risk being labeled anti-Semitic. Hillquit's triumph was a personal one, however.

A day after his election the same convention ousted his fellow New York, predominantly Jewish supporters from their control of the party's powerful National Executive Committee.[23]

It was not only at the leadership level that the pursuit of Americans and Americanization had consequences for the Left's relationship to Jews and anti-Semitism. The Marxist parties in the United States tried hard to recruit blacks and industrial workers. Both of these groups in the North were tainted with anti-Semitism. In fact, partially in response to this and out of a more general desire to create a less Jewish image, Jewish organizers who took party names always assumed non-Jewish ones like Gates, Allen, and Dobbs.[24]

The Marxist Left did little to educate the blacks and industrial workers to the dangers of anti-Semitism. The socialists wanted to attract and keep these groups in the movement and presumably did not wish to risk alienating them on non-vital issues, such as their anti-Semitic attitudes. Perhaps after being educated in Marxism they would then be able to correct the error of their anti-Semitic ways. As one Socialist party activist informed me: "The Socialist party was never known for its militant opposition to anti-Semitism. Sections and locals of the Party . . . were known to be hotbeds of anti-Semitism even into the fifties."[25]

It was the Communist party, however, that most openly challenged Jewish sensibilities and was the one most likely to open itself to charges of anti-Semitism. The party, in its "third period" from the late 1920s through the early 1930s, vigorously attacked organized religion and ethnic separatism, including Judaism and Christianity as well as ethnic loyalties on the parts of Jews, Finns, and Slavic groups. Given the prominence of Jews in the party and among the leadership and polemicists, it is not too surprising that things Jewish came under severe attack. Pushing long-held Marxist themes pertaining to Jews to an extreme, the party roundly struck at collective expressions that Jews, even some within the organization, valued. Judaism, Zionism, and even Yiddish were denounced as forces that weakened the Jewish working-class consciousness and separated them from their non-Jewish brethren.[26] (Finns, another very prominent group within the Communist party, also suffered strong attacks on their ethnic loyalty and language.)

The party, however, was not always careful in how it waged the campaign against things Jewish. At times, the anti-Semitic images of the money-hungry Jew and the sinister rabbi burst forth. For example, the Communist party's newspaper, the *Daily Worker*, of November 30, 1925, stated: "The Talmud Torah is a free religious school where ancient rabbis are poisoning the minds of working class children . . . with religious ceremonies and superstitions. . . . Knowing the value of such organizations for keeping workers mentally enslaved, the rich Jews are donating freely. They have plenty of cold cash exploited from their workers either in the factories or in their stores and pawnshops."

Such a vicious attack could have easily been made by virtually any anti-Semitic organization. From the Communist party's viewpoint, this was not an anti-Semitic attack. Like other articles in the same vein, it was written by a Jew and appeared in a paper largely edited by Jews. Similar attacks also appeared in the party's Yiddish language paper, the *Freiheit*, including scurrilous Jewish cartoon caricatures by the Jewish artist William Gropper. Second, Judaism and Jewish collective expressions were not singled out for special attack; others, particularly the Finns, were also harshly dealt with. Third, comparable kinds of attacks had previously been conducted within the context of entirely Jewish leftist organizations. Many Jews were familiar with such invectives from contact with militant Bundists and Jewish anarchists of an earlier day. Fourth, the primary audience that the party hoped to influence was a Jewish one. The Communist party had no intent to injure Jews as Jews. The objective was to rally the Jewish working class against the religious obscurantists and exploiters in their own community. A latent message, of course, was that Jewish workers could and should owe no allegiance to Judaism.

All things considered, it would be difficult to label this particular article, and the campaign of which it was only one expression, as anti-Semitic. Essentially, this campaign should be seen as a political competition for Jewish workers conducted largely by Jews in a crude, irresponsible, and insensitive manner.

From the early 1930s until the Soviet Union's entrance into World War II, the socialist movement in America, which basically meant the Communist party, shifted its policy toward Jews and adopted an aggressively philo-Semitic stance. The American Communist party championed the rights of Jews and vociferously denounced anti-Semitism. Points of friction such as opposition to Zionism were downplayed. This change in policy largely stemmed from the Soviet Union's desire to have local Communist parties build as many alliances as possible in the struggle against fascism.

Conflict between Jews and the Left was not totally absent during this period. The most important confrontation revolved around the Left's position on America's involvement in World War II. The Socialist party, under the leadership of Norman Thomas, took a principled position against participation in what it regarded as a war of competing imperialist rivalries. The Communist party, for its part, encouraged the U.S. to gird itself for battle until Soviet policy dramatically changed in August 1939 with the signing of the Nazi-Soviet non-aggression pact. From then until the Soviet Union was invaded on June 21, 1941, the American Communist party aggressively opposed U.S. support of the allies and any move to enter the fray.

The anti-war position of both the Socialist and Communist parties enraged the Jewish community. Although such a position was obviously injurious to Jewish concerns, it was not anti-Semitic in itself nor a product of anti-Semitic machinations. At the same time, however, it should be noted that the Left's anti-war stance did throw it into tacit alliance with anti-Semitic rightist and isolationist elements.

From Russia's entry into World War II through the mid 1960s, the issue of anti-Semitism within the American Left lay largely dormant. This was not true for the Soviet Union, the focal point of international Communism. The Soviet-inspired, anti-Jewish actions in its eastern European satellites and the Stalinist atrocities against Jews and Jewish culture in Russia itself evoked charges of anti-Semitism against the Soviet authorities. The U.S. Communist party, while itself not a participant in these events, suffered the wrath of Jews both in and out of its organization as it first denied and then rationalized these Stalinist actions. This proved to be the only consequential point of contention between the Left and Jews in the United States until the mid 1960s.

Before turning to the post-1967 period, we should pause to give some balance to the relationship between the Left and the Jews in the United States from 1900 to 1967. The focus has been on the negative association between these two camps and the eruptions of anti-Semitism or near anti-Semitism that did occur. This, however, only reveals and assesses part of the story. In the interest of historical accuracy some attention should be paid to the other part, the more positive component of the relationship between Jews and the Left in this century prior to 1967.

The anti-Semitism and hatred of Jews and things Jewish on the American Left, while deplorable, was almost inconsequential compared to those phenomena on the Right or in the rest of the society. The Left played no role in imposing quotas against Jews at Ivy League and professional schools. The Left was not involved in restricting the access of Jews to professions and prestigious careers. The Left was not represented among the employers who refused to hire Jews. Leftists were not those who barred Jews from private clubs, resorts, and certain residential areas. It was not the Left who refused Jews sanctuary in this country when they sought refuge from the racists bent on first harming, then murdering them.

It was not simply a question of the American Left lacking power and thus not being in the positions to discriminate against Jews in employment, residence, or entry. The Left in the United States was an important opponent of anti-Semitism and a champion of the rights of Jews as individuals. In part, especially in the case of the U.S. Communist party, this philo-Semitism may have been tactical rather than principled, influenced by the desire to attract and keep a Jewish constituency. For whatever the reason, the Left did generally take a philo-Semitic line (with the exceptions noted above). In fact, after the Communist party's "third period," this organization stood out as the most aggressively philo-Semitic party in the United States. It even campaigned to make anti-Semitism a punishable crime in the United States. Also, the Communists as well as the Socialists and the Socialist Workers (Trotskyists) were among the nation's staunchest advocates of opening the doors to Jewish refugees from Fascism. By 1948, the Communist party had moved so far in its pro-Jewish stance that it emerged as one of the staunchest supporters in American politics for the creation of Israel.

The post–World War II years through the mid-1960s were a virtual Golden Age for American Jewry. Jews prospered. They moved upward in the occupational hierarchy, into better housing, and sent their children to quality schools. There was also a massive decline in overt anti-Semitism. The Holocaust, sustained postwar prosperity, and a more educated American public appeared to have combined to make anti-Semitism an insignificant phenomenon.[27] Indeed, some authorities like Nathan Glazer claimed that by the early 1960s, "Anti-Semitism seemed to have become almost invisible."[28]

The post–World War II years, however, were not a Golden Age for the American Left or the Old Left, which largely meant the Communist party. By 1956, the Old Left, battered by governmental oppression, undermined by economic prosperity and the upward mobility of important constituent groups, weakened by the association with Stalinism, and suffering from a lack of ideological direction and internecine warfare, became an insignificant political force. Throughout this period, which extended into the mid-1960s, the Old Left, with some exceptions, did maintain a *relatively* friendly relationship with American Jewry basking on its wartime record and efforts on behalf of Israel in its early years. Jews, for example, constituted the single largest ethnic component of the Communist party and the religio-ethnic group most tolerant of the Communist party.

The year 1967 marked a turning point in the relationship between the Left and the American Jewish community. Until then little of significance had occurred since 1956—the year of Khrushchev's revelations and the Suez War—to cause either group to consider the other as a threat. The Anti-Defamation League, for example, in its reports on anti-Semitism scarcely if ever mentioned the Left as it focused almost entirely upon the Right. The larger American Jewish community relative to other religious and ethnic communities continued to display (albeit in a more attenuated form) its traditional support for causes and organizations on the liberal to left end of the political spectrum. American Jewry remained (and remains) the most liberal constituency in the white community. As of 1967, as in earlier years, American Jews constituted the single largest source for members and particularly activists of the (white) Left.[29]

The Left, both Old and New, for its part, scarcely dealt with Israel or other issues concerning Jews prior to 1967. The *Militant*, for example, the organ of the Old Left Trotskyist movement, did not publish one article or editorial in 1966 dealing with Israel or Jews. When the Communist party's *Worker* occasionally addressed matters pertaining to Jews, it was usually favorable, typically with a piece attacking anti-Semitism or demonstrating how non-anti-Semitic the Soviet Union was. Even with respect to the Arab-

Israeli conflict, the little attention given to it prior to the Six Day War was moderate and fairly evenhanded. For example, a few days before the war, the *Worker* was appealing to Arab governments to ". . . stop the acts of terror and the adventurer plans of 'Al Fatah,' of the 'PLO,' etc. and also cut off the resources of encouragement and aid that are feeding these warmongering bodies." Israel, on the other hand, was gently admonished to ". . . abandon the method of military reprisal, the military forays into the territory of the neighboring countries."[30]

The New Left, similar to the Old, paid scant public attention to Israel or things Jewish prior to 1967. Jews and Israel appeared secure. This disproportionately Jewish movement focused on more pressing issues like civil rights and the Vietnam War.[31]

After 1967, the relationship between the Old and New Left and the Jewish community rapidly deteriorated. Jewish communal leaders charged the Far Left—which meant almost any organization or grouping to the left of the moderate Socialists around Michael Harrington—and militant blacks, primarily the Student Non-Violent Coordinating Committee (SNCC) and the Black Panthers, with being anti-Israel and hostile to Jewish concerns. By 1972, the situation had so deteriorated that the Anti-Defamation League (ADL), one of the leading responsible Jewish defense agencies, publicly accused the Far Left of being anti-Semitic. Indeed, in the eyes of the organized Jewish community, the Radical or Far Left surpassed the Right as the major political threat to Israel and to Jewry.[32]

The charge of Left anti-Semitism has not been limited to those who were a part of or tied to the Jewish establishment. Since coming from this quarter, it has also been put forth by Leftists and former Leftists, both Jewish and non-Jewish. Chutzpah, a leading Jewish socialist organization, made its own condemnation of Left anti-Semitism in 1974.[33] Later, the black militant, Amiri Baraka (formerly Leroy Jones), openly confessed to being anti-Semitic in his more militant days.[34] This charge from the mid-1970s through the early 1980s has appeared in a variety of liberal and Left publications including the *New York Times, Ms., Plexus, Dissent, Village Voice,* the *Berkely Barb,* and *Jewish Currents.*

The accusation of anti-Semitism leveled against the Left did not suddenly spring forth on the American political scene; it was actually the culmination of a rapid deterioration of relations between the Left and the Jewish community. Before examining the bases of the charges against the Left, it is first necessary to consider the factors that contributed to the overall decline in the relationship. There were three overlapping issues involved—Marxism, race relations, and Israel—a mix that affected Jews as Jews and as white, middle-class Americans.

The Marxist shift of the New Left which occurred in the late 1960s increasingly alienated many Jews from this movement. Earlier, they, along with other middle-class non-Jews, had been attracted to it in part on the basis of the New Left's idealism and vague reformist notions. Then, Marxist Leninism moved to the fore. The enemy changed from the "system" or "bureaucracy" to the bourgeoisie, particularly white-skinned, liberal bourgeoisie. The vanguard force for change shifted from students and intellectuals to oppressed minorities and the Third World peoples. This ideological development made the New Left into an unpleasant milieu for whites from middle-class backgrounds, a disproportionate number of whom were Jews.

At approximately the same time, the metamorphosis from civil rights to black power in the 1960s strained relations between blacks and whites in general and Jews and blacks in particular. White New Leftists and liberals who had worked with blacks on behalf of their civil rights felt rejected when their allies demanded that the struggle for the realization of black interests be carried on in the context of separate all-white and all-black organizations. Jewish New Leftists and liberals were most likely to feel this rejection as they were disproportionately in the forefront of the civil rights struggle and had had the most direct contact with blacks. The strain for Jews was compounded after 1967 by blacks' well publicized attacks on Israel and Zionism, as well as on Jews in America as exploiters and oppressors of blacks. The concomitance of all of these factors, plus the Left's at times virtually uncritical acceptance of black demands and charges drove some Jews from the New Left and weakened the commitment and support of numerous others.

Probably the single most important factor in the denouement between the Left and the Jews occurred over Israel. The Six Day War and the continued occupation of Arab territory moved Israel from the wings of the Left to the center of its stage. The Left, particularly the New Left which attracted much more media coverage than the Old, took a critical stance toward Israel. There was actually a variety of Left and New Left criticisms of Israel ranging from moderate to severe. The one that attracted the most attention and caused the most furor emanated from the National New Politics Convention (NNPC) in September 1967. This convention's policy statement on Israel was virtually dictated by a militant Black Caucus. The policy statement put the New Left on record as condemning Israel for its "imperialist Zionist war." This definition of Israel as "a theocratic, racist, expansionist and aggressive State" (to use the Communist party's words) continued to be propagated by segments of the Left and some militant blacks for the next fifteen years.[35]

The Left's condemnation of Israel infuriated the Jewish community. The war had not only heightened the already considerable commitment of American Jews to Israel, but it also had propelled them, as Rabbi Arthur Hertzberg expressed it, toward "the sense of belonging to a worldwide Jewish people, of which Israel is the center."[36] In addition, the Six Day War reawakened or reinforced memories of the Holocaust and the perceived precarious position of Israel. By this time, organized American Jewry was solidly officered by an anti-radical leadership ready to smite any Leftist threat to Israel. Thus, when various segments of the Left condemned Israel and used inflammatory language in doing so, the reaction was swift and certain: the Left was identified as the principal enemy of Jews in America and in the world.

Those most pained by the confrontation between American Jewry on one side and the anti-Israel Left on the other were Jewish members and supporters of the radical movement. Many felt placed in an untenable position: to be pro-Israel was to be anti-Left. Torn by such a conflict, numerous Jews withdrew from the Left, and some who remained and argued for a more moderate position on Israel were subsequently forced out by their more ardently anti-Israeli colleagues.[37]

The Charges

The primary basis for the charge of anti-Semitism within the Left stems from its stance and rhetoric pertaining to Israel. On this point, there is a consensus that spans the Jewish establishment to the Jewish Left. The case against the Left was probably most succinctly made by the Jewish socialist organization Chutzpah in the following terms: "We believe that the form and content of most Left criticism of Israel is inescapably anti-Semitic. . . . The central feature of Left anti-Zionism is that it denies to Jews the right of self-determination. . . . Any ideology which seeks to thwart our people's legitimate aspirations is anti-Semitic. Thus, the Left, in its anti-Zionism, is anti-Semitic because it would deny to Jews those rights which it promises to all other peoples."[38]

The accusation of anti-Semitism against Leftists has had an accompanying secondary focus: the rhetoric which blurs the distinction between Jews and Zionists and attributes the "sins" of Zionism to Jews. In the denunciation of Zionism, references are sometimes made in Leftist publications to "the Jewish controlled media" or "Jewish financial interests." Take, for example, the following which appeared in the U.S. Communist party's *Daily World* on June 22, 1979: "Has nationalism wrapped in money turned all the 'leaders' of the Jewish people into stone?" This type of language, the Left's critics contend, either is anti-Semitic itself and/or contributes to anti-Semitism through reinforcement of traditional anti-Semitic stereotypes.

The central issue here is not the rhetoric, unfortunate though it may be, but the affixing of the label of anti-Semitism to the position that argues for the denial of Jewish national self-determination. It is clear that adherents of such a position need not ipso facto be anti-Semites.

It is important to place the position of the contemporary Left with respect to Israel in some perspective. There is a Marxist, Leninist, Trotskyist, and Stalinist legacy which denied that Jews were a people and that long opposed Jewish nationalism; however, current leftist parties in the U.S. do not uniformly conform to this tradition. The Democratic Socialists of America, a member of the Second International, has been a consistent supporter of Israel and when critical of particular policies has been so in a moderate fashion. The American Communist party, like its counterpart in the Soviet Union, while often hostile to the Israeli government and its actions, has never denied the right of Israel to exist. The Trotskyist Socialist Workers party, on the other hand, is quite explicit in denying Israel's legitimacy. At various times, though, the uncompromising hostility and the heated rhetoric on the part of segments of the Left toward Israel has given the impression to Jewish observers that despite disclaimers these parties or factions truly favor Israel's demise.[39]

Opposition to the establishment of a Jewish state or even *the* Jewish state is not limited to various Leftists. It can also be found historically and currently within the Jewish community as well. In the early years of the Zionist movement, the rabbinate was one of its most important enemies. Similarly, adherents of Reform Judaism long opposed Zionism and denied that Jews were a people. In the United States until the 1960s a significant portion of American Jewry chose to define itself as a religious community and not as a people. A major wing of the Hasidic movement long fought against the establishment of Israel and continues today to withhold de jure recognition of its existence. Among non-religious Jews, the Bund, a Jewish socialist movement founded at the turn of the century and distinguished by its courageous defense of Jewish lives and propogation of Jewish values, long stood in opposition to a Jewish state. It should be noted that it wasn't until the commencement of the Holocaust that Zionism ceased to be a small minority movement among American Jews.[40]

Accusations of anti-Semitism were more likely to be lodged against those denying Jewish peoplehood and statehood in the post–World War II era than before. Two interwoven historical facts account for this: the Holocaust and the creation of the state of Israel. The slaughter of 6 million Jews and the failure of any nation-state to provide sanctuary to any significant number reinforced Jews' conception of themselves as a people and made of Diaspora Jewry fervent supporters of a Jewish state. Indeed, in a short period of time, commitment to Israel and its survival as a belated sanctuary came to be a central feature of Jewish identity. Given this constellation, to be hostile to Israel was perceived by Jews as being hostile to Jewry and thus anti-Semitic.

It is in this context—a context shaped by history and the leaders of American and Israeli Jewry—that the Left receives the appellation of anti-Semitic. The position of the American Jewish establishment on this subject was expressed by top officials of the Anti-Defamation League, Arnold Foster and Benjamin Epstein: ". . . in a world that still harbors anti-Semitism, a world in which for Jews, at least the memory of the Holocaust cannot fade, Jewish security is inextricably intertwined with the survival of Israel as a sovereign state; Jews will neither feel nor *be* safe in a world which acquiesces in the destruction of the Jewish state, either all at once or piece by piece. In its assault on Israel's right to exist, the Radical Left engages in what is perhaps the ultimate anti-Semitism."[41] It is important to note here that this is not only the point of view of the Jewish establishment; it is also shared by Jewish liberals and Leftists. The liberal feminist editor of *Ms.*, Letty Cottin Pogrebin, echoed this sentiment when she declared, ". . . Like many Jews, I have come to consider anti-Zionism tantamount to anti-Semitism because the political reality is that the bottom line is an end to the Jews."[42] On this point, the Jewish Left, Center, and Right as well are in strong agreement: the Left's denial of the legitimacy of Israel is necessary and sufficient grounds to label it anti-Semitic.

One's position with respect to Israel has become the crucial criterion in assessing anti-Semitism. Other indicators such as negative opinions about Jews and Judaism or the usage of hostile Jewish stereotypes pale in comparison to the Israeli criterion. Thus, for segments of the Jewish establishment at least, the negative stereotypes of Jews held by members and leaders of the Moral Majority are relatively insignificant compared to that movement's ardent support of Israel.[43] Conversely, the Socialist Workers party is placed firmly in the anti-Semitic camp despite its record of fighting traditional anti-Semitism and struggling for the rights of Jewish individuals. Its position on Israel by itself is reason enough to label it anti-Semitic in the judgment of Jewish opinion leaders of all political persuasions.

The "Israeli criterion" as the key indicator in assessing anti-Semitism has increasingly been widened. The label of anti-Semite is no longer limited to those who reject the legitimacy of the Jewish state. Criticism of Israeli governmental policies and actions has also entered into the calculus. Even further, for some such as the leadership of the ADL, another factor encompassed by this criterion is the assessed impact of an individual or group's policy on the military strength of Israel. As the "Israeli criterion" for evaluating anti-Semitism has become broader, it has more and more impaled individuals and groups on the liberal-to-left of the political spectrum on the charge of anti-Semitism.

The ever-encompassing "Israeli criterion" and its ensnaring of liberals as well as Leftists can be observed in the case of the attack upon former senator and chairman of the Foreign Relations

Committee Frank Church by Nathan Perlmutter, the national director of the ADL. Perlmutter, in his book *The Real Anti-Semitism,* strongly implies that Church can be perceived as (in my term) a "functional" anti-Semite. Perlmutter openly acknowledges that Church is a sincere friend of Israel and a stalwart in the fight to free Russian Jewry. What troubles the national director of the ADL is Church's stance on the Soviet Union and disarmament. Church, in Perlmutter's opinion, is simply too soft on both matters. Should Church's view prevail in the U.S., then American hostility toward the Soviet Union would diminish along with our military capability. Such developments would lead to a weaker America and to less military and political support for Israel, a foe of Soviet-backed client states. It is through this circuitous reasoning that Church and other like-minded liberals endanger Israel's security and ultimately its survival. Thus, those who would weaken the United State's resolve and defense capability vis-à-vis the Soviet Union, regardless of their well intentioned motives or concern for Israel, are tantamount to being "functional" anti-Semites. Perlmutter succinctly lays out this line of attack on liberals as embodied in the person of the former Idaho Senator: "Church, the credentialed liberal, symbolizes within his very political gestalt problems for Jewish interests, which while not as readily recognizable as those of the hard core Left [which Perlmutter had already labeled anti-Semitic] for being relatively more centrist contains seeds of future mischief for Jews.[44]

The accusation of anti-Semitism against the Left has not been limited solely to its critical or anti-Zionist position on Israel. Jewish liberals and Leftists have charged the Left with being anti-Semitic stemming from its *insensitivity* to Jews and their problems, particularly anti-Semitism.[45] This charge has been most vociferously made by Jewish feminists. (See Elinor Lerner's work in this volume.) The failure of feminists to deal with or treat seriously contemporary Jewish oppression, they contend, is real, serious, and tantamount to being anti-Semitic.[46]

The "insensitivity" thesis of leftist anti-Semitism was probably best approached by the liberal writer of the *Village Voice,* Jack Newfield, who in a very controversial article entitled "Anti-Semitism and the Crime of Silence" wrote:

The thing that troubles me about part of the American Left doesn't have a name. It's more than anti-Zionism, and different from traditional anti-Semitism. Its impact is often in omissions—the injustice not mentioned, the article not written, the petition not signed. It is often communicated in code words. But it is essentially a series of dual standards. It is a dual standard for the human rights of Jews in certain countries. It is a dual standard that questions Israel's right to exist by denying to Zionism the same moral legitimacy that is granted to every other expression of nationalism in the world. And it is an amnesia of conscience about the creation of Israel, and about the Holocaust. . . .[47]

The insensitivity thesis has little to do with anti-Semitism and much to do with the context of the times and the heightened sense of ethnic and religious consciousness among Jewish liberals and Leftists. For several decades after World War II until the later 1960s, there was relatively little attention paid to the Holocaust, anti-Semitism, or Israel by Jews or non-Jews including those on the left of the political spectrum. There was scant reason to deal with these phenomena. Anti-Semitism declined in this period as American Jewry prospered. Israel appeared to be a secure social democratic society. The pain, the enormity, and the recency of the Holocaust made it a difficult subject to broach publicly or privately. In short, there was little pressure coming from the Jewish community for greater attention to be paid to Jewish issues and concerns, past or present. The liberal/Left community, Jewish and non-Jewish, in the 1950s and 1960s had more pressing issues to concern them including civil rights, civil liberties, the Cold War, nuclear disarmament, and the war in Vietnam.

After 1967, the situation changed and a confluence of forces helped to produce an ethnically conscious and assertive body of young Jewish liberals and Leftists. This amalgam was produced by forces that worked upon both their political and ethnic identities, including the overlapping rise of the black power, feminist, and self-awareness movements along with the fragmentation and decline of a humanistic and universalistic New Left. The rise and decline of these movements heightened the particularistic and personalistic consciousness of a variety of social and ethnic groups, including Jews. A Jewish identity was specifically strengthened by the dramatic attention that the Left gave to Israel and its vociferous attacks on Israeli policies and actions. This occurred during the same period that considerably more public attention was paid to the Holocaust and its contemporary relevance. It was also the period in which sectors of the organized Jewish community made special efforts to influence the Jewish consciousness of Jewish liberals and Leftists on American campuses. The cumulative weight of all of these factors gave rise to an ethnically sensitive and assertive Jewish liberal and Left population.

These new types of Jewish liberals and Leftists were more active in asserting their Jewishness than were previous generations. This meant that they did not limit their concern to responding to real and imagined attacks on Jews and things Jewish; it also meant a desire to have a Jewish identity and presence affirmatively recognized by their peers in the Left. Non-Jews as well as "non-Jewish" Jews on the Left were inadequately prepared to deal with or understand the needs and concerns of these more conscious Jews, a new element in the Left and feminist movements. The mix of assertive Jews on one hand and Leftists on the other operating under the old ground rules pertaining to Jewish issues led to confusion, bitterness, and charges of insensitivity or anti-Semitism.[48]

It is difficult to assess the extent and degree of anti-Semitism in the American Left either in the present or in the past. What is evident is the antagonistic relationship that has developed between sectors of the Left and segments of the American Jewish community, particularly among its organized components. Commencing in the mid-1960s, these two entities moved on a collision course as each pursued positions the other regarded as inimical to its interests. American Jewry, an increasingly middle-class community, assertively endorsed its commitment to the prevailing merit system regarding access to schooling and jobs and even more assertively supported Israel and Israeli policies. Much of the more visible and vocal left at the same time became more avowedly Marxist and hostile to the bourgeoisie, highly supportive of programs that challenged the merit system in favor of quotas on behalf of underprivileged minorities, and stridently anti-Israel. In this context of clashing interests and perceptions as well as heightened emotions, it was predictable that charges of anti-Semitism would emerge.

The importance of the Holocaust and Israel in the shaping of Jewish consciousness and reaction to anti-Semitism is essential for our understanding of the deteriorating relationship between Jews and the Left. As it wove its way into the Jewish psyche, the slaughter of the 6 million heightened the consciousness and sensitivity of Jews toward Jewish interests and concerns. It is also clear that by the late 1960s, after several Arab-Israeli wars, the survival of Israel became a major priority for virtually all Jews. Given this context, it became difficult for Jews to perceive criticism, particularly vulgar and uninformed criticism, of Jewish peoplehood and Israel in a detached fashion.

Ironically, the antagonism between Jews and the Left can also be perceived as flowing from the many years of positive associations between the two. Given the political history of mutual support, Jews expected more sympathy and understanding from the Left. The Left, using the same historical reference points, held Jews to different or higher standards than it did less enlightened ethnic communities. Thus, when the Left broke the virtual public moratorium on criticism of Israel and on issues pertaining to Jews that the Holocaust had inspired, American Jews reacted sharply, many feeling that either Leftist anti-Semites were coming out of hiding and/or Leftists were unlocking the doors that had previously barred anti-Semites from spreading their poison.

In conclusion, anti-Semitism exists and has existed in the Left. It is not solely the product of Jewish perceptions. It is also probably true that anti-Semitic elements and comments are more visible now than in the past. These observations, however, should not obscure certain basics. Anti-Semitism was never a major aspect of the American Left at any time in its history. On the contrary, throughout much of the twentieth century, the Left was in the vanguard of the fight for Jewish rights. The Left at present continues to struggle against anti-Semitism, which remains largely based still in the movements and ideologies of the Right. These central facts must be kept in mind.

Notes

1. Anti-Semitism as used here refers to the holding of irrationally negative attitudes or opinions about Jews and/or engaging in hostile actions against Jews because of the fact that they are perceived to be Jews. Anti-Semitism can be direct or indirect and personal or institutional. Anti-Semitism can have a variety of bases, including ideological, political, economic, social, psychological, and religious.

The term "Left" typically refers to a political ideology informed to some significant extent by some variant of Marxism. At times, as used here, it will also encompass Populism. Left will be employed to characterize collectively the various groups, organizations, parties, and movements that were inspired by Marxism and/or a vision of a radically more egalitarian and socially just America.

2. This Left anti-Semitism in Europe is discussed in the following: Hannah Arendt, *The Origins of Totalitarianism* (New York, 1960), pp. 42–49; George Lichteim, "Socialism and the Jews," *Dissent* (July-Aug. 1968), pp. 314–42; Arthur Liebman, *Jews and the Left* (New York, 1979), pp. 89–92, 517–21; Seymour Martin Lipset, *"The Socialism of Fools": The Left, the Jews and Israel* (New York, 1969), pp. 7–12, 17–18; Paul Massing, *Rehearsal for Destruction* (New York, 1949), pp. 151–83; Robert S. Wistrich, *Revolutionary Jews from Marx to Trotsky* (New York, 1976), pp. 1–22, 98–129, Wistrich, *Socialism and the Jews* (Rutherford, N.J., 1982).

3. Karl Marx, "On the Jewish Question," in *Karl Marx: Early Writings,* ed. T. B. Bottomore (New York, 1964), p. 34.

4. Hal Draper, *Karl Marx's Theory of Revolution: State and Bureaucracy,* Pt. 1 (New York, 1977), pp. 591–608.

5. See n. 2.

6. Quoted in Edmund Silberner, "German Social Democracy and the Jewish Problem Prior to World War I," *Historia Judaica* 15 (Apr. 1953): 11–12.

7. Quoted in Erich Goldenhagen, "The Ethnic Consciousness of Early Russian Jewish Socialists," *Judaism* 23 (Fall 1974): 493.

8. Quoted in Massing, *Rehearsal for Destruction,* pp. 311–12.

9. Lenin's views on the Jewish question are conveniently compiled in Hyman Lumer, ed., *Lenin on the Jewish Question* (New York: International Publishers, 1974). The basic socialist text arguing assimilation as the answer to the Jewish problem is Karl Kautsky's *Are the Jews a Race?* (New York, 1926). This was first published in German in 1914. See also Morris U. Schappes, "The Jewish Question and the Left—Old and New," *Jewish Currents* (June 1970), pp. 3–21. The duality or ambivalence of European socialism was aptly described by the German Marxist scholar, Paul Massing, in discussing the pre-World War II German Socialists:

> In theory and practice socialist labor was opposed to anti-Semitism. The Socialists never wavered in their stand against all attempts to deprive Jews of their civil rights. . . . They never gave in to temptation—considerable at times—to gain followers by making concessions to anti-Jewish prejudice. From the rise of the socialist labor movement in the 1860s to the time of its defeat by National Socialism it was characterized by an . . . unswerving opposition to any kind of discrimination against Jews. On the other hand, socialist labor was indifferent, if not actually hostile, toward all efforts to preserve and revitalize autonomous Jewish religious, cultural, or national traditions. Marxism, its guiding philosophy, had as little use for the Jewish religion as it did for the Christian. Eager to have the processes of industrial society do their work of obliterating cultural differences, socialist labor could see no more than an obsolete religious heritage in the beliefs of orthodox Jewry and had even less sympathy for conscious attempts to revive the Jewish nation. (Massing, *Rehearsal for Destruction,* p. 151)

10. Michael N. Dobkowski, *The Tarnished Dream: The Basis of an American Anti-Semitism* (Westport, Conn., 1979); Oscar Handlin, "American Views of the Jew at the Opening of the Twentieth Century," *Publications of the American Jewish Historical Society* 40 (June 1951): 323–25; and John Higham, *Send These to Me* (New York, 1975), pp. 120–37, 147–51.

11. Higham, *Send These to Me*, p. 129.

12. Ibid., pp. 130–37.

13. Those who have argued the case of Populist Anti-Semitism include Daniel Bell, "The Face of Tomorrow," *Jewish Frontier* 12 (June 1944): 16–17; Richard Hofstadter, *The Age of Reform* (New York, 1955), pp. 77–81; Handlin, "American Views of the Jew," pp. 340–44; Peter Vierick, "The Revolt Against the Elite" in Daniel Bell, ed., *The Radical Right* (Garden City, N.Y., 1963), pp. 163–64.

14. Dobkowski, *The Tarnished Dream*, pp. 174–84.

15. Walter K. Nugent, *The Tolerant Populists: Kansas Populism and Nativism* (Chicago, 1963), devotes his whole book to proving how tolerant were the Populists. See also Norman Pollack, "The Myth of Populist Anti-Semitism," *American Historical Review* 68 (Oct. 1962): 76–80.

16. Lawrence Goodwyn, *Democratic Promise: The Populist Movement in America* (New York, 1976); John D. Hicks, *The Populist Revolt* (Minneapolis, 1931).

17. For an extensive treatment of the relationship of the Jews and the Left in the United States, see Arthur Liebman, *Jews and the Left.*

18. James Weinstein, *The Decline of Socialism in America 1912–1925* (New York, 1969), p. 182.

19. Liebman, *Jews and the Left*, pp. 57–66, 492–501.

20. Quoted in Daniel Aaron, *Writers on the Left* (New York, 1965), p. 150.

21. Joseph Nedava, *Trotsky and the Jews* (Philadelphia, 1972), pp. 174–82.

22. Walter Laqueur, "Zionism, the Marxist Critique, and the Left," *Dissent* (Dec. 1971), p. 564.

23. Liebman, *Jews and the Left*, pp. 486–87.

24. Harvey Klehr, *Communist Cadre* (Stanford, Calif., 1978), pp. 40–41.

25. Interview with Socialist party activist Martin Oppenheimer, Nov. 13, 1974.

26. Melech Epstein, *The Jew and Communism* (New York, 1959), pp. 252–61; Ralph L. Roy, *Communism and the Churches* (New York, 1960), pp. 33, 38, 58, 59.

27. Charles H. Stember, et al., *Jews in the Mind of America* (New York, 1966), pp. 208–10. A study based on a national survey conducted in 1964 indicated that a third of the population was anti-Semitic, and only 16 percent were principled opponents. Survey researchers may have detected this but it certainly did not seem that bad to Jewish defense agencies or Jews in general. Irving Howe, *World of Our Fathers* (New York, 1976), pp. 608–34, shares this general perception.

28. Nathan Glazer, *American Judaism*, 2nd ed. (Chicago, 1972), p. 167.

29. Nathan Glazer, "The Jewish Role in Student Activism," *Fortune* 79 (Jan. 1969): 112; Kirkpatrick Sale, *SDS* (New York, 1973), pp. 89, 658–64.

30. *The Worker*, June 4, 1967.

31. Liebman, *Jews and the Left*, pp. 559–67.

32. "Danger on the Left," *FACTS* 21 (Nov. 1972): 549–60.

33. Steve Lubet and Jeffry (Shaye) Mallow, "That's Funny, You Don't Look Anti-Semitic: Perspective on the American Left," in *Chutzpah: A Jewish Liberation Anthology* (San Francisco, 1977), pp. 52–53.

34. Amira Baraka, "Confessions of a Former Anti-Semite," *Village Voice* 25 (Dec. 17–23, 1980): 1, 19–23.

35. Herbert Aptheker, "Anti-Semitism and Racism," *Political Affairs* 48 (Apr. 1969), p. 37.

36. Cited in Bernard Avishai, "Breaking Faith: *Commentary* and the American Jews," *Dissent* (Spring 1981), p. 241.

37. Liebman, *Jews and the Left*, pp. 514–26, 568–87.

38. Lubet and Mallow, "That's Funny, You Don't Look Anti-Semitic," pp. 52–53.

39. Peter Siedman, *Socialists and the Fight Against Anti-Semitism* (New York, 1973), p. 4.

40. Liebman, *Jews and the Left*, pp. 6, 78, 93, 115, 123–25, 163, 263–65.

41. Arnold Foster and Benjamin R. Epstein, *The New Anti-Semitism* (New York, 1974), p. 152.

42. Letty Cottin Pogrebin, "Anti-Semitism in the Women's Movement," *Ms.* 10 (June 1982): 65.

43. Earl Raab, for example, a prominent Jewish communal leader and analyst, dismisses the hostility of the Moral Majority toward Jews arguing "the Moral Majority is *not* featured by anti-Semitism or bigotry." He then proceeds to mention that the Moral Majority would like "to Christianize America." Earl Raab, "Fundamentalists: Real and Phantom Concerns," *ADL Bulletin* (Jan. 1982), p. 14.

44. Nathan Perlmutter and Ruth Ann Perlmutter, *The Real Anti-Semitism* (New York, 1982), pp. 134–35.

45. See, for example, the articles by liberal Jack Newfield and socialist Roger S. Gottlieb. Jack Newfield, "Anti-Semitism and the Crime of Silence," *Village Voice* (June 17–23, 1981), pp. 1, 13–17, 97; Roger S. Gottlieb, "Zionism, Anti-Semitism, and the Left," *Socialist Review* 47 (Sept.-Oct. 1979): 26–31.

46. Pogrebin, "Anti-Semitism in the Women's Movement, '62," and Irena Klepfisz, "Anti-Semitism in the Lesbian/Feminist Movement," in *Nice Jewish Girls: A Lesbian Anthology*, ed. Evelyn Torton Beck (Watertown, Mass., 1982), p. 46. See also the bitter exchange of letters in the radical feminist newspaper, *Off Our Backs*, Nov. and Dec. 1979.

47. Newfield, "Anti-Semitism and the Crime of Silence," p. 97.

48. A general discussion of this phenomenon at the time can be found in Liebman, *Jews and the Left*, pp. 559–87. For a personal view of a participant see Paul Cowan, *An Orphan in History: Retrieving a Jewish Legacy* (Garden City, N.Y., 1982), pp. 101–246.

Toward Christian Reevaluation and Interfaith Dialogue

Egal Feldman

American Protestant Theologians on the Frontiers of Jewish-Christian Relations, 1922–82

From the very beginning of American history a degree of ambivalence marked Protestant attitudes toward Jews.[1] Admired at times as descendants from and inheritors of a biblical tradition, at other times they were resented for their stubborn refusal to acknowledge Christian teachings and their resistance to conversion. Despite American Protestantism's evangelical and missionary outlook, its relationship with Jews, especially with individual Jews, evolved harmoniously.

Conceived in an age of religious laxity and suspicion of ecclesiastical authority, America's socioreligious and political institutions inhibited the growth of officially sanctioned anti-Semitism. From the very birth of the United States, Jews were accorded an unprecedented measure of hospitality and constitutional guarantees of religious freedom. Separation of church and state assured the small handful of Jews a religious security unusual in Western history. What is more, Protestant creedal and denominational diversity prevented the majority from realizing its potential potency and granted the Jewish people additional protection.[2]

American Protestants did, however, share with universal Christendom a common outlook toward Judaism. The Jewish rejection of Jesus as the Messiah and its alleged responsibility for the Crucifixion were matters strongly imbedded in American Protestant teaching. The conviction that the "New Israel" had superseded the "Old" and that Judaism was a religion of "Laws" which had achieved their fulfillment with the coming of Jesus were not debatable matters. These notions were accepted by many of the most prominent leaders of American Protestantism throughout the nineteenth and early twentieth centuries. Lyman Abbott, for example, one of the most respected voices of late nineteenth-century Protestantism, recognized little value in Judaism except insofar as it provided mankind a bridge to cross "from paganism . . . to Christianity."[3] The Jews, he was convinced, were responsible for the death of the Savior. "The Jewish church was corrupt . . . and the corrupt church hates the reformer and the purifier," he wrote in 1903.[4] Even Walter Rauschenbusch, the most important Protestant theologian in the early twentiety century, attributed any lingering anti-social elements in Christianity to the influence of Judaism. Like his co-religionists, Rauschenbusch presented Jesus as a leader who challenged the authority of the Jews, a people whose "piety was not piety," whose "law inadequate." The Jews, he observed in 1918, "were the active agents in the legal steps which led to the Christian Savior's death."[5]

The studies of Charles Glock and Rodney Stark, published in 1966, suggest that such thinking continued in Protestant circles well into the twentieth century. Their discovery that Sunday School texts repeat the deicide myth and the ancient Christian idea that Jewish suffering for this act will persist until its collective conversion surprised them. "We expected that this religious process had become more or less vestigial," remarked the authors of *Christian Beliefs and Anti-Semitism.* "We were entirely unprepared to find these old religious traditions so potent and so widespread in modern society."[6]

Three Protestant theologians have challenged such thinking: George F. Moore, Reinhold Niebuhr, and A. Roy Eckardt. While each one represents a different era in our recent past—Moore, the decade of the 1920s; Niebuhr, the time of Nazism, World War II, and its aftermath; and Eckardt our own post-Holocaust generation—insofar as their vision of Judaism is concerned, none speaks for the Protestant majority. Centuries of persecution, not to mention the cataclysmic and historic events that have overwhelmed the Jewish people in recent years—their almost total destruction and political rebirth—have as yet done little to alter Christian thinking about Jews. In this sense the works of Moore, Niebuhr, and Eckhardt are exceptional and stand as reminders that, at least in selected cases, traditional attitudes are capable of significant transformation.

Few eras in American history have been more justifiably disassociated with progress in the area of ethnic, racial, and religious relations than the decade of the 1920s. Remembered primarily for its religious fundamentalism, the Ku Klux Klan, and immigration restriction movement, which among other things unabashedly singled out Jews as a threat to the stability of American institutions, it was also the decade in which George F. Moore (1851–1931) offered a significant challenge to anti-Semitic thinking. His attack was indirect, for he did so by producing a series of studies which enabled Christian biblical scholars to view Judaism from a fresh and more sympathetic perspective.

A graduate of Union Theological Seminary in 1877 and ordained a Presbyterian minister in the following year, Moore taught at Andover until 1902 and later at Harvard as a professor of Hebrew, Bible, and Rabbinics.[7] A careful, meticulous, and dedicated scholar, he did more than anyone of his generation to disabuse his co-religionists of the accumulated misinformation about the Jewish religious heritage. Although he was not an active crusader against anti-Semitism, Moore was sympathetic toward those who sought to eradicate it. Jews "have small reason to admire Christian ethics in application, whether ecclesiastical, political, social, or individual," he wrote in 1923. "Judging the tree by the fruit it has borne in eighteen centuries of persecution, they not unnaturally resent Christian assertions of its preeminence."[8]

Moore was chiefly a scholar, a student of Talmudic literature, who labored a lifetime to disengage the Jewish historical record from Christian sources and interpretations. His primary effort was to convince the historians of early Christianity that their vision of Judaism was faulty since it was based upon a foundation of ignorance of Rabbinic literature. He complained in 1921 that Christian writing about Jews has been primarily "apologetic or polemic rather than historical."[9] He was critical of Catholic and Protestant scholarship which for centuries saw little else in Rabbinic literature beyond a mine in which to search for superstitions, "unholy rites," and blasphemies against Christianity.[10] Moore lamented that even recent and contemporary scholars found little else beyond arid "legalism" in the sacred Jewish sources. The argument that runs consistently throughout his work is that Judaism can be understood only on its own merits, by a study of its own sources and not by an attempt to find its relationship to the Christian faith.[11] He urged his readers to approach Rabbinic literature with the same reverence accorded to the Synoptic Gospels.[12]

He was also critical of Old Testament scholarship; here, too, Moore recognized the inability of Christian biblicists to accept the Jewish scripture on its own terms, but only as they believed it to be related to the Gospels. He was appalled, for example, at Christian efforts to seek in the Old Testament and its commentaries "a figure corresponding to the Son, or the Word (Logos)" or "a divine being, intermediary between God the Father and the world."[13] It was clear to Moore that no such figure or symbol could be discovered in sacred Jewish literature and urged Christians not to spend their time searching for it.

Moore's two volume work, *Judaism in the First Centuries of the Christian Era* (1927), continues to stand among the clearest expositions of Rabbinic Judaism produced by an American Christian scholar. His stress upon the formative years of modern Judaism stands in sharp contrast to the traditional practice of Christian scholars to disregard post-biblical Jewish history. He was not disturbed by the thought that "the completion of the New Testament" was of no significance to the early rabbis; that it had no impact on their own achievements. He recognized that any meaningful comprehension of "the creation of a normative type of Judaism" will fail to materialize without a thorough study of the creative accomplishments of the early Talmudic age.[14]

Moore's view of the Pharisees, as the most significant religious body in the Judaism of the early Christian Era, grew out of his familiarity with the Rabbinic sources. Unlike other Christian writers (even Reinhold Niebuhr, as will be seen, was uneasy with the Pharisees) Moore does not capitulate to the deprecation of the Pharisees found in the Gospels. He understood that Jewish survival depended upon their intelligent guidance, that because of the groundwork which they established, "unity of belief and observance among Jews in all their wide dispersion has been attained in later centuries."[15]

Aware of the differences which have evolved between Christians and Jews, Moore warns his readers that "Judaism must be allowed to speak for itself" and not be viewed as "a background, an environment" or "a contrast" to Christianity.[16] Christian ignorance about Judaism has invariably resulted in confusion and misunderstanding about such important designations as "law," a term which Moore considers "a poor English rendering" for *Torah*, or "original sin—an alien doctrine" for believing Jews. Its employment, Moore insists, served no useful purpose in enhancing Jewish-Christian relations.[17]

Moore represented a lonely voice in a generation captivated by the idea of triumphant Christianity when he suggested that both Judaism and Christianity, each in its own unique way, represented a valid road to God. "Both Rabbis and Church Fathers," he writes, were "convinced that they were showing men exactly how to conform to the revelation of God."[18] Moore stopped short of demanding a reevaluation of Christian theology in regard to its treatment of Jews, a task which would be left to others of a later generation.

It is difficult to gauge precisely the extent of influence that Moore's scholarship had upon American Protestant thought. The noted biblical scholar Samuel Sandmel believed that Moore's "eminence has been such that it has created a new tone in the Christian assessment of Judaism" but that its influence has been most pronounced among "Christian Biblical scholars."[19] How far it extended beyond this exclusive circle or filtered down from it, is another question; it was probably not very far. Moore's writings, found primarily in specialized journals with small circulations, possessed limited popular appeal. Still, as a Christian student of Judaism, Moore towered above his contemporaries.

In Reinhold Niebuhr (1892–1971) we meet a much more popular figure; unlike Moore, he was not a systematic theologian but a prolific and influential author. His writings grew primarily from his observations of the troubled world about him. "I must confess," he remarked in 1939, "that the gradual unfolding of my theological ideas has come not so much through study as through the pressure of world events."[20] In 1929, after serving thirteen years as a pastor in Detroit, he accepted a professorship at the Union Theological Seminary, where he remained until his retirement. His life was characterized by an active involvement in a variety of social and political issues of the day.[21]

Early in his career Niebuhr became disenchanted with the views of Christian liberals, especially with their belief of the inherent goodness of human beings. He concluded that the fundamental assumptions of the eighteenth century Enlightenment and the Social Gospel of the nineteenth, especially as these related to the moral decisions which individuals made about social and political matters, were unrealistic. He recalled in 1941 that "between Versailles and Munich I underwent a conversion which involved rejection of almost all the liberal theological ideas with which I first ventured forth."[22]

Niebuhr's name soon became associated with the idea of "Christian Realism," a point of view which enabled him to better grasp and cope with the discordant and complex issues of the 1930s and 1940s. His keen observation and extensive reading convinced him of at least two things: first, that democratic institutions were not capable of altering the self-seeking behavior of individuals,[23] and, second, that "a sharp distinction must be drawn between the moral and social behavior of individuals and of social groups, national, racial and economic." As Niebuhr saw it, human behavior was most brutal in its collective form. To him "the perennial tragedy of human history is that those who cultivate the spiritual elements usually do so by divorcing themselves from . . . the problems of collective man."[24] His was a new social gospel, rooted not in confidence but in suspicion of collective behavior. Indeed, it was the striking social consciousness of the Jewish people that attracted him to them. "The glory of their religion is that they are really not thinking so much of 'salvation' as of a saved society," he wrote while still a pastor in Detroit in 1928. It was a thought to which he would return repeatedly.[25]

By 1930 Niebuhr already sensed the ominous potential of German Nazism.[26] His periodic visits to Germany as a special correspondent confirmed his initial anxiety. "With unexampled and primitive ferocity," Jews were being "arrested, beaten and murdered, with no public protest," he reported back to the *Christian Century*.[27] The capitulation of the German churches, Protestant and Catholic, to Nazism and Jew-hatred disturbed him greatly.

He was appalled at the reichbishop's insistence "that Jesus was the first anti-semite and that he lost his life in his fight against Judaism."[28] Niebuhr traced to Luther's teaching German Protestantism's rapid fall to the dark forces of "blood and race."[29]

He also found inexcusable the indifference of American churches to the German atrocities of the 1930s. He urged his fellow Christians to issue "public pronouncements," organize public meetings, and "apply pressure upon the Washington government." "We must," he wrote in 1933, "in spite of our own sins, do what we can to inform the German people of the impression which their actions make upon sane people."[30] He rejected a style of Christianity "which transcended the whole sphere of sociological relationships" and ignored the evil around it.[31] It is therefore understandable why he deplored and viewed as heretical the Roman Catholic tilt towards Nazism as a defense against Communism. The rationalization that "fascism does not intend to destroy the Church while Communism does" he considered spurious.[32]

Similarly, Niebuhr's rejection of the thought that pacifism in the face of evil was a Christian virtue set him apart from the multitude of American Christians during the 1930s. From his perspective of "Christian Realism," Niebuhr had lost faith in the notion that pacifism was a useful instrument in international disputes as early as 1927.[33] In 1934, because of its isolationist position, he resigned from the Fellowship of Reconciliation, a pacifist organization with ties to the Quakers. Pacifism, "which he called 'the devil of hypocrisy,'" was no weapon against the brutality of Nazism. The latter, he counseled, could be met only with "the devil of vengeance."[34] Niebuhr was unimpressed with the "kind of Christianity" which "prompted the Archbishop of Canterbury to hail the victory of Hitler in Austria because it was 'bloodless.'"[35] Moral force had its place, but not as a weapon against Hitler's Germany, he told a group of isolationist Protestant ministers in 1940. He urged those who were morally repelled by the thought of meeting force with force "to retire to the monastery where medieval perfectionists found their asylum."[36] Colonel Charles Lindberg, who wished to avoid war with Germany "and other appeasers of his type," he viewed as dangerously misinformed. The avoidance of conflict with tyranny had nothing to do with "the Christian law of love," he wrote in 1940.[37] As the world crisis deepened he became increasingly irked at Christian pacifism's inability "to distinguish between the peace of capitulation to tyranny and the peace of the Kingdom of God."[38] For their hesitancy to voice criticism of Nazism, American churches, he believed, had entered a stage of spiritual and moral decline. There was more than cynicism in his recommendation that as a reward for their pacifism, American churches substitute for their crucifixes "three little monkeys who counsel men to 'speak no evil, hear no evil, see no evil.' "[39]

Observing Germany's anti-Semitic fury, Niebuhr became convinced that the United States must ultimately adopt a pluralistic social ideal. The melting-pot concept, he became increasingly convinced, was an illusion. He argued that ethnic and racial groups have not only a right, but a duty, to remain different from the majority, to be themselves. "There is a curious, partly unconscious, cultural imperialism in theories of tolerance which look forward to a complete destruction of all racial distinctions," he wrote in 1942.[40]

A logical outgrowth of Niebuhr's rejection of the assimilationist ideal was his disdain for Protestant efforts to convert Jews to Christianity. With its large Jewish population, New York City was not the place for Billy Graham's crusade, he declared on one occasion.[41] He was particularly annoyed with Gentile hypocrisy which practiced tolerance toward Jews "provisionally in the hope that it will encourage assimilation ethnically and conversion religiously." He warned that proselytizing will invariably end in disappointment as it always had in the past.[42] "It is not our business to convert Jews to Christianity," he told a group of worshippers on Palm Sunday in 1962.[43] Like Moore, Niebuhr rejected the Christian claim that it had a monopoly on salvation. He countered such assertions with his belief that there was more than one way to God, more than one road to salvation.[44] He believed that efforts to convert the Jews were not only unnecessary but socially and psychologically disruptive. The symbol of Christ might be spiritually uplifting for Christians, but it could not induce a similar emotion for Jews, he told his co-religionists. "We are reminded daily of the penchant of anti-Semitic . . . groups claiming the name of Christ for their campaign of hatred."[45]

Niebuhr recognized that anti-Semitism was rooted in an ancient legacy of Christian misrepresentation of the meaning of the Jewish heritage. Like Moore he challenged the prevailing tendency to reduce the difference between the two belief systems to "a religion of the law and a religion of the spirit,"[46] or of viewing the New Testament as the embodiment of a "religion of the spirit" in contrast to the Old Testament as a "religion of the law."[47] The "Love Commandment," which Christianity claimed as its invention," he wrote in 1958, "is taken from the Old Testament and the Rabbis have taught consistently that love is the fulfillment of the law."[48]

As a proponent of pluralism, it followed that Niebuhr would emerge as a vocal supporter of the Zionist movement. He entertained little sympathy for the liberal, universalistic presuppositions prevalent among Christians and some Jews, who rejected a national solution. Niebuhr became aware of the ethnopolitical realities of life sooner than most of his co-religionists. "A collective survival impulse is as legitimate a 'right' as an individual one," he wrote in 1942.[49]

Even before knowledge of the European holocaust dawned on the public imagination, Niebuhr recognized the inappropriateness of the European environment for postwar Jewry. This realization reinforced his conviction about a Zionist solution. Jews, he argued in 1942, were a "nationality and not merely a cultural group" and were entitled to a homeland, a place where they could be neither "understood nor misunderstood . . . appreciated nor condemned, but where they could be what they are."[50] In 1944 Niebuhr helped initiate the pro-Zionist American Christian Palestine Committee, serving as its first treasurer and for many years as a member of its executive committee.[51] Like Supreme Court Justice Louis D. Brandeis, whom he admired, Niebuhr saw no incompatibility between Zionism and loyalty to the United States.[52] He viewed the Zionist solution not only as a way to alleviate the plight of postwar Jews, but also as an opportunity, denied Jews for centuries, for an uninhibited cultural and religious expression.[53] Neither did he detect a contradiction between a two-thousand-year dispersion and the Jewish claim to nationality. On the contrary, with its biblical roots "grounded in a religious covenant experience" he saw Jewish nationhood as one of the oldest and most legitimate in history.[54] "No nation," he wrote, "has ever been 'so conceived and so dedicated' by such a variety of social, moral, and religious forces and factors."[55]

As the Jews of Palestine, the *Yishuv*, prepared for statehood, Niebuhr's voice was conspicuous among American Protestants in offers of encouragement and support. He testified on Zionism's behalf in Washington and publically criticized British bungling and callousness.[56] In the years that followed Israel's independence in 1948, his support for the new state remained consistent. For example, he applauded Israel's refusal to evacuate captured Egyptian territories following the Suez War of 1957, in defiance of both the United Nations and the United States, before it was assured of substantive guarantees for its security. Israel, he declared, had every right to suspect the "legalistic logic which asserted that its security could not be guaranteed until it had purged itself of defiance." Instead of censure, Niebuhr requested from Washington "an unequivocal" voice that it "will not allow the state to be annihilated" by its Arab neighbors.[57] It was more than sympathy that drew Niebuhr to Israel's cause. He also saw in its survival a "strategic anchor for a democratic world" and an asset to America's national interests in the Middle East.[58]

Although disabled by a long illness, Niebuhr mustered sufficient strength in 1967, as six Arab armies prepared to obliterate the Jewish state, to write, "No simile better fits the war between Israel and the Arabs . . . than the legend of David and Goliath." Israel's preemptive strike, he declared, was fully justified. "A nation that knows it is in danger of strangulation will use its fists."[59] These remarks appeared in *Christianity and Crisis*, a journal Niebuhr founded in 1941 "to rally American Christians against Nazism," and which he edited for many years. Nevertheless, because of its intolerance toward Israel following the 1967 victory, Niebuhr broke his association with the magazine. Shortly after his death, when the magazine printed an article charging Israel's annexation of East Jerusalem as immoral, Niebuhr's widow requested that *Christianity and Crisis* remove her late husband's name from the masthead of the journal.[60] The gesture was in keeping with Niebuhr's long and dedicated support for the Jewish state.

Steeped primarily in Christian sources and lacking the profound knowledge of early Judaism attained by Moore, Niebuhr's writings were not totally free, however, of signs of ambivalence about Judaism. This was especially true of his earlier works which reflected, for example, an acceptance of the Christian story of the crucifixion[61] and were interspersed with deprecations of the Pharisees and their "Judaistic-legalistic tradition."[62] Even his strong support for the State of Israel was on occasion weakened by an exaggerated concern about its theocratic potential.[63] Too close in time to the extermination of Europe's Jews, Niebuhr also represented a generation of Christians not yet ready to formulate a theological reaction to the Final Solution. Nonetheless, when measured against the support and understanding he offered Jews during one of the most difficult periods of their history, these lapses fade into relative unimportance.

How the Holocaust and the rise of the Jewish state are molding contemporary Christian thought about Jews can be seen in the writings of the theologian A. Roy Eckardt.[64]

Inspired by his mentor Niebuhr, Eckardt, a Methodist clergyman, was among the first to probe the Christian roots of the European catastrophe.[65] From his post at Lehigh University, where he served for many years as professor and chairman of the Department of Religion, Eckardt has conducted a relentless attack on Christian responsibility for anti-Semitism. "Opposition to Jews is the one constant of Christian history," its one unifying theme throughout the centuries. The Christian world, he believes, is responsible for the invention of anti-Semitism.[66] No other prejudice, racial or ethnic animosity, can be compared to it. What is more, recourse to historical explanations alone or to the theories of the social sciences will explain neither its character nor its persistence.[67]

For Eckardt, the attack upon the Jewish people mirrors the ambivalence with which Christians view their own faith. Envied for their chosenness, hated for their alleged rejection and murder of the Christian Savior, the Jews emerge as the only group through which the Christian is able to " 'get back at' Christ" for the challenge he makes upon his life. Unable to divest himself of the Christian burden, the Christian strikes out at God's chosen people, the Jews, who are accessible and vulnerable.[68]

Neither does Eckardt find the rhetoric of the New Testament blameless. Indeed, he is among the first Christian theologians to trace the origin of anti-Semitism to the "word of God."[69] "To shut our eyes to the antisemitic proclivities of the Christian Scripture is indefensible," he wrote in 1971.[70] Within this context, the false and evil charge of deicide, flung at the Jewish people for centuries, and accepted even today by leading representatives of Christendom, is understandably high on his list of Christological myths marked for elimination.[71] The charge of deicide, according to Eckardt, cannot be viewed merely as an historic event, for its power is such that it continues to haunt Jewish-Christian relations.[72] For this reason Eckardt is deeply disappointed at the Second Vatican Council's Declaration of 1965 which purportedly absolved the Jewish people of the charge of deicide. He finds the document weakly worded, even declaring that some Jews were guilty of the crucifixion. Its puny efforts came too late to have genuine meaning, lacking "the slightest mark of Christian contrition." "Could there be a more damning judgment upon the church of our century than this one—that not until after the day of Auschwitz did Christians see fit to fabricate a correction of the record?"[73]

Like Niebuhr, but with less hesitation, Eckardt challenges the Christian denegration of Jewish "law." Juxtaposing *Torah* and Christian love, according to Eckardt, can only result in the strengthening of the foundation of Christian anti-Semitism.[74] Similarly, Eckardt's assault upon the notion that the "New Israel" has displaced the "Old" goes far beyond what is seen in traditional theological texts. Eckardt views the theology of displacement as an "affront to the Ruler of the Universe."[75]

It is understandable why Eckardt's repudiation of the "supersessionist-triumphalist Christology of the Crucifixion and Resurrection"[76] leads him to an emphatic rejection of Christian missionary activity among Jews. Like Niebuhr, but more strongly, he acknowledges that Jews need no Christian guidance along the road to salvation.[77] Most importantly, Eckardt believes that the end of anti-Semitism will begin only when Christians refrain from missionary acitivity. In this, the post-Holocaust age, Eckardt equates any attempt to convert Jews with a "spiritual Final Solution."[78]

Like other thoughtful Christians of recent years, Eckardt's imagination has been captivated by a search for meaning in the European catastrophe, the *Shoah* (Hebrew: Holocaust). Because of this event, he wonders about, and on occasion despairs of, the possibility of a future genuine relationship between Christians and Jews.[79] He admits sadly that the Nazi gas chambers represented the logical outcome of centuries of Christian teaching about Jews,[80] and for that reason believes that the Final Solution has also altered forever the central meaning of the Christian faith.

In one of his boldest assertions Eckardt declares, "After Auschwitz, the Crucifixion cannot be accepted as the determinative symbol of redemptive suffering"; it cannot be seen anymore as the ultimate and "absolute horror upon which the Christian faith can and should, dialectically, build its hope." In the face of burning Jewish children "the death of Jesus upon the Cross fades into comparative moral triviality."[81]

Christians must henceforth accept the Final Solution as a central event in their own lives, an event which could not have occurred without their complicity.[82] "Many of the Nazi executions of Jews," Eckardt repeatedly reminds his readers, "were carried out by believing Christians." Neither should the *Shoah* be reduced to "an aberration," "a nightmare," or a peculiar historical mutation, he warns; on the contrary, it should be seen as the culmination of Christian history.[83]

So that this singular act of inhumanity, described by Eckardt as one of "transcending uniqueness," be permanently implanted upon the Christian memory, Eckardt marks the year 1941 as the dividing time between "two epochs": "B.S." being "the age before the *Shoah*" and "A.S." "the age of the *Shoah* and its aftermath." The division, Eckardt explains, will serve also to separate humanity into those "who take the *Shoah*-event with absolute seriousness" and "those who do not."[84] Without a genuine expression of repentance Eckardt sees no future for Jewish-Christian relations.[85]

Eckardt is not oblivious to the risk involved in reminding Christians of their complicity. He admits that it may evoke resentment, give sadistic pleasure to sick minds, and even serve to perpetuate anti-Semitism. "In gazing down the abyss, may we not open the abyss within ourselves?" The risk, he is convinced, is worth taking, for he sees a much greater danger in silence and ignorance about the most tragic event in the history of Western civilization.[86] It is the latter that concerns him most, for too few have as yet pondered the meaning of the Holocaust. Most Christians, Eckardt laments, continue to live as if there had never been a Final Solution. Anti-Semites even deny that the event had occurred. In its own way, such a denial, by robbing the victims of their tragedy, underscores further the transcendent singularity of the Final Solution.[87]

Like Niebuhr, Eckardt is a staunch supporter of the Jewish state and, even more so than his mentor, probes for meaning in its emergence and impact upon the Christian world. He sees the two events—Holocaust and national rebirth—as altering forever the relationship of Christians and Jews. Jewish statehood, he believes, has put a final end to "the dreadful epoch of Jewish martyrdom."[88]

He has little sympathy for Christians perplexed by the theological meaning of the birth of the Jewish state, who believe that the Jewish return to their ancestral home is a dreadful miscalculation, a "violation of Christian eschatology."[89] Eckardt, on the contrary, sees the birth of Israel as a repudiation of the "Christian fantasy" that Jews are doomed to perpetual dispersion and rootlessness.[90] What is more, Christian support for Israel's survival, he believes, constitutes the only meaningful gesture of atonement for their past mistreatment of the Jewish people.[91]

Throughout the years Eckardt has repeatedly challenged the Arab denial of Israel's right to a sovereign existence.[92] "To contend that Jews have a right to exist as an ethnic ... or a religious community ... but not as a sovereign nation ... is an example of antisemitism," he recently stated, for it denies the Jewish people a basic human need accorded to all other collective groups.[93]

The Arab world's yearning for Israel's demise and its repeated efforts to destroy the Jewish state Eckardt views as politicide, another form of genocide.[94] He is, therefore, skeptical about the future relationship of Israel and her neighbors. He is convinced that in the Arab mind, peace with Israel is equated with the abolition of Israel. Israel's aspiration for survival is matched by Arab dreams of its extinction. "No reconciliation or compromise is possible," he notes, "between antagonists one of whom rejects the reality of the other."[95] Eckardt sees hatred of the Jewish state as another form of anti-Semitism. "*It is impossible to separate Arab anti-Israelism and anti-Zionism from antisemitism. They are mutually reinforcing.*" What is more, Arab hatred of the Jewish state has much in common with Nazism, from which the Arabs have borrowed heavily.[96] Only hatred of Israel has been able to unite the Arab world, as it has for centuries united the Christian. Islam, with little discouragement from the West, has inherited Christianity's animosity toward Israel and the Jewish people.[97]

Neither does Eckardt absolve the Western world, including the United States, for duplicity in their dealings with the Jewish state. Western deceitfulness manifests itself by a "general schizophrenia which judges Israel at one moment by superhuman standards . . . and at the next moment by subhuman standards." In the United Nations Israel is condemned repeatedly for defending herself, while her Arab and terrorist aggressors escape even mild rebuke.[98] Even more regrettable, according to Eckardt, is that in regard to Israel, American church organizations and their leaders have adopted a similar double standard. He points to the American Friends Service Committee, a Quaker organization, The World Council of Churches, and the editors of the widely read *Christian Century* as examples of Christian groups ever ready to "lecture Israel" on the slightest pretext, but who are quick to tolerate and forgive the most heinous acts of Arab terror. Why is it, he asks, that no other nation but Israel "is told to practice universal saint-hood?"[99] "Why is it that the Christian world has challenged no other nation's right to exist in the way it has Israel's?"[100] Is it possible, he wonders, if the Church conceals a hidden desire, "a secret wish for the demise of Israel?"[101]

In the hours of her peril, while the Arab world stood ready to annihilate the Jewish state, first in 1948, then in 1967, and in 1973, American Portestants and Catholics, as did world Christianity in general, looked on with passive indifference. Assaulted by Egyptian and Syrian forces on the Day of Atonement, October 1973, Father Daniel Berrigan accused Israel of behaving like a "criminal" and "racist state," while Henry P. van Deusan, former president of the Union Theological Seminary, compared the Jewish commonwealth to Nazi Germany. It appears, Eckardt notes perceptively, that "whenever Israel is assailed, certain suppressed, macabre elements in the Christian soul are stirred to sympathy with the assailants."[102] He is left to conclude that in the Christian mind, the State of Israel, repeatedly reproached for its militancy, aggressiveness, inflexibility, vengefulness, and irreligiosity, has replaced the mythical Jew.[103] Clearly, the Christian world has drawn few lessons from the Holocaust.

Eckardt also views Christian attempts to read theological meaning in the founding and history of Israel as a form of anti-Semitism, perhaps even a more sinister strain because it is disguised. He agrees with Niebuhr that the "theologization of politics is a guarantor of immorality," for it makes unnatural demands upon Jews and invests their misfortunes with biblical meaning. He warns Christians against the temptation to lecture Israelis "as if they were biblical prophets"[104]

For this reason Eckardt finds the theology of "Christian Zionism" disturbing. Despite the guise of friendship that the conservative wing of Christendom assumes toward the Jewish state, its adherents see little value in its emergence except as it might serve as a preparation for the "second coming." Christian Zionists invest Israel with a divine importance, theologize its political existence, and in the process rob it of its humanity and its dignity.[105]

This is not to say that Christianity's liberal Left has not also erred in its view of Jewish nationalism. Unlike the "evangelicals," who picture Israel as a "political church," the liberal Left views Judaism exclusively in religious rather than in cultural and national terms, consequently, it sees no need for a Jewish state at all. Because of their attitudes, both wings of Christianity, the right and left, are guilty of anti-Semitism, for each, in its own way, denies the Jewish people a basic human requirement: the need to pursue a normal collective and political existence.[106]

Tension between the two faiths will continue, Eckardt believes, until Christianity acknowledges the self-sufficiency of the Jewish system of belief, that Christianity is not for the Jews, and that the two faiths, each in its own inimitable way, are separate and complete.[107] "Exodus-Sinai is for Israel what the life, death, and resurrection of Jesus Christ are for the Church." Indeed, the Jewish people deserve praise for their centuries of resistance and stubborn refusal to succumb to the pressures of Christianity. "Jewish non-acceptance of Jesus," Eckardt declares, "remains the most sublime and heroic instance of Israel's faithfulness to her Covenant with God."[108] Christians must know that for Jews Christianity "is in essence false."[109]

Christianity's inability to sever its ties with the Jewish faith, out of which it was born and with which it feels intertwined, has made it difficult for it to accept Jews "simply as people, ordinary people." Since for understandable reasons this Christian perspective will continue to create uneasiness among Jews, Eckardt wonders if a permanent parting of the ways may not be the best solution. Like Jews, Christians must also learn to accept their autonomy and disassociate their identity and eschatological thinking from that of the living Jews. "I do know," he has recently written, "that loved ones part from one another and go their different ways—though they need not thereby cease their loving or their caring."[110] This latter admission must have been difficult for Eckardt to make. Certainly his willingness to re-think some of the most sacred assumptions of his own belief places him today in the forefront of the Christian crusade against anti-Semitism.

To a somewhat lesser degree Moore and Niebuhr share also in this achievement. Moore's pioneering and lonely efforts to restore the dignity of the early Rabbinic writings in Christian eyes and grant their work the centrality it has long been denied undoubtedly prodded his selective group of readers to re-think some fundamental suppositions about Jews. Niebuhr, on the other hand, although not primarily preoccupied with the subject of Jewish-Christian relations, was nevertheless compelled by German brutalities and Christian indifference to re-examine the question of anti-Semitism. In the process he challenged long-held Christian beliefs about Jews, criticized their conversionist practices, and emerged as a leading ally of Zionism and of the State of Israel.

In the movement to improve Christian attitudes toward Jews, Niebuhr's was the most prominent Protestant voice of his generation. His efforts provided a place for contemporary Jewish problems in Christian theology. To be sure, not all of his co-religionists welcomed his new departure. Niebuhr's support for the Zionist movement and the State of Israel alienated a number of his former admirers. The socialist leader Norman Thomas, for example, broke his association with him, yet few could completely escape his influence.[111] Most importantly, his efforts provided American Jews the support of a leading American theologian at a critical moment in their history.

With Eckardt we meet a contemporary figure whose work is still unfolding. He represents a growing circle of American Christians stunned by the Final Solution, awed and challenged by the rise of Jewish sovereignty.[112] He is a leading participant in a quiet revolution, the impact of which has yet to be felt. It has been suggested that because of his work and of others like him, writers of Sunday School tracts must now proceed with greater caution. The stereotypical images of old and modern Judaism have been severely cracked because of such efforts.[113] More so than his predecessors and most of his contemporaries, Eckardt's writings raise penetrating questions about Christian responsibility for the *Shoah*, and his call for a reevaluation of long-held Christian beliefs about Jews has opened new vistas for thoughtful Christians and all concerned persons as well.

Notes

1. In this connection see Michael N. Dobkowski's *The Tarnished Dream: The Basis of American Anti-Semitism.* (Westport, Conn., 1979), pp. 11–15.

2. Egal Feldman, "Protestant-Jewish Relations in the United States," *Encyclopedia Judaica* 13 (Jerusalem, 1972): 1253–54.

3. Lyman Abbott, "Paganism, Judaism, and Christianity," *Outlook* 40 (Jan. 14, 1899): 107.

4. Lyman Abbott, "Was Jesus Christ a Jew?" *Outlook* 70 (June 6, 1903): 311.

5. Walter Rauschenbusch, *A Theology for the Social Gospel* (New York, 1918), pp. 31–32, 248–52.

6. Charles Y. Glock and Rodney Stark, *Christian Beliefs and Anti-Semitism* (New York, 1966), pp. 207–8.

7. "Moore, George Foot," *Encyclopaedia Judaica* 12 (Jerusalem, 1972): 294.

8. Quoted in Samuel Sandmel, *We Jews and Jesus* (New York, 1965), pp. 115–16.

9. George Foot Moore, "Christian Writers on Judaism," *Harvard Theological Review* 14 (July 1921): 197.

10. Ibid., pp. 198, 213–14, 221, 230.

11. Ibid., pp. 239–40.

12. Ibid., p. 253.

13. George Foot Moore, "Intermediaries in Jewish Theology, Memra, Shekina, Metatron," *Harvard Theological Review* 15 (July 1922): 41.

14. George Foot Moore, *Judaism in the First Centuries of the Christian Era* (New York, 1971 ed.), pp. vii–viii, 3, 39.

15. Ibid., pp. 110–11. The English biblical scholar R. Travers Herford, a contemporary of Moore, also defended the Pharisees in his *The Pharisees*, first published in 1913 and reissued in a larger edition in 1924.

16. Moore, *Judaism in the First Centuries*, pp. 128–29.

17. Ibid., pp. 263, 479, 483.

18. Ibid., p. 60.

19. Sandmel, *We Jews and Jesus*, pp. 100–101.

20. Reinhold Niebuhr, "Ten Years That Shook My World," *Christian Century* 56 (Apr. 26, 1939): 542–46.

21. For biographical information, I have relied upon June Bingham, *Courage to Change: An Introduction to the Life and Thought of Reinhold Niebuhr* (New York, 1961), pp. 49, 51; Nathan A. Scott, *Reinhold Niebuhr* (Minneapolis, 1963), pp. 10, 12–13; Reinhold Niebuhr, "Some Things I Have Learned," *Saturday Review* 48 (Nov. 6, 1965): 21.

22. Quoted in *Time* 37 (Mar. 24, 1941): 38.

23. Niebuhr, "Some Things I Have Learned," p. 21.

24. Reinhold Niebuhr, *Moral Man and Immoral Society. A Study in Ethics and Politics* (New York, 1932), pp. ix, 256.

25. Quoted in Reinhold Niebuhr, *Leaves From the Notebook of a Tamed Cynic* (New York, 1930), p. 187; see, for example, his *Moral Man and Immoral Society,* p. 61, *Reflections on the End of an Era* (New York, 1934), pp. 132–33, *Man's Nature and His Communities* (New York, 1965), pp. 17–19, *Christianity and Power Politics* (New York, 1969 ed.), p. 199, and *Pious and Secular America* (New York, 1958), pp. 91–94.

26. Reinhold Niebuhr, "The German Crisis," *Nation* 131 (Oct. 1, 1930): 360.

27. Reinhold Niebuhr, "Germany Must Be Told!" *Christian Century* 50 (Aug. 7, 1933): 1104. See also his "The Germans: Unhappy Philosophers in Politics," *American Scholar* 2 (Oct. 1933): 411–12.

28. Quotation from Niebuhr, "Germany Must Be Told," p. 1015. See also his "The Catholic Heresy," *Christian Century* 54 (Dec. 8, 1937): 1524.

29. Reinhold Niebuhr, "Church Currents in Germany," *Christian Century* 50 (June 28, 1933), pp. 843–44, and "The Churches in Germany," *American Scholar* 3 (Summer 1934): 348–49. For a discussion of the political implications of Lutheranism, see Niebuhr, *Christianity and Power Politics,* pp. 49–51.

30. Niebuhr, "Germany Must Be Told," p. 1015.

31. Reinhold Niebuhr, "Barthianism and Political Reaction," *Christian Century* 51 (June 6, 1934): 757, 759.

32. Niebuhr, "The Catholic Heresy," p. 1524.

33. Reinhold Niebuhr, "A Critique of Pacifism," *Atlantic Monthly* 139 (May 1927): 641.

34. Reinhold Niebuhr, "Why I Leave the F.O.R.," *Christian Century* 51 (Jan. 3, 1934): 17–19. For further thoughts on Niebuhr's pacifism, see his *Beyond Tragedy: Essays on the Christian Interpretation of History* (New York, 1937), p. 181.

35. Reinhold Niebuhr, "Must Democracy Use Force?" *Nation* 148 (Jan. 28, 1939): 118. See also his "Idealists as Cynics," *Nation* 150 (Jan. 20, 1940): 72.

36. Reinhold Niebuhr, "An End to Illusion," *Nation* 150 (June 29, 1940): 779.

37. Reinhold Niebuhr, "Ten Answers," *Christian Century* 57 (Dec. 18, 1940): 159.

38. Niebuhr, *Christianity and Power Politics,* p. xi.

39. Ibid., p. 33.

40. Reinhold Niebuhr, "Jews After the War," Pt. 1, *Nation* 154 (Feb. 21, 1942): 215.

41. Reinhold Niebuhr, "Proposal to Billy Graham," *Christian Century* 73 (Aug. 8, 1956): 921; Patrick Granfield, "An Interview with Reinhold Niebuhr," *Commonwealth* 85 (Dec. 6, 1966): 319; *New York Times,* June 2, 1957, p. 38.

42. Niebuhr, *Pious and Secular America,* p. 88; *New York Times,* Apr. 5, 1958, p. 10.

43. Reinhold Niebuhr, "The Son of Man Must Suffer," in *Justice and Mercy*, ed. Ursula M. Niebuhr, (New York, 1974), p. 85.

44. Reinhold Niebuhr, *The Children of Light and the Children of Darkness* (New York, 1944), pp. 134–35, and *Pious and Secular America*, pp. 98–99, 105.

45. Niebuhr, *Pious and Secular America*, p. 108.

46. Reinhold Niebuhr, "Rosenzweig's Message," *Commentary*, 15 (Mar. 1953): 312.

47. Reinhold Niebuhr, *The Self and the Dramas of History* (New York, 1955), p. 88.

48. Niebuhr, *Pious and Secular America*, p. 102. Niebuhr, however, was not always consistent in these assertions; see, for example, ibid., pp. 105–6.

49. Niebuhr, "Jews After the War," Pt. 1, p. 216. See also his "Toward a Program for Jews," Part I: "Survival and Religion," *Contemporary Jewish Record* 7 (June 1944): 241.

50. Niebuhr, "Jews After the War," Pt. 1, pp. 214–16.

51. Bingham, *Courage to Change*, pp. 284–85.

52. Reinhold Niebuhr, "Jews After the War," Pt. 2, *Nation* 154 (Feb. 28, 1942): 352–54.

53. Niebuhr, "Toward a Program for Jews, Part I," p. 245.

54. Reinhold Niebuhr, *Discerning the Signs of the Times: Sermons for Today and Tomorrow* (New York, 1946), pp. 75–76; Niebuhr, *The Self and the Dramas of History*, pp. 40, 87; Niebuhr, *The Structure of Nations and Empires* (New York, 1959), pp. 161–62.

55. Niebuhr, *Structure of Nations and Empires*, pp. 161–62.

56. Hertzel Fishman, *American Protestantism and a Jewish State* (Detroit, 1973), pp. 78–80; Reinhold Niebuhr, "Palestine: British-American Dilemma," *Nation* 136 (Aug. 31, 1946): 239.

57. Reinhold Niebuhr, "The U.N. is Not a World Government," *Reporter* 16 (Mar. 7, 1957): 32, and "Our Stake in the State of Israel," *New Republic* 136 (Feb. 4, 1957): 11–12.

58. Niebuhr, "Our Stake in the State of Israel," p. 12; *New York Times*, May 18, 1951, p. 26.

59. Reinhold Niebuhr, "David and Goliath," *Christianity and Crisis. A Journal of Christian Opinion* 27 (June 26, 1967): 141.

60. A. Roy Eckardt, "A Tribute to Reinhold Niebuhr," *Midstream* 17 (June/July, 1971): 16; *New York Times*, May 8, 1972, p. 9.

61. See, for example, Niebuhr, *Leaves From a Notebook of a Tamed Cynic*, p. 28, and "At Oberramergau," *Christian Century* 47 (Aug. 13, 1930): 984.

62. See Niebuhr, *Christianity and Power Politics*, p. 19; Niebuhr, "Religion and Action," in University of Pennsylvania Bicentennial Conference, *Religion and the Modern World* (Philadelphia, 1941), p. 93; Niebuhr, *The Nature and Destiny of Man: A Christian Interpretation* (New York, 1949), pp. 41, 58, 215–16.

63. Niebuhr, "Toward a Program for Jews, Part I," p. 242, and "Our Stake in the State of Israel," p. 10.

64. Other theologians, both Protestant and Catholic, whose thinking has

been affected by these events and whose work I have found impressive, include Alan T. Davies, Eva Fleischner, Franklin H. Littell, Bernard E. Olson, John T. Paulikowski, and Rosemary Ruether.

65. Eckardt also acknowledges his debt to the historians Salo W. Baron and James Parkes. See A. Roy Eckardt, "Theological Approaches to anti-Semitism," *Jewish Social Studies* 33 (Oct. 1971): 272; Robert Evans' review of A. Roy Eckardt's *Your People, My People: The Meeting of Christians and Jews* (New York, 1974) in *Jewish Social Studies* 37 (Jan. 1975): 90. As will be evident in the notes below, a few of Eckardt's books have been co-authored with his wife, Alice L. Eckardt. For the sake of stylistic consistency my references through the text are to "Eckardt."

66. Eckardt, *Your People, My People*, p. 79, and "The Devil and Yom Kippur," *Midstream* 20 (Aug./Sept. 1974): 70.

67. A. Roy Eckardt, *Christianity and the Children of Israel* (New York, 1948), pp. 3–13; Eckardt, "Christian Faith and the Jews," *Journal of Religion* 30 (Oct. 1950): 239–40; Eckardt, "Can There be a Jewish-Christian Relationship?" *Journal of Bible and Religion* 33 (Apr. 1965): 122. Following the suggestion of James Parkes ("the noted British historian, Anglican Clergyman, and pioneering scholar in Jewish-Christian understanding"), Eckardt concludes that the spelling "anti-Semitism" is inappropriate. Since most of the people of Southwestern Asia are "Semites," the term implies far more than Jew-hatred. The non-capitalized and non-hyphenated version, "antisemitism" (in actuality a new word) is more appropriate. Parkes and Eckardt assert that the spelling "anti-Semitism" is " 'pseudo-scientific, mumbo-jumbo.' " It implies " 'that the phenomenon in question is somehow a movement directed against an actual quality' " called Semitism. On the other hand, since the word antisemitism makes no pretense to a scientific designation, "it is entitled to neither a hyphen nor a capital." See Eckardt, "The Nemesis of Christian Antisemitism," *Journal of Church and State* 13 (Spring 1971): 227. In spelling "antisemitism," I had wished to follow Eckardt's suggestion, but have used the conventional spelling for the sake of consistency with the rest of this collection.

68. Eckardt, *Christianity and the Children of Israel*, pp. 43–45, 50–56; Eckardt, "Theological Approaches to Anti-Semitism," *Jewish Social Studies* 33 (Oct. 1971): 275–77, 283; Eckardt, *Your People, My People*, p. 80.

69. Eckardt, "Can There Be a Jewish-Christian Relationship?" pp. 126–27; Eckardt with Alice L. Eckardt, *Long Night's Journey Into Day: Life and Faith After the Holocaust* (Detroit, 1982), p. 114; Eckardt, "The Nemesis of Christian Anti-Semitism," pp. 231–32.

70. Eckardt, "Theological Approaches to Anti-Semitism," p. 282, and *Your People, My People*, p. 38.

71. Eckardt, *Christianity and the Children of Israel*, pp. 1–2; Eckardt, *Elder and Younger Brothers: The Encounter of Jews and Christians* (New York, 1967), pp. 116–17.

72. Eckardt, *Elder and Younger Brothers*, pp. 118–19, and *Your People, My People*, p. 12.

73. Eckardt, "Can There Be a Jewish-Christian Relationship?" pp. 123–24, and *Your People, My People*, pp. 42–45.

74. A. Roy Eckardt, "Jürgen Moltmann, the Jewish People and the Holocaust," *Journal of the American Academy of Religion* 44 (Dec. 1976): 681.

75. Eckardt, "Can There Be a Jewish-Christian Relationship?" p. 127, and *Long Night's Journey Into Day*, p. 118; see also his *Elder and Younger Brothers*, pp. 51, 129–30, 158.

76. A. Roy Eckardt, "Contemporary Christian Theology and a Protestant Witness for the Shoah," *Shoah: A Review of Holocaust Studies and Commemorations* 2 (Spring 1980): 11.

77. Eckardt, *Elder and Younger Brothers*, pp. 141, 152–53.

78. A. Roy Eckardt, "Christian Responses to the *Endlösung*," *Religion in Life* 48 (Spring 1978): 39; see also his "Christians and Jews, Along a Theological Frontier," *Encounter* 40 (Spring 1979): 98, 126.

79. Eckardt, "Can There Be a Jewish-Christian Relationship?" p. 122.

80. Eckardt, *Elder and Younger Brothers*, pp. 12–14.

81. Eckardt, "Jürgen Montmann," pp. 686–87; Eckardt, "The Recantation of the Covenant?" in *Confronting The Holocaust: the Impact of Elie Wiesel,* ed. Alvin H. Rosenfeld and Irving Greenburg (Bloomington, Ind., 1978), pp. 102–4; Eckardt, *Long Night's Journey*, pp. 99–104.

82. Eckardt, "Christian Responses to the *Endlösung*," pp. 34–35; Eckardt, "Christians and Jews: Along a Theological Frontier," p. 92.

83. Eckardt, *Long Night's Journey*, pp. 17, 23.

84. Eckardt, "Christians and Jews: Along a Theological Frontier," p. 95, and "Contemporary Christian Theology," pp. 12–13; see also his *Long Night's Journey*, pp. 45–47.

85. A. Roy Eckardt and Alice L. Eckardt, *Encounter with Israel: A Challenge to Conscience* (New York, 1979), p. 256.

86. Eckardt, *Long Night's Journey*, pp. 28–30.

87. Eckardt, "Christian Responses to the Endlösung," pp. 34, 41; see also his "Christians and Jews: Along a Theological Frontier," p. 95.

88. A. Roy Eckardt, "Eretz Israel: A Christian Affirmation," *Midstream* 14 (Mar. 1968): 12, and "Toward an Authentic Jewish-Christian Relationship," *Journal of Church and State* 13 (Spring 1971): 271.

89. A. Roy Eckardt and Alice L. Eckardt, "Silence in the Churches," *Midstream* 13 (Oct. 1967): 28.

90. Eckardt, "Eretz Israel: A Christian Affirmation," p. 11, and *Encounter with Israel*, p. 261.

91. A. Roy Eckardt, "The Fantasy of Reconciliation in the Middle East," *Christian Century* 48 (Oct. 13, 1971): 1202.

92. Eckardt, *Christianity and the Children of Israel*, p. 170, and *Encounter with Israel*, p. 194.

93. Eckardt, *Encounter with Israel*, p. 231.

94. Ibid., pp. 200–202; see also his "The Fantasy of Reconciliation in the Middle East," p. 1200.

95. Eckardt, "The Fantasy of Reconciliation in the Middle East," p. 1199.

96. Eckardt, *Encounter with Israel*, pp. 219, 222, Eckardt's italics.

97. Eckardt, "The Devil and Yom Kippur," p. 69.

98. Eckardt, "Eretz Israel: A Christian Affirmation," p. 10, and *Encounter with Israel*, pp. 184, 205.

99. Eckardt, *Encounter with Israel*, p. 208, and "The Devil and Yom Kippur," p. 72.

100. Eckardt, *Your People, My People*, p. 141.

101. Eckardt, "Christians and Jews: Along a Theological Frontier," p. 121.

102. Eckardt, "Silence in the Churches," pp. 28, 32; Eckardt, "The Protestant View of Israel," *Encyclopaedia Judaica Year Book, 1974* (Jerusalem, 1974), p. 162; Eckardt, "The Devil and Yom Kippur," pp. 67–68, 71, 73–74; see also, *New York Times*, Oct. 11, 1972, p. 44.

103. A. Roy Eckardt, "Christian Perspectives on Israel," *Midstream* 18, (Oct. 1972): 40–41, and "The Nemesis of Christian antisemitism," p. 239.

104. Eckardt, "The Nemesis of Christian antisemitism," p. 237; Eckardt, *Long Night's Journey*, p. 106; Eckardt, "Christian Perspectives on Israel," pp. 44–45.

105. Alice and Roy Eckardt, "The Achievements and Trials of Interfaith," *Judaism* 27 (Summer 1978): 320; see also his "Toward a Secular Theology of Israel," *Religion in Life* 68 (Winter 1979): 462, 466.

106. Eckardt, "Toward a Secular Theology of Israel," p. 467.

107. Eckardt, *Christianity and the Children of Israel*, p. 46; see also his "The Mystery of the Jews' Rejection of Christ," *Theology Today* 18 (Apr. 1961): 55.

108. Eckardt, *Elder and Younger Brothers*, pp. 105, 135, 242, and "Christians and Jews: Along a Theological Frontier," p. 96.

109. Eckardt, *Elder and Younger Brothers*, p. 160, and "A Response to Rabbi Olan," *Religion in Life* 62 (Autumn 1973): 404.

110. Eckardt, *Long Night's Journey*, p. 122, and "A Response to Rabbi Olan," p. 404.

111. For Niebuhr's impact on American Protestantism, I am indebted to a conversation with Dr. Carl Hermann Voss, Aug. 8, 1982.

112. This circle includes such names as Alan T. Davies, Eugene J. Fisher, Franklin A. Littell, and Paul M. Van Buren.

113. The suggestion comes from a conversation with Father John T. Pawlikowski, July 26, 1982.

David G. Singer

From St. Paul's Abrogation of the Old Covenant to Hitler's War against the Jews: The Responses of American Catholic Thinkers to the Holocaust, 1945–76

On October 28, 1965, the bishops of Vatican Council II voted almost unanimously to accept a schema entitled "A Declaration on the Church's Attitude toward Non-Christian Religions" (*Nostra Aetate*). It absolves contemporary Jews of any guilt for the crucifixion of Jesus and repudiates the belief that God rejected the Jews because they stubbornly refused and still refuse to accept Jesus as the savior. Except for the most reactionary elements in the Church, Catholic thinkers everywhere hailed the declaration as a major advance in the correction of Christian attitudes toward the Jews and as a framework for a meaningful dialogue between Jews and Catholics.

Among the episcopal delegations to Vatican II, the American bishops played a particularly important role in winning the council's approval of the declaration, and in March 1967, the American bishops issued their own guidelines for a Catholic dialogue with the Jews.[1] The significance of these developments is heightened by the fact that the American bishops are the spiritual leaders of one of the wealthiest and largest Catholic communities in the world; indeed, Catholics comprise the largest single religious community in the United States.

These official revisions in the Church's attitudes toward and doctrines concerning the Jews, at Vatican II and in the United States, call for a closer investigation of the attitudes of American Catholics toward the Jews. In the past, Catholic theologians and churchmen often described the Jews and their religion in unflattering, even hateful terms, and thereby stimulated Christian hatred of Jews. Now, in the middle of the twentieth century, the Church sought to modify traditional Christian beliefs concerning the Jewish religion and to improve its relations with the Jews. The attitudes and relations of Catholics toward and with Jews during the years 1945–1976—from the surrender of Nazi Germany to the interfaith discussions that followed the Yom Kippur War—often centered around the relationship between Christian theology and anti-Semitism and in particular, the attitudes and policies of the Church during the Holocaust.

Contrary to popular belief, neither the Jewish nor the Catholic communities are monolithic ones, and wide differences of opinion concerning various social and theological issues exist among American Jews and Catholics. There are three general trends of thought about the Jews among American Catholic intellectuals: the first and by far the largest group is conservative and traditional; the second group consists of a few very articulate revisionists who stand at the other end of the spectrum of Catholic thought; and between these two extremes is a group of moderate reformers. Each of these three groups of Catholic thinkers has markedly different attitudes toward Jews, toward the Jewish religion, toward the issues that divide Jews and Catholics, and, indeed, toward the Catholic Church itself. The boundary lines between these three groups are not rigid and clear ones, so the same writer may adhere to orthodox Christian theology while having serious doubts concerning Pope Pius XII's diplomatic policy during the Holocaust.

Traditional Catholics fervently believe in all of the basic doctrines and teachings of their Church and ardently defend the papacy against any political criticism. Therefore, traditional Catholics, whose thought is the dominant one in American Catholicism, accept the anti-Judaic passages in the New Testament at face value but deny that there is any connection between Christianity and anti-Semitism. Many traditional Catholic thinkers are members of the Catholic hierarchy or are closely associated with it as teachers at Church-affiliated colleges and universities and as writers for the Catholic press.

Traditional Catholic intellectuals reflect the attitudes of a sizable number, probably a majority, of American Catholics, many of whose forefathers came from countries like Ireland and Poland where Catholicism and national survival were deemed to be synonymous. In the United States, the Catholic Church successfully built its own separate religious and educational institutions in a predominantly Protestant country where Catholics, like nineteenth-century Irish immigrants, sometimes encountered economic, social, and religious discrimination. These factors heightened the attachment of many American Catholics to the traditional teachings and doctrines of their Church.

As a result of the pontificate of John XXIII and Vatican Council II, a group of Catholic clergy and lay intellectuals were motivated to rethink the theological relationship between Christianity and Judaism. This group of moderate, reform-minded Catholics concluded that Christianity does indeed harbor an anti-Jewish element, but that this bias can be expunged from the Church through a re-interpretation and shift in emphasis of Christian teaching and doctrines.

No doubt, these moderate Catholic thinkers reflect the growing religious tolerance and ecumenicism that developed in post–World War II American society. As Catholicism grew in strength and found acceptance as a truly American religion, an increasing number of the hierarchy felt confident enough about the status and future of their Church to enter into ecumenical discussions with the leaders of other religions in the United States.

Many among the Catholic laity supported such discussions or were themselves willing to enter into interfaith discussions with Protestants and Jews. These Catholics had risen socially and gained in political power as a result of the reforms of the New Deal and the postwar period, and in many of the newly affluent residential areas, there was an atmosphere of religious tolerance and understanding.

A handful of highly educated Catholic thinkers called for a total revision of Christian doctrines and beliefs concerning Jews and Judaism. With a few notable exceptions, these revisionists are lay Catholics who are on the fringes of mainstream Catholic thought. Indeed, Rosemary Radford Ruether, the most prominent of the revisionists, teaches at Garrett Evangelical Seminary in Evanston, Illinois.

The Nazi extermination of 6 million European Jews was not only a deep blow and a terrible shock to world Jewry, but it also caused thoughtful Christians to question and re-examine some of the basic institutions and beliefs of Western civilization—including the Christian religion and the Catholic and Protestant churches— and their relationship to the Holocaust. Christian intellectuals could not ignore the truth that millions of people were murdered simply because they were Jews, and that their slayers were born and reared as Christians. Moreover, many believing Christians remained silent or even tacitly supported the Nazi extermination of the Jews. Because it is the largest and best organized branch of Christianity, the Catholic Church and its policies toward the Jews during the years 1933–45 are particularly important. If the Church had taken a vigorous and firm stand against the Nazi persecution and extermination of the Jews, it is possible that many of them might have been saved from the death camps.

The vast majority of Catholic thinkers repudiate the allegation that the Catholic Church ignored the suffering of the Jews during the reign of the Third Reich and assert that the Church did all that it could do, under very difficult circumstances, to save as many Jews as possible. The most troublesome question with regard to this matter concerns the alleged failure of Pius XII to act directly and effectively on behalf of the trapped Jews of Nazi-occupied Europe.

The Jesuits who published *America*, possibly the foremost journal of Catholic opinion in the United States, were particularly ardent in their defense of the late pope and of the entire wartime record of the Church. The Jesuits asserted that the late pontiff made every effort to save the Jews of Rome from deportation to Auschwitz, and this was only one example of his many attempts to help the Jews during World War II, but the question of Pius's policy toward the Jews could not be so easily laid to rest. In his play *The Deputy*, the German writer Rolf Hochhuth alleged that Pius XII was indifferent to the fate of the Jews because he was obsessed by the Bolshevik threat to Europe, that he did not want to interfere with Germany's wartime aims because they included the destruction of Soviet Russia. In 1963 and 1964, the Jesuits of *America* bitterly criticized the play both as bad art and as a "vilifying portrayal" of a man who had done much to help save the Jews of Europe.[2] Despite these protestations, most historians who have examined Pius XII's wartime policy acknowledge his silence with regard to the extermination of Europe's Jews.

The Jesuits of *America* are particularly sensitive to any criticism of the Holy See because, like all members of their religious order, they take a special vow of obedience to the pope. Because of its influence on both Catholic and non-Catholic opinion in the United States, the editors of *America* think that they must uphold the reputation of the late pope lest the reputation of the entire Church suffer.

At the other end of the spectrum of Catholic thought is a small group of intellectuals who realize that most Christians, including Pius XII, remained silent while the Nazis slaughtered the Jews. Prominent among these intellectuals are Father Edward Flannery and the sociologist and pacifist, Gordon Zahn.[3]

While he decried Christian anti-Semitism, Flannery advised against any effort to single out the pope for his indifference to the Jews. The leaders of other Christian churches and many Western statesmen also kept silent even after they were informed about the Nazi genocidal operations, Flannery pointed out. Zahn, however, took a more radical position and was an outspoken critic of the Church as an institution. In 1964, he wrote that the Catholic Church was the only religious institution that could have effectively resisted Hitler, and in failing to do this, it failed in its moral duty and standards.[4]

The Jesuits were unmoved by men like Zahn and consistently defended the Church's wartime record. The Jesuits asserted that even in Germany many of the Catholic laity and several bishops resisted the Nazis. These include Michael Cardinal Faulhaber who was eulogized by the Jesuits of *America* as one who had consistently and repeatedly denounced the Nazi persecution of the Jews during the entire twelve-year reign of the Third Reich. However, soon after Hitler became the chancellor of Germany, Cardinal Faulhaber delivered a sermon wherein he declared that "after the death of Christ, Israel was dismissed from the service of Revelation. She had not known the time of her visitation. She had repudiated and rejected the Lord's Annointed, had driven Him to the Cross. Then the veil of the Temple was rent, and with it the covenant between the Lord and His people. The Daughters of Sion received the bill of divorce, and from that forth Assureus wanders forever restless over the face of the earth."[5]

Cardinal Faulhaber's sermon raises a fundamental question: what is the relationship between traditional Christian doctrines and theology concerning the Jews and all forms of hostility toward them, including modern anti-Semitism which reached its dreadful climax in the Nazi slaughter of 6 million Jews? In his book *The Anguish of the Jews*, Edward Flannery emphasizes pre-Christian, Greco-Roman hostility to the Jews that was introduced into the Church when the Roman Empire was converted to Christianity.[6] In the same vein, another Catholic thinker pointed out that the relations of the Jews of Alexandria with the pagan Greek and Egyptian populations of that city were marked by a degree of hatred, occasionally erupting into violence, that was far worse than anything that the Jews later had to endure at the hands of the Christians.[7]

Nevertheless, the sad record of medieval Christendom vis-à-vis the Jews cannot be so easily explained away. Then at the height of its political power and intellectual influence, the Catholic Church exerted great pressure on the Jews to convert to Christianity. Although individual Jews did accept baptism, the Church failed to convert the Jews en masse. Subsequently, religious hostility and economic cupidity led Christian princes to expel the Jews from their domains and Christian mobs to attack the Jews and seize their property. Although some of the Catholic hierarchy protested these outrages, it was the Church that created the anti-Jewish intellectual milieu wherein they took place. (Thoughtful Catholics recognize this but plead that the medieval Church must be understood in terms of the total cultural and social environment which then prevailed in Europe.)

In the same year that Vatican Council II approved *Nostra Aetate*, Edward Synan, a priest and advocate of a rapprochement between Jews and Catholics, wrote that the anti-Judaic policy of Pope Innocent III must be judged in the context of his time, which was the age of the Holy Roman Emperor Frederick II, who cynically used the Church for his own political purposes, as well as the age of St. Francis of Assisi.[8] It was an age of ruthless, even barbaric, political intrigues and machinations as well as one of deep and sincere religious feelings and piety. Synan further emphasized that both medieval Jews and Christians regarded sin as a collective and not an individual matter.

One unfortunate result of this collective view of sin, in Synan's estimation, was the medieval identification of all Jews with that small number of Jews who had called for the crucifixion of Jesus. This was a deplorable development, comments Father George Tavard, because it led to the physical segregation of the Jews, and thereby made it easier for Christian mobs to single out and attack them.[9] On the other hand, the medieval Church "still respected the privileged status of Israel in the period that was inaugurated by the New Covenant."[10] Indeed, Christian scholars often consulted their Jewish counterparts, who were regarded as the heirs of the Old Covenant, in matters of philosophy and even of religion, according to Tavard. It is a fact that during the so-called golden age of medieval Spanish history, Christians and Jews often met each other on an equal, even cordial, basis, but this came to an end in 1492 when the entire Jewish population was expelled from Spain.

Tavard explains, "The medieval mind that made no distinction between Church and State would make none among Jews. This explains the status of Judaism as a state within the state during the Middle Ages."[11] States are often in conflict, Tavard continues, and when the Spanish monarchs Ferdinand and Isabella expelled the Jews, they did so because of the medieval view that the Jews constituted a state within the state.

In the nineteenth and twentieth centuries, Tavard notes, the decline of Christianity is concurrent with a waning in the religious animosity towards the Jews. At the same time, the economic and political aspects of anti-Semitism have grown in importance; political anti-Semitism stems from a pagan concept of racial purity which is expressed as a national blood brotherhood. Hitler popularized these ideas in a Germany that was suffering from military defeat and economic depression. Although Tavard denies that there is a direct link between Christianity and the Holocaust, he ultimately acknowledges that there is an indirect link—albeit a vague one—between the Holocaust and Christian beliefs concerning the Jews.[12]

Throughout the years 1946–76, the Jesuits of *America* consistently maintained the opposite point of view: there is no connection between Christianity and contemporary anti-Semitism. In October 1948, the editors of this journal reminded its readers of Pius XII's opposition to the Nazi persecution of the Jews and recalled that in 1938, a year prior to becoming pope, he had commented, "Spiritually we are all Semites."[13] This and similar statements and actions of both Pius XI and his successor, Pius XII, prove that the Church is philo-Semitic, according to the Jesuits. In their opinion, modern anti-Semitism has its origin not in Christianity, but in unbridled nationalism and racism, and these movements sharply conflict with basic Christian values.

Tavard shares this view of the conflict between Christianity and anti-Semitism, but at the same time he admits that some segments of the Catholic population of the United States are anti-Semitic.[14] Again, the Jesuits protested that Catholicism is not responsible for this social development. Everywhere in the world, they pointed out, minorities may encounter discrimination, and this includes both Catholics and Jews in the United States and the United Kingdom.[15] The majority of the American people are Protestant, and although anti-Catholicism has diminished in the United States, it still lingers on as a political, even social, aspect of American culture. Some American Protestants regarded the Catholic Church as an alien, authoritarian institution, and in 1946, a writer in *America* compared these Protestant allegations with Hitler's verbal attacks on the Jews.[16] Nevertheless, despite these protestations, the editors and some of the writers of *America* ultimately acknowledged that some American Catholics were anti-Semitic, but they attributed this bias to the anti-Jewish attitudes that permeate Anglo-American Protestant society.[17]

Most traditional Catholic thinkers concluded that if there is an element of anti-Semitism in the universal Church, it is an historical aberration and an ideological error that crept into the Christian church at an early date in its development. Once more they emphasized that neither the basic doctrines nor the hierarchy of the Church is anti-Semitic because the Christian religion and the racial theory of modern anti-Semitism are diametrically opposed to each other. Therefore, the truly believing Christian cannot possibly hold anti-Semitic attitudes. After having again recalled Pius XII's oft-quoted statement, "Spiritually we are all Semites," traditional Catholic intellectuals vigorously denounced blatant anti-Semitism.[18]

The Gospels, however, are permeated with anti-Judaic statements; e.g., the Evangelists wrote that the Pharisees opposed Jesus
and that the Jewish priests conspired to kill him. At the same
time that traditional Catholic intellectuals condemned political
anti-Semitism, they emphasized the importance of traditional
Christian theology and this includes the belief that the Jews rejected
Jesus as the Messiah.[19]

The New Testament narrative of the crucifixion is an even
more serious attack on the Jews than their alleged repudiation
of Jesus. Here, too, traditional Catholic thinkers adhere to the
literal narrative of Christ's passion, and at the same time they
ardently deny any connection between it and modern anti-Semitism.
This is particularly true in the years before Vatican II approved
Nostra Aetate; nevertheless, rigidly traditional Catholic thinkers
continued to hold the same view of the role of the Jews in the
crucifixion both before and after Vatican II.[20]

In an effort to reduce the tensions between Judaism and
Christianity, Monsignor John Oesterreicher vehemently denied in
1964 that the New Testament narratives of Jesus' suffering in
themselves are the basic cause of anti-Semitism, but he also admitted,
"Many times the distorted telling of the story of the Passion has
stirred up anti-Jewish feeling and . . . the story itself has been
used as a pretext for persecuting the Jews."[21] Thus Oesterreicher
emphasized the distinction between the true meaning of Christ's
sacrifice on the cross as it had been understood by educated,
faithful Christians, and his crucifixion as it had been popularly
interpreted by the masses of Christians. Christian thinkers developed
the doctrine that Christ offered himself as a voluntary sacrifice
on the cross to ransom mankind from original sin. Oesterreicher
wrote that educated, sincere Christians always understood that
the Jews were only passive actors in this divine drama, but often
the Christian masses misunderstood the meaning of Christ's passion
and held the Jews responsible for the crucifixion.

It would seem, however, that Pope Paul VI did not conclude
that the Jews can be exonerated for the condemnation and crucifixion of Jesus. On Palm Sunday in 1965, the pontiff spoke of
"the clash between Christ and the Jews" and stated that "the
Jewish people were responsible for the tragic events leading to
the death of Christ."[22] In an effort to soften the impact of the
pope's sermon, moderate Catholic thinkers explained that when

the New Testament, and particularly the Gospel of John, refers to the Jews, it has reference to only a small group of Jews that includes the several Jewish sects, the ruling clique of Judaea, and the crowds of Jerusalem.[23] Educated Catholics, Michael Zeik wrote, are aware of this, and they know, too, that at the time of Jesus, only a small fraction of all the Jews in the world had even heard of him, much less participated in his crucifixion.

Such an exegesis of the Gospels is typical of the third strain in the Church: those American Catholic intellectuals who want both to retain the literal text of the New Testament and to purge it of any anti-Semitic implications. According to such Catholic reformers, the attainment of this goal merely involves the modification of an incorrect or wrong interpretation of various passages in the Christian scriptures. With regard to the crucifixion, this group of Catholic thinkers find themselves in a dilemma: they can neither exonerate the Jews of any responsibility for the death of Jesus nor can they hold them responsible for it.

This dilemma is evident in Father Gerard Sloyan's book *Jesus On Trial*. On the one hand, Sloyan wrote, the Evangelists, and John in particular, unjustly placed most of the responsibility for the crucifixion on the Jewish leaders, and especially on the priests.[24] This tendency to blame the Jewish political and religious leaders for the crucifixion—and exonerate the Roman governor—grew stronger as Jewish Christianity declined, and the Church became increasingly a Gentile institution.[25]

On the other hand, Sloyan emphasized that the Jewish priests misunderstood the apolitical nature and the pacific meaning of Jesus' teaching, and they contrived to kill him on the basis of a false but plausible political charge. (It was the Roman governor, however, who actually condemned Jesus to death.[26]) Now Sloyan concludes with these words: "When we finally have all the historical facts concerning the crucifixion, they will not redound to the credit of the band of threatened men of both nations, Israel and Rome."[27] Although scholars like Sloyan may differentiate between this small band of Jews and Romans who carried out the crucifixion and the Judaean and Roman masses, the distinction tends, in reality, to blur because most people make little distinction between a group of people and their leaders.

At the far end of the spectrum of Catholic thought, a small group of men and women assert that there is a clear link between

Christian doctrines concerning the Jews and anti-Semitism, and that two thousand years of Christian Jew-hatred created the social and intellectual climate that permitted the Nazis to kill 6 million Jews. Although the Christian churches and the Nazis were indeed often opposed to each other, Hitler and his followers built their program of racial and political anti-Semitism on Christian religious hostility to the Jews, writes Rosemary Radford Ruether, the most articulate and outspoken of the revisionist Catholic thinkers.[28]

Unlike their traditional co-religionists, revisionist Catholics maintain that Christian hostility toward Jews has an origin different from pagan antagonism toward them. Pagan anti-Semitism, Ruether wrote in 1974, was a reaction to an exclusive Jewish monotheism and a strict anti-paganism on the part of the Jews, but this antipathy toward them was "kept in check and balanced by Roman practicality and Hellenistic Jewish cultural apologetics. . . . The pagan might regard the Jew with puzzlement or contempt, but the polytheism of pagan culture did not lend itself to fanatical hatred of the Jews."[29] The triumph of Christianity as the official religion of the Roman Empire marked the rise of anti-Semitism as a persistent cultural component of Western civilization, in the opinion of Reuther and other revisionist Catholic thinkers.

Reuther argues that although the Church absorbed the Greco-Roman dislike of the Jews in the process of converting the Roman Empire, such anti-Semitism did not greatly influence the Church because the pagans initially regarded Christianity as simply another monotheistic, exclusive, and anti-pagan Jewish sect. Ironically, it was the Jewish Christians (the first Christians, of course, were those Jews who believed that Jesus was the Messiah) who introduced the seeds of anti-Semitism in Christianity. Although the Jewish Christians did not blame their fellow Jews for the crucifixion of Jesus, they developed the doctrine that God had abrogated his covenant with the degenerate Jews and had established a new one with the new Israel, the followers of Christ.[30]

The apostle Paul opened Christianity to the Gentiles and led the attack on those Christians who taught that a potential convert must first become Jewish in order to know Christ.[31] As the Christian church increasingly became a gentile one, Paul and his followers advanced the doctrine that God had chosen the gentiles and rejected the Jews as the chosen people.[32] The Fathers of the Church (e.g.

Saints John Chrysostom, Augustine, and Ambrose) further developed these and other anti-Jewish doctrines.[33]

Revisionist Catholic intellectuals viewed the role of the Church in the Middle and Modern Ages as well as in the early history of Christianity from a different perspective than that of traditional Catholics. After the collapse of the western part of the Roman Empire, the Catholic Church successfully converted the Germanic peoples to orthodox Christianity. (Earlier, many of the Germanic tribes had accepted Arian Christianity which taught that Jesus was more than man but less than God.) The Germanic peoples, many of whom had never even heard of the Jews before, were now exposed to Christian anti-Judaism.[34]

In modern times, the main attack upon the Jews has been not religious in nature but racial and economic; nevertheless, revisionist Catholic thinkers trace this new form of anti-Semitism to attitudes of medieval Christendom toward Jews. Faced with Jewish refusal to convert to Christianity en masse, according to Rosemary Ruether, the medieval Church developed the myth that the Jews are carnal, devoid of religious idealism, and exist solely as a testimony to God's wrathful judgement.[35] Although not racism, this Christian myth of a carnal Israel was transposed into racial hatred of the Jews.

Catholic Spain is the foremost example of this development, she wrote. After centuries of struggle and warfare, the last Moslem stronghold—Granada—surrendered in 1492 to the Catholic monarchs Isabella and Ferdinand, and in the same year, all Jews were told to accept baptism or leave the country. Many Jews converted to Christianity, but these new Christians still faced social discrimination in a society that was obsessed by "purity of blood." Whether one was a secret Judaizer or devout Catholic, if he aspired to a position in government or the Church, he had to submit genealogical charts to the Inquisition that proved he had no Jewish ancestors. In this way, even the most sincere Jewish converts and their descendents were effectively barred from full participation in Spanish society.

The Church must also bear much of the blame for the growth of economic hostility toward the Jews, according to revisionist Catholic intellectuals. Some pagan writers ridiculed the Jewish religion and criticized the Jews for keeping apart from other peoples, but only after the advent of Christianity were they attacked as materialistic and greedy people who were dishonest in their business dealings.[36] Medieval Christian society forbad the Jews from owning land, tilling it for a feudal lord, and joining craft guilds so that "no vocation except finance remained open to them. Thus, at the dawn of urban civilization the Jews had become businessmen—not by choice like Lombards, Greeks, or other Christians, but for lack of alternatives."[37] As a result of these social pressures, the economic position of the Jews eventually came to correspond to the Christian religious image of them, an image that the Church had created centuries earlier.[38]

In the twentieth century, anti-Semitic movements did not have to create anything new but only to build upon this inheritance of religious, economic, and racial hatred. Indeed, when two Catholic bishops raised the question of his anti-Jewish policy in the 1930s, Hitler replied that he was only putting into effect what Christianity had preached and practiced for almost 2,000 years.[39] According to a small group of Catholic intellectuals, the truth of this statement is borne out by the failure of the Vatican to take effective action on behalf of the doomed Jews of Europe during the years 1941–45.[40] Even after the Holocaust, these Catholics contend their Church continues to teach hatred of the Jews in the United States as well as in other countries.[41]

Thus the complexity and the wide range of American Catholic attitudes toward the Jews can be seen: Catholic intellectuals hold widely differing opinions concerning the relationship between Christian theology and anti-Semitism, the role of Jews in the crucifixion of Jesus, and the Vatican's efforts to save the doomed Jews of Europe during World War II. From a broad point of view, one can understand why traditional Catholic thinkers, whose thought is dominant in the Church, defend its wartime policy towards the Jews: people often defend and justify every aspect of the institutions to which they belong and with which they identify themselves. The more completely that one believes in the fundamental beliefs and structure of an institution, the less one is inclined to question any aspect or policy of that institution. Therefore, those Catholics who unquestioningly accept the New Testament accounts of the Jews' role in the crucifixion and the conflict between the early Church and the synagogue are also inclined to defend the wartime policy of their Church and to believe that Pius XII tried to save as many lives as possible—including Jewish ones.

Although the historical record is not completely clear, it appears that the Catholic hierarchy—including Pius XII—made only a minimal effort to save the Jews of Europe from the hands of the Nazis. On the other hand, few writers have noted that the Church's first responsibility, like any other institution's first duty, was to those groups and individuals who were integral members of that institution, i.e., baptized Catholics. This, too, was a time when Catholics found themselves on opposite sides of the battle lines, and entire Catholic groups, for example, the Catholic population of Poland, faced possible extermination. Ultimately, many Catholics as well as Jews did perish during World War II, and there was little that the Vatican could do to save the Polish Catholic intelligentsia, among whom were many priests, let alone save the Jews. If the Holy See had taken a strong stand against the Nazis and their racial policies, it was possible that this might have caused many German Catholics to leave the Church, and thereby its moral authority in Germany might have been greatly reduced.

It should not be forgotten, too, that many individual Christians, including members of the Catholic hierarchy, assisted the Jews in a variety of ways during the twelve-year reign of the Third Reich. Furthermore, these Christians risked their own lives when they acted and spoke out on behalf of the Jews of Europe.

Despite these observations, the sad fact remains that twenty centuries of Christian hostility toward Jews and Judaism made it possible for the Nazis to carry out the near-destruction of European Jewry. It is also true that there is a direct line—albeit an unclear one at times—between Christian religious hostility to the Jews and modern economic and racial anti-Semitism. It is difficult to see how traditional and moderate Catholics can conduct a meaningful dialogue with the Jews when they fail to recognize these facts of history. Because revisionist Catholics recognize these facts, thoughtful Jews who are aware of the historically negative relationship between Christianity and Judaism but who now want to open a dialogue with Christians welcome the conclusions of thinkers like Rosemary Ruether.

Are all trenchant theological discussions between Jews and Catholics limited to revisionist and moderate, reform-minded Catholics? Are Jews and traditional Catholic thinkers destined to simply go through the motions of a theological dialogue, or should they simply ignore the entire question of religion and only discuss their common social concerns? Is there any hope that Jews and traditional Catholics, who are in the mainstream of Catholic thought, can truly speak to each other, or are all discussions between the religions destined to remain on a superficial level, on the level of a truce in the two thousand-year-old conflict between the Church and the synagogue?

A truly meaningful and trenchant dialogue between Judaism and Catholicism can take place only if the Church renounces and purges itself of all anti-Judaic doctrines and anti-Jewish attitudes. This would be no easy task because such doctrines and beliefs lie at the basic intellectual foundations of Christianity. In order to solve this problem, Catholic thinkers must first acknowledge the anti-Judaic bias in Christianity.

Christians often are not even aware of the anti-Judaic cast of Christian thought. Father Ronald Knox, an English author, theologian, and dignitary of the Catholic Church, is best known for his translation of and commentary on the Bible. With regard to Matthew 27:11–26, Knox commented, "Mark and Luke may have been acquainted with the facts [concerning the crucifixion], and nevertheless decided to pass them over in silence. They probably wrote at Rome . . . and the Roman Church held a precarious balance between a Jewish and Gentile element. No need, then, to underline the responsibility of the Jewish people for our Lord's death."[42] Knox's book was declared free of theological and moral errors by Archbishop Richard J. Cushing of Boston in September 1952.[43]

Such approval by Archbishop Cushing, who later became Cardinal Cushing, does not imply that he personally was anti-Semitic; on the contrary, he was active in interfaith discussions, including those between Catholics and Jews. As a believing Catholic and a prelate of the Church, however, the archbishop's foremost aim was to strengthen the level of Christian faith in the United States, and so he approved Knox's book.

Another Catholic writer and theologian, Father Gregory Baum, a convert from Judaism to Catholicism, ultimately acknowledged the link between Christian anti-Judaism and modern anti-Semitism. Initially, Baum wrote that this anti-Judaism is an ideological error that crept into the Church because of a misunderstanding of the

New Testament. When the Evangelists condemned the Jews, Baum wrote, they referred only to the Jewish political and religious leaders of Jesus' time and to those among the Jewish masses who actually participated in his condemnation and crucifixion.[44] It is in this light that the Gospels of John and Matthew 27:25 ("His blood be on us and our children") as well as other negative references to the Jews in the Gospels should be interpreted.

Over a period of ten years, Baum's thinking underwent a gradual but decisive change. In 1971, Baum exonerated the Jewish leaders of Jerusalem of any responsibility for the crucifixion of Jesus. They simply failed to understand that the advent of Jesus was an entirely new and unique event in the history of the world. After all, the ruling circle of Jerusalem knew of other men who had claimed to be the Messiah, had performed miracles, and had misled the masses with false hope that provoked the anger of Rome.[45] Ultimately, in 1974, Baum commented, "While it would be historically untruthful to blame the Christian Church for Hitler's anti-Semitism and the monstrous crimes committed by him and his followers, what is true, alas, is that the Church has provided an abiding contempt among Christians for Jews and all things Jewish, a contempt that aided Hitler's purpose."[46] In 1974, Baum retracted, too, his earlier argument that "the anti-Jewish trends in Christianity were peripheral and accidental, not grounded in the New Testament itself, but due to later developments, and that it would consequently be fairly easy to purify the Church from anti-Jewish bias. Since then, especially under the influence of Rosemary Ruether's writings, I have had to change my mind."[47] What is the well-meaning and sincere Catholic to do after he acknowledges that the New Testament has an anti-Judiac bias? It logically follows that any Catholic who wishes to establish a truly meaningful dialogue between Judaism and Catholicism would try to remove all implicit as well as explicit anti-Judaic elements from Christianity. Such an effort is beset with serious difficulties.

As we have seen, the foremost Christian assault on Judaism centers on the role of the Jews in the crucifixion of Jesus. In her monumental book, *Faith and Fratricide*, Rosemary Ruether wrote that the early Christians, and the author of the Gospel of John in particular, falsified the events surrounding the crucifixion when they shifted the blame for this act from the Roman political authorities to the Jewish religious ones. In support of this contention,

Ruether and Catholic scholars point out that recent studies have clearly shown the New Testament accounts of Jewish participation in the crucifixion to be historically untenable.[48]

One of these Catholic scholars, Dominic Crossan, urged that the Catholic Church purge itself of all anti-Judaic statements and beliefs, including those in the New Testament[49]; traditional Catholic thinkers retorted, however, that the New Testament clearly and emphatically states that the Jews of both Palestine and the Diaspora rejected Christianity, and neither Church council nor pope can delete such statements from the Christian scriptures, including Matthew 27:25.[50] Here is the root of the problem facing those Catholic thinkers who sincerely wish to purge the Church of its anti-Judaic strain and enter into a meaningful dialogue with the Jews: the Gospels emphatically state that the Jews rejected Jesus and that their leaders plotted to have him crucified.[51]

Nevertheless, there is hope that the Church will change and modify or even completely delete all anti-Jewish statements in its theology and teachings. During the pontificate of John XXIII, changes were introduced in the Good Friday service that presaged further changes in the Church's attitude toward the Jews.

As has been emphasized, traditional Catholic thinkers refuted the charge that Christian theology is anti-Judaic and denied that the pre-1959 reference to the Jews in the Catholic Good Friday service was anti-Semitic.[52] Monsignor John Oesterreicher was prominent among those who argued that the Latin phrase in the missal *pro perfidis Judaeis* is not a derogatory one. He asserted that the word *perfidis* means disbelieving and not perfidious, but he admitted that most Catholics think that it has the latter meaning.[53]

Although Oesterreicher deplored this popular translation of *perfidis*, he predicted that the Church would not alter or delete these words from the Good Friday service because the Church is the guardian of the truth, and as such it must describe the life of Christ in a truthful and correct manner.[54] Furthermore, the Church would actually do a great disservice to the Jews if it attempted to hide the source of the Jews' unrest and unhappiness from them—their rejection of Christ.[55] But on March 25, 1959, Pope John XXIII decreed that the phrase *pro perfidis Judaeis* must be deleted from the Good Friday service, and, oddly, one of those who warmly greeted this decree was Monsignor John Oesterreicher.[56]

Although some Catholic intellectuals as well as many Jews may have wished the Catholic Church to go further in the revision of its theology and teachings about the Jews, both Jews and Catholics are encouraged by *Nostra Aetate* and the removal of the phrase *pro perfidis Judaeis* from the Good Friday service as welcome steps in the diminution of Christian hostility to the Jewish religion and people. In this light, *Nostra Aetate* did not represent a decisive change in the Church's attitude toward the Jewish religion and people but may signal a continuous process of re-evaluation and growth in the relations between Catholicism and Judaism.

Notes

1. Esther Yolles Feldblum, *The American Catholic Press and the Jewish State, 1917–1959* (New York, 1977), p. 111; Arthur Gilbert, *The Vatican Council and the Jews* (New York, 1968), pp. 44–45, 289–91; Vincent A. Yzermans, ed., *American Participation in the Second Vatican Council* (New York, 1967), p. 570.

2. Thurston N. Davis, "Of Many Things," *America* 109 (July 27, 1963): 84.

3. Edward H. Flannery, "Anti-Zionism and the Christian Psyche," *Journal of Ecumenical Studies* 6 (Spring 1969): 174–75: Gordon Zahn, *Hitler's Wars and Germany's Catholics* (New York, 1962). In 1967, Flannery was appointed as the executive secretary of the Secretariat for Catholic-Jewish Relations of the Roman Catholic Bishops' Committee for Ecumenical and Interreligious Affairs.

4. Gordon Zahn, "The Church under Hitler," *Commonweal* 80 (July 3, 1964): 448.

5. Alan T. Davies, *Anti-Semitism and the Christian Mind: The Crisis of Conscience After Auschwitz* (New York, 1969), p. 70. Moreover, the Jewish historian Guenter Lewy wrote that "the passivity of the German episcopate in the face of the Jewish tragedy stands in marked contrast to the conduct of French, Belgian, and Dutch bishops," in *The Star and the Cross: Essays on Jewish-Christian Relations*, ed. Katherine T. Hargrove (Milwaukee, 1966), p. 168. Lewy's statement was unchallenged in this collection of essays by Catholic and Jewish writers.

6. Edward H. Flannery, *The Anguish of the Jews* (New York, 1963), pp. 268–77; Edward H. Peters, "New Books: *The Anguish of the Jews,*" *Catholic World* 203 (Apr. 1966): 60–61.

7. Herbert Musurillo, "Books: *Judaism and the Early Christian Mind,*" *Thought* 47 (Spring 1972): 149.

8. Edward A. Synan, *The Pope and the Jews in the Middle Ages* (New York: 1965), p. 152. Synan asserts that Pius XII must also be seen against the background of the time in which he lived; he must be juxtaposed alongside such men as Churchill, Einstein, and Stalin for a balanced evaluation of his life; ibid., p. 164.

9. George Tavard, *The Church, the Layman, and the Modern World* (New York, 1959), p. 80. Tavard further emphasizes that the Jews were relatively free within the ghetto to conduct their own affairs and to live their own lives.

10. Ibid., p. 78.

11. Ibid., p. 79.

12. Ibid., p. 80.

13. "Church Attitude Clarified," *America* 80 (Oct. 16, 1948): 30.

14. Tavard, *The Church, the Layman, and the Modern World*, p. 80.

15. Walter O'Hearn, "Books: England through Jewish Eyes," *America* 83 (July 15, 1950): 339; "Current Comment: Speaking of Prejudice," ibid., 84 (Feb. 17, 1951): 576; "Current Comment: Spirit of the Klan," ibid., 86 (Mar. 1, 1952): 580; "Current Comment: Hate and Censorship," ibid., 100 (Feb. 28, 1959): 619.

16. Louis Baldwin, "Eyes Upon the Foil," ibid., 76 (Oct. 19, 1946): 69.

17. "Current Comment: The Banks and the Jews," ibid., 115 (Sept. 24, 1966): 309; Benjamin L. Masse, "Ethnic Patterns in Management," ibid., 112 (Apr. 24, 1968): 612; "Editorials: Discrimination and Executives,' ibid., 120 (May 31, 1969): 642; Marion Mitchell Stancioff, "How I Remember Ezra Pound," ibid., 128 (Mar. 17, 1973): 240–41; Frank Annunziata, "Book Reviews: Father Coughlin," ibid., 129 (Sept. 29, 1973): 224.

18. M. Raphael Simon, *The Glory of Thy People: The Story of a Conversion* (New York, 1948), p. 97; Edward Arbez, "Books and Reviews: *The Jewish People and Christ*," *Theological Studies* 12 (1951): 596; Vincent P. McCorry, "The Word: Moral Indignation," *America* 115 (Oct. 22, 1966): 496.

19. William A. Donaghy, "The Word," *America* 76 (Jan. 11, 1947): 415; John J. Scanlon, "The Word," ibid., 85 (Sept. 22, 1951): 609; William J. Read, "The Word," ibid., 87 (Aug. 2, 1952): 445; Vincent McCorry, "The Word," ibid., 120 (Feb. 8, 1969), 176–77.

20. McCorry, "The Word," ibid., 91 (Apr. 3, 1954): 24; "The Word," ibid. 121 (Sept. 27, 1969): 248.

21. John M. Oesterreicher, *The Brotherhood of Christians and Jews: An Address Given at the Jewish Community House of Taunton, Massachusetts on February 16, 1964* (Newark, 1964), p. 13. Msgr. Oesterreicher was converted to Catholicism while he was a medical student at the University of Vienna and, subsequently, became a priest. Between 1934 and 1938 he was active in missionary work among the Jews as director of the Opus Sancti Pauli in Vienna and the director of *Die Erfüllung*. In 1940 he came to the United States where he founded and directs the Institute for Judeo-Christian Studies at Seton Hall University.

22. Michael D. Zeik, "The Pope and the Jews," *Commonweal* 82 (Apr. 30, 1965): 181–82.

23. Ibid.; Irwin St. John Tucker, "The Lost Sheep." *America* 118 (Feb. 3, 1968): 158.

24. Gerard Sloyan, *The Trial of Jesus: The Development of the Passion*

Narratives and Their Historical and Ecumenical Implications (Philadelphia, 1973), pp. 125, 127.

25. Ibid., pp. 133–34.

26. Ibid., p. 127.

27. Ibid., p. 134.

28. Rosemary Radford Ruether, *Faith and Fratricide: The Theological Roots of Anti-Semitism* (New York, 1974), p. 184.

29. Ibid., p. 30.

30. Ibid., p. 94.

31. James J. Magee, "Jews and the Early Church," *New Catholic World* 214 (Dec. 1971): 113.

32. Ruether, *Faith and Fratricide*, p. 83.

33. J. Bruce Long, ed., *Judaism and the Christian Seminary Curriculum* (Chicago, 1966), p. 90; Magee, "Jews and the Early Church," pp. 114–15; Ruether, *Faith and Fratricide*, p. 230.

34. Claire H. Bishop, *How Catholics Look at Jews: Inquiries into Italian, Spanish, and French Teaching Materials* (New York, 1974), p. 103.

35. Ruether, *Faith and Fratricide*, p. 56.

36. Bishop, *How Catholics Look at Jews*, pp. 101–3. According to Bishop, pagan anti-Semitic writers often complained that the Jews were too poor.

37. Ibid., p. 104.

38. Ruether, *Faith and Fratricide*, pp. 223–24.

39. Ibid. Ruether had reference to a meeting that took place in Berlin on April 26, 1933, between the bishop of Osnabrück, the vicar general of Berlin, and Hitler who had called the meeting. At this meeting, Hitler told the prelates that "National Socialism was committed to joining the Church in its struggles against Bolshevism and Judaism. In its anti-Semitic program, Hitler insisted, the Nazi regime was only continuing the 1500-year-old policies of the Church vis-à-vis the Jews." In *Encountering the Holocaust: An Interdisciplinary Survey*, ed. Byron L. Sherwin and Susan G. Amend (Chicago, 1979), p. 27.

40. Thomas P. Anderson, "Christian Anti-Semitism," *Continuum* 4 (Autumn 1966): 38; Edward T. Gargan, "The Lesson of Eichmann," ibid., 5 (Winter-Spring 1967): 396.

41. Louis F. Doyle, "Irish Cavalcade," *Catholic World* 166 (Mar. 1948): 527; Bishop, *How Catholics Look at Jews*, pp. 119, 274; Bishop, "Learning Bigotry," *Commonweal* 80 (May 22, 1964): 264–67; John T. Pawlikowski, *Catechetics and Prejudice: How Catholic Teaching Materials View Jews, Protestants, and Racial Minorities* (New York, 1973), pp. 19, 80–81; Pawlikowski, "Christian-Jewish Relations and Catholic Teaching Materials," *Catholic Library World* 46 (Dec. 1973): 227–32; Pawlikowski, "Catholics Look at Jews," *Commonweal* 101 (Jan. 31, 1975): 364–65.

42. Ronald Knox, *A Commentary on the Gospels*, 3 vols. (New York, 1952), 1: 68.

43. Ibid., p. iv.

44. Gregory Baum, "How Anti-Semitism Found a Home in Christian Teaching," *Commonweal* 80 (June 12, 1964): 372, and *Is the New Testament Anti-Semitic?* (Glen Rock, N.J., 1965), pp. 8, 85, 105, 132.

45. Gregory Baum, "The 'New' in The Church and Its Ministry," *Journal of Ecumenical Studies* 8 (Spring 1971): 345–46.

46. Ruether, *Faith and Fratricide*, p. 7.

47. Ibid., p. 3.

48. Ibid., pp. 86, 87, 111; Jeffrey B. Sobosian, "The Trial of Jesus," *The Journal of Ecumenical Studies* 10 (Winter 1973): 70–93; Dominic M. Crossan, "Anti-Semitism and The Gospel," *Theological Studies* 26 (June 1965): 189–214.

49. Crossan, "Anti-Semitism and the Gospel," p. 189.

50. Gerald G. O'Collins, "Notes: Anti-Semitism in the Gospels," *Theological Studies* 26 (Dec. 1956): 663–66; Joseph A. Fitzmyer, "Notes: Anti-Semitism and The Cry of 'All The People'," ibid., 26 (Dec. 1956): 667–71.

51. In 1973, Fr. John Pawlikowski reported that Catholic seminaries in the United States were still teaching the traditional Christian doctrine that the Jews rejected Christianity, that they played an important role in the crucifixion of Jesus, and that because of this, the Jews suffer under a divine curse. Pawlikowski, *Catechetics and Prejudice*, p. 81.

52. "Comment on the Week: The Church and the Jews," *America* 76 (Mar. 29, 1947): 704; "Comment on the Week: Church Attitude Clarified," ibid., 80 (Oct. 16, 1948): 30; John M. Oesterreicher, ed., *The Bridge: A Yearbook of Judaeo-Christian Studies*, 5 vols. (New York, 1956), 2: 212–23; "The Inner Forum," *Commonweal* 45 (Apr. 4, 1947): 622.

53. Oesterreicher, "*Pro Perfidis Judaeis*," *Theological Studies* 8 (1947): 80.

54. Ibid., p. ;95.

55. Ibid.

56. "Current Comment: Pray for the Jews," *America* 101 (Apr. 18, 1959): 214–15.

Contributors

Richard D. Breitman is a member of the History Department at The American University where he teaches European History. His articles have appeared in *Central European History* and the *Journal of Contemporary History*. He is also the author of *German Socialism and Weimar Democracy* (1981, and co-author of *American Refugee Policy and European Jewry, 1933–1945* (1987).

Leonard Dinnerstein is a History Department faculty member at the University of Arizona and the author of a number of books in American ethnic and Jewish history, including *The Leo Frank Case* (1968). He is also the author of the important recent work *America and the Survivors of the Holocaust* (1982).

Egal Feldman is a member of the History faculty at the University of Wisconsin-Superior. He has published a number of articles on Jewish-Christian relations and is the author of *The Dreyfus Affair and the American Conscience* (1981).

David A. Gerber is a member of the History Department at the State University of New York at Buffalo. He is the author of *Black Ohio and the Color Line* (1976) and of recent articles in *Civil War History*, *Comparative Studies in Society and History*, the *Journal of American Ethnic History*, and the *Journal of Social History*.

Glen Jeansonne is a History Department faculty member at the University of Wisconsin-Milwaukee. He has written extensively on southern history including *Race, Religion, and Politics: The Louisiana Gubernatorial Elections of 1954–60* (1977) and *Leander Perez: Boss of the Delta* (1977). He will soon complete a biography of Gerald L. K. Smith.

Contributors

Alan M. Kraut is a member of the History faculty at The American University and writes on American Jewish and immigration history as well as on antebellum political history. He is the author of numerous articles and of *The Huddled Masses: The Immigrant and American Society, 1880–1921* (1981); he is also the editor of *Crusaders and Compromisers: Essays on the Relationship of the Antislavery Struggle to the Antebellum Party System* (1984), and co-author of *American Refugee Policy and European Jewry, 1933–1945* (1987).

Elinor Lerner is a member of the Sociology Department at Stockton State College in New Jersey. Her articles have appeared in *American Jewish History*, the *Insurgent Sociologist*, and other journals. Her doctoral dissertation, "Working-Class and Immigrant Involvement in the New York Woman Suffrage Movement, 1905–1918," was recently completed at the University of California at Berkeley.

Arthur Liebman was a member of the Sociology Department at the State University of New York at Binghamton. He was the author of the much-acclaimed *Jews and the Left* (1979) as well as a number of books and articles on American Jews and on politics and student life in Latin America. Professor Liebman died in February 1985. May his memory be for a blessing.

Jonathan D. Sarna, a History Department faculty member at Hebrew Union College-Jewish Institute of Religion, is also the Director of the Center for the Study of the American Jewish Experience. His articles have appeared in the *Journal of American History, Ethnicity,* and *American Jewish History* among many others, and he is the author of *Jacksonian Jew: The Two Worlds of Mordecai Noah* (1981).

Ellen Schiff is a faculty member of the French and Comparative Literature departments at North Adams State College in Massachusetts. She has published and lectured extensively on Jews in literature and drama. Her articles on drama have appeared in the *New York Times, Modern Drama*, and *American Jewish History*. She is the author of *From Stereotype to Metaphor: The Jew in Contemporary Drama* (1982).

Edward Shapiro is a faculty member in History at Seton Hall University. His articles and reviews have appeared in many publications, including the *Journal of American History, Catholic Historical Review, American Quarterly, American Jewish History*, and *American Studies*.

David G. Singer has taught at Loyola University of Chicago and the Spertus College of Judaica. He has published articles on Catholics and Jews in *American Jewish History* and *Contemporary Jewry*, and is currently writing a history of American Protestant attitudes toward Jews.

Robert Singerman is curator of the Price Library of Judaica at the University of Florida. He is currently completing for publication his fourth, book-length bibliography, *Jewish Serials of the World: A Research Bibliography of Secondary Sources*. His previous book, *Antisemitic Propaganda: An Annotated Bibliography and Research Guide* (1982), is a major guide to the literature of anti-Semitism in the modern era.

Marcia Graham Synnott is a member of the History Department of the University of South Carolina at Columbia. Among her works in the history of higher education are *The Half-Opened Door: Discrimination and Admissions at Harvard, Yale, and Princeton, 1900–1970* (1979) and articles in the *History of Education Quarterly* and the *American Archivist*.

Index

Other Titles of Interest

Daily Bread
Poems and Photographs
MARC KAMINSKY and LEON SUPRANER

Plain Folk
The Life Stories of Undistinguished Americans
DAVID M. KATZMAN and WILLIAM M. TUTTLE, Jr.

Trial of Judaism in Contemporary Jewish Writing
JOSEPHINE ZADOVSKY KNOPP

Forgotten Friendship
Israel and the Soviet Bloc, 1947-53
ARNOLD KRAMMER

The Jews Were Expendable
Free World Diplomacy and the Holocaust
MONTY NOAM PENKOWER

Israel and the American National Interest
A Critical Examination
CHERYL A. RUBENBERG

Tenement Songs
The Popular Music of the Jewish Immigrants
MARK SLOBIN

American Education and the European Immigrant, 1840-1940
BERNARD J. WEISS

For more information please write or call the University of Illinois Press, 54 East Gregory Drive, Champaign, IL 61820, 217/244-0626.